A CONCISE

America and Its People

VOLUME ONE TO 1877

James Kirby Martin
University of Houston

Randy Roberts
Purdue University

Steven Mintz
University of Houston

Linda O. McMurry
North Carolina State University

James H. Jones
University of Houston
and

Sam W. Haynes
University of Texas at Arlington

 HarperCollins *CollegePublishers*

For Our Students

Executive Editor: Bruce Borland
Director of Development: Betty Slack
Cover Design: Kay Petronio
Cover Illustration: Jane Sterrett
Photo Researcher: Judy Ladendorf/Ellen Berman
Electronic Production Manager: Angel Gonzalez Jr.
Publishing Services: Ruttle, Shaw & Wetherill, Inc.
Electronic Page Makeup: Ruttle Graphics, Inc.
Printer and Binder: RR Donnelley & Sons Company
Cover Printer: RR Donnelley & Sons Company

A Concise History of America and Its People, Volume One To 1877

Library of Congress Cataloging-in-Publication Data
A concise history of America and its people/James Kirby Martin . . .
    [et al.].
    p. cm.
    Includes bibliographical references (p.) and index.
    ISBN 0-673-46781-3
    1. United States—History. I. Martin, James Kirby
E178.1.C74   1995
973—dc20   94-20138
                                                    CIP

95 96 97   9 8 7 6 5 4 3 2

Brief Contents

VOLUME ONE ENDS

$\mathcal{D}$etailed Contents

*At the end of each chapter are a Chronology of Key Events, a Conclusion, and Suggestions for
Further Reading.

Maps, Charts, Figures, and Tables

Preface

A *Concise History of America and Its People,* a newly abridged version of the full-length *America and Its People* (2nd edition), has been designed with both instructors and students of the U.S. history survey in mind. It is hoped that this text will serve the needs of teachers who require a brief overview of American history, one which will allow them to develop particular themes and issues through the use of supplemental readings such as primary sources, monographs, novels, and the like. At the same time, the authors have not lost sight of the primary task of any textbook: to engage students and hold their interest. A history text which merely synopsizes the past does so at the risk of losing the richness, color, and drama of the American experience. The challenge of the authors in *A Concise History of America and Its People,* then, has been to streamline the full-length text without compromising its effectiveness as a pedagogical tool.

In addition to retaining the style and flavor of the original, *A Concise History of America and Its People* resembles its parent in terms of organization and structure. Although more than a third shorter than the full-length text, this abridgement contains many of the distinctive and popular features of *America and Its People.* The anecdotes that open each chapter, which frame the chapter's central themes and draw students into the material, have been retained with only minor revisions. Readers will find in the abridged text more than half of the original's maps and illustrations, as well as the useful Chronology of Events at the end of each chapter. Although the Special Features section has been dropped from the format in this brief edition, some material has been rewoven into the main text, albeit in abbreviated form.

As with all books there is always room for improvement, and we have worked hard to fine-tune this new version of *America and Its People.* A number of key events have been clarified, and every effort has been made to incorporate the findings of significant recent scholarship. To improve the narrative flow and emphasize the causative effects of national affairs on American foreign policy, the sequence of chapters covering the late nineteenth century has been changed. "Imperial America," a chapter which deals with such issues as the United States' search for markets and the Spanish-American War, now follows the chapter entitled "End of the Century Crisis," which covers politics in the Gilded Age, Populism and the Panic of 1893. Whereas the second edition of the full-length text ends with the election of 1992, the final chapter (Chapter 31) of the abridged text now includes a discussion of the Clinton administration. Bibliographies at the end of each chapter have also been updated.

Most important, this abridgement of the full-length text strives to remain true to the purpose of the original: to provide students with a "people-centered" approach to the American past. By focusing on people, both the great and the ordinary, the authors endeavor to highlight the dramatic conflict among individuals and groups that has so often produced meaningful change. Both the full-length and abridged versions of *America and Its People* attempt to go beyond the study of major historical figures and their impact on national affairs; both texts seek to show how ordinary people lived their lives, and to do so in ways that students will find meaningful and relevant to their own experience. It is the authors' belief that ethnicity, gender, and race should not be treated as adjunct information, tacked onto the end of a political narrative, but rather should be presented as an integral part of American history. It is our hope that this book has succeeded in presenting a compelling, balanced, and sensitive account of a nation and its people.

The Authors

Supplements

For Instructors

Instructors Resource Manual

This extensive resource by Mark Newman of the University of Illinois at Chicago, begins with essays on teaching history through maps, film, and primary sources. Each chapter contains a synopsis, sample discussion questions, lecture supplements called "Connections and Extensions," and instructional flowcharts. The manual includes a special reproducible set of map exercises by James Conrad of Nichols College, designed to teach basic geographic literacy.

America Through the Eyes of Its People: A Collection of Primary Sources

Prepared by Carol Brown, this one-volume collection of primary documents portraying the rich and varied tapestry of American life contains documents concerning women, Native Americans, African-Americans, Hispanics, and others who helped to shape the course of U.S. history. Designed to be duplicated by instructors for student use, the documents have accompanying student exercises.

A Guide to Teaching American History through Film

Created by Randy Roberts of Purdue University, this guide provides instructors with a creative and practical tool for stimulating classroom discussions. The sections include: "American Films: A Historian's Perspective," a listing of "Films for Specific Periods of American History," "Practical Suggestions," and "Bibliography." The film listing is in a narrative form, explaining the connection between each film and the topics being studied.

Video Lecture Launchers

Prepared by Mark Newman, University of Illinois at Chicago, these video lecture launchers (each 2 to 5 minutes in duration) cover key issues in American history from 1877 to the present. The launchers are accompanied by an Instructor's Manual.

American Impressions: A CD-ROM for U.S. History

This unique, ground-breaking product for the Introduction to U.S. History course is organized in a topical/thematic framework which allows an in-depth coverage for each topic with a media-centered focus. Hundreds of photos, maps, art, graphics, and historical film clips are organized into narrated vignettes and interactive activities to create a tool for both professors and students. This first volume of a series includes: When Three Cultures Meet, The Constitution, Labor and Reform, and Democracy and Diversity: The History of Civil Rights. Each topic is explored through three major themes, Politics, Culture and Society, and Science and Health. Available for Macintosh and Windows formats.

Visual Archives of American History, 2/e

This two-sided video laserdisc explores history from a meeting of three cultures to the present and is an encyclopedic chronology of U.S. History offering hundreds of photographs and illustrations, a variety of source and reference maps—several of which are animated—plus approximately 50 minutes of video clips. For ease in planning lectures, a manual listing barcodes for scanning and frame numbers for all the content will be provided.

Transparencies

A set of over 30 map transparencies drawn from the text of *America and Its People.*

Discovering American History Through Maps and Views

Created by Gerald Danzer of the University of Illinois at Chicago, the recipient of the AHA's 1990 James Harvey Robinson Prize for his work in the development of map transparencies—this set of 140 four-color acetates is a unique instructional tool. It contains an introduction on teaching history through maps and a detailed commentary on each transparency. The collection includes cartographic and pictorial maps, views and photos, urban plans, building diagrams, and works of art.

Test Bank

This *Test Bank,* prepared by Ken Weatherbie of Del Mar College, contains over 2,000 test items, including multiple-choice, true/false and essay questions, and map exercises. The questions are keyed to topic, difficulty level, cognitive type, and relevant text page.

TestMaster Computerized Testing System

This flexible, easy-to-master computer test bank includes all the test items in the printed test bank. The *TestMaster* software allows you to edit existing questions and add your own items. Tests can be printed in several different formats and can include figures such as graphs and tables. Available for IBM and Macintosh computers.

QuizMaster

This new program enables you to design *TestMaster* generated tests that your students can take on a computer rather than in printed form. *QuizMaster* is available separately from *TestMaster* and can be obtained free through your sales representative.

Grades

A grade-keeping and classroom management software program that maintains data for up to 200 students.

For Students

Study Guide and Practice Tests

This two-volume study guide, by Ken Chiaro of Pima Community College, is designed to provide students with a comprehensive review of text material and to encourage application and critical analysis of the

material. Each chapter contains a student introduction, reading comprehension and geography exercises, true-false, completion, and multiple-
choice "Practice Tests."

Learning to Think Critically: Films and Myths About American History

Randy Roberts and Robert May of Purdue University use well-known
films such as *Gone with the Wind* and *Casablanca* to explore some common myths about America and its past. Many widely held assumptions
about our country's past come from or are perpetuated by popular films.
Which are true? Which are patently not true? And how does a student of
history approach documents, sources, and textbooks with a critical and
discerning eye? This short handbook subjects some popular beliefs to
historical scrutiny in order to help students develop a method of inquiry
for approaching the subject of history in general.

Mapping American History: Student Activities

Written by Gerald Danzer of the University of Illinois at Chicago, this
free map workbook for students features exercises designed to teach students to interpret and analyze cartographic materials as historical documents. The instructor is entitled to a free copy of the workbook for each
copy of the text purchased from HarperCollins.

TimeLink Computer Atlas of American History

This atlas, compiled by William Hamblin of Brigham Young University,
is an introductory software tutorial and textbook companion. This
Macintosh program presents the historical geography of the continental
United States from colonial times to the settling of the West and the
admission of the last continental state in 1912. The program covers territories in different time periods, provides quizzes, and includes a special
Civil War module.

About the Authors

JAMES KIRBY MARTIN is a member of the Department of History at the University of Houston. A graduate of Hiram College in Ohio, he earned his Ph.D. degree at the University of Wisconsin in 1969, specializing in Early American history. His interests also include American social and military history. Among his publications are *Men in Rebellion* (1973), *In the Course of Human Events* (1979), *A Respectable Army* (1982), and *Drinking in America: A History*, rev. ed. (1987), the latter two volumes in collaboration with Mark E. Lender. Martin serves as general editor of the *American Social Experience* series, New York University Press. He recently was a senior fellow at the Philadelphia Center for Early American Studies, University of Pennsylvania, as well as scholar-in-residence at the David Library of the American Revolution, Washington Crossing, Pennsylvania. He is completing a biography of Benedict Arnold.

RANDY ROBERTS earned his Ph.D degree in 1978 from Louisiana State University. His areas of specialization include modern U.S. history and the history of American popular culture and sports. He is a member of the Department of History at Purdue University, where he recently won the Murphy Award for outstanding undergraduate teaching. His publications include *Jack Dempsey: The Manassa Mauler* (1979), *Papa Jack: Jack Johnson and the Era of White Hopes* (1983), and, in collaboration with James S. Olson, *Playing for Keeps: Sports and American Society, 1945 to the Present* (1989) and *Where the Domino Fell: America and Vietnam, 1945–1990* (1991). Roberts serves as co-editor of the *Studies in Sports and Society* series, University of Illinois Press, and is on the editorial board of the *Journal of Sports History*. His current research and writing interests include a biographical investigation of Hollywood actor John Wayne.

STEVEN MINTZ graduated from Oberlin College in Ohio before earning his Ph.D. degree at Yale University in 1979. His special interests include American social history with particular reference to families, women, children, and communities. Mintz is a member of the Department of History at the University of Houston. From 1989 to 1990 he was a visiting scholar at Harvard University's Center for European Studies, and has served as a consultant to the Smithsonian Institution's National Museum of American History. His books include *A Prison of Expectations: The Family in Victorian Culture* (1983), and, in collaboration with Susan Kellogg, *Domestic Revolutions: A Social History of American Family Life* (1988). Mintz is an editor of the *American Social Experience* series, New York University Press, and is completing a book on pre-Civil War American reform.

LINDA O. McMURRY is a member of the Department of History at North Carolina State University. She completed her undergraduate studies at Auburn University, where she also earned her Ph.D. degree in 1976. Her fields of specialization include nineteenth- and twentieth-century U.S. history with an emphasis on the African-American experience and the New South. A recipient of a Rockefeller Foundation Humanities fellowship, she has written *George Washington Carver: Scientist and Symbol* (1981), and *Recorder of the Black Experience: A Biography of Monroe Nathan Work* (1985). McMurry has been active as a consultant to public television stations and museums on topics relating to black history, and is currently completing a study of biracial organizations in the South from the Reconstruction era to World War II.

JAMES H. JONES earned his Ph.D. degree at Indiana University in 1972. His areas of specialization include modern U.S. history, the history of medical ethics and medicine, and the history of sexual behavior. A member of the Department of History at the University of Houston, Jones has been a senior fellow of the National Endowment for the Humanities, a Kennedy fellow at Harvard University, a senior research fellow at the Kennedy Institute of Ethics, Georgetown University, and a Rockefeller fellow at the University of Texas Medical Branch, Galveston. His published writings include *Bad Blood: The Tuskegee Syphilis Experiment* (1981), and he is currently finishing a book on Alfred C. Kinsey and the emergence of scientific research dealing with human sexual behavior.

SAM W. HAYNES received his B.A. from Columbia University and his Ph.D. from the University of Houston in 1988. He is the author of *Soldiers of Misfortune: The Somervell and Mier Expeditions* (1990) and the editor of Thomas Jefferson Green's memoir *Journal of the Texian Expedition Against Mier* (1993). In 1993 he received a Dobie-Paisano

Fellowship awarded by the Texas Institute of Letters. He is currently completing a biography of James K. Polk. His areas of specialization include nineteenth-century U.S. expansionism, early Texas history, and the American Southwest. He is a member of the history faculty at the University of Texas at Arlington, where he also serves as a Fellow at the Center for Greater Southwestern Studies.

Chapter *I*

The Peopling and Unpeopling of America

Each Thanksgiving Americans remember Squanto as the valued Native American friend who saved the suffering Pilgrims from starvation. Few know the other ways in which Squanto's life reflected the disastrous collision of human beings occurring in the wake of Christopher Columbus's first voyage of discovery to America in 1492. What the Europeans called the "new world" had in fact been the home of millions of people for many centuries. The tragic story of Squanto and his tribe, the Patuxets of eastern Massachusetts, vividly portrays what happened when the two cultures came into contact.

Born about 1590, Squanto acquired the values of his Algonquian-speaking elders before experiencing much contact with adventurers from overseas. Tribal fathers taught him that personal dignity came from respecting the bounties of nature and serving one's clan and village, not from acquiring material possessions. To be accepted as an adult, he had to undergo a series of trials, which included spending a harrowing winter alone in the wilderness and eating poisonous herbs. When he had demonstrated his fortitude, tribal members declared him a man.

Living among 2,000 souls in the Patuxets' principal village, Squanto may well have foreseen trouble ahead when fair-skinned Europeans started visiting the region. First there were French fishermen; more fatefully, English vessels from the Jamestown settlement in Virginia passed through in 1614. One of the captains lured 20 Indians, among them Squanto, on board his ship and, without warning, set his course for the slave market in Malaga, Spain.

Somehow Squanto avoided a lifetime of slavery. By 1617 he was in England, where he devoted himself to mastering the English tongue. When asked to serve as an interpreter and guide for yet another New England expedition, Squanto, anxious to return home, readily agreed. In 1619, when the party put in at Plymouth Bay, a shocked Squanto discovered that nothing remained of his once-thriving village, except overgrown fields and rotting human bones. As if swept away by some unnamed force, the Patuxets had disappeared from the face of the earth. Thousands of Indians had died in the Cape Cod vicinity, the victims of diseases heretofore unknown in New England and probably carried there from Europe by fishermen and explorers. When these diseases struck, the native populace, lacking antibodies, had no way of fending them off.

Squanto was living with the Pokanoket Indians when the Pilgrims stepped ashore in December 1620 at the site of his old village. The Pilgrims endured a terrible winter in which half their numbers died. Then in the early spring of 1621 a lone Indian, Samoset, appeared in Plymouth Colony. He spoke halting English and told of another who had actually lived in England. Within a week Squanto arrived and agreed to stay and

Squanto is best remembered for the assistance he gave the Pilgrims in providing the necessities of life, but his own life—and death—illustrate the tensions and problems created by contact between Native American and European cultures.

help the Pilgrims produce the necessities of life. He taught them how to grow Indian corn (maize), a crop unknown in Europe, and how to catch great quantities of fish. His efforts resulted in an abundance of food, celebrated in the first Thanksgiving feast during the fall of 1621.

The story does not have a pleasant ending. Contact with the English had changed Squanto, and he adopted some of their practices. In violation of his childhood training, he started to serve himself. As future Pilgrim Governor William Bradford recorded, Squanto told neighboring Indian tribes that the Pilgrims would make war on them unless they gave him gifts. By the summer of 1622 Squanto had become a problem for the Pilgrims, who were anxious for peace. Then he fell sick, "bleeding much at the nose," and died within a few days, another victim of some European disease.

As demonstrated by Squanto's life, white–Indian contacts did not point toward a fusing of Native American and European customs, values, and ideals. Rather, the westward movement of peoples destroyed Indian societies and replaced them with European-based communities. Native Americans experienced chaos and death when they came into contact with Europeans. By the time of the Pilgrims' arrival, the Indian population had declined by as much as 90 percent.

The First Discovery of America

The world was a much colder place 75,000 years ago. A great ice age, known as the Wisconsin glaciation, had begun. Year after year, water being drawn from the oceans formed into mighty ice caps, which in turn spread over vast reaches of land. This process dramatically lowered ocean levels. In the area of the Bering Straits, where today 56 miles of ocean separate Siberia from Alaska, a land bridge emerged, which at times may have been 1,000 miles wide. This corridor, most experts believe, provided the pathway used by early humans to enter a new world.

These people, known as Paleo-Indians, were nomads and predators. With stone-tipped spears, they hunted mastodons, woolly mammoths, giant beavers, giant sloths, and bighorn bison, as well as many smaller animals. The mammals led prehistoric men and women to America up to 30,000 or more years ago. For generations, these humans roamed Alaska in small bands, gathering seeds and berries when not hunting the big game or attacking and killing one another.

Eventually, corridors opened through the Rocky Mountains as the ice started to recede. Humans and animals trekked southward and eastward, reaching the bottom of South America and the east coast of North America by about 8000 B.C. It had been a long journey, covering thousands of miles, and in the process Paleo-Indians had become Native Americans.

The Early Americans

With the passing of time, the atmosphere began to warm as the ice age came to an end. Mammoths, mastodons, and other giant mammals did not survive the warming climate and needless overkilling. The first Americans now faced a serious food crisis. Beginning in Central America between roughly 8000 and 5000 B.C., groups of humans started cultivating plant life as an alternate food source. They soon mastered the basics of agriculture. They raked the earth with stone hoes and planted seeds that produced crops as varied as maize, potatoes, squashes, pumpkins, and tomatoes.

This agricultural revolution profoundly affected Native American life. Those who engaged in farming were no longer as nomadic. They constructed villages and ordered their religious beliefs around such elements of nature as the sun and rain. With dependable food supplies, they had more children, resulting in a population explosion. These cultures ultimately evolved into complex societies, the most sophisticated of which appeared in Central America and the Ohio and Mississippi river valleys.

Emerging before A.D. 300, the Mayas of Mexico and Guatemala built elaborate cities and temples. Their craft workers produced jewelry of gold and silver, and their merchants developed extensive trading networks. Their intellectuals devised forms of hieroglyphic writing, mathematical systems, and several calendars, one of which was the most accurate in the world at that time. After A.D. 1000 warlike peoples from the north began to conquer their cities. First came the Toltecs, then the Aztecs. The Aztecs called their principal city Tenochtitlán (the site of present-day Mexico City). At its zenith just before the Spanish conquistadores appeared in 1519, Tenochtitlán contained a population of 300,000, making it one of the largest cities in the world at that time. Although imitators of Mayan culture, the Aztecs brutally exacted tribute, both in wealth and lives, from subject tribes. Their priests reveled in human sacrifice, since Huitzilopochtli, the Aztec war god, voraciously craved human hearts. At one temple dedication, Aztec priests sacrificed some 20,000 subject peoples. Not surprisingly, these tribes hated their oppressors. Many later cooperated with the Spanish in destroying the Aztecs.

Other mighty civilizations also emerged, such as the Incas of Peru, who came into prominence after A.D. 1100. Settling in the Andes Mountains, the Incas built an extensive road system and developed a sophisticated food supply network. The Incas were even wealthier than the Aztecs. They mined gold and silver in huge quantities, which made them a special target for Spanish conquerors.

In North America the Mound Builders (Adena and Hopewell peoples) appeared in the Ohio River valley around 1000 B.C. and lasted until A.D. 700. These natives hunted and gathered food, but they obtained most of their diet from agriculture. Their merchants traded far and wide. Fascinated with death, they built elaborate burial sites, such as the Great Serpent Mound in Ohio. In time they gave way to the Temple Mound Builders (Mississippian peoples), who constructed large cities, including a huge site near Cahokia, Illinois, where as many as 75,000 people lived amid 85 large temple mounds. For unknown reasons the Mississippian culture broke apart before European contact. Remnant groups may have included the Choctaws and Creeks of Mississippi and Alabama, as well as the Natchez Indians. All but exterminated by the French in the 1730s, the Natchez were the last of the Mound Builders in North America.

Indians on the Eve of Contact

Beginning with the agricultural revolution, population in the Americas increased rapidly. Estimates vary widely, and one authority has claimed a native populace of up to 120 million persons by the 1490s. Other experts consider this estimate too high, suggesting a figure of 50 to 80 million, with 5 to 8 million inhabitants living in North America. Europe's population, by comparison, was roughly 75 million at the time of Columbus, which underscores the mistaken impression among European explorers that America was a "virgin" or "vacant" land.

The explorers encountered a world of immense cultural diversity. At the time of Columbian contact, some 550 to 650 languages were in use in Central and North America. Developing life-styles to fit their environments, native groups varied greatly. Tribes in Oregon and Washington, such as the Chinooks, did some farming, but fishing for salmon was their primary means of subsistence. In the Great Plains region, Indians such as the Arapahos and Pawnees pursued wild game within more or less fixed hunting zones. Men concentrated on bringing in meat, and women functioned as gatherers of berries and seeds. In the Southwest, the Hopi and Zuñi tribes relied upon agriculture since edible plant and animal life was scarce in their desert environment. These Indians even practiced irrigation. Perhaps they are best known for their flat-roofed, multitiered villages that the Spanish called *pueblos.*

In the East, where English explorers and settlers first made contact with Native Americans, there were dozens of small tribal groups. Southeastern natives, including Cherokees, Chickasaws, Creeks, Choctaws, and Seminoles, were more attuned to agriculture because of lengthy growing seasons. Northeastern tribes, such as the Mahicans and Micmacs, placed more emphasis upon hunting and gathering.

Eastern Woodland Indians spoke several different languages but held many cultural traits in common. Essential to their religious values was the notion of an animate universe. They considered trees, plants, and animals to be spiritually alive. Tribal *shamans,* or medicine men, communicated with these spirits and prescribed elaborate rules, or taboos, regarding the treatment of plants and animals. Indian parents, having mastered such customs, taught children like Squanto that nature contained the resources of life. Although there was intertribal trading and much gift-giving in pottery, baskets, jewelry, furs, and wampum (conch and clam shells), religious values deterred tribal members from exploiting the landscape for the sake of acquiring great personal wealth.

Eastern Woodland parents introduced their children to many other concepts. There was no individual ownership of land. Tribal boundaries consisted of geographic locales large enough to provide for basic food supplies. Although individual dignity did matter, cooperation with tribal members rather than individual competitiveness was the essential ideal, even in sports. The refinement of athletic skills also represented useful training for war. Intertribal warfare was sporadic and resulted from any number of factors, such as competition over valued hunting grounds. Festering tensions and language barriers worked against intertribal cooperation in repelling the Europeans.

Even though males served as warriors, they did not always control tribal decision making. Among the powerful Five Nations of Iroquois in central New York, tribal organization was matrilineal. Women headed individual family units that in turn formed into clans. Clan leaders were also women, and they decided which males would sit on tribal councils that considered policies regarding diplomacy and war. Among other Eastern Woodland Indians, women occasionally served as tribal *sachems* (chiefs), much to the shock of Europeans.

When European fishermen and explorers started making contact, there were 500,000 to 800,000 Indians inhabiting the region between the North Atlantic coastline and the Appalachian Mountains. The Europeans were initially curious as well as fearful, but these feelings soon gave way to expressions of contempt. Judging all people by European standards, they regarded the Indians as inferior. Native Americans looked and dressed differently. Their religious conceptions did not conform to European forms of Christianity. The men seemed lazy since women did the bulk of the farming, and there was no consuming drive to acquire personal wealth.

To make matters worse, the natives, like those of Squanto's tribe, quickly began to die in huge numbers, which further confirmed European perceptions that Indian peoples were inferior rather than merely different. These native "savages" were blocking the path of a more advanced civilization desirous of expansion, or so Europeans argued. Thus commenced what many historians have come to call the "invasion" of America.

Preparing Europe for Westward Expansion

Nearly 500 years before Columbus's first westward voyage in 1492, Europeans made their first known contacts with North America. Around A.D. 1000, the Vikings (Scandinavians) explored barren regions of the North Atlantic. Eric the Red led an expedition of Vikings to Greenland, and one of his sons, Leif Ericson, continued exploring south and westward, stopping at Baffin Island, Labrador, and Newfoundland (described as *Vinland*). There were some settlement attempts, but they did not endure.

Crusades, Commerce, and the New Learning

The Viking voyages had no long-term impact because Europe was not yet ripe for westward expansion. Nonetheless, Europeans were slowly gathering knowledge about previously unknown peoples and places. The Crusades, designed to oust the Muslim "infidels" from such Christian holy sites as Jerusalem, broadened their geographic horizons. Sanctioned by the Roman Catholic church and begun in 1095, the Crusades lasted for two centuries. Although unsuccessful in their military objectives, European warriors learned of spices that would preserve meats over long winters, fruits that would bring greater balance to diets, silk and velvet clothing, handcrafted rugs, delicate glassware, and dozens of other commodities that would make European lives more comfortable.

Italian merchants, living in independent city-states such as Venice and Genoa, took the lead in developing the Mediterranean trade. The new wealth displayed by these great merchants promoted a pervasive spirit of material acquisition. It also helped underwrite a resurgence of the arts and sciences, known as the *Renaissance*. Beginning in Italy, the Renaissance soon captivated much of Continental Europe. The new spirit of learning resulted in enhanced geographical knowledge and developments in naval science. By the mid-fifteenth century educated Europeans knew the world was not flat. Receptive to new ideas, they learned from the Muslims about the astrolabe and sextant and their uses as basic navigational instruments. Contact with the Arabs also introduced Europeans to more advanced ship and sail designs. These breakthroughs heightened prospects for worldwide exploration in the ongoing search for valuable trading commodities.

The adventures of Marco Polo underscored the new learning and exemplified its relationship to commerce and exploration. Late in the thirteenth century, this young Venetian trader traveled throughout the Orient. He recorded his findings and told of unbelievable wealth in Asian kingdoms such as Cathay (China). Around 1450, Johannes Gutenberg, a German printer, perfected movable type, making it possible to reprint limitless copies of manuscripts. The first printed edition of Marco Polo's *Journals* appeared in 1477. Merchants and explorers alike, among them Christopher Columbus, read Polo's *Journals,* which spurred them on in the prospect of gaining complete access to Oriental riches.

Nation-States Support the First Explorations

The breakdown of feudal institutions and the consolidation of feudal domains into larger, more powerful nation-states also helped make transoceanic exploration possible. The process of forming modern nation-states commenced during the fifteenth century. The marriage of Ferdinand of Aragon to Isabella of Castile in 1469 represented the beginnings of national unity in Spain. These joint monarchs hired mercenary soldiers to break the power of defiant nobles. In 1492 they also crushed the Muslims (Moors) inhabiting southern Spain, driving them as well as Jewish inhabitants out of the country. Working closely with the Roman Catholic church, Ferdinand and Isabella used the Inquisition torture chambers to break the will of others whose loyalty they doubted. By 1500 their subjects owed first allegiance to Spain, not to local manor lords.

Spain's neighbor Portugal also led the way in the process of nation-building. Consolidating his realm in the 1380s, King John I was able to support his son, Prince Henry, called "the Navigator," in the latter's efforts to learn more about the world. Henry set up a school of navigation, and with official state support he sent out ships on exploratory missions. When the crews returned, they worked to improve maps, sailing techniques, navigational procedures, and ship designs.

Initially, the emphasis was on learning, but then it shifted to a quest for valuable trade goods as Henry's mariners conquered such islands as the Azores and brought back gold, silver, and ivory from the west coast of Africa. The lure of wealth drove Portuguese sailors farther south along the African coast. Bartholomeu Dias made it to the Cape of Good Hope in 1487. Ten years later, Vasco da Gama took a small flotilla around the lower tip of Africa and on to the riches of India. Da Gama's expedition led to the development of Portugal's Far Eastern empire. None of this would have been possible without a unified Portuguese government able to tax the populace and thus sponsor Prince Henry's attempts to probe the boundaries of the unknown.

Ferdinand and Isabella were intensely aware of Portugal's triumphs when Christopher Columbus, a young mariner from the Italian city-state of Genoa, asked them to underwrite his dream of sailing west to reach the Orient. Too consumed with their struggle for internal unification, they refused him, but Columbus persisted. He had already contacted Portugal, France, and England but gained no sponsorship. Finally, Queen Isabella, less occupied with internal problems after the unification of Spain, reconsidered. She met Columbus's terms, which included 10 percent of all profits from his discoveries, and proclaimed him "Admiral of the Ocean Sea."

On August 3, 1492, Columbus and some 90 mariners set sail from Palos, Spain, in the *Niña, Pinta,* and *Santa María.* On October 12 they landed on a small island in the Bahamas, which Columbus named San Salvador (holy savior). He called the natives Indians, a misnomer that stuck, because he believed that he was near Asia (the Indies). Proceeding on, Columbus landed on Cuba, which he thought was Japan, and then on Hispaniola, where he traded for gold-laden native jewelry. In 1493 Columbus and his crew returned home to a hero's welcome and to funding for three more expeditions to America.

Explorers, Conquerors, and the Making of New Spain

A fearless explorer, Columbus turned out to be an ineffective administrator and a poor geographer. He ended up in debtors' prison, and to his dying day in 1506 he claimed he had reached Asia, not an unknown geographic entity. Geographers named the western continents after another mariner, Amerigo Vespucci, a merchant from Florence who participated in a Portuguese expedition to South America in 1501. In a widely reprinted letter, Vespucci claimed that a new world had been found, and it was his name that caught on.

Columbus's significance lay elsewhere. His 1492 venture garnered enough extractable wealth to excite the Spanish monarchs. They did not care whether Columbus had reached Asia, only that further exploratory voyages might produce unimaginable riches. Because they feared Portuguese interference, Ferdinand and Isabella moved quickly to solidify their interests. They went to Pope Alexander VI, who issued a papal bull that divided the unknown world between Portugal and Spain. In 1494 they worked out a formal agreement with Portugal in the Treaty of Tordesillas, drawing a line some 1100 miles west of the Cape Verde Islands. All undiscovered lands to the west of the demarcation line belonged to Spain. Those to the east were Portugal's.

Ferdinand and Isabella used their strong army, seasoned by its struggle for unification, to conquer the Americas. The Spanish *conquistadores* did so with relish. Befitting their crusader's ideology, they agreed to subdue the natives and, with the support of church leaders, to convert them to Roman Catholicism. Bravery and courage, these warriors believed, would bring distinction to themselves and to their nation. Further, they could gain much personal wealth, even if shared with the Crown. Gold, glory, and the gospel formed a triad of factors motivating the Spanish conquistadores, and their efforts resulted in a far-flung empire known as New Spain.

Conquistadores Overrun Native Americans

Before 1510 the Spanish confined their explorations and settlements to the Caribbean islands. Unwittingly, the conquistadores carried with them microbic weapons against the Indians. European diseases such as small-

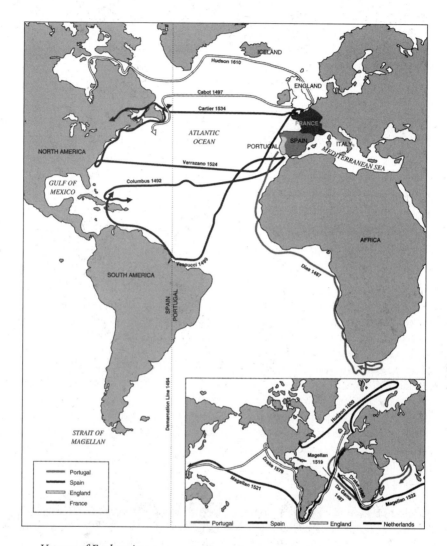

Voyages of Exploration

Except for abortive attempts by Norsemen in the late tenth century, contact between North America and Europe began at the end of the 1400s. In the 1500s settlements were founded by Spain in Mexico and Florida, and in the early 1600s France, England, Sweden, and Holland claimed territory along the Atlantic coast.

pox, typhoid, diphtheria, the measles, and various plagues and fevers took a rapid toll. In 1492, for example, more than 200,000 Indians inhabited Hispaniola. Just 20 years later, there were fewer than 30,000.

After 1510 the conquistadores moved onto the mainland. Vasco Núñez de Balboa reached Panama in 1513. He became the first European to see the Pacific Ocean, which he dutifully claimed for Spain. The same year Juan Ponce de León led a party to Florida in search of gold and a rumored fountain of youth. Although disappointed on both counts, he claimed Florida for Spain. Then in 1519 Hernando Cortés landed on the Mexican coast with 600 soldiers and marched toward Tenochtitlán, the site of modern-day Mexico City.

Aztec emperor Montezuma II offered Cortés mounds of gold and silver to keep out of Tenochtitlán, but this gesture only intensified the conquistadores' greed. They boldly marched into the city and took Montezuma prisoner. The Aztecs finally drove off Cortés's army in 1520, but less than a year later the Spaniards retook Tenochtitlán and claimed all Aztec wealth and political authority as their prize.

Cortés's stunning victory spurred on many other conquistadores, such as aggressive Francisco Pizarro. With fewer than 200 soldiers, he overwhelmed thousands of Incas in Peru, seizing the capital city of Cuzco in 1533 after hardly any fighting. Again, diseases stalked wherever Pizarro went. Showing no mercy, he executed the great chief Atahualpa and proclaimed Spain's sovereignty. By the 1550s the Spanish had conquered much of the rest of South America.

To the north, various expeditions scoured the landscape but found nothing comparable to the wealth of the Aztecs and Incas. Four hundred men under Pánfilo de Narváez began a disastrous adventure in 1528. They landed in Florida and searched the Gulf Coast region before being shipwrecked in what is now Texas. Only four men survived, one of whom, Cabeza de Vaca, wrote a tract telling of seven great cities laden with gold. His writings stimulated Hernando de Soto to investigate the lower Mississippi River valley. In 1540 another party under Francisco Vásquez de Coronado began exploring parts of New Mexico, Texas, Oklahoma, and Kansas. They were the first Europeans to see the Grand Canyon. Two years later, Spanish vessels sailed along the California coast as far north as Oregon. None of these groups ever located the fabled cities, but they advanced geographic knowledge of North America while claiming everything they came in contact with for Spain.

Constructing the Spanish Empire

To keep out intruders and to maintain order in New Spain, the Spanish Crown set up two home-based administrative agencies in Madrid. The

Columbus first landed on the Bahamian island which he named San Salvador. He described the local natives as peaceful and generous, an image that changed rapidly as *conquistadores* swept over the native populace in their rush to tap into the riches of the Americas.

House of Trade formulated economic policies and provided for annual convoys of galleons, called plate fleets, to haul American booty back to Spain. The Council for the Indies controlled all political matters in what became an autocratic, rigidly managed empire for the exclusive benefit of the parent state.

The Council for the Indies ruled through viceroys that headed four regional areas of administration. Viceroys, in turn, consulted with *audiencias* (appointed councils) on matters of local concern, but there were no popularly based representative assemblies. Normally, only pure-blooded Spaniards could influence decision making—and only if they had ties to councilors or viceroys. Those who questioned their political superiors soon learned there was little tolerance for divergent opinions.

During the sixteenth century about 200,000 Spaniards, a modest number, migrated to the Americas. Most migrants were young males looking for adventure and material riches. They did not find much of either, but some became wealthy as manor holders, ranchers, miners, and government officials. From the very outset, Spanish settlers complained about a shortage of laborers. One solution was the *encomienda* system. As *encomenderos,* or landlords, favored warriors and settlers received titles to Indian villages and the surrounding countryside as well as portions of annual crops and other forms of tribute. In exchange, the *encomenderos* were to educate the natives and instruct them in the Roman Catholic faith.

There were serious problems with the *encomienda* system. Landlords regularly abused the Indians, treating them like slave property. There was so much exploitation and death that one Dominican priest, Bartolomé de Las Casas, repeatedly begged officials in Madrid to stop such barbarities. In 1542 the Crown outlawed both the *encomienda* system and the enslavement of Indians, but this ruling did not change matters that much. Governing officials continued to award pure-blooded Spaniards vast landed estates (*haciendas*), on which Indians lived in a state of peonage, cultivating the soil and sharing their crops with their landlords (*hacendados*).

Since the native populace also kept dying off from contact with European diseases, a second solution to the labor problem was to import Africans. In 1501 the Crown authorized the first shipment of slaves to the Caribbean islands, a small beginning to what became a vast, forced migration of some ten million human beings to the Americas.

Slavery as it developed in New Spain was harsh. *Hacienda* owners and mine operators wanted only young males who could literally be worked to death, then replaced by new shiploads of Africans. On the other hand, Spanish law and Roman Catholic doctrine restrained some brutality. The Church believed that all souls should be saved, and it recognized marriage as a sacrament, meaning that slaves could wed and aspire to family life. Spanish law even permitted slaves to purchase their freedom. Such allowances were well beyond those made in future English-speaking colonies, and many blacks, particularly those who became artisans and house servants in the cities, did gain their independence.

Also easing slavery's harsh realities was the matter of skin color gradation: the lighter the skin, the greater the privileges. Since so many of the first Spanish migrants were males, they often intermarried with Indians or Africans. The mixture of skin colors in New Spain helped Africans escape some of the racial contempt experienced by blacks in English North

America, where there was less skin color variation because of legal restrictions against racial intermarriage.

Success Breeds Envy and Contempt

As Spanish authority spread north into areas that are now known as New Mexico, Arizona, and California, Franciscan, Dominican, and Jesuit friars opened missions and offered protection to natives who would accept Roman Catholic beliefs. Quite often local Indians simply incorporated Catholic doctrines into their own belief systems. When in the late 1660s and early 1670s a prolonged drought followed by a devastating epidemic ravaged Pueblos living in the upper Rio Grande valley of New Mexico, these natives openly questioned their new Catholic faith. Inspired by a native spiritual leader named Popé, they rose in rebellion in 1680 and killed or drove some 2,500 Spanish inhabitants out of New Mexico. By 1700 Spain had reconquered the region, maiming and killing hundreds of Pueblos in the process. With their numbers already in rapid decline, the Pueblos never again seriously challenged Spanish rule.

The flow of wealth from the Americas made Spain the most powerful—and envied—nation in Europe during the sixteenth century. Such success also became a source of contempt. When Las Casas, for example, wrote a book listing Spanish atrocities against the Indians, his charges became the basis of the "Black Legend," a tale that other Europeans used as a rationale for challenging Spain's New World supremacy. Spain's European rivals promised to treat Native Americans more humanely, but in reality their primary motivation was to garner a share of America's riches for themselves.

Challengers for North America: France and England

When Henry VII of England realized how successful Columbus had been, he chose to ignore the Treaty of Tordesillas and underwrote another Italian explorer, Giovanni Caboto (John Cabot), to seek Cathay (China) on behalf of the Tudor monarchy. Cabot's was the first exploratory expedition to touch North America since the Viking voyages. He landed on Newfoundland and Cape Breton Island in 1497. A second expedition in 1498 ended in disaster when Cabot was lost at sea. Still, his voyages served as the basis for English claims to North America.

Soon France joined the exploration race. In 1524 King Francis I sponsored yet another Italian mariner, Giovanni da Verrazzano, who sailed along the American coast from North Carolina to Maine. More important for later French claims, Jacques Cartier mounted three expeditions to the St. Lawrence River area, beginning in 1534, scouting as far inland as modern-day Quebec and Montreal.

The Protestant Reformation

Religious turmoil at home was one reason why the monarchs of England and France did not directly challenge Spain's supremacy in the Americas. There were too many problems at home, such as those related to religious turmoil. The Roman Catholic church had long been the wealthiest and most powerful institution in Europe. The greatest challenge to its authority came in 1517, when Martin Luther, an obscure German friar of the Augustinian order, criticized the church for what he thought were a number of unscriptural practices, particularly the selling of "indulgences" in the form of cash payments to the church to make amends for sins. As a form of penance, individuals could purchase indulgences for themselves or for others, such as deceased loved ones to assure quick journeys through purgatory to heaven.

Luther found no biblical basis for indulgences, and he despised the corrupt agents who sold them. As a professor of Scripture at the University of Wittenberg, Luther had agonized for years over the ways to earn God's grace, and he had concluded that faith was all that mattered, not ritual or good works. He insisted that people did not need priests to interpret scriptures for them but should be allowed to read the Bible for themselves in developing their own faith in God. Luther thus advocated a "priesthood of all believers" in comprehending the mysteries of Christianity. By the 1550s the doctrines of Lutheranism had taken firm hold in parts of Germany and the Scandinavian countries, often in the wake of enormous social turmoil.

Once underway, the Protestant Reformation, as the movement that Luther spawned became known, gained rapid momentum. It also took on many forms. In England, where politics rather than theology dictated the split with Rome, Henry VIII at first condemned Luther for arguing in favor of only two sacraments—baptism and communion. At the same time, Henry worried about not having a male heir to assure perpetuation of the Tudor line. In 1527 he asked Pope Clement VII to annul his marriage to Catherine of Aragon. When the pope refused, Henry severed all ties with Rome. Through a series of parliamentary acts, Henry closed monasteries and seized church property. In the 1534 Act of Supremacy he formally repudiated the pope and declared himself God's regent over England. Henceforth, all subjects would belong to the Anglican (English)

Church. The Church of England, unlike the Lutheran church, was similar to its predecessor in doctrine and ritual.

The Protestant leader whose beliefs were destined to have the greatest impact on the English colonies was John Calvin, a French lawyer who had fled to Switzerland in 1534 because of his controversial theological ideas. A brilliant and persuasive man, he soon controlled Geneva and ordered life there according to his understanding of scripture. Calvin believed God to be both all-powerful and wrathful. To avoid eternal damnation, it was necessary to gain His grace through a conversion experience denoted by accepting Jesus Christ as one's savior. However, while all had to seek, God had already predestined who would be saved and who would be damned. Since it was difficult to discern God's chosen "saints," Calvin taught that correct moral behavior according to the Bible and outward prosperity—physical and mental as well as material—represented possible signs of divine favor.

Calvin's disciples quickly spread the doctrine throughout Europe. Their numbers included founders of the German and Dutch Reformed churches, as well as Huguenots who eventually suffered from organized state persecution back in France. John Knox, another follower of Calvin, established the Presbyterian church in Scotland. In England, many Calvinists were called "Puritans." They wanted to continue Henry's reformation, but now along theological lines. Fiercely dedicated to their beliefs, they had a startling impact on the course of English history, particularly after the reign of Elizabeth I, when some of them moved to North America and others precipitated a civil war.

Defying the Supremacy of Spain

Spain's success in the Americas, combined with religious strife between Protestants and Catholics, fostered unending turmoil among European nation-states. Throughout the sixteenth century French, Dutch, and English freebooters attacked Spanish commerce or traded covertly within the Spanish empire. The most daring of the "sea dogs" were Englishmen like John Hawkins and Francis Drake. During the 1560s and 1570s Hawkins smuggled goods and raided for booty in New Spain. Drake's adventures were even more dramatic. With private financial backing, Drake attacked Spanish ports of call during the course of a three-year voyage which began in 1577. He became the first Englishman to circumnavigate the globe.

Queen Elizabeth's professions of innocence to the contrary, King Philip II of Spain suspected her of actively supporting the sea dogs. Further, he was furious with the English for giving military aid to the Protestant Dutch, who since 1567 had been fighting to free themselves from

Spanish rule. In 1588 Philip launched an armada of 130 vessels against England. The expedition ended in disaster for the Spanish when a host of English ships, most of them smaller but far more maneuverable than Philip's slow-moving galleons, appeared in the English Channel and offered battle under Drake's command. Then a fierce storm—the famous "Protestant Wind"— took over and blew the Spanish Armada to bits. The war with Spain did not officially end until 1604, but the destruction of the Armada established England's reputation as a naval power. It also demonstrated that little England, heretofore a minor kingdom, could prevail over Europe's most powerful nation, which encouraged some English subjects to press forward in securing territories in North America.

England Prepares for Westward Expansion

Besides the diminished Spanish threat, other factors helped to pave the way for England's westward expansion. None was more important than rapid population growth, which supplied a large pool of potential migrants. During the sixteenth century, England's population doubled in size, reaching four million people by the 1590s. Yet opportunities for employment or decent wages lagged behind the population explosion. The phenomenal growth of the woolen industry, for instance, forced peasants from the land as manor lords fenced in their fields to make pastures for sheep, a process known as the "enclosure movement." Meantime, cities such as London exploded in size as displaced persons poured in from the countryside and subsisted as best they could, some by working as day laborers for pitiful wages and others by begging and stealing.

Not only the uprooted peasants faced serious economic difficulties. Everyone confronted the major problem of rapid inflation. Between 1500 and 1600 the cost of goods and services spiraled upward by up to five times. The principal inflationary culprit was an overabundance of precious metal, mostly Spanish silver mined in America (seven million pounds in weight by about 1650) and then pumped into the European economy in exchange for various commodities. The money in circulation expanded more quickly than did the supply of goods or services. As a result, prices jumped dramatically.

In England even farmers owning their own land struggled to make ends meet since the cost of most necessities rose faster than what they received in the marketplace for their agricultural produce. A prolonged decline in real income on top of heavy taxes under the Tudors left many yeoman farmers destitute. In time, the abundant land of America attracted great numbers of England's failing independent farmers and permanently poor (or sturdy beggars).

The presence of so much poverty and suffering became a powerful argument for westward expansion. Besides putting beggars and other indigents back to work, colonies could serve as a source of valuable commodities. They would likewise stimulate England's shipbuilding industry and in other ways build up the power of the realm. On the other hand, Elizabeth was a tight-fisted Tudor monarch who remained unwilling to plunge vast sums of royal funds into highly speculative New World ventures. She preferred to let her favored courtiers, such as those who were currently subduing Ireland, expend their own capital and energies in searching for riches across the Atlantic Ocean.

Joining in the Invasion of America

Sir Humphrey Gilbert was a visionary who dreamed of finding a northwest passage through North America to the Orient, and who was willing to risk his personal fortune in the quest. Gilbert had other dreams as well, including the effective occupation of North America and the founding of American colonies. He appealed to Elizabeth for exclusive rights to carry out his plans, and she acceded in 1578.

The Roanoke Disaster

Gilbert did not live to see his dreams fulfilled. He disappeared in a North Atlantic storm after searching for the Northwest Passage. In 1584 his half-brother, Sir Walter Raleigh, received permission to carry on Gilbert's work. Raleigh sent out a reconnoitering party to explore the North Carolina coast and survey Roanoke Island. Then in 1585 he sponsored an expedition of 600 men. After some raiding for booty in New Spain, Raleigh's adventurers sailed north and dropped off 107 men at the chosen site.

The local Croatoan and Roanoak Indians initially welcomed the strangers, but relations quickly deteriorated as unknown diseases wreaked havoc on the native population. Warfare broke out, and the settlement had to be abandoned. Raleigh persisted, and in the summer of 1587 Governor John White and 114 others arrived on Roanoke Island. In mid-August White's daughter Elinor gave birth to Virginia Dare, the first English subject born in America. A few days later, the governor sailed back to England to obtain additional supplies. The outbreak of war with Spain delayed his return, and he did not get back to Roanoke until 1590. Nothing was left, except the word CROATOAN carved on a tree. What happened to the lost colony will never be known. No European ever saw the settlers again. Local Indians either killed or absorbed them into their tribes.

The Founding of Virginia

A few sixteenth-century English subjects did prosper in the wake of economic dislocation and spiraling inflation. Among these fortunate few were manufacturers of woolen goods and merchants who made all of Eu-

John White captured the life-style of the natives of Roanoke Island in his famous drawings.

rope a marketplace for English cloth. With their profits, these men started pooling their capital and sponsoring risky overseas business ventures by investing in *joint-stock* trading companies. Queen Elizabeth liked this model of business organization because private capital rather than royal assets would be marshaled to finance England's economic—and eventually political—expansion abroad. The Crown, of course, would share in any profits.

During the 1590s, English courtiers and merchant capitalists did not pick up on Raleigh's failed efforts. The ongoing war with Spain took precedence, and profits came easily from capturing Spanish vessels on the high seas. Once the war ended, influential merchants were anxious to pool their capital, spread the financial risk, and pursue Raleigh's patent. They took their case to the new king, the Stuart monarch James I, who willingly granted them a generous trading company charter in 1606.

In December 1606 they sent out 144 adventurers. The crossing was difficult, and 39 men died. In May 1607 the survivors located on an island some 30 miles up the James River off Chesapeake Bay. They called their settlement, really meant as a trading post, Jamestown. In its early days, Jamestown functioned as an outpost in another alien environment. The early participants were not settlers. They wanted to get in, gain access to easy forms of wealth, and get out before losing their lives.

It is amazing that Jamestown lasted at all. Many company adventurers were second and third sons of English noblemen. When Jamestown ran short of food, they still avoided agricultural work, preferring to search for gold and silver. The expedition also included valets and footmen, whose duties extended only to waiting on their aristocratic masters. Then there were goldsmiths and jewelers, plus a collection of ne'er-do-wells who apparently functioned as soldiers under gentleman officers. Hopelessly miscast for survival in the wilderness, many starved to death. Only 38 Englishmen were still alive by the early spring of 1608.

Another problem was the settlement site. Company directors had ordered the adventurers to locate on high ground far enough inland so as to go undetected by the Spanish. Jamestown Island met the second requirement, but it was a low, swampy place lying at a point on the James River where salt and fresh water mingled. The brackish water was "full of slime and filth," as one observer noted. The water could cause salt poisoning and was also a breeding ground for malaria, typhoid fever, and dysentery.

Several factors saved the Jamestown settlement. The local Indians under Powhatan, an Algonquian-speaking Pamunkey, initially offered sustenance. Powhatan had organized a confederacy of some 30 coastal tribes, numbering 20,000 people, to defend themselves against aggressive interior neighbors. Powhatan tried to stay clear of the Jamestown adventurers, but he could not help but notice their large ships, gaudy body

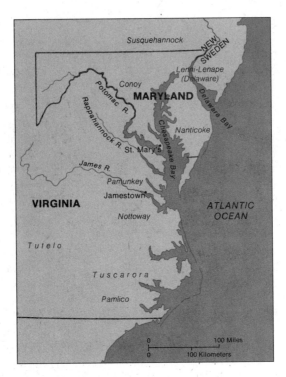

Chesapeake Settlements, 1650

armor, and noisy (though less-than-deadly) firearms. He viewed the English as potential allies in warfare with interior tribes, a faulty evaluation but one that kept him from wiping out the weakened adventurers.

At the same time, company investors in London refused to quit. They kept sending out supplies and adventurers, as many as 800 more young men plus a few women in 1608 and 1609. Upon their arrival, however, many quickly died of such diseases as malaria. Others, so debilitated from illnesses, were unable to work. They became a drain on Jamestown's precarious food supply.

At that time, the dynamic and ruthless local leadership of Captain John Smith kept the Jamestown outpost from totally collapsing. Once in Jamestown, he emerged as a virtual dictator. Smith helped save many lives by imposing discipline and forcing everyone—gentleman or servant, sick or well—to adhere to one rule: "He who works not, eats not."

In October 1609 Smith returned to England. Lacking authoritarian leadership, the adventurers experienced a tragic "starving time" during the winter of 1609–1610. Hundreds died as food supplies, described as "moldy, rotten, full of cobwebs and maggots," gave out. Only about 60 survived by eating everything from rats to snakes, and there was even an alleged instance of cannibalism. One man completely lost his mind; he murdered his wife, then "powdered [salted] her up to eat her, for which he was burned" at the stake.

Back in England, Virginia Company stockholders refused to concede defeat. By 1610 they realized that mineral wealth was an illusion but still they sent out more people. One of them, John Rolfe, experimented with local tobacco plants and produced a harsh-tasting crop. Rolfe, like the company, persisted. He procured some plants from Trinidad in the West Indies and grew a milder, more flavorful leaf. Tobacco soon became Virginia's gold and silver. The colony now had a valuable trading commodity, and settlements quickly spread along the banks of the James River. Englishmen had found an economic reason to stay in the Americas.

Dutch and French Adventurers

In the early 1600s the Spanish contented themselves with drawing wealth from their Caribbean basin empire. They did not challenge various European interlopers seeking to stake North American claims. Ultimately, Dutch settlements in New York were seized by the English, but France's efforts resulted in a Canadian empire capable of rivaling those of Spain and England.

Once fully liberated from Spanish domination at home, the Dutch grabbed at a portion of North America. In 1609 they sent out an English sea captain, Henry Hudson, to search for the Northwest Passage. Sailing up the New York waterway that bears his name, Hudson made contact with the Iroquois Indians and talked of trade in furs (broad-brimmed beaver hats were the fashion rage in Europe). The Dutch established trading stations on Manhattan Island (later called New Amsterdam) and Albany (Fort Orange) in 1624. The Iroquois did their part in delivering furs, and the colony of New Netherland took hold under the auspices of the Dutch West India Company.

Profits from furs also helped to motivate the French. In 1608 Samuel de Champlain set up an outpost at Quebec on the St. Lawrence River, and he found local Indians ready to trade. Yet only after 1663, when the Crown took control of managing the colony, did the French population in Canada grow significantly, reaching 10,000 by the 1680s. Following Champlain's lead, the French Canadians were energetic, exploring everywhere and claiming everything in sight. Few in number, they could not completely impose their cultural values on the Indians, so they established harmonious relations with dozens of different tribes. They even joined in native wars as a way of solidifying trading ties. They did use the natives for their own purposes, but they also showed respect, which paid off handsomely when their many Indian allies willingly fought beside them in a series of imperial wars that beset America beginning in 1689.

Conclusion

Except in Canada, the Europeans who explored the Americas and began colonies after 1492 acted as foreign invaders. Although a few were at first curious, they generally viewed the natives as their adversaries, describing them as "worse than those beasts which are of the most wild and savage nature." Judgments of cultural superiority seemed to justify the destruction of Native Americans.

Still, there was a "Columbian exchange" of sorts. The Indians taught the Europeans about tobacco, corn, potatoes, varieties of beans, peanuts, tomatoes, and many other crops then unknown in Europe. In return, Europeans introduced the native populace to wheat, oats, barley, and rice, as well as to grapes for wine and various melons. The Europeans also brought over domesticated animals, including horses, pigs, sheep, goats, and cattle. Horses proved to be important, particularly for Great Plains Indians, who used them in fighting against future generations of white settlers, just as tobacco production in the Chesapeake area had the unintended effect of attracting enough Europeans to end native control of that area.

Perhaps more than anything else, killer diseases served to unbalance the exchange. From the first moments of contact, great civilizations like the Aztecs and more humble groups like Squanto's Patuxets faced devastation. In some cases the Indians who survived, as in New Spain, had to accept the status of peons. Along the Atlantic coastline, survivors were drawn into the European trading network. In exchange for furs, the Indians wanted firearms to kill yet more animals whose pelts could be traded for still more guns and for alcohol to help them forget, even for a moment, what was happening to their way of life in the wake of European westward expansion.

The English would send the most settlers. They left home for various reasons. Some, like the Pilgrims, crossed the Atlantic to avoid further religious persecution. Others, such as the Puritans, sought to build a holy community that would shine as a light upon Europe. Still others, including colonists in the Chesapeake Bay area, desired land for growing tobacco. The latter group wanted laborers to help them raise their crops. Unable to enslave the Indians, they ultimately borrowed from the Spanish model and enslaved Africans. In so doing, they forced blacks to enter their settlements in chains and to become a part of a peopling and unpeopling process that helped to shape the contours of life in colonial America.

*C*hronology *of Key Events*

30,000–20,000 B.C.	First humans arrive in North America from Asia
A.D. 300–900	Mayan civilization flourishes in present-day Mexico and Guatemala
C. 900	Toltecs rise to power in the Valley of Mexico
C. 1000	Vikings reach Labrador and Newfoundland (*Vinland*)
1095	European Christians launch the Crusades to capture the Holy Lands
C. 1100	Inca civilization emerges in what is now Peru
1271	Marco Polo begins a 20-year journey to China
1420s	Portugal sends mariners to explore Africa's western coast
C. 1450	Johannes Gutenberg develops movable type, the basis of modern printing
1469	Marriage of Ferdinand and Isabella; beginning of Spanish unification
1492	Columbus makes the first of his voyages to the Americas
1494	Treaty of Tordesillas divides known world between Portugal and Spain
1497–1498	John Cabot voyages to Newfoundland and Cape Breton Island
1517	Protestant Reformation begins
1519	Conquest of the Aztec empire by Hernando Cortés and Spanish *conquistadores*
1527–1533	Anglican Reformation; Henry VIII severs ties with Roman Catholic Church
1531–1533	Conquest of the Inca empire by Francisco Pizarro
1534	Jacques Cartier explores the St. Lawrence River and claims the region for France
1585–1587	Sir Walter Raleigh sponsors Roanoke Island settlement
1607	First permanent English settlement at Jamestown established

Suggestions for Further Reading

On the pre-Columbian history of the Americas see Brian M. Fagan, *The Great Journey: The Peopling of Ancient America* (1987); and Alvin M. Josephy, Jr., ed., *America in 1492* (1991).

Useful accounts of Europe during the Age of Exploration are Charles R. Boxer, *The Portuguese Seaborne Empire* (1969); Carl Bridenbaugh, *Vexed and Troubled Englishmen, 1590–1642* (1968); Paul H. Chapman, *The Norse Discovery of America* (1981); Samuel E. Morison, *The European Discovery of America* (1971); and Wallace Notestein, *The English People on the Eve of Colonization*, (1954).

Studies of the clash of cultures in the Americas after 1492 include James Axtell, *After Columbus: Essays in the Ethnohistory of Colonial North America* (1988), *The European and the Indian* (1981), and *The Invasion Within: The Contest of Cultures in Colonial North America* (1985); William Cronon, *Changes in the Land: Indians, Colonists, and the Ecology of New England* (1983); Alfred W. Crosby, *The Columbian Exchange* (1972); Francis Jennings, *The Invasion of America: Indians, Colonialism, and the Cant of Conquest* (1975); Calvin Martin, *Keepers of the Game: Indian–Animal Relationships and the Fur Trade* (1978); and Timothy Silver, *A New Face on the Countryside: Indians, Colonists, and Slaves in the South Atlantic Forests, 1500–1800* (1990).

For information on early European efforts to colonize the Americas consult Daniel J. Boorstin, *The Americans: The Colonial Experience* (1958); Carl Bridenbaugh, *Jamestown, 1544–1699* (1980); Charles Gibson, *The Aztecs under Spanish Rule* (1964), and *Spain in America* (1966); Karen O. Kupperman, *Roanoke: The Abandoned Colony* (1984); David B. Quinn, *Set Fair for Roanoke, 1584–1606* (1985).

Useful biographies include Roland H. Bainton, *Here I Stand: Martin Luther* (1950); William J. Bouwsma, *John Calvin* (1988); Samuel E. Morison, *Christopher Columbus, Mariner* (1955); Alden T. Vaughan, *American Genesis: Captain John Smith and Virginia* (1975).

Chapter 2

Plantations and Cities upon a Hill, 1620–1700

John Punch wanted his freedom. He was a black indentured servant who joined two white servants and tried to flee Virginia in 1640, only to be caught by local residents. Brought before the Governor's council, the colony's highest court, the judges ordered the flogging of each runaway—30 lashes well laid on. Then in a telling ruling, these officials also revealed their thinking about the future status of blacks in England's North American colonies. The two whites had their terms of service extended by four years, but John Punch was sentenced to a life of slavery.

Persons of African heritage were first transported to Virginia in 1619. Since English law did not recognize human slavery, Virginia's first white settlers did not automatically assume that transplanted Africans were permanently unfree. They treated some blacks as indentured servants, a status that conveyed the prospect of personal freedom after four to seven years of laboring for someone else.

Into the 1630s some black Virginians did gain their personal freedom. Others not only owned land but held servants of African origin as well. By the 1640s, however, blacks faced a deteriorating legal status, ultimately leaving them outside the bounds of English liberty. In 1639 the new colony of Maryland guaranteed "all . . . Christians (slaves excepted)" the same "rights, liberties, . . . and free customs" as enjoyed by "any natural born subject of England." In 1643 the same assembly decreed that black women, like all adult males, would henceforth be "tithables"—those counted for local taxes because they worked in the fields. Black female servants planted, tended, and harvested tobacco crops while white female servants mainly performed household work—further evidence of discrimination based on skin color.

Between 1640 and 1670 the distinction between short-term servitude for whites and permanent, inheritable slavery for blacks became firmly fixed. In appearance and by cultural and religious tradition, Africans were not like the English. As with the "wild" Irish and Indian "savages," noticeable differences translated into assumptions of inferiority, and blacks became "beastly heathens," not quite human.

Such thinking helped justify the mixing of words like "black" and "slave," so that by the 1690s slavery in the English colonies had emerged as a caste status for blacks only. Now fully excluded from the tradition of English liberty, local law defined Africans as chattels (movable property), and their masters now had absolute control over their lives.

John Punch was among the first blacks in the Chesapeake Bay area who felt the stinging transition from servitude to slavery. He was also among the thousands of Europeans and Africans who helped settle England's North American colonies between 1620 and 1700. The societies and life-styles of these migrants had many differences, as comparisons between the founding of the northern and southern colonies demonstrate. There was, however, a common point for all migrants, regardless of status or condition; they faced a titanic struggle to survive in an alien land. Although thousands died, some 250,000 settlers inhabited England's mainland colonies by 1700, which resulted in the formation of another powerful European empire in the Americas.

From Settlements to Societies in the South

Smoking or chewing tobacco, wrote King James I, was "loathsome to the eye, hateful to the nose, harmful to the brain, and dangerous to the lungs." Despite the king's admonition, John Rolfe's experiments saved the Virginia Company—at least temporarily—by providing the struggling colony with an economic base. By the mid-1630s Virginians were selling a million pounds a year, and by the mid-1660s annual tobacco crops for export reached 15 million pounds. Virginia's climate and soil were ideal for raising tobacco. Also, new land for cultivation was plentiful, since the "stinking weed" quickly depleted the soil of its minerals. The London investors soon hailed tobacco as the savior of their venture. Other difficulties, however, cost the directors their charter, but not before company activities laid the basis for England's first enduring colony in North America.

Searching for Laborers

Life in early Virginia presented constant hardships. Migrants quickly succumbed to a variety of diseases. Survival, it seemed, depended upon "seasoning," or getting used to an inhospitable climate. Bad relations with Powhatan's Indians also caused mayhem and death, since the English and Native Americans fought in many isolated clashes. All told, the company convinced nearly 14,000 persons to attempt a new life in America, but only about 1,150 were still alive and residing in the James River area in 1624, the year the company lost its charter.

To encourage prospective laborers, company directors developed a system of indentured servitude. In theory, the system held out the opportunity of potential economic independence for England's rapidly growing numbers of landless farm servants and the urban poor. Individuals without money needed only to sign contracts in which they legally exchanged up to seven years of labor in return for passage costs. After completing their terms of service, their masters owed them "freedom dues," including clothing, farm tools, and in some cases land on which to begin anew as free persons.

The system of indentured servitude slowly took shape after 1609. At first, the company offered free passage along with shares of stock to those who signed up for seven years of labor. When terms were up, workers were to gain title to 100 acres of land as well as any stock dividends. The bait was eventual economic freedom, but even with high numbers of unemployed everywhere in England, few persons applied. Getting by marginally or facing a hangman's noose remained more attractive than an early—and often unmerciful—death in America.

Stories of brutal living conditions and high mortality rates undercut company efforts to secure a steady flow of laborers. In an effort to make settlement more attractive, the English government granted Virginia a new charter in 1618, which established a local representative assembly, the House of Burgesses. Its first deliberations took place in July 1619, a small cornerstone gathering pointing toward governments with a popular voice in England's North American colonies.

The charter also offered economic incentives. Heretofore, the company controlled all acreage, but now potential settlers could purchase land without first serving as company laborers. Fifty acres per person would be given to those who migrated or those who paid for the passage of others to Virginia. These "headrights" would permit English families with funds to relocate and get title to enough property to grow tobacco and, perhaps, prosper.

Even with these reforms, Virginia's unhealthful reputation kept families from migrating. Three-fourths of all English settlers entering seventeenth-century Virginia were indentured servants. The vast bulk of these migrants were single males under the age of 25 with no employment prospects in England. As a result, stable family life was not a characteristic of the rough-and-tumble frontier society of early Virginia.

Crushing Powhatan's Confederacy

Bickering, bloodshed, and death denoted relations with Powhatan's Indians as the English located tobacco farms along the James River. John Rolfe's marriage to Powhatan's daughter, Pocahontas, in 1614, which implied a political alliance of sorts, eased tensions, but only briefly. Rolfe soon took Pocahontas to England, where she became an instant celebrity, and both of them encouraged settlement in Virginia. Unfortunately, while preparing to return home in 1616, Pocahontas contracted smallpox or a lung disease and died.

Two years later, Powhatan also died. His more militant half-brother Opechancanough decided that slaughtering the intruders was the only means left to save his people. On Good Friday, March 22, 1622, his warriors struck everywhere. By the time the massacre was over, the Indians had killed 347 settlers, or about one-third of the English colonists, including John Rolfe. Opechancanough, however, had failed to exterminate the enemy, and in many ways the massacre was the beginning of the end for Virginia's coastal natives. White settlers, now more convinced than ever that Indians were savages, took vengeance whenever they could.

Opechancanough waited 22 years before striking again. The attack came in April 1644, and another 300 or more colonists died. The 1644 massacre was a last desperate gasp by Virginia's coastal natives. The numbers of whites were now too overwhelming for total destruction. After Opechancanough was shot to death in 1646, Confederacy chiefs signed a treaty agreeing to submit to English rule. The survivors of Powhatan's once-mighty league eventually accepted life on a reservation, as so many other remnant Indian tribes would be forced to do when Europeans pushed westward across the North American continent.

In 1624, King James I voided the debt-ridden Virginia Company's charter and declared the area a royal colony. He canceled the privilege of a local assembly and sent out his own governor, whom he authorized to rule absolutely. Virginia's planters, however, would not be denied a voice in government. To ease tensions, royal officials shrewdly called upon locally prominent men to serve as advisory councilors, and also held conventions to deal with local problems. Finally in 1639, King Charles relieved some of the pressure by permanently granting Virginians a representative assembly, thereby assuring some local participation in colony-related decision making. Unlike the Spanish and French, English subjects had refused to accept total political control by a far-off parent state. They would share in the decision making that affected their lives as colonists in America.

Proprietary Maryland and the Carolinas

The Stuart kings realized that assuring basic rights would attract more settlers, which in turn meant larger tobacco crops and more tax revenues for the Crown. Founding additional colonies, moreover, would enhance England's stature among the nations of Europe, and these same settlements could be used as dumping grounds for troublesome groups in England, such as the Puritans. Vast stretches of territory could also be granted to court favorites.

Sir George Calvert was one such favored courtier. In 1632 Charles I awarded Calvert, a Roman Catholic, title to ten million acres surrounding the northern end of Chesapeake Bay. Calvert soon died, but his son Cecilius took charge and established the colony, known as Maryland, as a haven for Roman Catholics. Maryland did not prohibit the settlement of Protestants, however, who soon represented a majority of the population. In an effort to protect the minority Catholics, Calvert proposed an Act of

Religious Toleration in 1649, which guaranteed all Christian adult males voting or officeholding rights. Although representing only a form of toleration, this act, which the assembly approved, was a key step toward liberty of conscience; yet the political bickering among Maryland's settlers continued for years to come. Regardless of the faith of early settlers, the colony soon bore a striking similarity to its Chesapeake neighbor Virginia, since Marylanders also devoted themselves to cultivating tobacco.

Meanwhile, religious warfare convulsed England. In the 1640s Puritan "Roundheads" rose up against Charles I, who had refused to let Parliament meet for several years. In 1649 the victorious Puritans beheaded Charles, and Oliver Cromwell, the leader of Puritan military forces, took political control of England as Lord Protector. Soon after Cromwell's death, Parliament invited Charles I's exiled son to reestablish the Stuart monarchy—in exchange for promises to assemble Parliament regularly and to support the Anglican church.

The restoration of Charles II in 1660 left the new king with many political debts, and in 1663 he paid off eight powerful gentlemen by awarding them title to the Carolinas—all lands lying south of Virginia and north of Spanish Florida. The new proprietors quickly set about the task of finding settlers. The Albemarle region of northeastern North Carolina developed as settlers spilled over from Virginia. Most inhabitants subsisted marginally by exporting tobacco and various timber-derived products, including pitch, tar, and potash. Focusing their efforts on settling South Carolina, the proprietors contacted small-scale English farmers on the island of Barbados, who founded Charleston (then known as Charles Town) in 1670. A steady trade in deerskins and horsehides soon developed with interior natives, but rice production eventually became the economic mainstay of the colony. By the end of the seventeenth century, English settlers in the southern colonies had constructed their lives around the exportation of cash crops, particularly tobacco and rice, supported increasingly by black slave labor. Over time the institution of slavery gave white southerners a common identity—with serious long-term consequences.

Religious Dissenters Colonize New England

English men and women migrated to North America for many reasons. Certainly the hope of economic betterment was a prime motivating factor, but in New England the initial emphasis reflected more directly on a communal desire to provide a hospitable environment for Calvinist religious values. Beginning in the 1620s New England emerged as a haven for religious dissenters of two types: separatists, such as the Pilgrims, and nonseparatists, such as the Puritans.

Separatists believed the Church of England to be so corrupt that it could not be salvaged. So as not to compromise their beliefs, their only course was to sever all ties with the Anglican church and establish their own religious communities. The intrepid band known as the Pilgrims were separatists from Scrooby Manor, a village in northeastern England. Facing official harassment, they fled to the Netherlands in 1608 but, finding life difficult there, sought a land grant to settle in America.

In September 1620 the first party of Pilgrims sailed west on the *Mayflower* under a land patent of the Virginia Company. Only one-third of the 102 migrants aboard were Pilgrims. The rest were employees of the London merchant who financed the venture. After surviving nine harrowing, storm-tossed weeks at sea, the *Mayflower* made first landfall on the northern tip of Cape Cod.

Knowing they were well to the north of Virginia territory, the Pilgrims drafted a plan of government, called the Mayflower Compact, before proceeding to the mainland in December 1620. The Compact guaranteed settlers the right to elect governing officials and a representative assembly, but only male Pilgrim "saints"—those who were church members—could vote. The Pilgrims would tolerate "strangers" in their midst and encourage them to seek God's grace—as long as they submitted to the authority of church members. In this sense the Compact was not an advanced statement of popular government; its purpose was to assure the Pilgrims full political control of Plymouth colony.

Plymouth Plantation struggled to survive; and under the effective, persistent leadership of Governor William Bradford, the settlers overcame all obstacles. Besides a deadly first winter, the Pilgrims had to reckon with no clear title to their land. In 1621 they obtained a proper patent, but it took them several years to fulfill their financial obligations to their sponsors. They did so mostly by shipping fish and furs back to England.

Slowly but surely the Pilgrim colony began to prosper. Through all of their adventures and travails, the Pilgrims never lost sight of their original purpose—freedom to worship God according to their own understanding of scriptures. Over time their numbers grew to 7,000 persons before being annexed in 1691 by the much more populous Puritan colony of Massachusetts Bay. They had endured for 70 years as the second oldest English colony in North America.

The Rise of Puritan Dissenters at Home

Far more numerous in Elizabethan England were nonseparatists who wanted to "purify" rather than separate from the Church of England. The Puritans, as these dissenters were known, have often been characterized as prudish, ignorant bigots who hated the thought of having a good time.

Modern historical research, however, has shattered this stereotype. The Puritans were reformers who, as recipients of John Calvin's legacy, took biblical matters seriously. They believed that God's word should order the steps of every person's life. What troubled them most about the Protestant Reformation in England was that it had not gone far enough. They decried the rituals and elaborate hierarchy of the Church of England. As a state-sponsored institution, the Church claimed all citizens as members, regardless of their spiritual nature. Many Anglican clergymen also seemed to lack piety, owing their positions to the influence of well-connected friends and relatives. The Puritans longed for far-reaching institutional change that would rid the Anglican church of its imperfections.

By the early 1600s the Puritans numbered in the hundreds of thousands. Their emphasis upon reading the Bible particularly appealed to literate members of the middle classes and lesser gentry. The Puritans prided themselves on hard work and the pursuit of one's "calling" as a way to glorify the Almighty. They also searched for signs that they had received God's saving grace, which all Puritans sought through a personal conversion experience. They testified in their prayer groups to these experiences—and hoped that others would agree that they had joined God's "visible saints" on earth. To be a visible saint meant that a person was fit for church membership.

King James I developed a decided distaste for religious dissenters. "I will harry them out of the land," he boldly proclaimed after becoming king of England, "or else do worse." But like Queen Elizabeth before him, James quietly endured the Puritans. He never felt secure enough in his own authority to test his will against their rapidly expanding influence. His son, Charles I, confronted the Puritans more boldly. He named William Laud, whom the Puritans considered a Roman Catholic in Anglican garb, as archbishop of the Church of England. In response, the Puritans pushed a bill through Parliament denouncing "popish" practices in church and state. Finally, Charles used his royal prerogatives to disband Parliament and tried to rule by himself between 1629 and 1640.

By the late 1620s a number of Puritans, weary of constant conflict with the Crown, decided upon an "errand into the wilderness." In 1629 they secured a joint-stock charter for the Massachusetts Bay Company. Investors knew that they were underwriting the peopling of a utopian religious experiment in America. As for King Charles, the prospect of ridding the realm of thousands of Puritans was incentive enough to give royal approval to the Bay Company charter.

Godly Mission to New England

The Puritans organized their venture carefully. They placed their settlement effort under John Winthrop, a prominent lawyer and landholder. In

1630 some 700 Puritans crowded onto 11 ships and joined Winthrop in sailing to Massachusetts. They were the vanguard of what became the *Great Migration,* or the movement of an estimated 20,000 persons to New England by 1642. These men and women did not cross the Atlantic as indentured servants but as families leaving behind the religious repression and worsening economic conditions of Charles I's England.

More than any other person, John Winthrop worked tirelessly to promote the Puritan errand. Aboard the flagship *Arbella* before landing in Massachusetts Bay, he delivered a sermon entitled "A Model of Christian Charity," in which he asserted: "We must consider that we shall be as a city upon a hill; the eyes of all people are upon us." The Puritan mission was to order human existence in the Bay Colony according to God's word. Such an example, Winthrop and other company leaders hoped, would inspire England and the rest of Europe, thereby causing the full realization of the Protestant Reformation.

Winthrop and other stockholders, once in Massachusetts, soon faced challenges to their authority. Typical was a protest in 1632 from settlers who refused to pay taxes under the "bondage" of no voice in government.

John Winthrop led the Puritans to New England, where he served several terms as governor of the Massachusetts Bay Colony.

The solution was to grant full citizenship and voting rights to male church members, or "freemen." The government of Massachusetts developed out of this arrangement. Freemen from each town sent delegates to Boston to represent local concerns in an elective assembly, the General Court. The governor, too, was elected on an annual basis, with John Winthrop holding the office almost continuously until his death in 1649. Town ministers were not eligible for political offices, so the government was not technically a theocracy. Clergymen, however, offered written advice to Winthrop and other leaders regarding religious issues, and their observations did affect political decision making.

Puritan town planners emphasized community control over individual lives. A 1635 law—later repealed—stated that inhabitants had to live within a half mile of the town church. Each family received a house lot near the village green, farmland away from the center of town, and access to pasture land and woodlots. Some towns perpetuated the European open-field system. Families gained title to strips of land in several fields and worked in common with other townspeople to bring in yearly crops. In other towns, families had all their farmland concentrated in one area.

These property arrangements reflected on English patterns of land distribution as well as the desire to promote godly behavior, especially since some first-generation settlers were not Puritans. To promote harmonious living conditions, town leaders set off lots for taverns, schools, and meetinghouses. Taverns served as community centers in which people socialized and cheerfully drank alcohol, which they believed was essential to good health. School lots satisfied concerns about education. The Puritans advocated literacy so that everyone could "understand the principles of religion and . . . laws of the country." Beginning in the 1640s, the General Court ordered each town to tax inhabitants to pay for formal schooling in reading and writing for all children. (The desire to have a learned clergy led to the founding of Harvard College in 1636.) The meetinghouse was the gathering place for town meetings and church services. It was the duty of church members to encourage non-Puritans in their midst to study the Bible, pray fervently, and seek God's grace so that they might also enjoy political and religious rights—as well as eternal salvation.

Testing the Limits of Toleration

The first generation of Puritans worked hard and prospered. Farming was the primary means of gaining a livelihood, although some coastal inhabitants took to shipbuilding, fishing, and mercantile activity. Prosperity did not stand in the way of serious internal controversies. These disagreements suggested how the Puritan system functioned on behalf of orthodoxy—and against diverse opinions—to assure adherence to the wilderness mission.

No Puritan was purer than Roger Williams. When this well-educated clergyman arrived in Boston in 1631, John Winthrop graciously welcomed him. Soon Williams received an offer to teach in the Boston church, but he refused because of rules about mandatory worship. To hold services with the unconverted in attendance was to be no purer than the Church of England. It "stinks in God's nostrils," Williams proclaimed.

So off Williams went, first to Salem and then to Plymouth Colony. Only the visible saints attended church services in Plymouth, but the Pilgrims soon dismissed Williams for his view of land ownership. He had become friendly with local Indians and had concluded that any Crown-based land patent was fraudulent—and that Puritans and Pilgrims alike were thieves because they had not purchased their land from the natives. Moving back to Salem, Williams next denounced Bay Colony leaders who meddled in church affairs. So long as churches were subject in any way to political influences, they would be as corrupt as the Church of England.

John Winthrop remained Williams's friend and kept advising him to keep his opinions to himself, but other Puritan leaders had endured enough. Orthodox adherence to the Puritan mission meant that Williams could not be tolerated. The General Court banished him in 1635. Williams fled to the Narragansett Indians from whom he eventually purchased land for a new community—Providence, Rhode Island. Partly because of his influence, the colony of Rhode Island became a center of religious toleration. Settlers there welcomed all faiths, including Judaism, and the government stayed out of matters of personal conscience. As for Williams, in his later years he became so concerned about not attempting to influence the religious beliefs of others that he rarely worshiped with anyone except his beloved wife. Personal conscience was truly sacred, he thought, which made him an advance agent for such concepts as religious freedom and separation of church and state.

Meanwhile others such as Anne Hutchinson tested the limits of orthodoxy. She was a woman of powerful mind and commanding presence who frightened leaders like John Winthrop. Hutchinson, the mother of 13 children, moved with her family to Boston in 1634, where she served as a midwife. She also spoke openly about her religious views. Hutchinson's frame of thought had a strong mystical element. Once humans experienced saving grace, she believed, God would offer direct revelation, meaning that true saints no longer needed the church or the state to help order their daily existence.

Hutchinson's ideas earned the label "Antinomian," which Puritans defined as against the laws of human governance. To Winthrop, who thought that God's revelation ended with scripture, Hutchinson appeared as an advocate of social anarchy. She was threatening to ruin the Puritan mission, since there would be no purpose to human institutions of any kind, except to control the unregenerate. In 1637 Bay Colony clergymen assembled in a synod and denounced Antinomianism as "blasphemous." Ordered to appear before the General Court, Hutchinson masterfully defended herself for two days, only to be declared guilty of sedition for dishonoring Winthrop and the other magistrates. As "a woman not fit for our society," she was banished and migrated to Rhode Island where she helped establish the community of Portsmouth.

"Hivings Out" Provoke Bloody Indian Relations

Also banished by the Bay Colony for his Antinomian views was Hutchinson's brother-in-law, John Wheelwright, who with his following went off to found Exeter, New Hampshire. Other venturesome souls had already established themselves along the coast of Maine. Massachusetts tried to maintain control of both areas, but in 1681 New Hampshire became a separate royal colony. The Bay Colony did sustain its authority over Maine by purchasing the land patents of rival claimants, and this territory remained a thinly settled appendage of Massachusetts until the granting of statehood in 1820.

Connecticut also started to emerge as a Puritan colony during the 1630s. The Reverend Thomas Hooker, who viewed John Winthrop as too dictatorial, led 100 settlers into the Connecticut River valley in May 1636. By year's end, another 700 Puritans had followed Hooker's path. The towns founded by Hooker adopted a plan of government which, while similar to that of the Bay Colony, gave voting rights to all adult male property holders, not just church members. Connecticut Puritans, however, had little interest in encouraging religious diversity; as in Massachusetts, the Congregational church dominated spiritual life.

These "hivings out" from Massachusetts, as Winthrop called them, adversely affected relations with the native populace. When Hooker's followers moved into the Connecticut River valley, they settled on land claimed by the Pequots, who decided to resist and struck at Wethersfield in April 1637, killing several people. A force of Puritans and Narragansett Indians, who hated the Pequots, retaliated a month later by surrounding and setting fire to the main Pequot village on the Mystic River. Some 400 men, women, and children died in the flames.

Warfare erupted again in the summer of 1675, when Metacomet, better known to the Puritans as King Philip, led various Indian tribes on raids along the Massachusetts-Connecticut frontier. By early 1676 all of

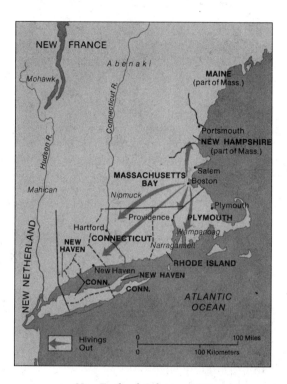

New England Colonies, 1650

New England was in chaos. Metacomet's forces even attacked towns within 20 miles of Boston. When an Indian convert shot and killed Metacomet, King Philip's War rapidly lost its momentum, but not before his warriors had leveled or done substantial damage to several towns. Some 2,000 Puritan settlers died in the war, as did about twice as many Indians, in what proved to be a futile effort to drive away the ever-expansive English. Still, King Philip's War was not the Indians' last gasp. In a few years remnant native groups began getting support from the French in Canada and once again started attacking New England's frontier towns.

Surviving in Early America

During the seventeenth century New England's population grew steadily by natural increase. Most of the 25,000 migrants crossed the ocean before the outbreak of England's civil war in the 1640s, yet by the end of the

century some 93,000 colonists inhabited New England. In the Chesapeake, by comparison, as many as 100,000 persons attempted settlement,
but only about 85,000 were living in Virginia and Maryland in 1700. If it
had not been for the constant influx of new migrants, these two colonies
might have ceased to exist.

Life and Death, North and South

The Chesapeake colonists experienced shorter, less fertile lives than their
New England counterparts. In 1640, for example, Chesapeake migrants
had no more than a 50 percent chance of surviving their first year in
America. Hot, steamy summers fostered repeated outbreaks of malaria
and typhoid fever, which, along with dysentery and poisoning from
brackish drinking water, killed thousands. New England's drinking water
was safer, although Puritans generally preferred home-brewed beer, and
the harsher winter climate helped to kill off deadly germs. As a result, the
Puritans enjoyed longer, healthier lives.

In New England 20 percent of all Puritan males who survived infancy
lived into their seventies. Even with the hazards of childbirth, Puritan
women lived almost as long. In Virginia and Maryland men who survived
into their early twenties had reached middle age; on the average, they
would not live beyond their mid-forties. For women in their early twenties, there was little likelihood of surviving beyond their late thirties.
Given an average life expectancy of 50 to 55 years back in England, the
Chesapeake region deserved its reputation as a human graveyard. In comparison, early New England represented a utopian health environment.

Good health among New Englanders sustained life and meant longer
marriages and more children. Longevity resulted in large families, averag-
ing seven to eight children per household. In some locales nine out of ten
children survived infant diseases and grew to adulthood knowing not only
their parents but their grandparents as well. Families with living grandparents were a unique characteristic of Puritan New England, reflecting
life spans more typical of modern America than early modern Europe.

From a demographic perspective, then, New England families were far
more stable and secure than those of the Chesapeake. Because Puritans
crossed the Atlantic in family units, the ratio of women to men was more
evenly balanced than in Virginia or Maryland, where most migrants were
not married. Planters seeking laborers for their tobacco fields preferred
young males, which skewed the sex ratio against women and retarded the
development of family life. Before 1640 only one woman migrated to the
Chesapeake for every six men; and as late as 1700, males still outnumbered
females by a ratio of more than three to two.

A unique characteristic of Puritan New England was families with living grand-parents, as illustrated in this portrait of Abigail Gerrish and her grandmother.

The system of indentured servitude also affected population patterns. Servants could not marry until they had completed their terms. Typically, women were in their mid-twenties before they first wed, which in combination with short adult life expectancies curbed the numbers of children they could bear. Seventeenth-century Chesapeake families averaged only two to three children, and a quarter of them did not survive their first year of life. Two-thirds of all surviving children lost one parent by the age of 18, and one-third lost both. Rarely did children know grandparents. For Chesapeake families, death was as much a daily reality as life, at least until the early eighteenth century when disease stopped wreaking such havoc.

Roles for Men, Women, and Children

The early Puritans looked at their mission as a family undertaking, and they referred to families as "little commonwealths." Not only were families to "be fruitful and multiply," but they also served as agencies of education and religious instruction as well as centers of vocational training and social welfare. Families cared for the destitute and elderly; they took in orphans; and they housed servants and apprentices—all under one roof and subject to the authority of the father.

The Puritans carried *patriarchal* values across the Atlantic and planted them in America. New England law, reflecting its English base, subscribed to the doctrine of *coverture,* or subordinating the legal identity of women in their husbands, who were the undisputed heads of households. Unless there were prenuptial agreements, all property brought by women to marriages belonged to their mates. Husbands, who by custom and law directed their families in prayer and scripture reading, were responsible for assuring decency and good order in family life. They also represented their families in all community political, economic, and religious activities.

Wives also had major family responsibilities. "For though the husband be the head of the wife," the Reverend Samuel Willard explained, "yet she is the head of the family." It was the particular calling of mothers to nurture their children in godly living, as well as to perform many other tasks—tending gardens, brewing beer, raising chickens, cooking, spinning, and sewing—when not helping in the planting and harvesting of crops.

Most Puritan marriages functioned in at least outward harmony. If serious problems arose, local churches and courts intervened to end the turmoil. Puritan law, again reflecting English precedent, made divorce quite difficult. The process required the petitioning of assemblies for bills of separation, and the only legal grounds were bigamy, desertion, and adultery. On occasion the courts brought unruly husbands under control, as in the case of one Maine husband who brutally clubbed his wife for refusing to feed the family pig.

Family friction arose from other sources as well, some of which stemmed from the absolute control that fathers exercised over property and inheritances. If sons wanted to marry and establish separate households, they had to conform to the will of their fathers, who controlled the land. Family patriarchs normally delayed the passing of property until sons had reached their mid-twenties and selected mates acceptable to parents. Since parents also bestowed dowries on daughters as their contributions to new family units, romantic love had less to do with mate selection than parental desires to unite particular family names and estates. Puritans expected brides and grooms to learn to love one another as they went about their duty of conceiving and raising the next generation of children.

Young adults who openly defied patriarchal authority were rare. Those who did could expect to hear what one angry Bay Colony father told his unwanted son-in-law: "As you married her without my consent, you shall keep her without my help." Also unusual were instances of illegitimate children, despite the lengthy gap between puberty and marriage. As measured by illegitimate births, premarital sex could not have been that common in early New England, not a surprising finding among people living in closely controlled communities and seeking to honor the Almighty by reforming human society.

The experiences of seventeenth-century Chesapeake colonists were very different, due primarily to high death rates in combination with an unbalanced sex ratio. These conditions may have, at least temporarily, enhanced the status of some Chesapeake women, permitting single adults and widows to own and manage property and households for themselves. The fragility of life also resulted in complex family genealogies, with some households containing children from three or four marriages. In some instances local Orphans' Courts had to take charge because all adult relatives had died. Because parents did not live that long, children quite often received their inheritances by their late teens, much earlier than in New England. This advantage only meant that economic independence, like death, came earlier in life.

For indentured servants in the Chesapeake region, life was even more difficult. Planters sought to get as much labor as possible out of servants, since 40 percent died before completing their contracts. Disease was the major killer, but hard-driving planters also contributed to many early deaths. For servants who resisted their masters, local laws specified harsh penalties. Besides floggings and brandings, insubordinate servants faced extensions of service, as one unfortunate man learned after he killed three pigs belonging to his master. The court added six years to his term of service. Since servants could not marry, indentured servitude also inhibited family life, and increased the likelihood of illicit sexual activity. Quite frequently, women became the unwilling sexual partners of lustful masters or male servants. Still, the fate of female and male servants was not always abuse or death. Many survived, gained title to land, and enjoyed, however briefly, personal freedom in America.

Commercial Values and the Rise of Chattel Slavery

By 1650 there were signs that the Puritan mission was in trouble. From the outset many non-Puritan settlers, including merchants in Boston, had shunned the religious values of the Bay Colony's founders. By the 1660s children and grandchildren of the migrating generation displayed less zeal

about earning God's grace; they were becoming more like southern settlers in their eagerness to get ahead economically. By 1700 their search for
worldly prosperity even brought some New Englanders into the international slave trade.

Declension in New England

Declension, or movement away from the ideals of the Bay Colony's founding fathers, resulted in tensions between settlers adhering to the original
mission and those attracted to rising commercial values. In 1662 clergymen proposed a major compromise known as the "Half-Way Covenant."
The covenant recognized that many children were not preparing for salvation, a necessary condition for full church membership, as their parents
had done. The question was how to keep them aspiring toward a spiritual
life. The solution was halfway membership, which permitted the baptism
of the children and grandchildren of professing saints. If still in the
church, ministers and full members could continue to urge them to focus
their lives on seeking God's eternal rewards. Many communities disdained the Half-Way Covenant because of what it suggested about changing values. But with the passage of time most accepted the covenant to
help preserve some semblance of a godly society in New England.

Spreading commercial values took hold for many reasons, including
the natural abundance of the New England environment and an inability
to sustain fervency of purpose among American-born offspring who had
not personally felt the religious repression of early Stuart England. Also,
Puritans back in England, after overthrowing Charles I, generally ignored
the model society in America; this left the impression that the errand had
been futile, that no one back in Europe really cared.

The transition in values occurred gradually. In farming communities,
some families bought and sold common field strips so that all of their
landholdings were in one place, then proceeded to build homes on their
property. This was certainly a more efficient way to practice agriculture, as
well as a statement that making one's living was more important than
daily participation in village life—with its emphasis on laboring together
in God's love. In Boston and other port towns, merchants gained increasing community stature because of their wealth. By the early eighteenth
century, some of them were earning profits by participating in the African
slave trade. Their newfound status was symbolized by retinues of household servants or, more properly, slaves taken from Africa.

Clergymen disapproved of these trends. Their sermons took on the
tone of "jeremiads," modeled on the prophet Jeremiah who kept urging
Israel to return to the path of godliness. In 1679 the ministers met in a

synod and listed several problems, everything from working on the sabbath to swearing in public and sleeping during sermons. Human competitiveness and contention, they sadly concluded, were in ascendance. Worse yet, the populace, in its rush to garner worldly riches, showed little concern that Winthrop's "city upon a hill" was becoming the home of the acquisitive Yankee trader.

Stabilizing Life in the Chesapeake Region

In Maryland and Virginia there were indications by 1675 that life could be something more than brief and unkind. The death rate dropped; more children survived; the gender ratio started to balance out; and life expectancy figures rose. By the early 1700s Chesapeake residents lived well into their fifties. This was comparable to longevity estimates for England but still 10 to 15 years shorter than in New England. These patterns suggested greater family stability, as shown by longer marriages and more children; the average union now produced seven to eight offspring with five to six children surviving into adulthood.

Not only did life become more stable, but an elite group of families, controlling significant property and wealth, had begun to emerge. By 1700 the great tidewater families—the Byrds, Carters, Fitzhughs, Lees, and Randolphs among others—were making their presence felt. These gentleman-planters imitated the life-style of England's rural gentry. They constructed lavish manor houses from which they ruled over their plantation estates, dispensing hospitality and wisdom as the most important local leaders of their tobacco-producing colony.

For every great planter, there were dozens of small farmers who lacked the wealth to obtain land, slaves, and high status in society. Most eked out bare livings, yet they dreamed of the day when they, or their children, might live in the style of the planter elite. Meanwhile, they deferred to their "betters," allowing the local gentry to dominate political and social affairs.

The Beginnings of American Slavery

The system of perpetual servitude that shaped the lives of persons of African heritage like John Punch had an ancient history. Slavery had been dying out in much of Europe by the fifteenth century, but revived when Portuguese mariners made contact with sub-Saharan African peoples, some of whom were willing to barter in human flesh as well as in gold and ivory. The first Portuguese expeditions represented the small beginnings of a trade that forcibly relocated an estimated ten million Africans to the Americas during the next 350 years.

Lavish estates like Westover, built by William Byrd II, illustrate the wealth and dominance of the gentleman-planters in Virginia.

These African kingdoms thrived on elaborate regional trading networks, which the Portuguese and other Europeans, offering guns and various iron products, tapped into easily. The Portuguese found that coastal chiefs were willing to trade slaves captured in tribal wars for European firearms, which they could use when attacking interior kingdoms. A new objective of this tribal warfare became the capturing of peoples who would then be transported back to the coast and sold into slavery in exchange for yet more European goods.

Once this vicious trading cycle began, there did not seem to be any way to stop it. During the sixteenth century the Spanish and Portuguese started pouring Africans into their colonies. Decade after decade, thousands of Africans experienced the agony of being shackled in collars and ankle chains, marched in gangs to the coast, thrown into slave pens, and then packed aboard ships destined for ports of call in the Americas. One slave, Olaudah Equiano, who made the voyage during the eighteenth century, recalled the "loathsomeness of the stench" from overcrowded conditions, which made him "so sick and low" that he neither was "able to eat, nor had . . . the desire to taste anything." About 15 percent of those forced onto slave ships did not survive. For those who did, there was the frightening realization of having lost everything familiar in their lives—and not knowing what might happen next.

Shifting to Slavery in Maryland and Virginia

The English North American colonies existed at the outer edge of the African slave trade until the very end of the seventeenth century. In 1650 the population of Virginia approached 15,000 settlers, including only 500 persons of African descent. By comparison, the English sugar colony of Barbados already held 10,000 slaves, a majority of the population. English Barbadians had started to model their economy on that of other Caribbean sugar islands whereas Virginians, with a steady supply of indentured servants, had not yet made the transition to slave labor.

Factors supporting a shift, however, were present by the 1640s, as evidenced in laws discriminating against Africans and court cases involving blacks like John Punch. During the same decade, a few Chesapeake planters started to invest in Africans. Slaves cost significantly more to purchase than indentured servants, yet those who invested owned their laborers for their lifetimes and did not have to pay "freedom dues." Further, they soon discovered that Africans, having built up immunities to tropical diseases like malaria and typhoid fever, generally lived longer than white servants. Resistance to such diseases made Africans a better long-term investment, at least for well-capitalized planters.

African Slave Trade

The destinations of slaves traded between 1520 and 1810 show the heaviest concentration in Central and South America.

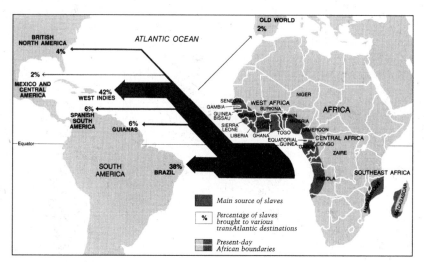

In the 1660s two additional factors encouraged the shift toward slave labor. First, Virginia legislators in 1662 decreed that slavery was an inheritable status. The law made yet unborn generations subject to slavery, a powerful incentive for risking an initial investment in human chattels. Second, the supply of new indentured servants began to shrink as economic conditions improved in England. With expanded opportunities for work, poorer citizens were less willing to risk life and limb for a chance at economic independence in America.

As a result, the slave population figures in the Chesapeake area increased dramatically. In 1750 white Virginians owned 120,000 slaves—about 40 percent of the total population. In Maryland there were 40,000 slaves—some 30 percent of the populace. Indentured servitude had become a moribund institution. White planters, great and small, now measured their wealth and status in terms of plantations and slaves owned and managed.

The World the Slaves Made

Historians once argued that slavery in English North America was harsher than the Spanish-American version. They pointed to the moderating influence of the Roman Catholic church, which mandated legal recognition of slave marriages as a sacramental right, and ancient legal precedents influencing Spanish law, which meant that slaves could earn wages for their labor in off hours and buy their freedom. Although Spanish laws may have been more humane, daily working and living conditions were not. Most slaves destined for Caribbean or South American settlements did not survive long enough to marry or enjoy other legal rights. By contrast, in North America where early deaths were not so pervasive among migrants, slaves more easily reconstructed meaningful lives for themselves.

About 90 percent of those Africans coming to the colonies labored in the South, mostly on small plantations where field work dominated their existence. There was little chance for family life, at least in the early years, because planters purchased an average of three males for every female. In addition, southern law did not recognize slave marriages—in case masters wanted to sell off some of their chattels. In New England, by contrast, the Congregational church insisted that slave marriages be recognized and respected by masters.

Southern slaves made separate lives for themselves, particularly on larger plantations where their numbers were large enough to form their own communities in the slave quarters. Here they maintained African cultural traditions and developed distinctive forms of music. In many places, female slaves managed slave quarter life, thus maintaining the matrilineal nature of African kinship ties.

Whenever possible, slaves selected mates and had large families, even if slave quarter marriages had no standing in law. As a consequence, the ratio of men to women balanced itself out over time, which in turn sped up natural population growth. Large families became a source of slave community pride. Natural increase also undercut the need to continue heavy importations of chattels. As a result, only 5 percent—399,000 persons—of all imported Africans ended up in English North America.

Such comparisons are relative. Nowhere in the Americas did slavery function in an uplifting fashion. Although blacks on large southern plantations carried on traditional cultural practices, they still had to face masters or overseers who might whip them, sell off their children, or maim or kill them if they tried to run away. Always present was the realization that whites considered them to be a subhuman species of property, which left scant room for human dignity in life beyond the slave quarters.

Conclusion

Although most blacks adapted to slavery, some remained defiant. They stole food, broke farm tools, or in a few cases poisoned their masters. In rare instances they resorted to rebellion. In September 1739 twenty slaves in the Stono River area of South Carolina rose up, seized some weapons, killed a few whites, and started marching toward Spanish Florida. Within a few days frightened planters rallied together and crushed the Stono uprising by shooting or hanging the rebels.

The South Carolina legislature soon approved a more repressive slave code, which all but restricted the movement of blacks from their home plantations. No legislator gave thought to the other possibility, which was to abandon the institution of slavery. Even though long in development, slavery now supported southern plantation agriculture and the production of such cash crops as tobacco and rice.

Just as the southern colonies had made a fateful shift from servitude to slavery, New Englanders experienced another kind of transition. Slowly but surely, they had forsaken their utopian, religiously oriented errand into the wilderness; service to mammon had replaced loyalty to God and community. The religious side would remain, but the fervor of a nobler spiritual mission was in rapid decline by 1700. Material gain was now a quality shared in common by white English colonists in America—North and South.

Prosperity, which had come after so much travail and death, promoted a sense of unlimited opportunity in profiting from the abundance of the American environment. Other realities, however, were also in the making. The colonists had learned that Crown officials now expected them to conform to new laws governing the emerging English empire.

*C*hronology of Key Events

1608	Pilgrims flee to Holland
1617	Virginia begins to export tobacco
1619	The first persons of African descent arrive in Virginia; first representative assembly in English North America meets in Jamestown
1620	Pilgrims cross the Atlantic Ocean on the *Mayflower* and establish a colony at Plymouth
1622	Opechancanough's Indians fail in an attempt to massacre all English settlers in Virginia
1624	New Netherland founded by the Dutch
1630	Puritans establish the Massachusetts Bay Colony
1632	Maryland becomes the first proprietary colony
1635	Roger Williams banished from Massachusetts Bay
1636	Harvard College founded
1637–1638	Anne Hutchinson convicted of heresy and banished from Massachusetts Bay
1644	Second attempted Indian massacre of Virginia settlers fails
1646	Powhatan's Confederacy accepts English rule
1649	Maryland Act of Toleration affirms religious freedom for all Christians in the colony
1660	Charles II restored to the English throne
1664	English conquer New Netherland
1675–1676	King Philip's (Metacomet's) War inflicts heavy casualties on New Englanders
1681–1682	William Penn founds Pennsylvania
1688	Glorious Revolution drives James II from England
1732	Georgia founded as haven for debtors
1739	Stono slave uprising occurs in South Carolina

Because of these imperial rules, much turmoil lay ahead for the people now inhabiting English North America.

Suggestions for Further Reading

For general surveys of family and community life in early America see David Hackett Fischer, *Albion's Seed: Four British Folkways in America* (1989); Philip Greven, *The Protestant Temperament* (1977); Nathan Huggins, *Black Odyssey: The Afro-American Ordeal in Slavery* (1977); Steven Mintz and Susan Kellogg, *Domestic Revolutions: A Social History of American Family Life* (1988); Helena M. Wall, *Fierce Communion: Family and Community in Early America* (1990).

Useful studies of New England colonial life are Bernard Bailyn, *The New England Merchants in the Seventeenth Century* (1955); John Demos, *A Little Commonwealth: Family Life in Plymouth Colony* (1970); Stephen Foster, *The Long Argument: English Puritanism and New England Culture, 1570–1700* (1991); Philip J. Greven, Jr., *Four Generations: Colonial Andover, Massachusetts* (1970); David D. Hall, *Worlds of Wonder, Days of Judgment: Popular Religious Belief in Early New England* (1989); Perry Miller, *The New England Mind: From Colony to Province* (1953); Robert Middlekauff, *The Mathers: Three Generations of Puritan Intellectuals* (1971); Edmund S. Morgan, *The Puritan Dilemma: The Story of John Winthrop* (1958), and *Visible Saints* (1963).

For general studies of slavery see David B. Davis, *The Problem of Slavery in Western Culture* (1966); Winthrop D. Jordan, *White Over Black* (1968). For the slave trade see Herbert S. Klein, *The Middle Passage* (1978); James Rawley, *The Transatlantic Slave Trade* (1981).

For Southern colonial society, consult Timothy H. Breen and Stephen Innes, *"Myne Owne Ground": Race and Freedom on Virginia's Eastern Shore,* (1980); Wesley Frank Craven, *The Southern Colonies in the Seventeenth Century* (1949); Allan Kulikoff, *Tobacco and Slaves* (1986); Gloria L. Main, *Tobacco Colony: Life in Early Maryland* (1982); Edmund S. Morgan, *American Slavery, American Freedom: The Ordeal of Colonial Virginia* (1975); Darrett B. Rutman and Anita H. Rutman, *A Place in Time: Middlesex County, Virginia* (1984); Peter H. Wood, *Black Majority: Negroes in Colonial South Carolina from 1670 Through the Stono Rebellion* (1974).

Chapter 3

Provincial America in Upheaval, 1660–1760

Hannah Dustan (1657–1736) and Eliza Lucas (1722–1793) never knew one another. Dustan lived in the town of Haverhill on the Massachusetts frontier, and Lucas spent her adult years in the vicinity of Charleston, South Carolina. Even though of different generations, both were inhabitants of England's developing North American empire. Like so many other colonists, perpetual imperial warfare affected their lives as England, France, and Spain repeatedly battled for supremacy in Europe and America between 1689 and 1763.

During the 1690s, as part of a war involving England and France, frontier New Englanders experienced devastating raids by French and Indian parties from Canada. On the morning of March 15, 1697, a band of Abenakis struck Haverhill. Hannah Dustan's husband and seven of her children saved themselves by racing for the community's blockhouse. Hannah, who had just given birth a few days before, was not so fortunate. The Abenakis captured her, as well as her baby and midwife Mary Neff.

After some discussion, the Indians killed the infant, but decided to spare Hannah and Mary along with a few other captives. The plan was to march them to the principal Abenaki village in Canada. A party of two male warriors, three women, and seven children escorted Hannah, Mary, and a young boy named Samuel Lenorson. Hannah struggled to maintain her composure as the party walked northward day after day, praying fervently for some means of escape. Just before dawn one morning, she awoke to find all her captors sound asleep. Seizing the moment, she roused Mary and Samuel, handed them hatchets, and told them to crush as many skulls as possible. Suddenly the Indians were dying, and only two, a badly wounded woman and a child, escaped.

Hannah then took a scalping knife and finished the bloody work. When she and the other captives got back to Haverhill, they had ten scalps, for which the Massachusetts General Court awarded them a bounty of £50. New Englanders hailed Hannah Dustan as a true heroine—a woman whose courage overcame the French and Indian enemies of England's empire in America. After a long and full life, Hannah Dustan died in 1736.

Two years later, George Lucas, a prosperous Antigua planter and an officer in the British army, moved to South Carolina, where he owned three rice plantations. He wanted to get his family away from the Caribbean region, since hostilities were brewing with Spain. When war required Lucas to return to military service in Antigua, he placed his 17-year-old daughter Eliza in charge of his Carolina properties. The responsibility did not faze her; she wrote regularly to her "Dear Papa" for advice, and the plantations prospered. The war, however, disrupted rice trading routes to the West Indies, and planters needed other cash crops to be sold elsewhere.

George Lucas was aware of the problem and sent Eliza seeds for indigo plants, the source of a valued deep-blue dye, to see whether indigo
could be grown profitably in South Carolina. With the help of knowl-
edgeable slaves, Eliza conducted successful experiments. In 1744 a major
dye broker in England rated her product as good as the best French indigo. Just 22 years old, Eliza had pioneered a cash crop that brought additional wealth to Carolina's planters and became a major trading staple of
the British empire.

Eliza ultimately married Charles Pinckney, a widower of great wealth
and high social standing. In later life she took pride in the success of her
children, one of whom served in the Constitutional Convention of 1787,
and another represented President Washington during 1795 in negotiating
an agreement that resolved western boundary questions with Spain. A her-
alded woman of her generation, Eliza Lucas Pinckney died at the end of
the revolutionary era, nearly 140 years after the birth of Hannah Dustan.

Dustan and Pickney both lived during years of turbulence and upheaval, as England built a mighty empire in North America. Despite new
imperial laws governing the lives of Americans and a series of wars with
France and Spain, the colonies grew and prospered. After 1760 the
colonists were in a position to question their subordinate relationship
with Britain. The coming of the American Revolution cannot be appreci-
ated without looking at the development of the British empire in America—and how that experience related to the lives of passing generations of
colonists like Hannah Dustan and Eliza Lucas Pinckney.

Designing England's North American Empire

During the 1760s Benjamin Franklin tried to explain why relations between England and the colonies had turned sour. He blamed British trade
policies designed to control American commerce, which had been implemented "for private advantage, under pretense of public good." The trade
system, he believed, had become both oppressive and corrupt. Little more
than a hundred years before, the colonists had traded as they pleased.
After 1650, however, Parliament designed trade policies that exerted
greater control over the activities of the American colonists.

To Benefit the Parent State

Certain key ideas underlay the new, more restrictive policies. Most important was the concept of *mercantilism* (although the term was not invented
until the late eighteenth century). Mercantilist thinkers believed the

world's supply of wealth was not infinite but fixed in quantity. Any nation that gained wealth automatically did so at the expense of another. In economic dealings, then, the most powerful nations always maintained a favorable balance of trade by exporting a greater value of goods than they imported. Governments controlling the most gold and silver would be the most self-sufficient and could use such wealth to stimulate internal economic development as well as strengthen military forces. This ensured not only national survival but ascendancy over other countries.

Mercantilist theory also demonstrated how colonies could best serve their parent nations. For England, the colonies could contribute to a favorable trade balance by producing such staple crops as tobacco, rice, and sugar, thus ending any need to import these goods from other countries. The American provinces, in addition, could supply valuable raw materials—for example, timber products for construction of a naval fleet. Great stands of American timber could also be fashioned into fine furniture and sold back to the colonists. Ideally, England's overseas colonies would serve as a source of raw materials and staple crops as well as a marketplace for manufactured goods.

Mercantilist reasoning affirmed the principle that the colonies existed to benefit and strengthen the parent nation. As such, provincial economic and political activities had to be closely managed. To effect these goals, Parliament passed a series of Navigation Acts (1651, 1660, 1663, and 1673), which formed the cornerstone of England's commercial relations with the colonies and the rest of the world. The acts banned foreign merchants and vessels from participating in the colonial trade; proclaimed that certain "enumerated" goods could only be shipped to England or other colonies (the first list included dyewoods, indigo, sugar, and tobacco, with furs, molasses, rice, and wood products added later); and specified that European goods destined for America had to pass through England.

Through the Navigation System, England became the central trading hub of the empire, which resulted in a great economic boom at home. After 1660 key industries like shipbuilding began to prosper as never before. By the late 1690s the English merchant fleet had outdistanced all competitors, including the Dutch.

In the colonies the Navigation Acts had mixed effects. New Englanders, taking advantage of nearby timber supplies, strengthened their economy by heavy involvement in shipbuilding. By the early 1700s Americans were constructing one-fourth or more of all English merchant vessels. In the Chesapeake Bay region, however, the enumeration of tobacco resulted in economic difficulties. By the 1660s planters were producing too much tobacco for consumption in the British Isles alone. Because of the costs of merchandising the crop through England, the price became too high to support large sales in Europe. Consequently, the glut of tobacco in England caused prices to decline, resulting in hard times and much furor among Chesapeake planters.

Seizing Dutch New Netherland

The Navigation Acts were only part of England's efforts to establish itself as an imperial power. Under Charles II, England also sought to challenge its European rivals in the Americas. A principal target was the Dutch colony of New Netherland, which served as a base for Holland's illegal trade with English settlers.

New Netherland was the handiwork of the Dutch West India Company, a joint-stock venture chartered in 1621. The company soon sent out a governor and employees to the Hudson River area to develop the fur trade with local Indians, particularly the Five Nations of Iroquois inhabiting upper New York. By 1660, New Netherland's population pushed toward 8,000, but the colony was internally weak and unstable. A series of unpopular and incompetent governors had stirred feelings of resentment among its many non-Dutch inhabitants. Denied a voice in government and freedom of worship, many settlers felt no great loyalty to Holland and its colonial administrators.

In 1664 King Charles gave his brother, James, the Duke of York, title to all Dutch lands in North America, on the obvious condition that they be conquered. James quickly organized a small invasion fleet. When the flotilla appeared before New Amsterdam in August 1664, Governor Peter Stuyvesant failed to rally the populace. With hardly an exchange of shots, New Netherland became the Duke of York's English province of New York.

James's proprietary charter had no clause mandating an assembly for his colony, but Puritans living on Long Island demanded some form of representative government. They refused to pay local taxes, arguing that they were "enslaved under an arbitrary power." The absence of a popularly based assembly for New York's colonists continued to be a source of friction. Finally, in the early 1680s James conceded the point, and an assembly met for the first time in 1683. Once he became king in 1685, however, James disallowed further assembly meetings, which was one reason for a local rebellion in 1689.

To make matters more confusing, James in 1664 turned over all his proprietary lands between the Hudson and Delaware rivers to two court favorites. Unfortunately, land patents in the eastern portion of what became the colony of New Jersey had already been offered to Puritan settlers, and questions regarding proprietary ownership plagued the colony's development for many years. Settlement proceeded slowly, with the population approaching 15,000 by 1700. Most colonists engaged in commercial farming and raised a variety of grain crops, which they marketed through New York City and Philadelphia. Because of ongoing confusion over land titles, as well as proprietary political authority, the Crown decided in 1702 that New Jersey would henceforth be a royal province.

Middle Colonies, 1685

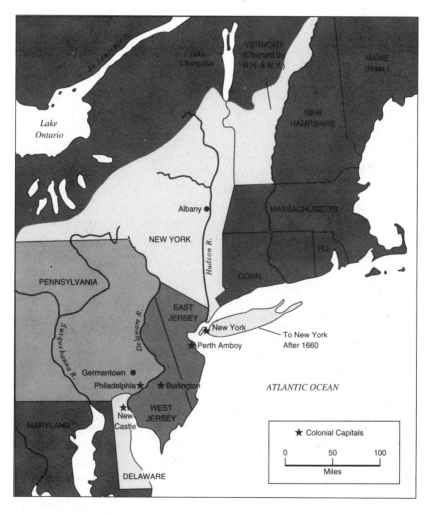

Planting William Penn's "Holy Experiment"

During the English Civil War of the 1640s a number of radical religious sects, among them the Quakers, began to appear in England. Adhering to many controversial ideas, the Quakers believed that all persons had a divine spark, or "inner light," which, when fully nurtured, allowed them to commune directly with God. Like Anne Hutchinson before them, they saw little need for human institutions. They had no ministers and downplayed the importance of the Bible, since they could order their lives according to revelation received directly from God.

In addition, the Quakers held a unique social vision. All humans, they argued, were equal in the sight of God. Thus they wore unadorned black clothing and refused to remove their broad-brimmed hats when social superiors passed by them. Women had full access to leadership positions and could serve as preachers and missionaries. Members of the sect also refused to take legal oaths, which they considered a form of swearing, and as pacifists they believed that warfare would never solve human problems. In time, Quakers became antislavery advocates, arguing that God did not hold some persons inferior because of skin color.

Early English Quakers were intensely fervent, and during the 1650s and 1660s they sent many witnesses of their faith to America. These individuals, about half of them women, fared poorly in the colonies. Puritan magistrates in Massachusetts told them of their "free liberty to keep away from us" and threw them out. Three Quakers were so persistent in coming back to Boston that officials hanged them, making them martyrs to their vision of a more harmonious world.

In 1681 Charles II gave William Penn, who had converted to the Quaker faith in the early 1660s while a student at Oxford, a land grant in America to pay off a debt owed to the estate of Penn's father. Pennsylvania, meaning Penn's woods, was a bountiful tract, and Penn wanted to make the most of it, both as a sanctuary for oppressed religious groups and as a source of personal income from quitrents (land taxes). Penn sent agents to Europe in search of settlers, offering generous land packages with low annual quitrents. He also wrote the colony's First Frame of Government, which guaranteed a legislative assembly and full freedom of religion. Determined to succeed, Penn sailed to America in 1682 to spend two years in the colony, during which time he established cordial relations with the Indians and mapped out Philadelphia.

Like the Puritans before him, Penn had a utopian vision. Unlike them, his "holy experiment" sought to mold a society in which peoples of diverse backgrounds and religious beliefs lived together harmoniously—a bold idea in an era not known for its toleration. During the next few years settlers not only from England but also from Wales, Scotland, Ireland, Holland, Germany, and Switzerland poured through the booming port of Philadelphia and then fanned out into the fertile countryside. There they established family farms, raising livestock and growing abundant grain crops, which they marketed to the West Indies and Europe. The settlers prospered, and Pennsylvania gained a reputation as "one of the best poor man's countries in the world." By the early 1700s the population exceeded 20,000.

Still, not all was perfect in the peaceable kingdom. Religious sects segregated themselves, wanting little to do with one another. Quakers dominated the government but fought endlessly over the prerogatives of power. Penn's pleas for harmony went unheeded. Equally disturbing from his point of view, settlers refused to pay quitrents, yet he kept funding the colony's development.

In his old age Penn considered the "holy experiment" a failure, concluding that peaceable kingdoms on earth lay beyond human reach. Having even endured prison for debts contracted on behalf of his colony, Penn died an embittered man in 1718. Nonetheless, peace, prosperity,

In his treaty with the Indians, William Penn sought to treat Native Americans fairly in negotiating land rights. However, Pennsylvania colonists and Penn's own officials wanted to push the native populace westward as rapidly as possible.

pluralism, and religious toleration were the hallmarks of his utopian vision. By seeking a better life for all peoples, he had infused a sense of high social purpose into the American experience.

Defying the Imperial Will: Provincial Convulsions and Rebellions

Besides standing up to the Dutch, Charles II and his advisers worked to build the emerging empire in other ways. Crown officials crossed the Atlantic to determine whether the colonists were cooperating with the Navigation System. They also sent the first customs officers to America to collect duties on enumerated goods being traded between colonies—and then to foreign ports. Increasingly, the Americans felt England's constraining hand, which in some locales helped to bring on violence.

Bacon's Bloody Rebellion in Virginia

With tobacco glutting the market in England, Virginia's economy went into a tailspin during the 1660s. The planters blamed the Navigation Acts, which stopped them from dealing directly with such foreign merchants as the Dutch; and it did not improve the planters' mood when, in 1667, Dutch war vessels captured virtually the whole English merchant fleet hauling the annual tobacco crop out of Chesapeake Bay, resulting in nearly the total loss of a year's worth of work.

The colony's economic woes were not the only problem. Some Virginians thought that their longtime royal governor, Sir William Berkeley, had become a tyrant. Berkeley handed out patronage jobs to a few preferred planters. Such favors allowed the governor to dominate the assembly and lay heavy taxes at a time when settlers were suffering economically. As a consequence, some planters lost their property, and young males just completing terms of indentured service saw few prospects for ever gaining title to land and achieving economic independence.

In 1674 Nathaniel Bacon, an ambitious and socially prominent young Englishman, arrived in Virginia. He promptly sought acceptance among Berkeley's favored friends, who controlled the lucrative Indian trade. He asked the governor for a trading license, but Berkeley denied the request, feeling that the young man had not yet proven his worth. Incensed by his rejection, Bacon started opposing Berkeley at every turn. He organized other substantial planters not favored by Berkeley, and he also appealed to Virginia's growing numbers of propertyless poor for support.

Stirrings among Indian tribes made matters worse. Far to the north in New York, the Five Nations of Iroquois had become more aggressive in their quest for furs. They started pushing other tribes southward toward Virginia, and some spilled onto frontier plantations, resulting in a few killings.

Bacon demanded reprisals, but Berkeley urged caution, noting that a war would only add to Virginia's tax burdens. Bacon asked for a military commission, stating that he would organize an army of volunteers. The governor refused, at which point Bacon charged his adversary with being more interested in protecting profits from his Indian trading monopoly than in saving settlers' lives. Bacon pulled together a force of over 1,000 men, described as "the scum of the country" by Berkeley's supporters, and indiscriminately started killing local Indians.

In response, Berkeley sent out militiamen to corral the volunteers, but Bacon's force eluded them. The governor also called a new assembly to pass reforms designed to pacify the "mutineers," but events had gone too far, and a shooting war broke out. Before the fighting ceased, Bacon's force burned Jamestown to the ground, and Berkeley fled across Chesapeake Bay.

Charles II promptly dispatched 1,000 troops from England to restore order, but by the time they arrived, Berkeley was back in control. Bacon's death from dysentery in October 1676 had already brought an end to the struggle. Royal advisers with the king's army, however, removed the aging governor from office on the grounds that his policies had helped to stir up trouble.

After 1676 the Crown started sending royal governors to Virginia with detailed instructions on managing the colony as an imperial enterprise—at times at the expense of local interests. In response, Virginia's leading gentleman-planters, previously divided into pro- and anti-Berkeley factions, settled their differences in the face of what they saw as threats to local autonomy. They rallied the people to their side, got themselves elected regularly to the House of Burgesses, and worked together to protect the colony's interests.

This fundamental recasting of political lines was an important development. No longer would rising planter elite leaders fight among themselves. They would stand united in defense of local rights and privileges, making it clear that the Crown, if it wanted harmony and stability, had to show at least some respect for the welfare of its colonists.

The Glorious Revolution Spills into America

The Crown's reactions to Bacon's Rebellion fit a larger pattern of asserting more authority over America. New England, with its independent ways, was an obvious target. The Crown revoked the Bay Colony's charter in 1684, and with the accession of James II to the throne the following year, set up an entirely new form of administration for the colonies, known as the Dominion of New England. Stretching from Nova Scotia to the Delaware River, the Dominion centralized political power in the hands of a governor and a large advisory council made up of Crown appointees. As a result, local representative assemblies would cease to exist.

From the outset the Dominion was a bad idea, perhaps made worse by naming as governor Sir Edmund Andros, a man of aristocratic bearing with impressive military credentials. Arriving in late 1686, Andros expected the Puritans to conform to the imperial will—and his autocratic rule. He announced plans to rewrite all land deeds and, then, to impose quitrents, which New Englanders had never paid. He announced import taxes to underwrite the expenses of his government, and he started prosecuting violators of the Navigation Acts.

Meanwhile, in England, James II had created an uproar by pushing royal authority too far. In defiance of England's Protestant tradition, he flaunted his Roman Catholic beliefs in public and declared that his newborn son, now next in line for the throne, would be raised a Roman Catholic. The thought of yet more religious turmoil was too much for influential English leaders to bear. In December 1688 they drove James from the realm and offered the throne to his Protestant daughter, Mary, and her Dutch husband, William of Orange. Ruling as joint monarchs, William and Mary agreed to give Parliament an equal, if not dominant, voice in Britain's political affairs.

When news of the Glorious Revolution reached Boston, local Puritan leaders went into action. Denouncing Andros and his followers as "bloody devotees of Rome,'" they seized the governor on April 18, 1689, threw him in jail, and then shipped him back to England. They did so, they insisted, to end Andros's arbitrary rule, and they asked William and Mary to restore their original corporate charter.

The coup in Massachusetts helped spark a rebellion in New York, where a volatile mix of ethnic and class tensions resulted in a violent upheaval. Jacob Leisler, a combative local merchant of German origin, took advantage of lower-class resentment toward Francis Nicholson, the Dominion's lieutenant governor, and the wealthy Dutch and English families who cooperated with his rule. When reports of the Massachusetts coup reached New York, Leisler organized a military force of 500 men and on May 31 captured Fort James that guarded New York harbor. Within a few days, Nicholson fled to England amid cries that all Dominion "popish dogs and devils" must be jailed. Leisler then set up an interim government and waited for advice from England, hoping that the new monarchs would make a permanent grant of a popularly based assembly. In addition, Leisler allowed mobs to harass and rob wealthy families.

The third colony jolted by a revolt in 1689 was Maryland, where quarrels between Roman Catholics and Protestants remained a perpetual source of tension. The proprietary governor, William Joseph, tried to contain the popish conspiracy rumors, but John Coode, a nervous local planter, organized the Protestant Association to defend Marylanders from the impending slaughter. Coode led 250 followers to St. Mary's, then Maryland's capital, where in July 1689 they removed Joseph from office, called their own assembly, and then sent representatives to England to plead for royal government.

In a chain reaction, three uprisings had occurred in the American colonies during a span of four months. Although each had its own local character, the common issue, besides the rumored Catholic conspiracy, was the question of how extensive colonial rights would be in the face of tightening imperial administration. All the colonists could do now was wait to hear from the new monarchs—and hope for the best.

New England's Witchcraft Hysteria

By the early 1690s New Englanders had lost their charter, lived under the Dominion, rebelled against Edmund Andros, and engaged in war with the hated French. These unsettled conditions may have made the populace overly suspicious and anxious about evil influences in their midst. Moreover, as New England's Puritan communities moved away from their original religious mission toward a commercial, profit-oriented society, tensions emerged which, according to some historians, manifested themselves in 1692 in an unusual form: the Salem witch trials.

Puritans, like most Europeans and colonists elsewhere, believed in witchcraft. They thought that the devil could materialize in various shapes and forms, damaging lives at will. Satan's agents included witches and wizards, women and men possessed by his evil spirits. Eighty-one New Englanders had faced accusations of practicing witchcraft before 1692, 16 of whom were put to death. These numbers were insignificant in comparison to accused witches hunted down and executed in Europe.

In 1692 the Salem area was a divided community. Salem Town, the port, was caught up in New England's commercial life, while outlying settlers around Salem Village remained quite traditional in seeking God's grace before material wealth. Resentment by the villagers was growing when, in early 1692, a few adolescent girls started having "fits." Anxious about their own lives, the girls had asked Tituba, a local slave woman from the West Indies, to tell them their fortunes. Soon thereafter the girls started acting hysterically, observers claimed, as if possessed by Satan's demons.

When asked to name possible witches, the girls did not stop with Tituba. They eventually made hundreds of accusations before a special court appointed to root the devil out of Massachusetts. With increasing frequency they pointed to prosperous citizens like those of Salem Town.

Some 50 defendants, among them Tituba, saved themselves by admitting their guilt; but 20 men and women were executed (19 by hanging and 1 by the crushing weight of stones) after steadfastly refusing to admit that they had practiced witchcraft.

By the end of the year the craze was over, probably because too many citizens of rank and influence, including the wife of the new royal governor, Sir William Phips, had been accused of doing the devil's work. In time, most participants in the Salem witchcraft trials admitted to being deluded. Although their victims could not be brought back to life, the episode stood as a cautionary reminder in the colonies about the dangers of mass hysteria. The incident also helped sustain New England's transition to a commercial society by making traditional folk beliefs—and those who espoused them—appear foolish.

Settling Anglo-American Differences

In 1691 William and Mary began to address colonial issues. As constitutional monarchs, they were not afraid of popularly based assemblies. In the case of Massachusetts they approved a royal charter that gave the Crown the authority to name royal governors and stated that all male property holders, not just church members, had the right to vote. The monarchs did not tamper with the established Congregational church, thereby reassuring old-line Puritans that conforming to the Church of England was not necessary so long as Bay Colony residents supported England's imperial aspirations. New York also gained permanent status as a royal colony in 1691, complete with a local representative assembly. Still in power, Jacob Leisler refused to step aside, which led to his arrest, trial, and execution for treason. In Maryland's case, the colony's proprietors, the Calvert family, temporarily lost political control in 1692 in favor of royal government, and shortly thereafter a Protestant assembly banned Roman Catholics from political office.

The transformation revealed a movement toward the royal model of government in which the colonies established legislative assemblies to express and defend their local concerns. Crown-appointed governors, in turn, pledged themselves to enforce the Navigation Acts and other imperial laws. So long as the colonists cooperated, they would not face autocratic forms of government. Nor would the Crown permit the kind of loose freedom of early colonial days because, in gaining basic rights the Americans also accepted responsibility for conducting their daily affairs within the imperial framework. The Glorious Revolution and its reverberations in America had made this compromise possible.

Maintaining the delicate balance between imperial intrusiveness and local autonomy was the major challenge of the eighteenth century. Until the 1760s both sides tried to make the compromise work. The Crown demonstrated its resolve by establishing the Board of Trade and Plantations in 1696 as a permanent administrative agency to advise England's leaders on colonial issues. It also mandated vice-admiralty courts in America to punish smugglers and others who violated the rules of trade.

The Board of Trade generally acted with discretion, even in recommending a few acts to restrain colonial manufacturers competing with home industries. Parliament in 1699 adopted the Woolen Act that outlawed any exportation of woolen products from America or from one colony to another. The intent was to get the colonists to buy finished woolens from manufacturers in England rather than to develop their own industry. In 1732 there was similar restrictive legislation (the Hat Act) concerning the production of beaver and felt hats. In 1750 Parliament passed the Iron Act that forbade the colonists from building new facilities or expanding old ones for the manufacture of finished iron or steel products. As a whole, this legislation had few adverse effects on the provincial economy. It simply reinforced fundamental mercantile notions regarding colonies as sources of raw materials and as markets for finished goods.

Occasionally, imperial administrators went too far, such as with the Molasses Act of 1733. In support of a thriving rum industry based mostly in New England, colonial merchants roamed the Caribbean for molasses, which cost less on French and Dutch West Indian islands. To placate British West Indian planters, Parliament tried to redirect the trade with a heavy duty (6 pence per gallon) on foreign molasses brought into the colonies. Enforcing the trade duty could have ruined the North American rum industry, but customs officers wisely ignored collecting the duty, a sensible solution to a potentially inflammatory issue.

As the eighteenth century progressed, imperial officials tried not to be overbearing. In certain instances they actually stimulated provincial economic activity by offering large cash bounties for growing such valued export commodities as the indigo originally produced by Eliza Lucas. Caught up as the empire was in warfare with France and Spain, home leaders did not want to tamper with a system that, by and large, worked. The colonists, for their part, gladly accepted what many have referred to as the "era of salutary neglect."

Maturing Colonial Societies in Unsettled Times

Besides the maintenance of stable relations with the parent state, other factors stimulated the maturing of the American provinces after 1700. Certainly the expanding population base, which saw a near doubling of numbers nearly every 20 years, strengthened the colonies, as did the pattern of widespread economic prosperity, even if not shared evenly among the populace. The important role American colonists played during a series of imperial wars also instilled a vital sense of self-confidence. By the 1760s provincial Americans took pride in what they had accomplished as subjects of the British empire in North America.

An Exploding Population Base

Between 1700 and 1760 the colonial population mushroomed from 250,000 to 1.6 million persons—and to 2.5 million by 1775. Longer lives were partly responsible for this growth, due to better health and agricultural abundance. Colonists had plentiful supplies of food. Nutritious diets led to improved overall health, making it easier for Americans to ward off virulent diseases.

Natural population increase was only one source of the population explosion. Equally significant was the introduction of non-English peoples. Between 1700 and 1775, for example, the British North American slave trade reached its peak, resulting in the involuntary entry of an estimated 250,000 Africans into the colonies. The black population grew from 28,000 in 1700 to over 500,000 in 1775, with most living as chattel slaves in the South. At least 40 to 50 percent of the African-American population increase was attributable to the booming slave trade.

Among European groups, the Scots-Irish and Germans were predominant, although a smattering of French Huguenot, Swiss, Scottish, Irish, and Jewish migrants joined the westward stream. The Scots-Irish had endured many privations. Originally Presbyterian lowlanders from Scotland, they had migrated to Ulster (Northern Ireland) in the seventeenth century at the invitation of the Crown. During the next several years they endured crop failures and huge rent increases from their English landlords. In a series of waves between 1725 and 1775 over 100,000 Scots-Irish descended upon North America. Many moved out into the southern backcountry where they squatted on open land and earned reputations as bloodthirsty Indian fighters.

Even before the first Scots-Irish wave, Germans from the area of the upper Rhine River began streaming into the Middle Colonies. Some, like Amish, Moravian, and Mennonite sectarians, were fleeing religious persecution; others were escaping crushing economic circumstances caused by overpopulation, crop failures, and heavy local taxes. By the eve of the American Revolution, some 100,000 German migrants had arrived in the colonies.

The "Europeanizing" of America

Compared to Europe, America was a land of boundless prosperity. To be sure, however, there were wide disparities in wealth, rank, and privilege that the colonists accepted as part of the natural order of life. They did so because of the pervasive influence of European values, such as the need for hierarchy and deference in social and political relations. The eighteenth century was still an era in which individuals believed in three distinct social orders—the monarchy, the aristocracy, and the "democracy" of common citizens. All persons had an identifiable place in society, fixed at birth; and to try to improve one's lot was to risk instability in the established rhythms of the universe.

Elite families set themselves apart from the rest of colonial society by imitating English aristocratic life-styles. Wealthy southern gentlemen utilized gangs of slaves to produce the staple crops that generated the income to construct lavish manor houses with elaborate formal gardens. Northern merchants built residences of Georgian design and filled them with fashionable furniture. Together, they thought of themselves as the "better sort," and they expected the "lower sort" to defer to their judgment in social and political decision making.

One characteristic, then, of the "Europeanizing" of colonial society was growing economic stratification, with extremes of wealth and poverty becoming more visible. Nevertheless, there was a large middle class, and it was still possible to get ahead in provincial America. Over 90 percent of the colonists lived in the countryside and made their livings from some form of agricultural production. By European standards, the ownership of property was widespread, yet there were also many instances of extreme poverty. Some of the worst cases were among urban dwellers, many of whom eked out the barest of livelihoods as unskilled day laborers or merchant seamen. These individuals at least enjoyed some personal freedom, which placed them above black slaves, who formed 20 percent of the population but enjoyed none of its prosperity or political rights.

With colonial wealth concentrated in fewer and fewer hands, another "Europeanizing" trend was toward the hardening of class lines. Elite families increasingly intermarried among themselves, and they spoke openly of an assumed right to serve as political stewards for the people.

Although widespread property holding allowed great numbers of free white males to vote, they most often chose members of the elite to represent them in elective offices, particularly in colonial assemblies. Once elected, these stewards did constant battle with Crown-appointed governors and councilors in upper houses over the prerogatives of local decision making. In colony after colony during the eighteenth century, elite leaders insisted on the same legislative rights in their respective territorial spheres as Parliament had over all British subjects.

More often than not, royal governors had only feeble backing from the home government and lost these disputes. As a result, the provincial assemblies gained many prerogatives, including the right to initiate all money and taxation bills. Because governors depended on the assemblies for their salaries, they often approved local legislation not in the best interests of the Crown in exchange for bills appropriating their annual salaries. By the 1760s the colonial assemblies had thus emerged as powerful agencies of government.

Intellectual and Religious Awakening

Besides politics, colonial leaders were fascinated by Europe's dawning Age of Reason, also called the Enlightenment. The approach to learning was secular, based on scientific inquiry and the systematic collection of information. Leading intellectuals sought to unlock the physical laws of nature and identify laws governing human behavior. In his *Essay Concerning Human Understanding* (1690), English political thinker John Locke described the human mind as a blank sheet (*tabula rasa*) at birth waiting to be influenced by the experiences of life. If people followed the insights of reason, social and political ills could somehow be reduced or eliminated from society, and each person, as well as humankind as a whole, could advance toward greater harmony and perfection.

The key watchword of the Enlightenment was *rationalism,* meaning a firm trust in the ability of the human mind to solve earthly problems—and much less faith in the centrality of God as an active, judgmental force in the universe. Whereas John Winthrop believed that earthquakes were signs of God's wrath, his great-great-grandson, John Winthrop IV, a professor of mathematics at Harvard College in the mid-1730s, argued that movements in the earth's surface had natural causes, which he explained in scientific terms.

Benjamin Franklin became the best-known provincial student of science. In 1743 he helped found the American Philosophical Society. With the aid of a kite, Franklin performed experiments with lightning, seeking to reveal the mysteries of electrical energy. After publishing his *Experiments and Observations on Electricity* (1751), Franklin's fame spread throughout the western world.

Many religious leaders viewed Enlightenment rationalism with great suspicion. It seemed to undermine orthodox religious values by reducing God to a prime mover who had set the universe in motion only to leave humans to chart their own destiny. (This system of thought was known as Deism.) Others worried about the loss of religious faith emphasizing the need for repentance, conversion, and God's saving grace. They felt that the populace, rushing to achieve material prosperity, had become too complacent, as if affluence and good works would guarantee eternal salvation. For some clergymen, then, the time was at hand for placing a renewed emphasis on vital religious faith.

During the 1720s and 1730s in Europe and America, some ministers started holding revivals. They did so in the face of declining popular interest in formal religion, as expressed by dwindling church attendance in many locales. Through impassioned sermons delivered from their hearts, they exhorted great numbers of people to seek God's saving grace. This was the first in a succession of revivals known collectively as the Great Awakening.

In 1734 Jonathan Edwards, a Congregational minister residing in Northampton, Massachusetts, initiated a series of revival meetings aimed at the youth of this community. Edwards was a learned student of the Enlightenment who argued that experiencing God's grace was essential to the comprehension of the universe and its laws. In one sermon Edwards reminded his congregation of the "abominations of your life," vividly picturing how each member was "wallowing in sensual filthiness, as swine in mire." Appealing to the senses more than to rational inquiry, Edwards felt, was the surest way to uplift individual lives, win souls for God, and improve society as a whole.

Such local revivals did not become broad and general until after the dynamic English preacher, George Whitefield, arrived in America. Whitefield was a disciple of John Wesley, the founder of the Methodist movement in England. Possessing a booming, melodious voice and a charismatic presence, Whitefield preached with great simplicity, always stressing the essentials of God's "free gift" of grace for those seeking conversion. He made seven preaching tours to the colonies, traveled thousands of miles, delivered hundreds of sermons, and spoke to gatherings as large as 30,000. Perhaps his most dramatic tour was to New England in the autumn of 1740. In Boston over 20,000 heard him preach in a three-day period. Concluding his tour in less than a month, Whitefield left behind churches full of congregants anxious to experience conversion and bask in the glow of fellowship with God.

Concerned with reviving vital religion, the Awakening soon became a source of great contention, splitting America's religious community into "new" and "old" light camps. Many revivalists advised their flocks to shun clergymen who, while well educated in formal theology, showed no visible signs of having gained God's saving grace. Thousands paid attention, and they started breaking away from congregations where ministers were suspect.

In response, Old Light clergymen began denouncing the Awakening as a fraudulent hoax being perpetrated by unlettered fools of no theological training. In New England, orthodox Congregational ministers got their legislative assemblies to adopt anti-itinerancy laws, which barred traveling evangelists like Whitefield from preaching in their communities.

All of the turmoil had significant long-term repercussions. Those feeling a new relationship with God were less willing to submit to established authority and more determined to speak out on behalf of basic liberties. Typical were colonists in New England who had started calling themselves Baptists. They demanded the right to separate completely from the established Congregational church, to which all citizens owed taxes, and the right to support their own ministers and churches. Theirs would be a long and hard-fought campaign for an end to state-supported religion.

The liberty to worship and support whatever church one pleased was a central concern of the Awakening movement, as was a desire to see clergymen properly trained. Prior to the 1740s, there were only three colonial colleges, Harvard, William and Mary, and Yale. In demanding toleration for diverse ideas, Presbyterian revivalists set up the College of New Jersey (later Princeton) to train New Light clergymen; Baptists founded the College of Rhode Island (later Brown); and the Dutch Reformed established Queen's College (later Rutgers). In 1769 a New Light Congregational minister, Eleazar Wheelock, received a charter for Dartmouth College to carry the new birth message to Native Americans.

As the Great Awakening spread into the South, it had a variety of lasting effects. During the late 1740s and 1750s the emergence of Presbyterian congregations in Virginia called into question the authority of the established Anglican church. By the mid-1750s swelling numbers of Baptists were displaying anything but a deferential regard for the mores of Virginia's planter elite. They started demanding, for example, the "entire banishment of *dancing, gaming,* and sabbath-day diversions."

The Awakening also stimulated Protestant forms of worship among blacks. They did not forsake their African religious traditions but blended them with Christian faith in a savior who offered eternal life through God's saving grace as well as hope for triumphing over oppression in their search for human freedom.

As the Great Awakening spread through the British North American provinces, then, its proponents questioned established authority at every turn and provoked movement toward a clearer definition of fundamental human rights as well as toleration of divergent ideas. The Awakening also served to direct the colonists toward the day when Americans would naturally accept religious pluralism, as expressed in the dramatic rise of such non-state-supported denominational groups as the Baptists and Presbyterians. Greater toleration of dissenters and diverse religious ideas were hall-mark legacies of the Awakening.

None of this came easily, and some of it, especially the emphasis on the search for personal liberty and freedom of conscience, along with the questioning of established authority, may have unwittingly served to pre-dispose many colonists to the political rebellion against Great Britain that lay in the not-too-distant future. Historians have divided opinions on this matter, but most would agree that the Awakening demonstrated that American communities showed considerable strength in weathering so much divisiveness. The provinces had indeed grown up and matured dur-ing the previous 100-year period, even if the British Crown failed to ap-preciate the newfound self-confidence of its North American colonists.

International Wars Beset America

Successful participation in a series of wars involving Britain and its two North American rivals, France and Spain, also contributed to the colonists' growing self-confidence. During the seventeenth century Spain maintained its grip on Florida as well as the Gulf coast. French Canadi-ans, operating from bases in Montreal and Quebec, explored throughout the Great Lakes region and then down into the Mississippi Valley. In 1682 an expedition headed by René-Robert Cavelier, Sieur de La Salle, reached the mouth of the Mississippi River. La Salle, who dreamed of a mighty French empire west of the Appalachian Mountains, claimed the whole region for his monarch, Louis XIV.

Despite these auspicious beginnings, New France grew slowly. Con-sumed by European affairs, the French Crown did not actively encourage settlement, and as late as 1760 no more than 75,000 French subjects lived in all of Canada and the Mississippi Valley. Some were farmers or fisher-men, and most others were fur traders. On the whole, they treated Native Americans with respect, and because the French population was so small, the Indians did not worry about losing ancient tribal lands. Sound rela-tions with the Indians certainly paid off, especially after European warfare spilled over into America. The advantage of having thousands of potential allies willing to join in combat against British settlers made the French Canadians a very dangerous enemy, as events proved during the imperial wars between 1689 and 1763.

The first of the four wars, known in the colonies as King William's War (1689–1697), was a limited conflict with no major battles in Amer-ica. What made this war so frightening were bloody border clashes in-volving Indians and colonists—typical was the attack on Hannah Dus-tan's Haverhill—that resulted in some 650 deaths among the English colonists. Five years later war erupted again, this time over French claims to the Spanish throne. Known as Queen Anne's War (1702–1713) in the colonies, the Anglo-Americans found themselves dueling with Spain as well as France and their Indian allies. In terms of casualties the war was not particularly bloody for the English colonists, who lost fewer than 500 people over an 11-year period. The Treaty of Utrecht, which ended the conflict in 1713, was a virtual declaration of Britain's growing imperial might. The British realized major territorial gains, including Hudson Bay, Newfoundland, and Nova Scotia in Canada.

Britain's triumph deterred additional warfare for 26 years, but further conflict seemed inevitable. To serve as a buffer between South Carolina and Spanish Florida, the Board of Trade in 1721 called for the creation of a military colony. General James Oglethorpe, a wealthy member of Parliament, decided to pursue the idea. A true philanthropist as well as imperialist, he hoped to roll back Spanish influence in America while improving the lot of England's downcast poor, especially imprisoned debtors. In 1732 King George II issued a charter for Georgia, granting 21 trustees all the land between the Savannah and Altamaha rivers for 21 years to develop the region, after which the colony would revert to the Crown and function under royal authority.

Colonists were hard to find, largely because of the rules devised by Oglethorpe and the other trustees. To assure good order, they outlawed liquor. To promote personal industry and hard work as well as spread out settlements in an effective defensive line, they limited individual land grants to 500 acres, and they banned slavery.

As a social experiment to uplift the poor, the colony was not successful. Some migrants wanted slaves; others, referring to Oglethorpe as "our perpetual dictator," called for a popular assembly; and they all demanded alcohol. The trustees acknowledged their failure by turning Georgia back to the Crown in 1752, a year ahead of schedule. By that time, they had already conceded on the issues of slavery and strong drink. Thereafter, Georgia looked more and more like South Carolina, with large rice and indigo plantations underpinning the local economy. By 1770, the colony's populace was almost 25,000, nearly half of whom were slaves.

Meanwhile, the conflict between the major European powers continued sporadically. James Oglethorpe mounted an unsuccessful expedition against Florida in 1740, and the following year a combined British-colonial force tried unsuccessfully to capture the major Spanish port of Cartagena. In 1744, England and France came to blows again over the legitimate heir to the Austrian throne, which in its American phase the colonists called King George's War. In June 1745 a New England army achieved a brilliant victory over the French, capturing the mighty fortress of Louisbourg that guarded the entrance to the St. Lawrence River.

The triumph at Louisbourg represented for the colonists the high point of a war that cost as many as 5,000 Anglo-American lives. But in the peace settlement that ended the war, Britain returned Louisbourg to the French. In exchange it received a port in India, which the king's negotiators reasoned was of much greater value as a center for imperial trade than a fortress in the American wilderness. The colonists were furious about this action, but they were powerless to do anything except complain among themselves about their subordinate—and unappreciated—status in the empire.

Showdown: The Great War for the Empire

When war broke out again, it resulted from conflicting interests in America. In 1748 fur traders from Pennsylvania and Virginia began establishing contacts with natives in the Ohio River valley. With the boom in colonial population, leading planters in Virginia were casting a covetous eye toward the development of the Ohio River Valley. With the backing of London merchants, one group formed the Ohio Company in 1747 and two years later secured a grant of 200,000 acres from the Crown.

Determined to secure the region against encroaching Anglo-American traders and land speculators, the French in the early 1750s started constructing a chain of forts in a line running southward from Lake Erie in western Pennsylvania. By 1753 the British ministry knew of these plans and ordered colonial governors to challenge the French advance and "repel force by force" if necessary.

Virginia's Governor Robert Dinwiddie, who happened to be an investor in the Ohio Company, acted quickly. In the spring of 1754 he sent a young major of militia, George Washington, with 200 men into western Pennsylvania. Foolishly, Washington skirmished with French troops, then hastily retreated and constructed Fort Necessity. A superior French and Indian force attacked on July 3. Washington surrendered and was allowed to lead his troops back to Virginia as prisoners of war.

While Washington was preparing to defend Fort Necessity, delegates from seven colonies had gathered in Albany, New York, to plan for their defense in case of war and to secure active support from the powerful Iroquois Indian Confederacy. At this meeting, delegates Benjamin Franklin and Thomas Hutchinson proposed an intercolonial plan of government, known as the Albany Plan of Union. The idea was to have a "grand council" made up of representatives from each colony who would work with a crown official, a "president general," to plan for defense and even to tax the provinces on an equitable basis in keeping the North American colonies secure from external enemies. The plan stirred little interest at the time, since the assemblies were not anxious to share their prerogatives, especially the power of taxation, with anyone.

Home government officials ignored the Albany Plan of Union, but the Fort Necessity debacle resulted in a fateful decision to send Major General Edward Braddock, an unimaginative 60-year-old British officer who had never commanded troops in battle, to Virginia. With a combined force of 3,000 redcoats and colonial militia—Washington came along as a volunteer officer—Braddock marched toward Fort Duquesne, the site of modern-day Pittsburgh. On July 9, 1755, about eight miles from the French fort, a much smaller French and Indian force, attacking from all sides, nearly destroyed the British column, leaving two-thirds of Braddock's soldiers dead or wounded. Braddock himself sustained mortal wounds, but before he died, he stated wryly: "We shall better know how to deal with them another time."

The ensuing conflict, widely known as the Seven Years' War and later referred to in America as the French and Indian War, was a showdown between France and England. William Pitt, the king's new chief minister, viewed America as the place "where England and Europe are to be fought for." Pitt's strategic plan was to let Prussia, Britain's ally, bear the brunt of warfare in Europe, while placing the bulk of England's military resources in America with the intent of strangling New France. He also advanced a

This woodcut, displayed in the *Pennsylvania Gazette,* failed to overcome long-standing jealousies that thwarted attempts at intercolonial cooperation.

young group of dynamic officers over the heads of less capable men. It all paid off in a series of carefully orchestrated military advances that saw Quebec fall to the British in September 1759. A year later, with hardly an exchange of musket fire, Montreal surrendered to British troops.

Conclusion

The fall of the French empire in North America took place in the face of growing antagonism between British military leaders and the colonists. Americans joined provincial regiments and fought beside British redcoats, but most did not care for the experience. They found the king's regulars to be rough, crude, and morally delinquent. They viewed the king's officers as needlessly overbearing and aristocratic. They resented being treated as inferiors.

Chronology of Key Events

1650–1673	Navigation Acts passed to ensure that colonies trade within the emerging English empire
1664	Dutch surrender New Netherland to the English, who rename the colony New York
1676	Bacon's Rebellion takes place in Virginia
1682	La Salle claims Louisiana for France
1684	England revokes the Massachusetts Bay Colony charter
1686	Dominion of New England established
1688	Glorious Revolution drives James II from throne
1689	Rebellions occur in Massachusetts, New York, and Maryland
1692	Witchcraft scare in Salem, Massachusetts, results in execution of 20 women and men
1739–1740	Great Awakening gains momentum
1754	Albany Congress draws up plan to bring unity to the 13 colonies; George Washington defends Fort Necessity
1759	British forces capture Quebec
1763	Treaty of Paris ends the Seven Years' War

Young George Washington explained how Virginia's recruits "behaved like men, and died like soldiers" during Braddock's defeat, as compared to the British regulars, who "behaved with more cowardice than it is possible to conceive." The Americans were proud of their contributions to the triumphant British empire. They hoped that the Crown would treat them with greater respect in the days ahead. The king's chief ministers, however, believed that the colonists had done more to serve themselves than the British empire during the Seven Years' War. Because of many problems related to the war, the Crown decided to crack down on the "obstinate and ungovernable" American colonists.

Apparently the king's ministers had not learned very much from the previous 100 years of Anglo-American history. Before 1690, as the laws by which the empire operated became too restrictive, serious colonial resistance ensued. After 1690 an accommodation of differences assured the Americans basic rights and some local autonomy, so long as they supported the empire's economic and political objectives. Now more self-assertive than ever before, provincial Americans would again resist imperial plans to make them more fully subordinate to the will of the parent nation. This time they would go so far as to break the bonds of empire.

Suggestions for Further Reading

For studies of Britain's North American empire see Lawrence H. Gipson, *The British Empire Before the American Revolution,* 15 vols. (1936–1970); Michael Kammen, *Empire and Interest: The American Colonies and the Politics of Mercantilism* (1970); David S. Lovejoy, *The Glorious Revolution in America* (1972); Stephen S. Webb, *The Governors-General: The English Army and the Definition of Empire, 1569–1681* (1979).

For a general overview of North America during the late seventeenth and early eighteenth centuries see Wesley Frank Craven, *The Colonies in Transition, 1660–1713* (1968). Studies of the New England witch hysteria during this period include Paul Boyer and Stephen Nissenbaum, *Salem Possessed* (1974); John Putnam Demos, *Entertaining Satan* (1982); Carol F. Karlsen, *The Devil in the Shape of a Woman* (1987). For studies of the Middle Colonies see Patricia U. Bonomi, *A Factious People: Politics and Society in Colonial New York* (1971); Gary B. Nash, *Quakers and Politics* (1968); Robert C. Ritchie, *The Duke's Province: Politics and Society in New York* (1977); Sally Schwartz, *"A Mixed Multitude": The Struggle for Toleration in Colonial Pennsylvania* (1987). On the southern colonies see Jack P. Greene, *The Quest for Power: The Lower Houses of Assembly in the Southern Colonies, 1689–1776* (1963); Rhys Isaac, *The Transformation of Virginia,* (1982); Wilcomb E. Washburn, *The Governor and the Rebel: A History of Bacon's Rebellion* (1957). The intellectual climate in the colonies is examined in

Henry F. May, *The Enlightenment in America* (1976); Alan Heimert, *Religion and the American Mind* (1966).

On the imperial conflict in North American see Fred Anderson, *A People's Army: Massachusetts in the Seven Years' War* (1984); John E. Ferling, *Struggle for a Continent: The Wars of Early America* (1993); Francis Jennings, *Empire of Fortune: Crown, Colonies, and Tribes in the Seven Years' War* (1988; Douglas E. Leach, *Roots of Conflict: British Armed Forces and Colonial Americans* (1986), and *Arms for Empire: A Military History of the Colonies, 1607–1763* (1973).

Chapter *4*

Breaking the Bonds of Empire, 1760–1775

S amuel Adams grew up with many advantages in life. His father was a prosperous businessman who wanted his son to become a Congregational minister, so he sent him off to Harvard College. In 1740 Samuel emerged with a bachelor's degree, a reputation for free spending and excessive drinking, and little desire to become a clergyman. Enormously proud of his Puritan heritage, Adams remained a lifelong student of scripture, but his primary vocational interest was politics.

The year 1740 turned out to be disastrous for Adams's father. As a community leader he had become deeply involved in a plan to provide citizens with paper currency for local business transactions. Adams and others established a "land bank" that would lend out money to individuals who put up collateral in the form of real estate. The bank's paper money could then be used to purchase goods and services—and even pay debts as legal tender.

The directors of the Massachusetts Land Bank believed that they were performing a public service. Wealthy merchants, however, thought otherwise. They viewed such paper currencies with great skepticism. Only money properly backed by specie, such as gold or silver, they argued, could hold its value in the marketplace. They did not want to have to accept what they feared would be rapidly depreciating land-bank notes in their commercial dealings or for debts. Under the leadership of a powerful local merchant, Thomas Hutchinson, they appealed to the royal governor, who declared the land bank illegal, a position sustained in 1741 by Parliament.

With the land bank's collapse, Adams's father lost tremendous sums of money that he had invested to help underwrite the venture. He never recovered financially. When he died in 1748, he left his son a legacy of bitterness toward arbitrary royal authority and those Crown favorites, such as Thomas Hutchinson, whose actions had destroyed his family's prosperity.

Having no desire to continue his father's business, Samuel barely kept his own family in food and clothing. What little income he earned came from a number of minor political offices. In 1756 he assumed duties as a collector of local taxes for the town government, but he found it difficult to collect taxes from hard-pressed local citizens who, like himself, were struggling to make ends meet. Adams regularly accepted any good explanation—the outbreak of illness in some families and the loss of jobs in others. Boston's economy was stagnant, and unskilled workers were especially hard-pressed. As Adams was also aware, each time he did not enforce a collection he made a friend. By the early 1760s he had built up a loyal following of admirers who fervently believed that he was a good and decent man committed to protecting their interests.

Even as he earned the gratitude of Boston's ordinary citizens, Adams did not lose sight of adversaries from his past. He particularly loathed

Thomas Hutchinson, whose stature as a wealthy merchant with wide-ranging imperial connections had helped him gain a number of prominent offices. In 1758 Hutchinson secured a Crown appointment as the Bay Colony's lieutenant governor. He was already holding a local probate judgeship, was the ranking local militia officer, and was serving as an elected member of the governor's council (the upper house of the General Court). Then in 1760 he gained appointment to the post of chief judge of the superior court. His combined annual salary from these offices was around £400 sterling, ten times the amount of an average family's yearly income.

In the years ahead when Hutchinson and other royal officials in Massachusetts tried to implement imperial policies, Adams was ready to protest and resist. His allies in the streets would be the ordinary people, and they set a particularly defiant tone for the broader resistance movement throughout the 13 provinces. Whether Samuel Adams acted out of personal rancor toward Hutchinson or purely to defend American liberties was one of the secrets he carried to his grave, even as his contemporaries remembered him both in Europe and America as "one of the prime movers of the late Revolution."

The actual outbreak of the American Revolution may be traced directly to the year 1763 when British leaders began to tighten the imperial reins. The colonists protested vigorously, and communications started to break down, so much so that a permanent rupture of political affections began to take place. No one in 1763 had any idea that the developing crisis would shatter the bonds of empire, but that is exactly what happened when the American colonists, after a dozen years of bitter contention with the parent nation, finally proceeded to open rebellion in 1775.

Provoking an Imperial Crisis

In 1763 British subjects everywhere toasted the Treaty of Paris that ended the worldwide Seven Years' War. The empire had gained territorial jurisdiction over French Canada and all territory east of the Mississippi River, except for a tiny strip of land around New Orleans that France deeded to Spain. The Spanish, in turn, who also took over French territory west of the Mississippi River, had to cede the Floridas to Britain to regain the Philippines and Cuba, the latter having fallen to a combined Anglo-American force in 1762. Britain likewise made substantial gains in India. Most important from the colonists' perspective, the French "menace" had been eradicated from North America, which should have signaled a new era of imperial harmony. That was not to be the case.

Samuel Adams, shown here in an engraving by Paul Revere. Adams believed
that royalist leaders in Massachusetts wanted to destroy American liberties. He
was a vigorous opponent of the Stamp Act, an organizer of the Sons of Liberty,
and, after independence, a long-term governor of Massachusetts.

A Legacy of War-Related Problems

For the chief ministers in Great Britain under the youthful and vigorous
monarch George III, who was 25 years old in 1763, the most pressing
problem was Britain's national debt. During the Seven Years' War it had
skyrocketed from £75 million to £137 million sterling. Advisers to the
Crown worried about ways to get the debt under control, a most difficult

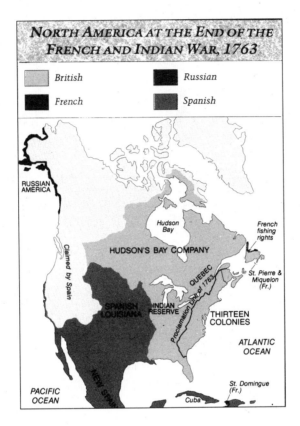

North America, 1763

With the signing of the Treaty of Paris, Great Britain received almost all of France's holdings in North America.

problem considering the newly won territories that the home government now had to govern.

Closely linked to the debt issue was the matter of American smuggling activity. Many colonial merchants, eager for profits of any kind, had traded illegally with the enemy during the war. Even though the Royal Navy had blockaded French and Spanish ports in the Caribbean, traders from New England and elsewhere used various pretexts to effect business deals.

A host of issues relating to newly won territories to the north and west of the Anglo-American settlements also concerned the king's ministers. Most important, they worried about the financial burden of prolonged warfare on the frontier, should land-hungry white settlers push into Indian hunting grounds too quickly. The vacuum created by the collapse of French authority combined with fears that British officials would ignore the encroachment of white settlers on tribal lands inspired Pontiac, an Ottawa war chief, to build an alliance of several western Indian tribes.

Beginning in May 1763, Pontiac's warriors struck with a vengeance, attacking white settlements running in a southwesterly arc from New York through western Pennsylvania to Virginia. Only a severe thrashing at Bushy Run, Pennsylvania, in August 1763 turned the tide of bloody frontier warfare against the Indians, and by autumn Pontiac's allies began drifting back to their villages.

It fell to George Grenville, who became the king's chief minister in April 1763, to solve these imperial problems. Grenville held strong anti-American feelings. As he proclaimed before Parliament, "Great Britain protects America; America is bound to yield obedience." An ominous moment in Anglo-American relations was at hand. The so-called era of salutary neglect, under which the colonists had thrived in relative freedom for so many years, was about to end.

Getting Tough with the Americans

Grenville was a mercantilist in his thinking and firmly believed that the colonists had forgotten their subordinate status in the empire. In early October 1763 he issued two administrative orders designed to bring the Americans to heel. The first, known as the Orders in Council of 1763, stationed British naval vessels in American waters for the purpose of running down and seizing all colonial merchant ships suspected of illegal trading activity. The goal was to end American smuggling and to force the colonists to start paying more trade duties into royal coffers.

The second order, known as the Proclamation of 1763, dealt with the West. It addressed matters of government for the new British territories, including the temporary organization of such provinces as Quebec. It also mandated that a line be drawn from north to south along "the heads or sources of any of the rivers which fell into the Atlantic Ocean from the west and northwest." No doubt much influenced by the news of Pontiac's uprising, the ministry's notion was to stop white incursions into Indian lands. Hence, territory west of the Proclamation line was forever to be "reserved to the Indians."

The Proclamation policy may have reflected some desire for humane treatment of Native Americans; however, the cabinet was far more concerned with avoiding costly Indian wars. There were some cabinet leaders, furthermore, who did not relish the prospect of American settlements spreading too far inland from the Atlantic coastline. If the colonists built communities across the mountains and out of the reach of the imperial trading network, they would of necessity begin manufacturing all sorts of products—and might, in time, start competing with the British Isles for control of seaboard markets. From the imperial perspective, it was in the parent nation's best interest to keep the colonists to the east of the Appalachian Mountains.

The Proclamation of 1763 also related to another policy decision of momentous consequence. To keep control over both white settlers and Indians, the cabinet had already decided to maintain up to 10,000 British regulars in North America. Pontiac's uprising and the Proclamation policy determined where the redcoats were to be located, at least initially. Most would be ordered out onto the frontier, but it was unclear who would pay for these redcoats—a crucial issue, indeed.

Determined that the colonists should pay for their own defense, Grenville came up with plans to tax His Majesty's subjects in America. In April 1764 Parliament adopted the Revenue Act, usually called the Sugar Act, which placed trade duties on a number of foreign goods—coffee, indigo, sugar, and wine—regularly purchased by the colonists. It also lowered the Molasses Act duty of 1733 from six to three pence a gallon with the hope that it would be easier to collect than in the past.

Grenville projected that the Sugar Act would produce an additional £40,000 in annual revenue to assist in covering the ongoing costs of imperial administration, in this case paying for Britain's military establishment in America. From the colonists' perspective, that was exactly the problem with this legislation. As the New York assembly pointed out, the purpose was something more than merely fixing a duty that would affect the flow of commerce. In 1763 the colonists had paid only an estimated £1,800 in trade duties associated with the Navigation Acts. (It actually cost the Crown £8,000 that year to run the customs service in America.) A projected £40,000 in yearly revenue, by comparison, made it clear that the intention was to tax the Americans.

Taxation was what Grenville had most in mind, but he also had other concerns, as embodied in Parliament's adoption of the Currency Act of April 1764. This act represented an expansion of legislation directed against New England in 1751. The paper money of all colonial governments could no longer be used as legal tender in payment of private debts. Nor could provincial governments issue any new paper bills, and they were expected to retire what money they had in circulation within a reasonable time period.

Unfortunately, the colonies were in the midst of a severe postwar depression in 1764. Limiting the currency supply only worsened matters by making it yet more difficult for citizens to obtain money to conduct business—let alone pay increased taxes. If nothing else, the timing of the Currency Act was terrible; it caused the home government to appear incredibly insensitive to promoting the economic welfare of its colonies.

Parliament Endorses Direct Taxes

George Grenville really did not care about the opinions of the colonists. His major goal was to raise a substantial tax revenue in the colonies. He got what he wanted with the Stamp Act of March 1765, the capstone of his imperial program. Through the Stamp Act, Parliament asserted for the first time its full authority to lay *direct* taxes, as opposed to *indirect* (or hidden taxes, such as trade duties), on the colonists.

As such, there was nothing subtle about the Stamp Act. This legislation required Americans to pay for stamps attached to some 50 items, everything from newspapers, pamphlets, almanacs, and playing cards to port clearance papers for ships, land deeds, and wills. The price of the stamps varied according to the value of the particular items to which they were affixed. Grenville estimated that the tax would yield about £100,000 a year. All stamps would have to be paid for in hard currency, a virtual impossibility since specie continually flowed to Britain to pay for imported goods. Also, violators could be prosecuted in juryless vice-admiralty courts, as well as in regular criminal courts.

Grenville knew that the colonists would not like the Stamp Act, but he believed the time had come for Americans to pay for the benefits of being part of the mightiest empire in the western world. Grenville was not asking the colonists to help reduce the home debt, only to assist in meeting the rising costs of imperial administration. For that reason, Parliament earmarked Stamp Act revenues for maintaining the redcoats in America.

To counter arguments about taxation without representation, Grenville employed the concept of "virtual representation," maintaining that all English subjects throughout the empire—by virtue of their citizenship—enjoyed representation in Parliament. In theory, members of Parliament were to promote the public good by representing not just particular constituents but all imperial subjects in legislative decision making.

But Grenville had failed to see the whole picture. From an economic point of view, if from no other, the colonies were invaluable to the British empire. The provinces so stimulated the home economy, particularly with regard to buying manufactured goods, that a serious trade deficit had developed for the Americans. The colonists had gotten into the habit of importing much more from the British Isles than they exported in return. By the early 1770s, provincial Americans owed more than £4 million to English and Scottish creditors. This was a major reason why hard money was so difficult to come by in America. It was being drained off constantly to pay these debts.

By only looking at specific governmental costs, Grenville had missed an essential point. Provincial subjects were not just taking from the empire; they also provided a ready, indeed, captive market for British-manufactured commodities. In this sense the Americans were paying a significant price, as measured by the trade deficit, in support of the parent nation.

"Liberty, Property, and No Stamps"

Certainly the colonists were not plotting independence in 1763. They were proud to be citizens of the far-flung British empire, stretching as it did from India in the East across the globe to some 30 American colonies in the West, including such Caribbean islands as Barbados and Jamaica. With the elimination of French authority in North America, the mainland colonists were also experiencing a buoyant new sensation of freedom. Paradoxically, the reinvigorated imperial program came at the very time when the colonists, feeling great pride but needing much less government protection from across the ocean, hoped for a continuation if not an expansion of the local autonomy to which they had become accustomed. Psychologically, they were ready for anything but new imperial constraints on their lives.

Emerging Patterns of Resistance

As the Grenville program took shape, the colonists experienced various emotions. Dismay gave way to disappointment and anger. Initial reactions involved petitioning King and Parliament for a redress of grievances. By the summer of 1765 colonial protest took an extralegal turn as Americans resorted to such tactics of resistance as crowd intimidation and violence, economic boycott, and outright defiance of imperial law. The colonists no longer liked to think of themselves as Britain's children. Through their tactics of resistance they were asking to be treated more like adults. Very few British officials seemed to understand this message, which in time resulted in the full rupture of British-American relations.

The first words of protest were quite mild, expressed in a flurry of petitions and pamphlets that laid out an American position with respect to essential political rights. In reaction to the Sugar Act of 1764, the New York Assembly complained about "all impositions" by Parliament, "whether they be internal taxes, or duties paid, for what we consume." In many ways protest by pamphlet and petition was so mild in tone during 1764 that it encouraged George Grenville to pursue more comprehensive taxation plans. The intensity of American ill feeling in reaction to the Stamp Act thus shocked the home government.

First news of the Stamp Act arrived in the provinces during April 1765, which left ample time to organize effective resistance before November 1, when the Act was to take effect. Colonial protest soon became very turbulent, with Samuel Adams's Boston taking the lead in stirring up resistance.

In Massachusetts, as in many other provinces, there were a small number of royal officials favored by the parent nation's patronage. This group held the most prominent offices in colonial government, and they were known as the "royalist" or "court" political faction. Besides Lieutenant Governor and Chief Justice Thomas Hutchinson, other leading members of the royalist faction were Governor Francis Bernard, Secretary and Councilor Andrew Oliver, and Associate Justice and Councilor Peter Oliver (Andrew's younger brother). Hutchinson and the Oliver brothers were natives of New England and had all graduated from Harvard College. They were interrelated by marriage, and they were among the wealthiest citizens in America.

Even though these gentlemen were at the apex of provincial society, their opponents in the "popular" or "country" faction did not defer to them. Samuel Adams and other local leaders such as James Otis, Jr., a brilliant lawyer, viewed the likes of Hutchinson and the Oliver brothers with contempt. Adams won his first term to the Assembly in 1765 as a representative from Boston. For him personally the emerging Stamp Act crisis represented an opportunity to launch a simultaneous attack on unacceptable imperial policies and old political adversaries. The twin assault unfolded in August 1765 shortly after citizens learned that none other than Andrew Oliver was the Bay Colony's proposed Stamp Act distributor.

Protest Takes a Violent Turn

Samuel Adams did not participate directly in crowd actions. Nor did the informal popular rights governing body, known as the Loyal Nine. To help organize popular protests, Adams enlisted the aid of Ebenezer Mackintosh, a shoemaker, and Henry Swift, a cobbler, leaders of Boston's workingmen's associations. The North End and South End "leather apron" gangs were in reality fraternal organizations providing fellowship for artisans, apprentices, and common day laborers. The two groups had for many years engaged in street brawls, but now agreed to stop fighting among themselves and unite in defense of essential political liberties. In time these workers would be called the Sons of Liberty, and their cooperation proved to be a critical step in ending any implementation of the Stamp Act in Massachusetts.

On the morning of August 14, 1765, the local populace awoke to find an effigy of Peter Oliver hanging in an elm tree—later called the Liberty Tree—in the South End of Boston. That evening a crowd numbering in the thousands gathered around the tree to watch Ebenezer Mackintosh solemnly remove the effigy and exhort everyone present to join in a march through the streets. Holding the effigy high on a staff, Mackintosh and Swift led what was an orderly procession. As they marched, the people shouted: "Liberty, Property, and No Stamps."

The crowd worked its way to the local dockyards, where the Sons of Liberty ripped apart a building recently constructed by Andrew Oliver. Rumor had it that Oliver intended to store his quota of stamped paper there. Next, the crowd moved toward Oliver's stately home. Some in the crowd tore up the fence, ransacked the first floor (the Oliver family had fled), and imbibed from the well-stocked wine cellar. Others gathered on a hill behind the Oliver residence. Materials from Oliver's building as well as his wooden fence provided kindling for a huge bonfire that ultimately consumed the effigies as the working men and women of Boston cheered. By midnight this crucial crowd action was over.

Early the next morning, the thoroughly intimidated Oliver resigned. Mackintosh's crowd, rather than Crown officials, were now in control of Boston. Had Boston's Sons of Liberty and their leaders been solely concerned with rendering the Stamp Act unenforceable, they would have ceased their rioting after Oliver's resignation; however, they had other accounts to settle. A misleading rumor began to circulate through the streets claiming that Thomas Hutchinson was very much in favor of the Stamp Act, indeed had even helped to write the tax plan. As a result, the Sons of Liberty came out again on the evening of August 26. After visiting a few others, the crowd descended upon Hutchinson's palatial home, one of the most magnificent in the province. They ripped it apart. As the lieutenant governor later described the scene, "they continued their possession until daylight; destroyed, carried away, or cast into the street, everything that was in the house; demolished every part of it, except for walls, as lay in their power."

Who started the rumor remains a moot point, but Hutchinson's political enemies were well known. Further, some Bostonians may have vented their frustrations with the depressed local economy by ransacking the property of a well-placed person with imperial connections who was prospering during difficult times. Whatever the explanation, royal authority in the Bay Colony had suffered another serious blow. The mere threat of crowd violence gave Samuel Adams and his popular rights faction a powerful weapon that Hutchinson and other royalist officials never overcame.

Resistance Spreads Across the Landscape

By rendering the office of stamp distributor powerless, Boston had established a model for resistance. Colonists elsewhere were quick to act. Within the next few months distributors in Rhode Island, Maryland, and Connecticut, fearful of mob violence, resigned their commissions. By November 1 there was virtually no one foolish or bold enough to distribute stamps in America. Only Georgians experienced a short-lived implementation of the despised tax.

Crowds protesting imperial policies, in this case burning stamped documents and newspapers, were normally made up of ordinary citizens, particularly the working poor.

While the colonists employed intimidation and violence, they also petitioned King and Parliament. Assembly after assembly prepared remonstrances stating that taxation without representation was a fundamental violation of the rights of English subjects. Patrick Henry, a young and aggressive backcountry Virginia lawyer, had a profound influence on these official petitions. As a member of the Virginia House of Burgesses (lower house of the Assembly), Henry proposed a series of resolutions in mid-May 1765. The House endorsed the first four, which reiterated the no taxation without representation theme, but it rejected the fifth as too categorical a denial of Parliament's authority. Henry did not bother to present his remaining two resolutions.

Some newspapers in other provinces reprinted all seven of Henry's resolutions. The fifth stated that the Virginia Assembly held "the only exclusive right and power to lay taxes and impositions upon the inhabitants of this colony." The sixth asserted that Virginians were "not bound to yield obedience to any law" not approved by their Assembly. The seventh indicated that anyone thinking otherwise would "be deemed an enemy by His Majesty's colony."

These three resolutions read as if the Virginia burgesses had denied King and Parliament all legislative authority over the American provinces. They seemed to be advocating some form of dual sovereignty in which the American assemblies held final authority over legislative matters in America—comparable in scope to Parliament's authority over the British Isles. This was a radical concept, in fact too radical for the Virginia burgesses. Yet the reprinting of all seven of the Virginia Resolutions, as they came to be known, encouraged other assemblies to prepare strongly worded petitions during the summer and fall of 1765.

An important example of intercolonial unity was the Stamp Act Congress, attended by delegates from nine colonies. Generally speaking, cautious gentlemen of the upper ranks dominated the Stamp Act Congress. Their "declarations" on behalf of American rights had a far more conciliatory tone than the Virginia Resolutions. The delegates proclaimed their loyalty to Great Britain, but respectfully requested that Parliament relinquish its right to tax the colonies to the provincial assemblies. The Stamp Act Congress demonstrated that leaders from different colonies could meet together and agree on common principles. The Congress also suggested that unified intercolonial resistance might be possible, should events ever make that necessary.

Another, more telling blow to the Stamp Act was an intercolonial economic boycott. Merchants in New York City were the first to act. They pledged not to order British goods "of any nature, kind, or quality" unless the Stamp Act was repealed. Within a month merchants in the other principal port towns, including Boston and Philadelphia, drafted similar agreements. A trade boycott of British goods, particularly with the remnants of economic depression still plaguing the empire, was bound to win support for repeal among merchants and manufacturers in Britain.

On November 1, 1765, commerce in the colonies came to a halt. Trading vessels remained in ports because no stamped clearance papers could be obtained. Courts ceased functioning, since so many legal documents required stamps. Newspapers stopped publication, at least temporarily. For all of their bravado the Americans really did not want to defy the law. As November gave way to December, however, popular leaders began to apply various forms of pressure on more timid citizens. By the beginning of 1766 colonial business and legal activity started returning to normal, and newspaper editors commenced printing again—all in open defiance of the Stamp Act.

George Grenville thus had grossly miscalculated. Not willing to be treated as errant children, the colonists, in defending their liberties, sent petitions to Parliament, intimidated and harassed royal officials, destroyed property, cut off the importation of British goods, and, finally, openly defied the law. Americans hoped for a return to the old days of salutary neglect, but they also wondered whether the king's ministers would understand and back down in the face of such determined resistance.

Parliament Retreats

Instability in the British cabinet, as much as American protest, helped to bring about repeal of the Stamp Act. George III had never liked Grenville. In July 1765 the king asked him to step aside in favor of the Marquis of Rockingham, who was more sympathetic toward the Americans. Rockingham's political coalition was brittle, and his term as chief minister lasted just long enough to bring about repeal.

Looking for political allies, Rockingham took advantage of pressure from English traders and manufacturers who were extremely worried about the American boycott. In March 1766 Parliament repealed the Stamp Act. Home government leaders had by no means accepted colonial arguments. They insisted upon a face-saving statement designed to make it clear that King and Parliament were the supreme legislative voices of empire. In conjunction with rescinding the Stamp Act, Parliament approved the Declaratory Act, which specifically denied the claims of American assemblies to "the sole and exclusive right of imposing duties and taxes . . . in the colonies." The Declaratory Act forcefully asserted that Parliament had "full power and authority to make laws and statutes . . . , *in all cases whatsoever.*" Having repealed the Stamp Act for the sake of imperial harmony, Parliament still had the right to tax all British subjects anytime it chose. It had stated its position—and in terms irreconcilable with the stance taken by the Americans.

A Second Crisis: The Townshend Duties

What was needed in 1766 was an extended cooling-off period, but that was not to happen. The Rockingham ministry, which would have been willing to leave the colonists alone, collapsed, giving way to a new ministry headed by William Pitt, who became the Earl of Chatham. As a member of the House of Lords, Pitt let others provide for legislation in the House of Commons. One person in particular, Chancellor of the Exchequer Charles Townshend, rushed forward to fill the void in leadership. To the amazement of many, Townshend proclaimed that he knew how to tax the colonists. The result was the ill-advised Townshend duties of 1767, which renewed tension between Britain and America.

Formulating a New Taxation Scheme

Benjamin Franklin, who was in England serving as an agent for various colonies, inadvertently helped to formulate Townshend's plan. In a lengthy interview before Parliament during the repeal debates, Franklin, who was out of touch with American sentiment, stated emphatically that the colonists only objected to *direct* or "internal" taxes, such as those embodied in the Stamp Act. They did not object, he claimed, to *indirect* or "external" taxes, which may be defined as duties placed on trade goods for the purpose of gaining imperial revenue. Pointing out that Franklin was the most respected colonist of the era, Charles Townshend seized upon this distinction and came up with his taxation scheme.

In June 1767 Parliament authorized the Townshend duties, which were nothing more than import duties on a short list of trade items: British-manufactured glass, paper and lead products, painters' colors, and a three-pence-a-pound duty on tea. Townshend proclaimed that his plan would net the Crown £35,000 to £40,000 per year. In time, once the colonists got used to the idea, the list of taxable products could be lengthened. Meantime, the revenue would help defray the costs of royal governments in America.

At first, it appeared that Townshend knew what he was doing. The plan was subtle and generated very little colonial opposition. Except for tea, the duties were on luxury items, rarely used by the majority of colonists. The tea tax could be evaded by opening illicit trading connections with Dutch tea merchants—and Americans were still quite adept at the art of smuggling.

Mustering Further American Resistance

Late in 1767 John Dickinson, a Philadelphia landholder and lawyer, began publishing a series of newspaper essays, later printed as a pamphlet entitled *Letters from a Farmer in Pennsylvania.* Dickinson assailed Townshend's logic. Americans, he pointed out, had not distinguished between internal and external taxes. Certainly they had long accepted duties designed "to regulate trade" and facilitate the flow of imperial commerce. They now faced trade duties "for the single purpose" of raising revenue. Taxes disguised as trade duties, warned a most suspicious Dickinson, were "a most dangerous innovation" with the potential for turning the colonists into "abject slaves." Yet Dickinson, a man of considerable wealth who feared the destructive potential of violent crowds, urged caution in resistance; he called for the colonial assemblies merely to petition Parliament, hoping that body would listen to reason.

Parliament nonetheless viewed these arguments as seditious. It was likewise angered by the rough treatment experienced by royal customs officials, particularly in Boston where the Crown had recently located a new five-man Board of Customs Commissioners to coordinate all customs collections in America. When members of the board arrived at the end of 1767, jeering crowds greeted them at the docks. The commissioners found it virtually impossible to walk the streets or carry out their official duties without harassment.

More serious trouble erupted in Boston during June 1768 when a crowd attacked local customs collectors who had seized John Hancock's sloop *Liberty* on charges of smuggling in a cargo of Madeira wine. (Hancock, a Boston merchant, was notorious for illegal trading.) The new commissioners fled to Fort Castle William in Boston harbor for personal safety, and they asked Parliament for military protection.

Meanwhile, the Secretary for American Affairs, Lord Hillsborough, had issued orders for four regiments of British troops to proceed to Boston. When the first redcoats arrived in the fall of 1768 without serious incident, members of the royalist political faction breathed more easily and went about their duties with new courage. It looked as if crowd rule, civil anarchy, and open harassment were tactics of the past.

Samuel Adams and the popular rights faction, however, kept demanding more resistance. On August 1, 1768, they convinced an enthusiastic town meeting to accept a nonimportation boycott of British goods. New Yorkers signed a similar document a few days later. Philadelphians, bowing to the pressure of influential merchants, hoped that a petition from the Pennsylvania Assembly would change Parliament's mind. Somewhat reluctantly, they finally joined the trade boycott in February 1769. Threats of crowd action forced the merchants of Charleston, South Carolina, into line during August 1769. It had taken a year, but now all the major port towns had endorsed yet another trade boycott in defense of political liberties.

The colonists did more than boycott. In some of the port towns there was talk about producing their own manufactured goods, such as woolen cloth, in direct defiance of imperial restrictions. With the boycott in full force, wealthier citizens could no longer get the most fashionable fabrics from London, and popular leaders encouraged them to join poorer colonists in wearing homespun cloth—a sign of personal sacrifice for the cause. Some leaders urged all "genteel ladies" to master the skills of spinning and weaving.

Upper-class women, by and large, were not persuaded. They did not like the itchy feeling of homespun, and they considered spinning and weaving to be beneath their station in society. For poorer women, particularly those in the port towns, the trade boycott generated opportunities for piecemeal work in the production of homespun cloth. This meant some extra income, but there was virtually no long-term effect in improving the lot of the poor in America. Homespun was abundant, and the market price remained quite low. While wealthier women itched, complained, and worried about losing their status, poorer women were virtually donating their labor to the defense of American rights. For them the term "sacrifice" held a special meaning.

A "Bloody Massacre" in Boston

The citizens of Boston deeply resented the redcoats in their midst. Besides symbolizing political tyranny, the soldiers also competed for scarce jobs because, when not on duty, their officers allowed them to work for extra wages on a piecemeal basis. As a result, the troops made hard economic times even harder for common day laborers, semiskilled workers, and other poorer Bostonians already suffering from the prolonged economic depression besetting their community.

Throughout 1769 troop baiting by Boston's working men and women had resulted in fistfights and bloodied faces. Then on March 2, 1770, a fight broke out between off-duty redcoats and employees of a ropemaking establishment. The ugly confrontation served to inflame tempers on both sides, prompting Boston's working people to challenge the redcoats' continued presence in their community. On the evening of

March 5, crowds of day laborers, apprentices, and merchant seamen began milling about in the streets. Slowly, but without an appearance of overall direction, these groups moved toward King Street, the site of the Customs House, where a small detachment of soldiers was on guard duty.

Suddenly, angry citizens began pelting the soldiers with mud, snowballs, rocks—indeed anything that could be thrown. Captain Thomas Preston tried to steady his detachment, but one of his soldiers, fearing for his life, panicked. He leveled his musket, and a shot rang out. Ignoring Preston's orders to stop, other soldiers also fired their weapons. Before the shooting ceased, five civilians lay dead or dying, including Crispus Attucks, an unemployed mulatto merchant seaman. Bostonians would soon hail these men as martyred heroes in the struggle to defend American liberties.

Effective propaganda, such as Paul Revere's engravings of the Boston Massacre, helped increase outrage over the event. Here, the British soldiers appear to be firing without provocation into an innocent-looking crowd of citizens.

Captain Preston and his troops faced trials for murder. The court found two soldiers guilty of manslaughter; the others were judged innocent on the grounds of having been forced into a life-threatening situation by an enraged crowd of citizens. Long before these verdicts, royal officials removed the hated redcoats from Boston. In this important sense the working citizens of Boston had won at the cost of five lives. They had freed their community of British regulars and unwanted economic competition. Just as important, the "Boston Massacre" caused colonists everywhere to ask just how far King and Parliament would go to sustain their policies.

Parliament Backs Down Again

The colonists' trade boycott seriously hurt merchants and manufacturers in the British Isles. By the beginning of 1770 the Townshend program had netted only about £20,000 in revenue, a paltry sum when compared to the loss in American trade, estimated to be as high as £7 million. Once again, the colonists had found the means to force Parliament to reevaluate its position.

In January 1770 George III asked amiable Lord Frederick North to form a new cabinet and give some direction to drifting governmental affairs. North, listening to the wrath of powerful British merchants and manufacturers, moved quickly to settle differences with America. He went before Parliament on March 5, 1770, and called for repeal of the Townshend duties, except for the tax on tea, which was to stand as a face-saving, symbolic reminder of Parliament's right to tax and legislate for the Americans in all cases whatsoever. As with the Stamp Act confrontation, the colonial trade boycott of 1768-1770 most certainly had a telling effect. King and Parliament had backed off again, but it was going to be their last retreat.

The Rupturing of Imperial Relations

Lord North was a sensible leader who wanted to avoid taxation schemes and other forms of legislation that could provoke more trouble. He knew that imperial relations had been strained almost to a breaking point by too many restrictive policies thrown at the colonists in too short a time after so many years of salutary neglect. North carefully avoided challenging the Americans between 1770 and 1773. In turn, the colonial resistance movement waned. For a brief period, then, there were no new issues to stir further conflict—only old problems needing to be resolved.

When Parliament stepped away from the Townshend duties, most colonists wanted to discontinue the boycott and return to normal trade relations, despite the irritating tax on tea. They knew that the duty could be avoided by the continued smuggling of Dutch tea. Slowly, economic relations with Britain improved, and His Majesty's subjects in England and America enjoyed a brief period of mutually supportive economic prosperity.

The Necessity of Vigilance

Political relations were not so resilient. Many colonists had become very suspicious of the intentions of home government officials. Provincial leaders tried to explain what had happened since 1763 by drawing on the thoughts of England's "radical" whig opposition writers of the early eighteenth century. Men such as John Trenchard and Thomas Gordon, who had penned a series of essays known as *Cato's Letters,* had repeatedly warned about corruption in government caused by high ministerial officials lusting after power. If not somehow checked, citizens like the colonists would find themselves stripped of all liberties and living in a state of tyranny (often described as "political slavery").

What took firm hold during the 1760s was an American worldview, or ideology, that saw liberties under attack by such grasping, power-hungry leaders as George Grenville and Charles Townshend in England and their royalist puppets in America, personified by such officials as Thomas Hutchinson and Andrew Oliver. In attempting to explain what had happened, the evidence of a conspiracy seemed overwhelming. There were his Majesty's regular troops along the frontier and in Boston, and there were ships of the Royal Navy patrolling in American waters, all during peacetime. The colonists had been cut off from frontier lands, and perhaps worst of all, there had been three willful attempts to tax them, literally to deprive them of property without any voice in the decision to do so.

As never before, great numbers of colonists doubted the goodwill of the home government. Even if Lord North was behaving himself and keeping Parliament in check, many suspected that ministerial inaction was only a ploy, nothing more than a trick designed to lull Americans into a false sense of security while conspiring royal officials devised new and even more insidious plans to strip away all political rights.

Popular leaders exhorted the citizenry to be vigilant at all times. They employed various devices to ensure that the defense of liberties was not forgotten. In Boston, for example, Samuel Adams and his political lieutenants declared March 5 to be an annual commemorative holiday to honor the five fallen martyrs of the Massacre. Each year there was a large public meeting and grand oration to stir memories and to remind the populace of the possible dangers of a new ministerial assault.

Local confrontations also kept emotions stirred up. One such incident occurred in June 1772 when a Royal Navy vessel that regularly patrolled for smugglers, the *Gaspée,* ran aground off Rhode Island. A crowd disguised as Indians descended upon the stranded ship and burned it. Crown officials were furious about the *Gaspée's* destruction. They set up a royal commission of inquiry but never obtained any useful information concerning the perpetrators. The episode prompted several provincial assemblies, fearful of further threats to colonial liberties, to establish committees of correspondence to communicate with each other. These committees were soon writing back and forth regarding serious problems over tea.

The Tea Crisis of 1773

The final assault on American rights, as the colonists perceived matters, grew out of a rather inconspicuous piece of legislation known as the Tea Act of 1773. When Lord North proposed this bill, he had no idea that it would precipitate a disastrous sequence of events; in fact, he was hardly even thinking about the American provinces. His prime concern was the East India Company, a joint-stock trading venture that dated back to the early seventeenth century whose officials ruled over British interests in India.

Having prospered for years, the company was in desperate economic straits in the early 1770s. One reason was that the recent colonial boycott had cost the company its place in the American tea market. With tea warehouses bulging, company directors won important marketing concessions from Parliament in 1773. They asked to have the authority to ship tea directly from India to America (instead of via England, which added significantly to the final market price). To reduce costs further, the company proceeded to name its own tea agents in the major American ports. The net effect of these changes was to make company tea much more competitive with, if not cheaper than, smuggled Dutch blends.

Lord North thought he had found a way to get the Americans to accept the tea tax—and symbolically, at least, recognize Parliament's sovereignty. North could not imagine that the colonists would stand on principle and keep purchasing more expensive Dutch tea just to avoid the three-pence-a-pound trade duty. Suspicious Americans, however, conditioned by years of warding off undesirable imperial legislation, were looking for signs of further conspiratorial acts. A small economic saving meant nothing in the face of what appeared to be another insidious measure to reduce the colonists to a state of political slavery. Although such a worldview may seem far-fetched today, popular leaders and the general populace were thinking in confrontational terms. East India Company tea had to be resisted.

Once again, the port city of Boston became the focal point of significant protest. In early November a crowd took to the streets and tried unsuccessfully to intimidate the tea agents into resigning. When the first tea ship, the *Dartmouth,* docked in Boston later that month, the local customs collectors, fearing reprisals, fled to Fort Castle William. The local committee of correspondence, headed by Samuel Adams and his associates, put guards on the *Dartmouth* and two other tea ships entering the port within the next few days. The popular rights faction repeatedly insisted that the three tea ships be sent back to England. But Governor Thomas Hutchinson refused. Deciding that a showdown was necessary, he called upon Royal Navy vessels in the vicinity to block off the port's entrance.

On December 16 a mass meeting of local citizens took place in Old South Church. The Adams faction sent a messenger to the governor with a very clear message: remove the tea ships or else. Hutchinson refused again. Late in the day, Adams appeared before the huge gathering and reportedly shouted: "This meeting can do no more to save the country." The moment for crowd action had been proclaimed. Several dozen artisans, apprentices, and day laborers, led by Ebenezer Mackintosh, went to the docks disguised as Indians. They jumped onto the tea ships and dumped 342 chests of tea valued at £10,000 into the harbor. It took nearly three hours to complete the work of the Boston Tea Party.

Tea confrontations occurred later in other ports, but none so destructively as in Boston. Philadelphians used the threat of tar and feathers to convince local officials to send back the first tea ships to arrive there. The governor of South Carolina managed to get the tea landed, but the company product lay rotting in a warehouse and was never sold. New Yorkers had to wait until the spring of 1774 for tea ships to appear in their port. They jeered loudly at the docks, and an intelligent sea captain raised anchor and fled for the high seas. Once again, then, the Bostonians stood out for their bold defiance of imperial law.

Parliament Adopts the Coercive Acts

The Boston Tea Party shocked Lord North and other British officials. North decided that the "rebellious" Bostonians simply had to be taught a lesson, and Parliament adopted a series of legislative bills, collectively known as the Coercive Acts. Although the home government directed these laws against Massachusetts, the Coercive Acts held implications for colonists elsewhere who believed that the tyrannical parent nation was only using the Tea Party as a pretext for the final destruction of American liberties.

King George III signed the first act, known as the Boston Port Bill, into law at the end of March 1774. This act closed the port of Boston, making trade illegal until such time as local citizens paid for the tea. In May Parliament adopted the Massachusetts Government Act. This bill suspended the colony's royal charter, vastly expanded the powers of the royal governor, abolished the elective council (upper house of the General Court), and replaced that body with appointed councilors of the Crown's choosing. Town meetings could only be held with the governor's permission, except for annual spring election gatherings.

As matters turned out, Governor Hutchinson never exercised this vastly expanded authority. Dismayed by the Tea Party, he asked for a leave of absence and went to England. The Crown replaced him with General Thomas Gage, Britain's North American military commander, who held the governorship until the final disruption of royal government in the Bay Colony.

Another bill, the Administration of Justice Act, provided greater protection for customs collectors and other imperial officials in Massachusetts. If they injured or killed anyone while carrying out their duties, the governor had the right to move trials to some other colony or to England. The assumption was that local juries were too biased to render fair judgments.

Finally, in early June 1774 Parliament sanctioned an amendment to the Quartering Act of 1765. The earlier law had outlined procedures relating to the provision of housing for redcoats and had specifically excluded the use of private dwellings of any kind. The 1774 amendment gave General Gage the power to billet his troops anywhere, including unoccupied private homes, so long as the army paid fair rental rates. Parliament passed this law because Gage was bringing several hundred troops to Boston with him.

The Quebec Act, also approved in June 1774, was seen by the colonists as another piece of coercive legislation. Actually, this bill mainly concerned itself with the territorial administration of Canada by providing for a royal governor and a large appointed advisory council, but no popularly elected assembly. Roman Catholicism was to remain the established religion for the French-speaking populace. In addition, the Ohio River was to become the new southwestern boundary of Quebec.

Ever-vigilant colonial leaders viewed the Quebec Act as confirming all the worst tendencies of imperial legislation over the past decade. Parliament had denied local representative government; it had ratified the establishment of a branch of the Christian faith that was repugnant to militantly Protestant Americans, especially New Englanders; and it had wiped out the claims of various colonial governments to millions of acres of western land, in this case all of the Ohio country. The latter decision particularly infuriated well-placed provincial land speculators, among them Benjamin Franklin and George Washington, who had fixed upon this region for future development and population expansion. The Quebec Act, thousands of Americans concluded, smacked of abject political slavery.

Even without the Quebec Act, Lord North had made a tactical error by encouraging Parliament to pass so much legislation. The Port Bill punishing Boston was one thing; some Americans felt that the Bostonians had gone too far and deserved some chastisement. The rest of the Coercive Acts, however, caused widespread concern because they seemed to violate the sanctity of local political institutions, to distort normal judicial procedures, and to favor military over civil authority. For most colonists the acts resulted in feelings of solidarity with the Bostonians, which was critical to mounting yet higher levels of unified resistance.

Hurling Back the Challenge: The First Continental Congress

News of the full array of Coercive Acts provoked an outburst of intercolonial activity, the most important expression of which was the calling of the First Continental Congress. This body assembled in Philadelphia on September 5, 1774, and gentlemen of all political persuasions were there (Georgia was the only colony not represented). Among the more radical delegates were Samuel Adams and his younger cousin John, as well as Patrick Henry. George Washington was present, mostly silent in debates but firmly committed to protecting fundamental liberties. More conservative delegates were also in attendance, such as Joseph Galloway of Pennsylvania and John Jay of New York. The central question facing all the delegates was how belligerent the Congress should be. The more cautious delegates wanted to find some means of settling differences with Britain, but the radicals believed that well-organized resistance could get King and Parliament to back down yet a third time.

Accounts of the work of the First Continental Congress make clear that Samuel Adams, Patrick Henry, and others of their more radical persuasion dominated the proceedings. Although they went along with the preparation of an elaborate petition to Parliament, known as the "The Declaration of Colonial Rights and Grievances," these experienced molders of the colonial protest movement demanded much more. They drew upon the weapons of resistance that had caused Parliament to retreat before and, just in case they could not convince Parliament to repeal the Coercive Acts, they argued that Americans should begin to prepare for war.

To assure that Congress moved in the right direction, Samuel Adams and his political allies back in Massachusetts had done some careful planning. Their efforts came to light on September 9, 1774, when a convention of citizens in Suffolk County (Boston and environs) adopted a series of resolutions written by Dr. Joseph Warren, a close political associate of Adams. Once approved, Paul Revere, talented silversmith and active member of Adams's popular rights faction, mounted his horse and rode hard for Philadelphia. Revere arrived in mid-September and laid the Suffolk Resolves before Congress. Not only did these statements strongly profess American rights, but they also called for a complete economic boycott and the rigorous training of local militia companies, just in case it became necessary to defend lives, liberty, and property against the redcoats led by Thomas Gage.

Congress approved the Suffolk Resolves—and with them the initial step in organization for possible military confrontation. The delegates also committed themselves to a comprehensive plan of economic boycott, which came to be called the Continental Association. The association called for the nonimportation and nonconsumption of British goods, to be phased in over the next few months, as well as the nonexportation of colonial products if Parliament did not retreat within a year.

The association also urged every American community to establish a local committee of observation and inspection charged with having all citizens subscribe to the boycott. In reality, the association was a loyalty test. Citizens who refused to sign were about to become outcasts from the cause of liberty. The term of derision applied to them was *tory;* however, they thought of themselves as *loyalists*—maintaining their allegiance to the Crown.

The only attempt at conciliation during the first Congress came from Joseph Galloway, a wealthy Philadelphia lawyer who had long served as Pennsylvania's speaker of the house. Galloway desperately wanted to maintain imperial ties because he feared what the "common sort" of citizens might do if that attachment was irrevocably severed. Galloway drew on the Albany Plan of Union of 1754 and proposed a central government based in America that would be superior to the provincial assemblies.

Galloway's Plan of Union represented a structural alternative allowing Americans a greater voice in imperial decision making affecting the colonies, and it foreshadowed the future commonwealth organization of the British empire. But the more radical delegates called the proposal impractical and belittled it as an idea that would divert everyone from the task of the moment, which was to get Parliament to rescind the Coercive Acts.

Later, at the urging of the radicals, all references to Galloway's plan were expunged from the official minutes of Congress in favor of displaying American unity to King and Parliament. As for Galloway, he faced growing harassment as a loyalist in the months ahead and eventually fled to the British army for protection.

When the First Continental Congress ended its deliberations in late October 1774, its program was one of continued defiance, certainly not conciliation or submission. The delegates understood the course they had chosen. One of their last acts was to call for the Second Continental Congress, to convene in Philadelphia on May 10, 1775, "unless the redress of grievances, which we have desired, be obtained before that time."

As autumn 1774 gave way to another cold winter, Americans awaited the verdict of King and Parliament. Local committees of observation and inspection were busily at work encouraging—and in some cases coercing—the populace to boycott British trade goods. Local militia companies were vigorously training. Even as they prepared for war, colonists everywhere waited anxiously for the reaction of King George III, Lord

*C*hronology of Key Events

1760	George III becomes king of England
1763	Treaty of Paris ends the Seven Years' War; Pontiac leads an unsuccessful rebellion on the western frontier; Proclamation of 1763 forbids white settlement west of the Appalachian Mountains
1764	Sugar Act; Currency Act prohibits colonial governments from issuing paper money
1765	Quartering Act; Stamp Act; Stamp Act Congress
1766	Parliament repeals the Stamp Act; Declaratory Act asserts Parliament's authority to tax the colonies
1767	Townsend duties Act imposes taxes on imported glass, lead, paint, paper, and tea
1768	British troops sent to Boston
1770	Boston Massacre
1772	British naval vessel *Gaspée* burned in Rhode Island
1773	Tea Act allows East India Company to sell tea directly to American retailers; Boston Boston Tea Party ensues
1774	Coercive Acts close port of Boston; Quebec Act extends boundaries of Quebec to Mississippi and Ohio rivers; First Continental Congress in Philadelphia protests Parliamentary legislation

North, and Parliament. They would soon learn that Britain's leaders had dismissed the work of the First Continental Congress, having concluded that the parent nation could not retreat a third time.

Conclusion

In September 1774 Lord North observed: "The die is now cast, the colonies must either submit or triumph." The once harmonious relations between Britain and America had become increasingly discordant between 1763 and the end of 1774. The colonists refused to accept undesirable imperial acts, and they successfully resisted such taxation plans as the Stamp Act and the Townshend duties. In the process they came to believe firmly that ministerial leaders in England were engaging in a deep-seated plot to deprive them of their fundamental liberties. When something as inconsequential as the Townshend duty on tea precipitated yet another crisis in 1773, neither side was willing to back down. By early 1775 both sides had decided to show their resolve.

A small incident that well illustrates the deteriorating situation occurred in Boston during March 1774. At the state funeral of Andrew Oliver, the Bay Colony's most recent lieutenant governor and former stamp distributor-designate, a large gathering of ordinary citizens came out to watch the solemn procession. As Oliver's coffin was slowly lowered into the ground, these Bostonians, many of them veterans of the American resistance movement, suddenly burst into loud cheers.

Such an open expression of bad will epitomized the acute strain in British-American relations. It was almost as if the cheers were for the burial of imperial authority in America. Certainly these colonists demonstrated contempt, not pride, in their British citizenship that day. Such striking changes in attitudes, over just a few years, pointed toward the fateful clash of arms known as the War for American Independence.

Suggestions for Further Reading

Overviews of the revolutionary period include Merrill Jensen, *The Founding of a Nation, 1763–1776* (1968); James Kirby Martin, *In the Course of Human Events* (1979); Edmund S. Morgan, *The Birth of the Republic,* rev. ed. (1977); Gordon S. Wood, *The Radicalism of the American Revolution* (1992); and Esmond Wright, *Fabric of Freedom, 1763–1800,* rev. ed. (1978).

For studies of the causes of the revolution consult Bernard Bailyn, *The Ideological Origins of the American Revolution* (1967); Robert A. Becker, *Revolution, Reform, and the Politics of American Taxation, 1763–1783* (1980); Michael Kammen, *A Rope of Sand: Colonial Agents, British Politics, and the Revolution* (1968); Dirk Hoerder, *Crowd Action in Revolutionary Massachusetts* (1977); Pauline R. Maier, *From Resistance to Revolution* (1972); James Kirby Martin, *Men in Rebellion* (1973); Edmund S. and Helen M. Morgan, *The Stamp Act Crisis*, rev. ed. (1962); Gary B. Nash, *The Urban Crucible* (1979). Other valuable works include David Ammerman, *In the Common Cause: American Response to the Coercive Acts* (1974); Benjamin W. Labaree, *The Boston Tea Party* (1964).

Useful biographies of the period include Bernard Bailyn, *The Ordeal of Thomas Hutchinson* (1974); Richard R. Beeman, *Patrick Henry* (1974); John Ferling, *The First of Men: George Washington* (1988), and *John Adams* (1992); John C. Miller, *Sam Adams: Pioneer in Propaganda* (1936).

Chapter 5

The Times That Tried Many Souls, 1775–1783

Joseph Plumb Martin was a dedicated patriot soldier, one of 11,000 men and women who formed the backbone of General George Washington's Continental forces. When that army entered its Valley Forge winter campsite in December 1777, Martin recorded despondently that the soldiers' trail could "be tracked by their blood upon the rough frozen ground." The Continentals were "now in a truly forlorn condition,—no clothing, no provisions, and as disheartened as need be."

While the British army enjoyed far more comfortable quarters in Philadelphia only 20 miles away, Washington's troops constructed miserable shanties to protect them from the bitterly cold weather. Making matters more difficult was the lack of food and clothing. Martin claimed that, upon first entering Valley Forge, he went a full day and two nights without anything to eat, "save half a small pumpkin, which I cooked by placing it upon a rock, the skin side uppermost, and making fire upon it." His comrades fared no better. Within two days of moving into Valley Forge, a common grumble could be heard everywhere: "No Meat! No Meat!" By the first of January the words had become more ominous: "No bread, no soldier!"

Thus began a tragic winter of desperation for Washington's Continentals. Some 2,500 soldiers, or nearly one-fourth of the troops, perished before the army broke camp in June 1778. They died from exposure to the elements, malnutrition, and such virulent diseases as typhus and smallpox. It was not uncommon for soldiers to languish for days in their rudely constructed huts because they were too weak to drill or to go on food-hunting expeditions. Sometimes for lack of straw and blankets, they simply froze to death in their beds. To add to the woes of the camp, more than 500 of the army's horses starved to death that winter. It was impossible to bury their carcasses in the frozen ground, which only magnified the deplorable sanitation conditions and the consequent spread of disease. Under such forsaken circumstances, hundreds of soldiers deserted.

The extreme suffering at Valley Forge has usually been attributed to the severe weather and a complete breakdown of the army's supply system. In fact, weather conditions were no worse than in other years. Certainly a major reason for the deprivation at Valley Forge was widespread indifference toward an army made up of the poor, the expendable, and the unfree in American society.

Joseph Plumb Martin clearly thought this was the case. He was a young man from Connecticut, without material resources, who had first enlisted during 1776 at the very peak of patriot enthusiasm for the war. He soon learned that there were few glories in soldiering. Camp life was both dull and dangerous, given the many killer diseases that ravaged armies of the era, and battle was a frightening experience. He did not

George Washington led a bedraggled, half-starved army of 11,000 men and women into Valley Forge in December 1777.

renew his enlistment and returned to Connecticut. For a poor, landless person, economic prospects at home were not much better than serving for promises of regular pay in the Continental army. In 1777 Martin stepped forth again and agreed to enlist as a substitute.

Martin's experiences typified those of so many others who performed long-term Continental service on behalf of the cause of liberty. After an initial rush to arms in defiance of British authority in 1775, the harsh realities of military life and pitched battles dampened patriot enthusiasm to the point that by December 1776 the Continental Army all but ceased to exist. Washington's major task became that of securing enough troop strength and material support to shape an army capable of standing up time after time to British forces.

The commander-in-chief found his long-term soldiers among the poor and deprived groups of revolutionary America. Major European nations like France, Spain, and Holland eventually came to the rescue with additional troops, supplies, and vital financial support. Working together, even in the face of so much popular indifference, these allies-in-arms outlasted the mighty land and sea forces of Great Britain, making possible a generous peace settlement in 1783 that guaranteed independence for the group of former British colonies that now called themselves the 13 United States.

Reconciliation or Independence

Crown officials in England gave scant attention to the acts of the First Continental Congress because they believed that the time had come to teach the American provincials a military lesson. George III explained why. The colonists, he asserted, "have boldly thrown off the mask and avowed nothing less than a total independence of the British legislature will satisfy them." This was an inaccurate perception, but it lay behind the decision to turn the most powerful military machine in the western world, based on its record in recent wars, against the troublemakers in America and to crush resistance to British authority once and for all.

The Shooting War Starts

During the winter of 1774–1775 the king's ministers prepared for what they thought would be nothing more than a brief demonstration of military force. General Gage received "secret" orders to employ the redcoats under his command to arrest the ringleaders of rebellion; however, if the likes of Samuel Adams, John Hancock, and Joseph Warren could not be captured, then Gage was to use any methods he deemed appropriate to put an end to unrest in Massachusetts.

During February 1775 the King and Parliament authorized funds for a larger force of regular troops in America and named three high-ranking generals—William Howe, Henry Clinton, and John Burgoyne—to sail to Boston and join Gage. They also declared Massachusetts to be in a state of rebellion, which permitted redcoats to shoot down suspected rebels on sight, should that be necessary to quell opposition. Eventually this act would be applied to all 13 provinces.

General Gage received the ministry's secret orders in mid-April 1775. Being on the scene, he was not quite as convinced as his superiors about American martial weakness. Gage had repeatedly urged caution in his reports to home officials, but now there was no choice; he had to act. Because some rebel leaders had already fled to the countryside, Gage decided to send a column of regulars to Concord, a town about 20 miles northwest of Boston that also served as a storage point for patriot military supplies. Once there, the troops were to seize or destroy as much weaponry and ammunition as possible. Gage hoped this maneuver could be effected without bloodshed, fearing full-scale warfare would follow if patriot lives were lost.

At dawn on April 19, 700 British troops under Lieutenant Colonel Francis Smith passed through Lexington, five miles east of Concord. Here they encountered 70 militiamen lined up across the village green. Obviously outnumbered, the Minutemen—so-called because they had been trained to respond at a moment's notice—were not there to exchange shots, but to warn the regulars against trespassing on the property of free-born British subjects. As the redcoats came closer, a mysterious shot rang out, causing British troops to level their arms and fire. Before order was restored, eight colonists had died in what was the opening volley of the War for American Independence.

The redcoats regrouped and continued their march to Concord. Once there, a detachment moved out to cross the Old North Bridge in search of weapons and gunpowder, but was repulsed by rallying militiamen. Lieutenant Colonel Smith began to fear that his column might be cut off by onrushing citizen-soldiers, so he ordered a retreat. The rest of the day turned into a rout as an aroused citizenry fired away at the British from behind trees and stone walls. Final casualty figures showed 273 redcoats dead or wounded, as compared to 95 colonists. Lexington and Concord were clear blows to the notion of the invincibility of British arms and suggested that American citizens, when defending their own property, could and would hold their own against better-trained British soldiers.

As word of the bloodshed spread, New Englanders rallied to the patriot banner. Within days thousands of colonists poured into hastily assembled military camps surrounding Boston. Thomas Gage and his soldiers were now trapped, and they could only hope that promised reinforcements would soon reach them.

Most colonists believed that it would be only a matter of weeks before the ministry regained its senses and restored all American rights. They did not realize that Crown leaders were irrevocably committed to eradicating all colonial resistance, or that the conflict would become a long and grueling full-scale war in which the fortitude to endure would determine the eventual winner.

Moderates Versus Radicals in Congress

The shadow of Lexington and Concord loomed heavily as the Second Continental Congress convened in Philadelphia in May 1775. Despite the recent bloodshed, very few delegates had become advocates of independence. New Englanders like Samuel and John Adams were leaning that way, but the majority held out hope for a resolution of differences. By the summer of 1775 two factions had emerged in Congress: the one led by New Englanders, favoring a formal declaration of independence, and the opposing moderate faction, whose strength lay in the Middle Colonies and whose most influential leader was John Dickinson of Pennsylvania.

The two factions debated every issue with regard to possible effects on the subject of independence. The moderates remained the dominant faction into the spring of 1776, but then the weight of the spreading rebellion swung the pendulum decisively toward those favoring independence.

Early congressional wrangling centered on the organization of a Continental army. In mid-June 1775 the delegates, at the urging of the New Englanders, voted to adopt the patriot forces around Boston as a Continental military establishment. They asked the other colonies to supply additional troops and unanimously named wealthy Virginia planter George Washington to serve as commander-in-chief. Washington did have qualifications for the job, including his combat experiences during the French and Indian War. Also, he was a southerner. His presence at the head of the army was a way to involve the other colonies, at least symbolically, in what was still a localized war being fought by New Englanders.

Congressional moderates were persons caught in a bind. Although deeply concerned about American rights, they also feared independence. Like many other colonists of substantial wealth, they envisioned internal chaos in the colonies without the stabilizing influence of British rule. They also doubted whether a weak, independent American nation could long survive among aggressive European powers.

The moderates thus tried to keep open the channels of communication with the British government. Characteristic of such attempts was John Dickinson's "Olive Branch" petition, approved by Congress in July 1775. This document implored George III to intercede with Parliament and find some means to preserve English liberties in America. Like other petitions before it, the "Olive Branch" had little impact in Britain. By the autumn of 1775 the home government was already mobilizing for full-scale war.

The Expanding Martial Conflict

No matter what they tried, congressional moderates accomplished little, except in delaying a declaration of independence. The rebellion kept spreading, making a formal renunciation of British allegiance seem almost anticlimactic. On May 10, 1775, for example, citizen-soldiers seized the once-mighty fortress of Ticonderoga at the southern end of Lake Champlain. This action netted the Americans more than 100 serviceable artillery pieces that would eventually be deployed to help drive British forces from Boston.

In an effort to lure Canada into the rebellion—many hoped that Quebec Province would become the fourteenth colony—Congress approved a two-pronged invasion in the late summer of 1775. One column under General Richard Montgomery traveled down Lake Champlain and seized Montreal. The second column under Colonel Benedict Arnold proceeded on a harrowing march through the woods of Maine and finally emerged before the walls of Quebec City. On the morning of December 31, 1775, combined forces under these two commanders boldly tried to take the city but were repulsed. Montgomery lost his life, Arnold was seriously wounded, and great numbers of patriot troops were killed or captured. The rebel attempt to seize Canada had failed. This aggressive effort, however, made it increasingly difficult to argue that the colonists were only interested in defending their homes and families until political differences with Britain could be resolved.

Back in Boston, meanwhile, General Gage resumed the offensive against the New Englanders. That opportunity came on June 17, 1775, in an attack on rebel fortifications on Breed's Hill, north of Boston. As citizens watched the misnamed Battle of Bunker Hill from rooftops, the British made three separate charges, finally dislodging the patriots, who were running out of ammunition. It was the bloodiest engagement of the whole war. The British suffered 1,054 casualties—40 percent of the redcoats engaged. American casualties amounted to 411, or 30 percent.

The realization that patriot soldiers had been driven from the field undermined the euphoria that followed the rout of the redcoats at Lexington and Concord. Still, the British gained little advantage because they had failed to pursue the fleeing rebels. They remained trapped in Boston, surrounded by thousands of armed and angry colonists.

Lord Dunmore's Proclamation of Emancipation

New England and Canada did not long remain the only theaters of war. Before the end of 1775 fighting erupted in the South. In Virginia the protagonist was John Murray, Lord Dunmore, the last royal governor of the Old Dominion. In May 1774 Dunmore had dissolved the Assembly because the burgesses had called for a day of fasting and prayer in support of the Bostonians. Incensed at Dunmore's arbitrary action, Virginia's gentleman-planters started meeting in provincial conventions, acting as if royal authority no longer existed.

Dunmore resented such impudence. In June 1775 he fled Williamsburg and announced that British subjects still loyal to the Crown should join him in bringing the planter elite to its senses. Very few citizens came forward. By autumn Dunmore had concluded that planter resistance could only be broken by turning slaves against masters. On November 7, 1775, he issued an emancipation proclamation.

Dunmore hoped that Virginia's slaves would break their chains and join with him, but the plan backfired. Irate planters suppressed copies of the proclamation and spread the rumor of a royal hoax designed to lure blacks into Dunmore's camp so that he could sell them to the owners of West Indian sugar plantations. As many as 2,000 slaves took their chances and escaped to the royal standard. They became a part of Dunmore's "Ethiopian" regiment, which made the mistake of engaging Virginia militiamen in a battle at Great Bridge in December 1775. Having had no time for even the fundamentals of military training, the regiment took a drubbing. This battle ended any semblance of royal authority in Virginia. Dunmore and his followers soon retreated to a flotilla of vessels in Chesapeake Bay, and in the summer of 1776 they sailed away, leaving behind a planter class that closely guarded its human property while demanding independence from those in Britain whom it denounced as tyrants.

Resolving the Independence Question

Lord Dunmore's experiences highlighted the collapse of British political authority. Beginning in the summer of 1775, colony after colony witnessed an end to royal government. During that same summer Massachusetts moved one step further by asking the Continental Congress for permission to establish a more enduring government based on a written constitution. After ousting its royal governor, New Hampshire followed suit. These requests forced Congress to act. The delegates did so in early November, stating that the colonies might adopt "such a form of government, as . . . will best produce the happiness of the people," but only until the present dispute with Great Britain was settled.

The moderates in Congress realized that new state governments, as much if not more than a separate army, had the appearance of de facto independence. They did everything they could to prevent a total rejection of British political authority in America. Provincial assemblies in Pennsylvania, New York, Delaware, Maryland, and South Carolina also continued to balk at an irrevocable split with the mother country. Thus there was to be no resolution of the independence question before 1776.

But events were about to overwhelm the moderates. In January 1776 Thomas Paine, a recent migrant from England, published a pamphlet entitled *Common Sense,* which became an instant best-seller. In forceful language, *Common Sense* communicated a sense of urgency about moving toward independence, and it attacked congressional moderates for not being bold enough to break with the past.

Paine likewise denounced the British monarchy. He wrote: "The folly of hereditary right in Kings, is that nature disapproves it . . . by giving mankind *an ass for a lion.*" *Common Sense* put severe pressure on the moderates, but they held on doggedly, hoping against hope that Great Britain would turn from its belligerent course and begin serious negotiations with Congress.

At the end of February 1776 a short, bloody battle between loyalists and patriot militia at Moore's Creek Bridge in North Carolina ended in a rout of local tories (a term of derision for those who maintained their allegiance to the Crown). North Carolina's provincial congress reversed orders to its congressional delegates and allowed them to discuss independence and vote on a plan of national government. Soon thereafter the Virginians, furious about Lord Dunmore's activities, issued similar instructions. Then leaders in Rhode Island, impatient with everyone else, boldly declared their own independence in early May. The moderates were rapidly losing their ability to block resolution of the independence question.

On June 7, 1776, Richard Henry Lee of Virginia, urging independence, presented formal resolutions to Congress which called for the creation of a national government and the formation of alliances with foreign nations in support of the war effort. Within a few days Congress established two committees, one headed by John Dickinson to produce a plan of central government and another to prepare a statement on independence. Thomas Jefferson, a tall, young, red-haired Virginian, agreed to write a draft text on independence, which the committee laid before Congress on Friday, June 28.

On Monday, July 1, John Dickinson spoke forcefully against a formal severance of ties with Great Britain. The delegates listened politely, but Dickinson was no longer in step with the mood of Congress. The next day, July 2, 12 states voted in favor of Lee's resolutions, thus technically declaring independence (New York abstained, having not yet received instructions from leaders back home).

Congress next turned to the consideration of Jefferson's draft, which one delegate in a classic understatement called "a pretty good one." The delegates made only a few changes. They deleted a controversial statement blaming the slave trade on the king as well as words repudiating friendship with the British people. By Thursday evening, July 4, 1776, everything was in place, and Congress quickly adopted Jefferson's document, a masterful explanation of the reasons why the colonists were seeking independence.

The Declaration of Independence proclaimed to the world that Americans had been terribly mistreated by the parent nation. Indeed, much of the text represents a summary list of grievances, ranging from

The Declaration of Independence came before Congress for debate on July 1, 1776, and was pronounced publicly on July 4.

misuse of a standing army and the abuse of the rights of colonial assemblies to starting an unjustified war against loyal subjects. The Declaration also blamed George III who, by failing to control his ministers, had abandoned his role as a true servant of the people.

Much more than a list of grievances, the Declaration also gave the revolution a clear and noble purpose. Since "all men are created equal" and have "certain unalienable rights," which Jefferson defined as "life, liberty, and the pursuit of happiness," Americans needed to dedicate themselves to the establishment of a whole new set of political relationships guaranteeing all citizens fundamental liberties. The great task facing the revolutionary generation would be to institute republican forms of government, based on the rule of law and human reason.

Through Jefferson's words, the patriots of 1776 committed themselves to uplifting humanity in a world overrun by greed and petty human ambition. None of these ideals was going to be realized, however, unless the means could be found to defeat the huge British military force arriving in America at the very time that Congress was debating and approving the Declaration of Independence.

Without Visible Allies: The War in the North

British officials had made a great blunder in 1775. Thinking of the colonists as "a set of upstart vagabonds, the dregs and scorn of the human species," they had woefully underestimated their opponent. Lexington and Concord drove home this reality. Although British leaders and generals continued to presume their superiority, they became far more serious about planning for the war. It was now clear that snuffing out the rebellion was a complex military assignment, given the sheer geographic size of the colonies and the absence of a strategically vital center, such as a national capital, which, if captured, would end the war. It was also clear that the use of an invading army was not the easiest way to regain the political allegiance of a people no longer placing such high value on being British subjects.

Britain's Massive Military Buildup

Directing the imperial war effort were King George, Lord North, and Lord George Germain, who became the American Secretary in 1775. Germain proved to be a surprisingly effective administrator and adept at working within England's complicated and inefficient military bureaucracy. His skills became evident in planning for the campaign of 1776—the largest land and sea offensive executed by any western nation until the Allied invasion of North Africa in 1942.

Step by step, Germain pulled the elements together. Of utmost importance was overall campaign strategy. It involved concentrating as many troops as possible on the port of New York, where great numbers of loyalists lived, then subduing the surrounding countryside as a food and supply base. Loyalists would be used to reinstitute royal government, and the king's forces would engage and destroy the rebel army. Germain believed that the American will to resist had to be shattered, and he hoped that it would take only one campaign season. The longer the rebels lasted, he argued, the greater would be their prospects for success.

Next came the matter of assembling the military forces. With the middle classes exempt from service because they were considered productive members of society, the rank and file were drawn from two sources. First, there were poorer, less productive citizens in the British Isles who would be recruited or dragooned into service. Since life in European armies was often brutal, it was not always possible to convince or coerce even the most destitute of subjects to sign enlistment papers. To ensure adequate troop strength, George III and his advisers turned to a second source, the principalities of Germany. Before the end of the war, six German states procured 30,000 soldiers, more than half from Hesse-Cassel, where the local head of state received direct cash payments from the British Crown for each soldier that he supplied. Hessians and downtrodden Britons, including many Irish subjects, thus made up the king's army.

Certainly as significant a matter as troop recruitment was military leadership. Viewing General Gage as too timid and too respectful of Americans, the king recalled him in October 1775 and named William Howe to replace him as overall commander-in-chief. William's brother Richard, Admiral Lord Howe, took charge of the naval flotilla that would carry thousands of troops to America.

Neither of the Howe brothers turned out to be hard-hitting military commanders. Politically, they identified with whig leaders in England who believed that the Americans had some legitimate grievances. They intended to move in careful steps, using the presence of so many well-trained regulars to persuade Americans to sign loyalty oaths and renounce the rebellion. In failing to achieve the strategic goal of wiping out patriot resistance in only one campaign season, the Howe brothers helped save the patriot cause from early extinction.

The Campaign for New York

Not yet aware of the scale of British mobilization, New Englanders cheered loudly in mid-March 1776 when General Howe took redcoats and loyalists in tow and fled by sea to Halifax, Nova Scotia. British control of Boston had become untenable because General Washington placed the cannons captured at Ticonderoga on Dorchester Heights overlooking the city. Howe's choice was to retreat or be bombarded into submission.

At the end of June Howe returned, sailing from Halifax to Staten Island, across the bay from Manhattan, with 10,000 soldiers. During July, even as Americans excitedly read their Declaration of Independence, more and more British troops appeared, another 20,000 by mid-August. Including seamen under Admiral Howe's command, the British had some 43,000 well-supplied, well-trained, and well-armed combatants. By comparison, George Washington had 28,000 troops on his muster rolls, but only 19,000 present and fit for duty. To make matters worse, the bulk of his army lacked good weapons or supplies and was deficient in training and discipline.

The decision to defend New York, which the Continental Congress insisted upon and to which Washington acceded, was one of the great rebel blunders of the war. Completely outnumbered, the American commander unwisely divided his soldiers between Manhattan and Brooklyn

Heights on Long Island. They took a severe beating in defending Brooklyn Heights, but Lord Howe allowed them to escape across the East River. Learning from this mistake, Washington would never place his troops in so potentially disastrous a position again.

The Howe brothers moved along indecisively through the rest of the campaign season. Every time they had the advantage, they failed to destroy the rebel army. Washington retreated into New Jersey, and by early December what remained of his army had crossed the Delaware River into Pennsylvania.

Saving the Cause at Trenton

Increasingly dispirited, hundreds of half-starving, battle-wearied patriot troops deserted. Others, ravaged by disease or wounded in battle, were left along the way with the hope of receiving decent treatment from their pursuers. Having virtually destroyed his prey, William Howe ordered his troops into winter camps and returned to New York City. He ignored his charge to end the rebellion in one campaign season, fully satisfied that mopping-up operations could be easily conducted in the spring of 1777.

George Washington assessed his desperate position and decided upon a bold counterstroke. The success of this maneuver might save his army; defeat would surely ruin it. With muster rolls showing only 6,000 troops, he divided his soldiers into three groups and tried to recross the icy Delaware River on Christmas evening. Their targets were British outposts in New Jersey. Of the three contingents, only Washington's near-frozen band of 2,400 soldiers accomplished this daring maneuver.

At dawn they reached Trenton, capturing almost 1,000 unsuspecting Hessians, who were still groggy with liquor from their Christmas celebration. Within another few days the elated Americans again outdueled British units at Princeton. In these two engagements Washington had done much more than just regain lost ground. He had saved the Continental Army from virtual extinction. Never again during the war would the British come so close to total victory—and all because of a failure to annihilate Washington's shattered forces when the opportunity was there. William Howe never seemed to understand this mistake. He relaxed in his winter quarters in New York and gloried in the knighthood awarded him for his victory at Brooklyn Heights.

Another error British military commanders committed was their unwillingness to make use of the king's friends in America. An estimated 20 percent of the populace, these loyal subjects stood ready to fight the rebels to assure a continuation of British rule. Before the war was over an estimated 50,000 loyalists enlisted, but royal commanders did not really take advantage of them. The official attitude seemed to be that loyalists were just colonists, a part of the "rude" American rabble.

On the rebel side, the Trenton and Princeton victories did not result in a revived outpouring of popular support for Washington's army. Thomas Paine begged the populace to rally at this moment of deep despair. "These are the times that try men's souls," Paine stated forcefully. "The summer soldier and the sunshine patriot will, in this crisis, shrink from the service of his country; but he that stands it now, deserves the love and thanks of man and woman."

The Real Continentals

One of the greatest problems facing Washington and the Continental Congress after 1776 was sustaining the rebel army's troop strength. In May 1777 the commander-in-chief only had 10,000 soldiers, of which 7,363 were present and fit for duty. This number increased substantially during the summer and fall, although only an estimated 11,000 Continentals entered Valley Forge. For the remainder of the war Washington's core of regulars rarely was more sizable. At times, as few as 5,000 soldiers stood with him.

After 1776 the rank and file of the Continental Army came to be made up of economically hard-pressed and unfree citizens. The bulk of Washington's long-term Continentals were young (ranging in age from

Northern Theater of War, 1775–1778

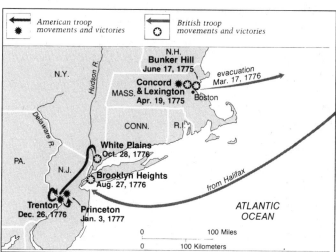

their early teens to mid-twenties), landless, and unskilled. Also well represented were indentured servants and slaves who stood as substitutes for their masters in return for guarantees of personal freedom at the war's end.

In 1777 Massachusetts became the first state to authorize the enlistment of blacks—both slaves and freemen. Rhode Island soon followed suit by raising two black regiments. Southern states were far more reluctant to allow slaves to substitute for their masters. Maryland and Virginia ultimately did so, which caused one patriot general to query why so many "sons of freedom" seemed so anxious "to trust their all to be defended by slaves." Add to these groups captured British soldiers and deserters, particularly Hessians and Irishmen, as well as tories and criminals who were often given a choice between military service or the gallows, and a composite portrait of the real Continental Army begins to emerge.

Eighteenth-century armies also accepted women in the ranks. Like their male counterparts, they were invariably living on the margins of society. These women must be differentiated from so-called camp followers—those who marched along with their husbands or were prostitutes. Women in service performed various functions, ranging from caring for the sick and wounded, cooking, and mending clothes to scavenging battlefields for clothing and equipment and burying the dead. On occasion they became directly involved in combat.

Whether male or female, a unifying characteristic of Washington's post-1776 Continentals was poverty and, in many cases, lack of personal freedom. In their social profile, they looked very much like their counterparts in the British army. As a group, they repeatedly risked their lives in return for promises of food, clothing, pay, and even land on which to make a decent living after the war. Their dreams of future prosperity depended upon the success of the rebellion, and that is one reason why they willingly endured, even though the far more prosperous civilian populace ignored their privation at such encampments as Valley Forge.

Rescuing the Patriots: Toward Global Conflict

The struggles of the American rebels did not go unobserved in European diplomatic circles. France and Spain, in particular, hoped that the rebellion would succeed. Territorial losses sustained during the Seven Years' War had swung the European balance of power decisively in Britain's favor. For France, post-1763 disagreements between Britain and America represented an opportunity to deflate the puffed-up British lion. Losing the colonies would weaken Britain immeasurably. French statesmen had little interest in fostering American political liberties. They hoped only to advance France's future while exacting revenge on an old and despised enemy.

France Offers Covert Assistance

Before 1775, the French sent spies to America to report on events, and when possible to help stir up ill will toward Britain. Once the war started, France provided covert assistance to the rebels while maintaining a public stance of disinterested neutrality. If the rebels demonstrated their long-term resolve and proved worthy in combat, then France would enter the war and help crush the British.

Secret French aid, which came in the form of cash subsidies and loans, strengthened the rebel cause immeasurably, thus helping the patriots to endure until the French government came out publicly against Great Britain. To promote American interests, the Continental Congress sent a three-person delegation to Paris which included Benjamin Franklin. Already well known among French intellectuals because of his electrical experiments, the aging Philadelphian became a popular celebrity. With his simple dress, witty personality, worldly charm, and shrewd mind, he embodied the ideals of republicanism. Working closely with the astute French foreign minister, the Comte de Vergennes, Franklin played his role well in helping secure a formal alliance with Britain's long-time enemy.

The British Seize Philadelphia

The home government's plan for 1777 was to send an army under "Gentleman Johnny" Burgoyne south from Canada through the Lake Champlain corridor. In turn, Howe was to move troops up the Hudson River, eventually linking with Burgoyne at Albany. Called the Hudson Highlands strategy, the goal was to cut off New England from the rest of the colonies before sweeping eastward to reconquer the very region that had been the seedbed of rebellion.

Sir William Howe, however, had ideas of his own about campaign strategy. He favored going after and destroying the main Continental Army. During June 1777 he tried to lure Washington into a major battle in New Jersey, but the American commander refused the bait. At this juncture Howe made a decision that may have cost Britain the war. All but abandoning the primary campaign goal of joining up with Burgoyne, he resolved to seize Philadelphia, hoping at the same time to catch and crush Washington's Continentals as they moved into eastern Pennsylvania to protect the rebel capital.

On September 11 the British mauled the Continentals at Brandywine Creek, southwest of Philadelphia, but the engagement did not destroy the rebel army. Within another two weeks Sir William proudly led his troops into Philadelphia; yet except for the establishment of comfortable winter quarters, the British commander had accomplished nothing of consequence. Although another patriot attack on British troops at Germantown on October 4 ended in failure, the Continental Congress had already moved westward to York, Pennsylvania. Howe's capture of the rebel's capital had been a hollow quest—and had cost the British dearly.

Capturing Burgoyne's Army at Saratoga

The 1777 British descent from Canada had been planned carefully, at least on paper. The army of General Burgoyne, strengthened by hundreds of Indians who had joined the British to put an end to colonial settlers' seizure of tribal lands, moved southward in mid-June. The main column of nearly 8,000 pushed into Lake Champlain and drove the rebels from Fort Ticonderoga in early July. A second column of 1,700 under Colonel Barry St. Leger proceeded up the St. Lawrence River and onto Lake Ontario, before sweeping south toward Fort Schuyler at the western end of the Mohawk Valley. St. Leger's troops were to act as a diversionary force. Soon they had 750 desperate rebel defenders of Fort Schuyler under siege. Seemingly, nothing could stop these two columns, which were to converge again in Albany.

After seizing Ticonderoga, Burgoyne became more tentative about his southward movement. Like William Howe in 1776, he did not take his colonial opponents seriously enough. The rebels blocked Burgoyne's path by cutting down trees, ripping up bridges, and moving boulders into fording points on streams. Soon the British advance had been slowed to less than a mile a day.

Meanwhile, St. Leger's diversionary force was running into trouble. Militiamen in the Mohawk Valley tried to break through to Fort Schuyler. On August 6, 1777, they clashed with St. Leger's loyalists and Indians at the bloody Battle of Oriskany. St. Leger's victory was only temporary. Upon hearing rumors of thousands of rebel soldiers moving rapidly toward Fort Schuyler, the Indians, satiated with the bloodshed at Oriskany, quickly broke camp and fled, leaving the British colonel no alternative but to retreat back into Canada.

Oriskany was the beginning of the end for the once-mighty Iroquois nation, whose tribes were now hopelessly divided and consuming each other in combat. When war chieftain Joseph Brant (Thayendanegea) of the Mohawks led numerous bloody frontier raids for the British, a Continental Army expedition under General John Sullivan marched into central New York during 1779 and destroyed every Iroquois village it came upon. After the war was over, the more aggressive Iroquois migrated north to Canada or west into the Ohio country, where they fought to keep out white frontiersmen; others, less militant, moved quietly onto reservations in western New York.

Burgoyne had now lost his diversionary force. He suffered yet another major setback on August 16 when New Hampshire militiamen overwhelmed some 900 Hessians who were out raiding for supplies near Bennington, Vermont. With little prospect of relief from New York City, Burgoyne's army was now all but entrapped some 30 miles north of Albany along the Hudson River. In two desperate battles (September 19 and October 7) the British force tried to find a way around the well-entrenched rebels, but the brilliant field generalship of Benedict Arnold inspired the Americans to victory. It was all over for Burgoyne, and at Saratoga he surrendered to General Horatio Gates on October 17, 1777.

Losing an army at Saratoga was an unnecessary disaster for Britain, caused primarily by William Howe's unwillingness to work in concert with Burgoyne and follow through on the Hudson Highlands strategy. The victory was a major triumph for the Americans. It convinced Vergennes that it was now safe for France to commit publicly to the rebel cause.

On February 6, 1778, the French government signed two treaties with the American commissioners. The Treaty of Amity and Commerce recognized American independence and encouraged the development of trading ties. The Treaty of Alliance established a military pact between the two allies should hostilities break out between France and Britain. On March 20 King Louis XVI formally greeted the American commissioners at court and announced that the new nation had gained France's diplomatic recognition. In June 1778 a naval battle in the English Channel between British and French warships resulted in formal declarations of war by both powers.

The World Turned Upside Down

When George Washington learned about the French alliance in May 1778, he declared a holiday for "rejoicing throughout the whole army." There was much to celebrate. The Americans had survived the winter, and they had also benefited from the rigorous field training of Baron Friedrich von Steuben, a pretended Prussian nobleman who had volunteered to teach the soldiery how to fight in a more disciplined fashion. With the announcement of open, direct aid from France, which would include land troops and naval reinforcements, the prospects for actually beating the British now appeared considerably brighter.

Revamping British Strategy

The alliance with France changed the fundamental character of the War for Independence. British officials realized that they were no longer just contending with upstart rebels in America. They were getting themselves ensnared in a world war. France, with its well-trained army and highly mobile navy, had the ability to strike British territories anytime and anywhere it chose. The British military problem became even more complex in 1779 when Spain joined the war, hoping to regain the Rock of Gibraltar. Then in late 1780 the British declared war on the Netherlands, partly so that they could capture the Dutch Caribbean island of St. Eustatius, a major source of war supplies for the American patriots.

The dawning reality of world war threatened the British empire with major territorial losses across the globe. One result was a redesigned war plan—the Southern strategy—for reconquering the rebellious American provinces. The assumption was that His Majesty's troops could no longer be massed against the American rebels; instead, they would have to be dispersed to threatened points, such as islands in the West Indies, and later Gibraltar.

The first step came in May 1778 when General Sir Henry Clinton, who had taken over as North American commander from a discredited William Howe, received orders to evacuate Philadelphia. In June Clinton's troops retreated to New York City, narrowly averting a disastrous defeat by Washington's pursuing Continentals at Monmouth Court House (June 28) in central New Jersey. Clinton was to hang on as best he could at the main British base, but he would have to accept a reduction in forces for campaigning elsewhere. The process of dispersal began during the autumn of 1778. Clinton avoided major battles with Washington's army in the North while he slowly implemented the Southern strategy.

Lord George Germain mistakenly assumed that loyalists existed in far greater numbers in the South than they actually did. The idea was to employ bands of armed loyalists, who would operate in conjunction with a main redcoat army to subdue all rebels, beginning in Georgia and then moving in carefully planned steps northward. When any previously rebel-dominated region had been fully secured, royal government would be reintroduced. Ultimately, the whole South would be brought back into the British fold, opening the way for eventual subjugation of the North. The Southern strategy required patience as well as careful nurturing of loyalist sentiment. Both seemed possible when a detachment of 3,500 redcoats quickly reconquered Georgia in December 1778.

Until the French alliance, the South was a secondary theater of war, although there had been sporadic fighting between loyalists and rebel militia. White-Indian relations were bloodier. Both sides maneuvered for the favor of the most powerful Indian nations. In the summer of 1776 the Cherokees attacked frontier settlements from Virginia to South Carolina, killing settlers who had unwisely moved onto traditional tribal hunting grounds. They were soon beaten back with equal ferocity by North Carolina and Virginia militiamen. The Cherokees agreed to forswear further assistance to the British, and the other major tribes, seeing what had happened, took little part in events after 1778.

The most serious setback for the American cause in the South came in 1780 when Sir Henry Clinton led an expedition by sea against Charleston, South Carolina. There General Benjamin Lincoln, with just 3,000 Continental regulars and a smattering of militia, found himself completely outnumbered and trapped when part of Clinton's force moved inland and cut off escape routes. Facing prospects of extermination, Lincoln surrendered without much of a fight on May 12.

Clinton's victory at Charleston was a second major advance in the Southern strategy. The British commander sailed back to New York in high spirits, leaving behind Charles, Lord Cornwallis, to secure all of South Carolina. Clinton had ordered Cornwallis to move forward with care, making sure that loyalist partisans always had firm control of territory behind his advancing army. Ironically, Cornwallis was one of the few aggressive British generals in America. His desire to rush forward and get on with the fight helped undermine the Southern strategy.

At first, Cornwallis's boldness reaped dividends. After learning about the fall of Charleston, the Continental Congress ordered Horatio Gates, now known as the "hero of Saratoga," to proceed south and check Cornwallis. Gates botched the assignment completely. He gathered troops, mostly raw militiamen, in Virginia and North Carolina, then hastily rushed his soldiers into the British lair. Early on the morning of August 16, 1780, Cornwallis's force intercepted Gates's column near Camden, South Carolina. Not only did the American troops lack training, but bad provisions had made them ill. Cornwallis's army devastated the rebels in yet another crushing American defeat in the South.

The Tide of War Turns at Last

During 1780 everything seemed to go wrong for the patriot cause. Besides major setbacks in the South, officers and soldiers directly under Washington's command were increasingly restive about long-overdue wages and inadequate supplies. In July 1780 the officers threatened mass resignations unless Congress did something—and speedily. In September a frustrated Benedict Arnold switched his allegiance back to the British. By the end of the year Continental army troop strength fell below 6,000. Then, as the new year dawned, Washington faced successive mutinies among his hardened veterans in the Pennsylvania and New Jersey lines. The Continental Army seemed to be disintegrating.

Quite simply, it looked as if the British were winning the endurance contest of wills. At no time during the war, except for those dark days just before Washington's counterstrike at Trenton, had the rebel cause appeared more forlorn. What could not be seen was that British successes in the South moved the redcoats toward a far greater failure. Encouraged by its victories, General Cornwallis's army overreached itself. After Camden, Cornwallis started pushing toward North Carolina. His left wing under Major Patrick Ferguson, whose soldiers were mostly loyalists, repeatedly shot down or hanged patriots who fell in their path. Pursued by growing numbers of frontiersmen grimly determined to protect their homesteads and families, Ferguson fell back to Kings Mountain in northern South Carolina. He calculated that he and his 1,100 followers could withstand any assault from atop the promontory. On October 7, 1780, frontier militia units attacked from all sides. Ferguson fell mortally wounded; the rest of his column was killed, wounded, or captured; and the frontiersmen hanged nine of Ferguson's loyalists as a warning to others who might fight for the king.

His left wing destroyed, Cornwallis was unable to bring all of South Carolina under British control. Whenever royal troops moved to a new locale, rebel guerrilla bands under such leaders as "Swamp Fox" Francis Marion emerged from their hiding places and wreaked vengeance on tory sympathizers. Once again, the British had not effectively protected citizens favorably disposed toward them, which in combination with the debacle at Kings Mountain cut deeply into the reservoir of loyalist support available to Cornwallis.

Like his fellow officers, Cornwallis held Americans in contempt, believing that it was only a matter of time until superior British arms would destroy the rebels. However, he did not bargain on facing the likes of General Nathanael Greene, who replaced Gates as the Southern Department commander. When Greene arrived in North Carolina he found very few troops available for duty, while the "appearance" of those in camp, he stated despondently, "was wretched beyond description."

Greene was a military genius. Violating the military maxim of concentrating troop strength, he decided to divide his soldiers into three groups. One rebel column headed by General Daniel Morgan lured the British into a trap at Hannah's Cowpens in western South Carolina on January 17, 1781. Only 140 of the some 1,100 British soldiers escaped being killed, captured, or wounded. Meanwhile, Cornwallis relentlessly pursued Greene, who kept retreating before him. Finally, on March 15, 1781, the rebels squared off for battle at Guilford Courthouse in central North Carolina. Cornwallis gained a technical victory, but sustained heavy casualties; his troops were exhausted, and the rebels were still very much in the field.

Franco-American Triumph at Yorktown

Cornwallis retreated to the seacoast to rest his army, then decided to take over British raiding operations in Virginia, which had begun in January

Southern Theater of War, 1780–1781

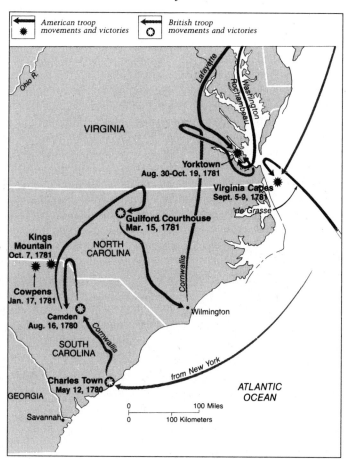

1781 under turncoat Benedict Arnold. In storming northward, Cornwallis totally abandoned the Southern strategy. Nathanael Greene was now free to reassert full patriot authority in the states south of Virginia.

Back in New York, Sir Henry Clinton fumed. He wanted to discipline his subordinate but lacked the courage. Instead, he sent Cornwallis orders in July to establish a defensive base and to refrain from conducting any offensive operations. Reluctantly, Cornwallis selected Yorktown, with easy access to Chesapeake Bay.

At this juncture everything fell into place for the Americans. Upon learning that a French naval fleet would be making its way north from the West Indies, Washington, in concert with French troops under the Comte de Rochambeau, started marching his soldiers south, leaving only enough troops behind in New York to keep Clinton tied down. In early September the French fleet, after dueling with British warships, took control of Chesapeake Bay, thus sealing off any escape for Cornwallis's army. As the month came to a close, some 7,800 French troops and 9,000 Continentals and militiamen surrounded the British army of 8,500 at Yorktown. Cornwallis wrote Clinton: "If you cannot relieve me very soon you must expect to hear the worst."

Using traditional siege tactics, Washington and Rochambeau squeezed Cornwallis into submission. It did not take long. On October 17 a lone British drummer marched toward the Franco-American lines with a white flag showing. Two days later the British force laid down its arms, while its musicians played an appropriate song, "The World Turned Upside Down." The surrender at Yorktown was an emotional scene. A second British army had been captured in America, and the question now was whether Great Britain still had the resolve to continue the war.

A Most Generous Peace Settlement

It was not the great Franco-American victory at Yorktown alone that brought the British to the peace table. It was the accumulation of wounds being inflicted by the Americans and their European allies, with Yorktown the most damaging, that forced the home ministers into peace negotiations.

As early as 1778 Britain had felt the effects of world war. Daring American seaman John Paul Jones conducted raids along the English and Scottish coasts, while French and Spanish warships were soon attacking British vessels at will in the English Channel. French warships threatened British possessions in the West Indies. France and Spain were about to launch a major expedition against Gibraltar. In the spring of 1781 a Spanish force under Bernardo de Gálvez captured a sizable British garrison at Pensacola, Florida, and the British soon experienced setbacks as far away as India. The allies had demonstrated that they could carry the war any-where, suggesting the prospect of disastrous consequences for the power-ful British empire.

In March 1782 Lord North's ministry collapsed, and a new cabinet opened negotiations in France with designated American peace commis-sioners Benjamin Franklin, John Adams, and John Jay. On November 30, 1782, the representatives agreed to preliminary peace terms. The other belligerents also started coming to terms, largely because the naval war had turned against France and Spain and British troops had saved Gibraltar. All parties signed the final peace accords at Paris on September 3, 1783.

The major European powers now recognized the independence of the 13 rebellious colonies. Further, the peace settlement established the Mis-sissippi River as the western boundary line of the new nation. Britain re-turned Florida to Spain. Although the American commissioners had tried and failed to gain Canada, they had obtained title to the vast reserve of In-dian territory lying between the Appalachian Mountains and the Missis-sippi River. All told, effective bargaining by the American peace commis-sioners gave the former colonists a huge geographic base on which to build their new republic.

The peace settlement was significant in several other respects. The treaty was silent about the rights of Indians, whose interests the British ig-nored, despite repeated promises during the war to protect the lands of Native Americans who joined the king's cause. Britain recognized Ameri-can fishing rights off the coast of eastern Canada, thus sustaining a major New England industry. The British demanded that prewar debts be paid in full to its merchants (few actually were) and insisted upon the complete restoration of the rights and property of loyalists. The American commis-sioners agreed to have Congress make such a recommendation to the states (which they generally ignored). The peace treaty, then, both established American independence and laid the groundwork for future conflict.

Conclusion

The Americans came out remarkably well in 1783. They emerged victori-ous not only in war but at the peace table as well. The young republic had endured over its parent nation, Great Britain, and, with invaluable assis-tance from foreign allies, particularly France, had earned its freedom from European monarchism and imperialism. On the other hand, it was far from certain whether the United States could sustain its independence or have much of a future as a nation, given the many internal problems fac-ing the 13 sovereign states.

Chronology of Key Events

1775	First military clashes between British troops and Colonists at Lexington and Concord; Second Continental Congress meets in Philadelphia; George Washington given command of Continental Army.
1776	Thomas Paine publishes *Common Sense;* Declaration of Independence adopted; British rout rebel soldiers in vicinity of New York City; British defeated at Battle of Trenton
1777	British forces seize Philadelphia; General Burgoyne surrenders at Saratoga
1778	Franco-American alliance; British troops conquer Savannah, Georgia
1779	Spain joins the war against Britain
1780	British capture Charleston; Battle of Camden, South Carolina, Battle of Kings Mountain; the Dutch enter the war against Britain
1781	British defeated at Hannah's Cowpens; Guilford Courthouse ends in a draw; British surrender at Yorktown, Virginia
1783	Treaty of Paris ends the War for American Independence

Among those who did not cheer heartily at the prospect of peace were the officers and soldiers of the Continental Army. They had made great personal sacrifices and had every reason to be proud of their accomplishments; however, they deeply resented the lack of civilian support that had plagued them throughout the long conflict. Even in leaving the service, wrote Private Joseph Plumb Martin, they were "turned adrift like old worn-out horses" without just financial compensation for their services. Still, they had the personal satisfaction of knowing that their pain and suffering had sustained the vision of a bright and glorious future for the infant United States, but only if revolutionary Americans resolved their own political differences—especially those relating to the implanting of republican ideals in institutions of government.

Suggestions for Further Reading

For an overview of the revolutionary war consult Don Higginbotham, *The War of American Independence* (1971); John R. Alden, *The American Revolution, 1775–1783* (1954). See also Marcus Cunliffe, *George Washington: Man and Monument,* rev. ed. (1982); James Kirby Martin, ed., *Ordinary Courage: The Revolutionary War Adventures of Joseph Plumb Martin* (1993).

On daily life on the eve of the Revolution see Robert A. Gross, *The Minutemen and Their World* (1976). On the composition of the Continental Army and its role in revolutionary society see James Kirby Martin and Mark Edward Lender, *A Respectable Army: The Military Origins of the Republic* (1982); Charles Royster, *A Revolutionary People at War* (1979). The military side of the revolution is examined in William M. Fowler, Jr., *Rebels under Sail: The American Navy During the Revolution* (1976); Ira Gruber, *The Howe Brothers and the American Revolution* (1972); W. Robert Higgins, ed., *The Revolutionary War in the South* (1979); Lee Kennett, *The French Forces in America, 1780–1783* (1977); Piers Mackesy, *The War for America, 1775–1783* (1964); Dave R. Palmer, *The Way of the Fox: American Strategy in the War for America* (1975).

On the diplomacy of the Revolution see Samuel F. Bemis, *The Diplomacy of the American Revolution,* rev. ed. (1957); Jonathan R. Dull, *A Diplomatic History of the American Revolution* (1985). On the Confederation period consult H. James Henderson, *Party Politics in the Continental Congress* (1974); Merrill Jensen, *The Articles of Confederation* (1940); Jackson Turner Main, *The Sovereign States* (1973); Jack N. Rakove, *The Beginnings of National Politics* (1979).

Chapter **6**

Securing the Republic and Its Ideals, 1776–1789

Nancy Shippen was a product of Philadelphia's best lineage. Although she was born in 1763, the political turmoil leading to rebellion did not affect her early life. As a privileged daughter in an upper-class family, it was her duty to blossom into a charming woman, admired for her beauty and social graces, rather than develop her intellect. Her education consisted of the refinement of skills that would please and entertain—dancing, cultivating her voice, playing musical instruments, painting on delicate china, and producing pieces of decorative needlework.

Three hundred miles away in Boston, Phillis Wheatley was also reckoning with the American Revolution. Her life had been very different from Nancy's. Born on Africa's West Coast around 1753, she had been snatched from her parents by slave catchers. At the Boston slave market, Mrs. Susannah Wheatley, looking for a young female slave to train in domestic service, noticed her. In Phillis the Wheatley family got much more; their new slave yearned to express her thoughts and feelings through poetry.

Conventional wisdom dictated that slaves should not be educated. Exposure to reading and writing might make them resentful, perhaps even rebellious. Sensing Phillis's talents, the Wheatley family defied convention. She mastered English and Latin, even preparing translations of ancient writings. By 1770 some of her poems had been published, followed in 1773 by a collection entitled *Poems on Various Subjects, Religious and Moral.*

Little as Phillis Wheatley and Nancy Shippen had in common, they lived during an era in which men thought of all women, regardless of their rank in society, as second-class human beings. In the case of Phillis, she carried the additional burden of being black in an openly racist society. Like other women in revolutionary America, they could only hope that the ideals of human liberty might someday apply to them.

For Nancy Shippen there were two male tyrants in her life. The first was her father, who in 1781 forced her into marriage with the son of one of New York's most powerful and wealthy families. The man she truly loved had only "honorable expectations" of a respectable income, so her father, to whom she legally belonged until marriage, insisted that she wed the second tyrant in her life—her husband Henry Beckman Livingston.

The marriage was a disaster, most likely because Henry was a known philanderer. Nancy eventually took her baby daughter and moved back to her family. She wanted full custody of the child, who by law was the property of her husband. Henry made it clear that he would never give up his legal rights to his daughter, should Nancy embarrass him in public by seeking a divorce. Even if she had defied him, divorces were very hard to get because they involved proving adultery or desertion.

Although they were from diverse cultures, Phillis Wheatley and Nancy Shippen
were considered second-class citizens because they were women.

To keep actual custody of her daughter, Nancy accepted her entrap-
ment. Several years later Henry relented and arranged for a divorce, but
by that time Nancy's spirit was broken. This former belle of Philadelphia
society lived on unhappily in hermitlike fashion until her death in 1841.
Having been so favored at birth, her adult years were a personal tragedy,
primarily because of her legal dependence on the will of men.

Phillis Wheatley, by comparison, enjoyed some personal freedom before she died in 1784. Emancipated upon the death of her owners, Phillis
married a free black man and bore him three children. But the family was
poor, and there was scant time for poetry. It was very difficult for free

blacks to get decent jobs, and Phillis struggled each day to help her family avoid destitution. She lived long enough to see slavery being challenged in the North; but she died knowing that African Americans, even when free, invariably faced discrimination based on race, forcing families like hers to exist on the margins of revolutionary society.

The experiences of Phillis Wheatley and Nancy Shippen raise basic questions about the character of the Revolution. Did the cause of liberty really change the lives of Americans? If it was truly a movement to end tyranny, secure human rights, and ensure equality of opportunity, then why did individuals like Wheatley and Shippen benefit so little? A major reason was that white, adult males of property and community standing put greater emphasis on setting up an independent nation between 1776 and 1789 than on securing human rights. Still, the ideology of liberty could not be denied. Primarily, the revolutionary era saw the creation of a new nation and the articulation of fundamental ideals regarding human freedom and dignity—ideals that have shaped the course of American history.

Establishing New Republican Governments

Winning the war and working out a favorable peace settlement represented two of three crucial elements that made for a successful rebellion. The third factor centered on the formation of stable governments. Everyone agreed that a monarchical system, indeed any form capable of producing political tyranny, was unacceptable. A second point of consensus was that governments should be republican in character. Sovereignty, or ultimate political authority, previously residing with King and Parliament, should be vested in the people. After all, political institutions presumably existed to serve them. As such, citizens should be governed by laws, and laws should be the product of collective deliberations of representatives elected by the citizenry.

Defining the core ideals of republicanism—popular sovereignty, rule by law, and legislation by elected representatives—was not a source of disagreement. Yet revolutionary leaders argued passionately about the organization and powers of new governments, both state and national, as well as the extent to which basic political rights should be put into practice. At the heart of the argument was the concept of *public virtue:* whether citizens were capable of subordinating their self-interest to the greater good of the whole community. Although some leaders answered in the affirmative, others did not. Their trust or distrust of the people directly affected how far they were willing to go in implementing republican ideals.

Leaders who believed that citizens could govern themselves and not abuse public privileges for private advantage were in the vanguard of political thinking in the western world. As such, they may be called radicals. On the other hand, more cautious, elitist revolutionary leaders feared what the masses might do without the restraints of central political authority. These leaders remained attached to traditional notions of hierarchy and deference in social and political relationships. They still thought that the "better sort" of citizens should be the stewards who guided the people. They wanted a strong central government to replace King and Parliament, a government controlled by more cautious revolutionaries in the interests of national political stability.

People Victorious: The New State Governments

In the wake of collapsing British authority during 1775 and 1776, radical and cautious revolutionaries squared off in constitutional conventions.

Their heated debates produced several new state constitutions by the end of 1777, plus a plan of national government written by the Continental Congress. Although the state constitution-makers varied in their commitment, free, white, adult male citizens (about 20 percent of the total population) gained expanded voting and officeholding rights. The movement clearly was toward greater popular participation in governmental decision making.

Pennsylvanians produced the most democratic of the first state constitutions. All white male citizens, with or without property, could now vote for legislators, who served in an annually elected unicameral, or one-chamber, assembly. By comparison, Maryland's constitution-framers were much less trusting. They maintained a three-tiered structure of government, reminiscent of the king and two houses of Parliament. Potential voters had to meet modest property-holding requirements. Those elected to the lower house had to own at least a 50-acre freehold farm while election to the upper house and governorship was restricted to the wealthiest members of society. In Pennsylvania ordinary citizens could control their own political destiny, but in Maryland the "better sort" were to act as stewards for the people, hence continuing the tradition of deferential politics.

The other state constitutions varied between these two extremes. Those of New Hampshire, North Carolina, and Georgia were more like Pennsylvania. New York, Virginia, and South Carolina resembled the Maryland plan more closely. Delaware and New Jersey were in the middle.

Only New Jersey defined the electorate without regard to gender. Its 1776 constitution gave the vote to "all free inhabitants" meeting minimal property qualifications. This permitted some women to vote. Since all property in marriage belonged to husbands, New Jersey had technically extended franchise rights only to widows and spinsters (very few divorced women were to be found anywhere in America). Nonetheless, great numbers of married women went to the polls regularly. Although the experiment worked, this concept proved too radical for the customary male-dominated political culture of revolutionary America, and in 1807 New Jersey disenfranchised females.

Because of the first state constitutions, male citizens with more ordinary family backgrounds, less personal wealth, and a greater diversity of occupations began to gain greater access to political offices after the Revolution started. Neither as well-educated nor as well-to-do as in the past, these leaders were, as one Virginian noted in 1776, "the people's men (and the people in general are right)." Radical leaders throughout the states heartily endorsed these sentiments.

The Articles of Confederation

In June 1776 the Continental Congress called for a plan of national government. John Dickinson, the well-known reluctant revolutionary who refused to vote for independence, took the lead. Concerned about losing the stabilizing influence of British authority, Dickinson proposed a muscular plan of central government to be called the Articles of Confederation for "THE UNITED STATES OF AMERICA," in which the states would have little actual authority.

The radical revolutionaries who dominated Congress in late 1776 and 1777 did not like this plan. They feared power too far removed from the people. After all, they had rebelled against a distant government that they had perceived as tyrannical. When Congress finally completed revisions of the Articles of Confederation in November 1777, the delegates made sure that the states retained their sovereignty. At most, the central government could coordinate activities among the states. It could manage the war, but it did not even have taxation authority to support that effort. If Congress needed money (it obviously did), it could "requisition" the states. The states, however, could decide for themselves whether they would send funds to Congress. As a testament to the sovereignty of the 13 states, each had to ratify the Articles before this plan could go into full operation.

Fundamentally penniless and powerless, the Confederation government represented the optimistic view that a virtuous citizenry did not require the constraining hand of central authority. This bold vision—fully in line with the rejection of King and Parliament as a far distant, autocratic central government—pleased radicals like Samuel Adams, Thomas Paine, and Thomas Jefferson. Cautious revolutionaries still harbored grave doubts, and events over the next few years convinced them that the first constitutional settlement had all but doomed the experiment in republicanism to failure.

Crises of the Confederation

The young American republic had to face many immediate challenges. These included ratifying the Articles of Confederation, establishing a national domain west of the Appalachians, finding some means to pay for the war, achieving stable diplomatic relations with foreign powers, and guarding against domestic insurrections.

Over time, those who advocated a strong central government formed an informal political bloc, since known as the *nationalists*. With each passing year the nationalists became more and more frustrated by the Confederation. Finally, in 1787 they overwhelmed their opposition by pressing for and getting a new plan of national government.

Struggle to Ratify the Articles

Given the wartime need for national unity in the face of a common enemy, Congress asked each state to approve the Articles of Confederation quickly. Overcoming much indifference, 12 states had finally ratified by January 1779—but Maryland still held out.

The propertied gentlemen who controlled Maryland's revolutionary government objected to one specific provision in the Articles. Although Dickinson's draft had designated all lands west of the Appalachian Mountains as a *national domain,* belonging to all of the people for future settlement, the final version left these lands in the hands of states having sea-to-sea clauses in their colonial charters. Maryland, having a fixed western boundary, had no such western claim; nor did Rhode Island, New Jersey, Pennsylvania, or Delaware.

Maryland's leaders simply refused to be cut off from western development. Many had invested in land companies trying to gain title to large parcels of western territory, and they stood to make substantial profits if the national Congress would recognize these claims. The Maryland assembly adamantly refused ratification unless the landed states turned over their charter titles to Congress. Virginia, which had the largest claim, including the vast region north of the Ohio River that came to be known as the "Old Northwest," faced the most pressure. Forsaking local land speculators for the national interest, the Virginia Assembly broke the deadlock in January 1781 by agreeing to cede its claims to Congress.

If self-interest had not been involved, ratification would have followed quickly; however, greedy Maryland leaders still held out. They pronounced Virginia's grant unacceptable because of a condition not permitting Congress to award lands on the basis of Indian deeds. Fortunately for the republic, the war intervened. In early 1781, with the British raiding in the Chesapeake Bay region, Marylanders became quite anxious about their defense. Congressional leaders urged ratification in exchange for promises of Continental military support. All but cornered, the Maryland Assembly reluctantly gave in and approved the Articles of Confederation.

Contention over Financing the War

From the very first, financial problems plagued the new central government. Under the Articles, Congress had no power of taxation; it repeatedly asked the states to pay a fair proportion of war costs. The states, also hard-pressed for funds, rarely sent in more than 50 percent of their requisitions. Meantime, soldiers like Joseph Plumb Martin endured shortages of food, clothing, camp equipment, and pay.

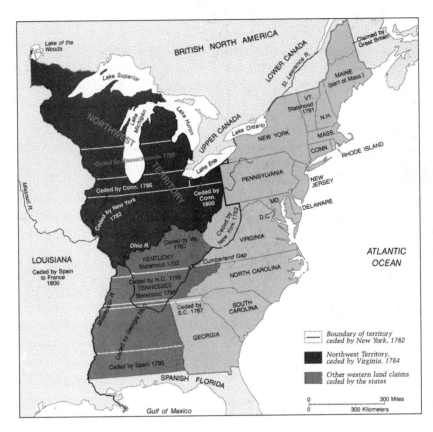

Western Land Claims Ceded by the States

The battle over conflicting state claims to western lands was a major issue
facing the Continental Congress.

The lack of tax revenues forced Congress to resort to various expedient measures to meet war costs. Between 1775 and 1780 it issued some
$220 million in paper money. Lacking any financial backing, these "Con-
tinentals" became so worthless by 1779 that irate army officers complained that "four months' pay of a private [soldier] will not procure his
wretched wife and children a single bushel of wheat." In addition, Congress, largely to get military supplies, issued interest-bearing certificates of
indebtedness. Without any means to pay interest, these notes, which also
circulated as money, rapidly lost value. If it had not been for financial assistance from allies like France and the Netherlands, the war effort might
well have floundered.

Deeply disturbed by these conditions, many nationalists in the Continental Congress acted forcefully to institute financial reform. Their leader was the wealthy Philadelphia merchant, Robert Morris, sometimes called the "financier of the Revolution." His assistant superintendent, Gouverneur Morris (no relation), a wealthy New Yorker then practicing law in Philadelphia, was also critical to shaping the events that lay ahead.

At the urging of the nationalists, congressional delegates approved the Impost Plan of 1781. It called for import duties of five percent on all foreign trade goods entering the United States, the revenues to belong to Congress. These funds could be used to pay the army, to back a stable national currency, and, ultimately, to meet foreign loan obligations. Because the plan involved giving Congress taxation authority, the delegates recommended it in the form of an amendment to the Articles. Amendments required the approval of all 13 states.

Reluctant as they were to share taxation powers with the central government, many state leaders agreed with Robert Morris. By the fall of 1782, 12 states had ratified. Only Rhode Island voted against ratification. Once again, one state had blocked the will of the other 12.

In this crucial matter the nationalists had allies. Most prominent were disgruntled officers in the Continental Army. Rarely had the soldiers been paid, for Congress lacked a fixed source of revenue to meet its obligations to its fighting men and women. After a group of high-ranking officers learned about Rhode Island's decision, they sent a menacing petition to Congress, insisting upon five years of full pay in lieu of promised half-pay pensions when mustering out of the service. They warned of "fatal effects" if their demands were not met.

Threatened Military Coup: The Newburgh Conspiracy

For years Continental officers and soldiers alike had been complaining about the ungenerous treatment they received from revolutionary leaders and civilians. Convinced that the general populace had lived well at home while the army endured privation, sickness, and death in the field, they spoke with impassioned feelings about the absence of citizen virtue. As one officer bluntly wrote: "I hate my countrymen." Personal sacrifice for the good of the whole community, it seemed to the Continentals, had been exacted only from those with the fortitude to fulfill the obligation of long-term military service.

After the British surrender at Yorktown, Washington moved 11,000 troops north to Newburgh, New York. From this campsite near the Hudson River, the Continental Army waited for peace terms and kept its eye on British forces in New York City. As peace negotiations dragged on, officers and soldiers worried about being demobilized without back pay and promised pensions.

When the congressional nationalists received the officers' hotly worded petition, they were more pleased than alarmed. They soon devised a scheme to use these threats to extort taxation authority from the states. If need be, they would encourage the army to go back into the field and threaten the civilian populace with a military uprising. The danger, of course, was that the army might get out of control, seize the reins of government, and push the revolution toward some form of military dictatorship.

Washington refused to cooperate in a military coup directed at the states and the people. Perhaps better than anyone in revolutionary America, he understood that military power had to remain subordinate to civilian authority, or the republic would never be free. Robert Morris and other congressional nationalists found General Horatio Gates, who dreamed of replacing Washington at the head of the army, much more receptive to their scheme, but without Washington's support the Newburgh conspiracy collapsed.

Nonetheless, dissension in the ranks, and dissatisfaction with the central government, continued unabated. After leaving the army one angry group of Pennsylvania Continentals marched on Philadelphia in June 1783. They surrounded Independence Hall where Congress held its sessions and refused to leave until they received back pay. The frightened delegates asked the Pennsylvania government for protection, but state officials turned down their request. Thoroughly humiliated by armed soldiers and a state government that would not defend them, the delegates first moved to Princeton, New Jersey, then to Annapolis, Maryland, and finally to New York City. The delicate fabric of the new nation seemed to be unraveling.

Drifting Toward Disunion

Despite the Paris peace settlement and the final removal of British troops, most citizens engaged in another battle beginning in late 1783—this one against a hard-hitting economic depression. Farmers in New England reeled from the effects of new British trade regulations which in essence turned the Navigation System against the independent Americans. The Orders in Council of 1783 prohibited the sale of many American agricultural products in the British West Indies, formerly a key market for New England goods, and required many commodities to be conveyed to and from the islands in British vessels. The orders represented a serious blow to New England's agricultural, shipping, and shipbuilding trades. Making matters even worse, merchants in all the states had purchased large quantities of British goods at war's end, only to discover they could not sell these commodities to citizens feeling the effects of the depression.

The central government could do little. It did send John Adams to Britain in 1785 as the first minister from the United States. Adams, however, made no headway in getting British officials to back off from the Orders in Council. He dejectedly reported to Congress that "they rely upon our disunion" to avoid negotiations.

Some merchants, primarily from the Middle Atlantic states, were anxious to break free of Britain's economic hold. An opportunity presented itself in 1784 when John Jay, Congress's newly appointed secretary for foreign affairs, started negotiations with Don Diego de Gardoqui, Spain's first minister to the United States. Spain, concerned that Americans, now streaming into the trans-Appalachian west, would in time covet its territory beyond the Mississippi, had closed that river to American commerce. Attempting to assuage possible bad feelings, Gardoqui offered an advantageous commercial treaty. Jay and a number of powerful merchants from the Middle Atlantic states saw merit in the Spanish proposal. They viewed southwestern development as a potential threat to eastern economic dominance. When Jay reported on his discussions to Congress in the summer of 1786, tempers flared. The southern states voted as a bloc against any such treaty, which ended the Jay-Gardoqui negotiations. But southerners and westerners still suspected that Jay and his eastern merchant allies would not hesitate to abandon them altogether for petty commercial gains.

Daniel Shays's Rebellion

Postwar economic conditions were so bad in several states that citizens began demanding tax relief from their governments. In western Massachusetts desperate farmers complained about huge property tax increases by the state government to pay off its war debt. Taxes on land rose by more than 60 percent in the period 1783–1786, exactly when a depressed postwar economy meant that farmers were getting little income from the sale of excess agricultural goods.

Local courts, in the absence of tax payments, started to seize the property of men like Daniel Shays, a revolutionary war veteran. Viewing their plight in terms of tyranny, the farmers of western Massachusetts believed that they had the right to break the chains of oppression, just as they had done in resisting British rule a few years before. This time, however, the enemy was their own state government.

In late August 1786 an estimated 1,000 farmers poured into Northampton and shut down the county court. This crowd action represented the first of many such closures. By popular mandate citizens would no longer permit judges to seize property or condemn people to debtors' prison as the penalty for not paying taxes. Frightened state leaders in Boston hastily organized an army to deal with the crisis.

The insurrection soon fizzled. On January 25, 1787, Shays and his followers attacked the federal arsenal at Springfield, but were driven off. In early February the army pursued the western rebels through a driving snowstorm and routed them at Petersham. These setbacks, along with tax relief from the assembly and amnesty for the leaders of the rebellion, ended the uprising.

Shays's Rebellion, however, held broader significance. Only a strong central government, nationalists believed, could save the republic from internal chaos. The nationalists now intensified their campaign for a new constitutional settlement, one designed to bring the self-serving sovereign states and the people under control.

Human Rights and Social Change

The years between 1776 and 1787 were not just a time of mounting political confrontation between nationalists and localists. The period also witnessed the establishment of many fundamental human rights. When Thomas Jefferson penned his famous words, "all men are created equal," he informed George III that kings were not superior to the people by some assumed right of birth. Jefferson went on to say that all human beings had "certain unalienable rights," or rights literally beyond governmental control. Republican governments had the responsibility to respect and guarantee these rights, including "life, liberty, and the pursuit of happiness" for all citizens.

At the same time Americans had waged civil war against Britain to preserve property rights. Tyrannical governments, for example, threatened property through taxation without representation. In trying to protect property rights while expanding human rights, revolutionary leaders learned that the two could clash. They found it much easier to guarantee human rights when property rights, such as those relating to the ownership of slaves, were not also at stake. Thus there were some striking contradictions in efforts to enshrine greater freedom for all inhabitants in revolutionary America.

In Pursuit of Religious Freedom

Since the days of the Great Awakening, dissenter religious groups had expressed opposition to established churches in the colonies. The Baptists were particularly outspoken. They wanted official toleration and an end to taxes used exclusively for state-supported churches. In 1786 Virginia passed its Statute of Religious Freedom, which not only provided for the separation of church and state, but guaranteed complete freedom of conscience. Jefferson would later be labeled an atheist for his efforts on behalf of this legislation, but for him the statute was just as significant as the Declaration of Independence, and he had these sentiments engraved on his tombstone.

Disestablishment quickly followed in other states, particularly in the South where the Anglican church (soon to become the Episcopal Church) had been dominant. In New England, only Rhode Islanders, following in the tradition of Roger Williams, had enjoyed full latitude in worship. With the Revolution the cause of religious freedom started to move forward in other New England states. Lawmakers began letting citizens decide which local church to support with their tax monies. This development represented a partial victory for individuals who preferred worshipping as Baptists or Presbyterians. However, dissenters still had to accept Congregationalism as the established state church; complete separation of church and state did not occur in New England until the early nineteenth century.

Freedom of religion was one among a number of fundamental rights to make headway during the revolutionary era. Several states adopted bills of rights similar to Virginia's, guaranteeing freedom of speech, assembly, and the press, as well as trials by jury. Other states started revising their legal codes, making penalties for crimes less harsh. Such feudal practices as primogeniture and entail (passing and committing property only to eldest sons through the generations) were abolished. Running through all these acts was the republican assumption that citizens should have the opportunity to lead productive lives, uninhibited by laws violating personal conscience or denying the opportunity to acquire property.

The Propertyless Poor and the West

For many Americans gaining property remained only a dream. At least 20 percent of the population lived at the poverty level or below, eking out precarious existences as unskilled laborers. Indeed, wealth was more unevenly distributed in 1800 than it had been in 1750. One reason for the increased concentration of wealth in fewer hands was the policy of state governments regarding the seizure of loyalist property. Anxious to obtain a source of wartime revenue, states sold these holdings, worth milllions, to the highest bidders. This practice favored men of wealth with investment capital and worked against any substantial redistribution of property.

Another missed opportunity lay with the enormous trans-Appalachian frontier awaiting development. Washington's Continental soldiers, who ranked among the poorest members of revolutionary society, had been promised western lands for long-term service. When they mustered out in 1783, they received land warrant certificates. In order to survive, most veterans soon exchanged these paper certificates for the bare necessities of life. As a result, very few were ever able to begin anew in the Ohio country, once military tracts had been set aside and surveyed.

Still, western lands remained a source of hope for economically downtrodden soldiers and civilians alike. In 1775 explorer Daniel Boone blazed open the "Wilderness Road" to Kentucky, which contained a population of 74,000 fifteen years later. Newly formed white settlements in Kentucky and Tennessee soon created pressures to open territory north of the Ohio River. After ceding the Old Northwest to the United States in 1783, however, the British did not abandon their military posts there. To maintain the lucrative fur trade, they bolstered the Indians with a steady supply of firearms. Whites foolish enough to venture north of the Ohio River rarely survived, and the region remained closed to large numbers of westward-moving settlers well into the 1790s.

Despite the British and Indians, Congress was eager to open the Ohio country. With this goal in mind the delegates approved three land ordinances. The 1784 Ordinance provided for territorial government and guaranteed settlers that they would not remain in permanent colonial status. When enough people (later specified at 60,000) had moved in, a constitution could be written, state boundaries set, and admission to the union as a full partner would follow. The 1785 Ordinance called for orderly surveying of the region. Townships of six miles square were to be laid out in gridlike fashion, containing 36 sections of 640 acres each. Proceeds from the sale of the sixteenth section were to be used to finance public education. The Northwest Ordinance of 1787 refined governmental arrangements, gave a bill of rights to prospective settlers, and proclaimed slavery forever banned north of the Ohio River. In providing for orderly development and eventual statehood, the land ordinances may well have been the most significant legislation of the Confederation-period Congress.

Even so, the ordinances were not fully enlightened. Congress, in its desperate search for revenue, viewed the Old Northwest as a source of long-term income. The smallest purchase individual settlers could make was 640 acres, priced at $1.00 per acre, and there were to be no purchases on credit. Families of modest means, let alone poorer ones, could not meet such terms. To survive, the poorest western settlers had no alternative but to squat on uninhabited land until they were driven off.

Women Appeal for Fundamental Liberties

Like the poor, women experienced little success in improving their lot during the revolutionary era. By law and social practice, women were legally dependent on men, as the case of Nancy Shippen so vividly illustrated. What held the greatest promise for women, at least for those of middling and affluent status, was the ideology of republicanism, which directly influenced family life by offering a broadened definition regarding the role of mothers. Patriot leaders repeatedly asserted that the republic would founder without virtuous citizens. Hence it became a special trust for mothers to implant strong moral character and civic virtue in their children, especially their sons, so that they would uphold the obligations of disinterested citizenship for the good of the nation.

The concept of "republican motherhood" had potentially liberating qualities. It became the calling of republican mothers to manage the domestic sphere of family life, just as husbands were to take responsibility for the family's economic welfare. This duty reduced traditional male dominance in all family matters. Elevating the role of women in family life may also have affected the nature of courtship by putting more emphasis upon affection than on parental control in the making of marriages. However, the immediate effect of this emerging tendency should not be exaggerated, as Nancy Shippen's experiences indicate.

If women were to be responsible for instilling proper values in future generations, they needed more and better schooling. During the 1780s and 1790s some states started taxing citizens for the support of elementary education. Massachusetts broke new ground in 1789 by requiring its citizens to pay for female as well as male elementary education. In addition, these two decades saw the opening of many new private schools, which offered more advanced education to daughters of well-to-do families in subjects traditionally reserved for males, such as mathematics, science, and history.

Still, the emphasis in expanding opportunities for middle- and upper-class women was upon service to the family and the republic, not on individual development. Most men in revolutionary America resisted further change for women. Although republican motherhood offered higher status, most men still thought of women as a form of property whose existence should be devoted to masculine welfare and happiness.

The Question of Race

Revolutionary ideology placed a premium on such terms as *liberty* and *equality*. Almost everyone recognized that it was inconsistent to use such terms while holding 500,000 African Americans (one-fifth of the population in 1776) in perpetual bondage. For generations, colonial Americans had taken slavery for granted, as if it were part of the natural order of life. All of the talk about liberty and political slavery during the 1760s and 1770s began to undermine this unquestioning attitude, so much so that even slaveholding patriots like Patrick Henry asked whether the institution was not "repugnant to humanity . . . and destructive to liberty?" Some revolutionary leaders decisively answered "yes."

In 1774 Philadelphians, among them Benjamin Franklin, organized an abolition society. Pressure from this group and from antislavery Quakers resulted in Pennsylvania becoming the first state (1780) to declare human bondage illegal. Soon other northern states followed, modeling their emancipation laws on Pennsylvania's, which specified that children born to slave mothers had to be set free by the age of 28. By 1800 slavery was a dying institution in the North.

Many revolutionary leaders hoped that the drive to abolish slavery would also extend into the South. During the 1780s there were some positive signs. After 1783 only South Carolina and Georgia were still involved in the international slave trade. States such as Maryland, Delaware, and Virginia passed laws making it easier for planters to manumit (free) individual slaves. George Washington was one of a few wealthy planters who took advantage of Virginia's manumission law. He referred to slavery as a "misfortune" that sullied revolutionary ideals, and in his will he made provision for the liberation of his slaves.

Washington, as in most other ways, was unusual. Far more typical was Thomas Jefferson. In his *Notes on the State of Virginia* (1785) Jefferson called slavery "a perpetual exercise" in "the most unremitting despotism," but he could not bring himself to free his own slaves. His chattels formed the economic base of his way of life. Their labor gave him the time that he needed for politics and, ironically, the time to work so persuasively on behalf of human liberty.

Support for his life-style was not the only reason Jefferson held back. He was representative of his times in believing blacks to be inherently inferior to whites. In his *Notes* he made a number of comparisons of ability detrimental to blacks, such as in the category of reasoning power (Jefferson scoffed at the poems of Phillis Wheatley, which he described as "below the dignity of criticism"). He thought, too, that the emancipation of all blacks would result in racial war. Thus, a man who labored so diligently for human rights in his own lifetime remained in bondage to the racist concepts of his era.

Negative racial attitudes were the norm in revolutionary America, as the growing number of freed blacks learned again and again. Because of the general abolition and individual manumission movements, the free black population approached 60,000 by 1790 and 108,000 by 1800 (11 percent of the total African-American population). Like the some 5,000 black Continental Army veterans, Phillis Wheatley, and George Washington's former slaves, these individuals repeatedly had to struggle to survive in a hostile society.

Slave Concentration, 1790

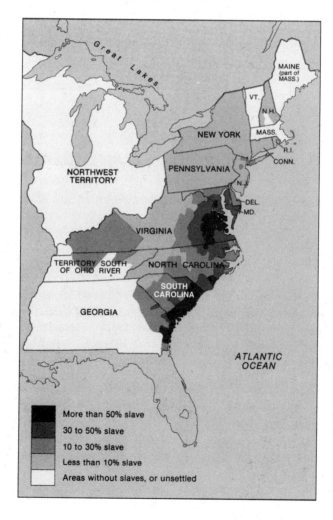

Many free blacks moved to the large northern port towns, where slavery was a fading threat. They built their own neighborhoods, and skilled workers opened shops to serve one another. Other urban free blacks performed domestic service at low wages for well-to-do white families, but they did so as free persons with the opportunity to fashion independent lives for themselves. Free African Americans also established their own churches, such as the African Methodist Episcopal Church, founded by Richard Allen in Philadelphia in 1786. African Baptist and African Presbyterian denominations also developed in the northern port towns, and these churches provided opportunities for formal education, since black children were rarely welcome in white schools.

Whether in the North or the South, the reality more often than not was open discrimination. As a group, free African Americans responded by providing for one another and believing in a better day when revolutionary ideals regarding human freedom and liberty would have full meaning in their lives. In this sense they still had much in common with their brethren in slavery.

Second New Beginning, New National Government

In 1787 many revolutionary leaders were more concerned about internal political stability than securing human rights. With all the talk of breaking up the Confederation, with Shays's Rebellion not yet completely quelled, and with the states arguing endlessly about almost everything, political leaders believed that matters of government should take primacy, or the republican experiment might be forever lost. Certainly the nationalists felt this way, and they were pushing hard for a revision of the first constitutional settlement.

In September 1786 representatives from five states met briefly in Annapolis, Maryland, to discuss pressing interstate commercial problems. Those present included such strong nationalists as Alexander Hamilton, John Dickinson, and James Madison. Since so few states were represented, the delegates abandoned their agenda in favor of an urgent plea asking all the states to send delegates to a special constitutional convention.

This time the states responded, largely because of the specter of civil turmoil associated with Shays's Rebellion. Twelve states—Rhode Island refused to participate—named 74 delegates, 55 of whom would attend the Constitutional Convention in Philadelphia. As the Continental Congress instructed the delegates in February 1787, their purpose was to revise the Articles of Confederation, making them "adequate to the exigencies . . . of the union." Some nationalists, however, had other ideas. They wanted a whole new plan of national government. Their ideas would dominate the proceedings from beginning to end, and their determination produced the Constitution of 1787.

The Framers of the Constitution

The men who gathered in Philadelphia were successful lawyers, planters, and merchants of education, wealth, and wide-ranging accomplishments, not ordinary citizens. They represented particular states, but most of them thought in national terms, based on experiences like serving in the Continental Congress and the Continental Army. They feared for the future of the republic, unless someone did something—and soon—to strengthen the weak central government as a means of containing the selfishness of particular states. Having for years been frustrated by the Revolution's first constitutional settlement, they seized the opportunity for change and made the most of it.

Among those present during the lengthy proceedings, which stretched from May 25 to September 17, was the revered George Washington, who served as the convention's president. Other notable leaders included James Madison, Alexander Hamilton, Gouverneur and Robert Morris, and John Dickinson. Benjamin Franklin, at 81, was the oldest delegate. He offered his finely tuned diplomatic tact in working out compromises that kept the proceedings moving forward.

Although the delegates disagreed vehemently, they never let differences over particular issues deflect them from their main purpose—to find the constitutional means for an enduring republic. The Constitution was not perfect, as Benjamin Franklin stated on the last day of the convention, but it did bring stability and energy to national government—and it has endured.

A Document Constructed by Compromises

If the nationalists had been doctrinaire, their deliberations would have collapsed. They held fast to their objective—providing for a strong central government—but were flexible about ways to achieve their goal. Thus they were able to compromise on critical issues. The first great points of difference dealt with the structure of government and whether states should be represented equally or according to population distribution. The eventual compromise required the abandonment of the Articles of Confederation.

Slight of build and reserved, James Madison of Virginia has been called the "father of the Constitution." He worked out a proposed plan of national government, then made arrangements to have it presented by Edmund Randolph, a more adept public speaker and Virginia's governor, at the outset of the convention. This strategy worked, and the delegates gave the "Virginia Plan" their undivided attention. The plan outlined a

James Madison, a strong nationalist, has been called the "father of the Constitution" for his plan of national government. He became the nation's fourth president.

three-tiered structure with an executive branch and two houses of Congress. Madison also envisioned a separate judicial branch.

Delegates from the less populous, smaller states objected. Under the Virginia Plan representatives to the two chambers of Congress would be apportioned to the states according to population, whereas under the Articles, each state, regardless of population, had an equal voice in national government. For such delegates as lawyer William Paterson of New Jersey, the latter practice ensured that the interests of the smaller states would not be sacrificed to those of the more populous, larger states. Thus Paterson countered with his "New Jersey Plan" on June 15. It retained equal voting in a unicameral national legislature, and it also vested far greater authority, including the powers of taxation and regulation of interstate and foreign commerce, in the central government.

On June 19 the delegates voted to adopt a three-tiered structure, but they did not resolve the question of how the states should be represented in the two new legislative branches. For several days it appeared as if the convention had reached an impasse, and some delegates were threatening to leave.

With Franklin and others calling for harmony, the delegates finally hammered out a settlement. Central to the "Great Compromise," which saved the convention from dissolving, was an agreement providing for proportional representation in the lower house (favoring the more populous states) and equality of representation in the upper house (favoring the less populous states). In the upper house each state would have two senators. Although the senators could vote independently of each other, they could also operate in tandem to protect state interests.

Having passed this crucial hurdle, the convention turned to other issues, not the least of which was slavery. Delegates from the Deep South wanted guarantees that would prevent any national tampering with their chattel property. Some northerners, however, including those who had supported abolition in their states, preferred constitutional restrictions on slavery. For a while, it looked as if there would be no compromise, but in the end both sides made concessions for the sake of union. By mutual agreement, the Constitution neither endorsed nor condemned slavery, nor can the word be found in the text. It did guarantee southerners that slaves would count as "three-fifths" of white persons for purposes of determining representation in the lower house. Although this meant more congressional seats for the South, direct taxes would be based on population, including "three-fifths of all other persons." Thus the South would pay more in taxes. The delegates also agreed that there would be no national legislation against the importation of slaves from abroad until at least 1808.

Although these clauses gave implicit recognition to slavery, it should be noted that the Northwest Land Ordinance of 1787, adopted by the Continental Congress in New York at the same time, forever barred slavery north of the Ohio River. The timing has led some historians to conclude that inhibiting the spread of slavery was also part of the compromise, representing a major concession to northern interests. The North-South Compromise kept the convention and the republic together by temporarily mollifying most delegates on an extremely divisive issue. Still, chattel slavery was so inconsistent with the ideals of human liberty that the problem could not be sidestepped for long.

A third set of issues provoking compromise had to do with the office of president. Nobody seemed sure what range of authority the national executive should have, how long the term of office should be, or how the president should be elected. By early September the delegates, fatigued by endless debates and extremely hot weather during three months of meetings, settled these questions quickly. The office of the president was potentially powerful. Besides serving as commander-in-chief of military forces, the incumbent could fashion treaties with foreign powers, subject to ratification by a two-thirds vote of the Senate. The president could veto congressional legislation, which both houses of Congress could only override with two-thirds majorities. Congress, in turn, had an important check on the president. It could impeach the executive if presidential powers were abused. Four years seemed like a reasonable term of office, and reelection would be possible.

To help insulate the president from manipulation by public opinion, the delegates made the office indirectly elective. They did so by creating the electoral college. Each state would have the same number of electors as representatives and senators. In states that permitted popular voting for the presidency, citizens would cast ballots for electors who favored particular candidates. In turn the electors would meet and each vote for the person they favored. The candidate with a majority of electoral college votes would become president. The person with the second highest total would become vice president. Should the electors fail to reach a majority decision, the election would be turned over to the House of Representatives, where each state would have one vote in choosing a president.

The subject of the presidency might have been more contentious had no person of George Washington's universally acclaimed stature been on the scene. Washington was the one authentic popular hero and symbol of national unity to emerge from the Revolution, and the delegates were already thinking of him as the first president. Since he was so fully trusted as a firm apostle of republican principles who had disdained the mantle of a military dictator, defining the mode of election and powers of the national executive were not insurmountable tasks.

The Ratification Struggle

Thirty-nine delegates affixed their signatures to the proposed Constitution on September 17, 1787. The delegates who signed knew there would be significant opposition because their plan cut so heavily into state authority. Before finishing their deliberations, they made the shrewd move of agreeing that only nine states needed to ratify the Constitution—through special state conventions rather than through state legislatures—to allow the new central government to commence operations. The nationalists were not going to let one or two states destroy months of work—and what they viewed as the best last hope for a languishing republic.

In another astute move, the nationalists started referring to themselves as *Federalists,* and they disarmed their opponents by calling them *Antifederalists.* Actually, the Antifederalists were the real federalists; they wanted to continue the confederation of sovereign states, and they sought to keep power as close as possible to the people, mostly in the hands of state governments. This confusion in terminology may have gotten some local Federalist candidates elected to state ratifying conventions, thus helping to secure victory for the Constitution.

The nationalists were also very effective in explaining the Convention's work. The essence of their argumentation appeared in *The Federalist Papers,* a series of 85 remarkably cogent newspaper essays written by James Madison, Alexander Hamilton, and John Jay on behalf of ratification in New York. Under the pseudonym "Publius," they discussed various aspects of the Constitution and tried to demonstrate how the document would ensure political stability and provide enlightened legislation.

The new government, they asserted, had been designed to protect the rights of all citizens. No one self-serving faction, whether representing a minority or majority of citizens, could take power completely and deprive others of their liberties and property. The Constitution would check and balance willful interest groups because basic powers would be divided among the various branches of government. And the system was truly federal, they argued, because much decision-making authority remained with the states as a further protection against power-hungry, self-serving factional interest groups.

Beyond these advantages, the Constitution embodied the principle of representative republicanism, as Madison explained in his famous *Federalist No. 10* essay. Large election districts for the House of Representatives would make it more difficult for factions to manipulate elections, enabling citizens of true merit to get elected and to enact laws beneficial for citizens everywhere.

The nationalists admitted that they were overturning the first constitutional settlement of 1776. The new emphasis on a strong central government was necessary, they believed, because the people had failed the test of public virtue. They had shown more interest in their individual welfare, for instance, than in making material or personal sacrifices to support the Continental war effort. They had formed into troublesome factions like the Maryland land speculators and the Massachusetts rebel followers of Daniel Shays, all to the detriment of the republic's political stability.

The nationalists, now expecting to function as the country's political stewards, did not repudiate the concept of popular sovereignty. Rather, they enshrined it in such concepts as representative republicanism. The people were to have a political voice, in the abstract at least. Their representatives, supposedly detached from selfish concerns, could now more easily check narrow interests inhibiting stable national development.

The Antifederalists viewed this new settlement with grave alarm. One writer feared that the Constitution would support "in practice a *permanent* ARISTOCRACY" of self-serving, wealthy citizens. Leading Antifederalists, among them Samuel Adams, Patrick Henry, and Richard Henry Lee, still had negative images of the distant British government, too far removed from the people to be checked in any effective way. Having rebelled against what they perceived as the tyranny of the British imperial government, they were not anxious to approve a plan for a new central government with enough power to threaten the states and the people with yet more political tyranny. They preferred life under the Articles of Confederation.

The Antifederalists failed to deflect nationalist momentum, even though there would be close calls in some ratifying conventions, such as in Massachusetts, New York, and Virginia. The well-organized nationalists were always ready to counter Antifederalist complaints. When there were objections about the absence of a national bill of rights guaranteeing each citizen fundamental liberties, they promised that the first Congress would prepare one. When there were cries for a second convention that would not overturn but modify the Articles of Confederation, they argued that the new government should first be given a chance. If it did not work, the nationalists stated, they would support another convention.

When the New Hampshire convention voted to ratify on June 21, 1788, the necessary nine states had given their approval. The two large states of Virginia and New York were still not in the fold, however, so everyone hesitated. Promises of a bill of rights helped bring the Virginia convention around in a close vote (89 yeas to 79 nays) on June 25. A month later, after much skillful Federalist maneuvering, the dominant

Antifederalists in New York conceded enough votes for ratification to occur by the slim margin of 30 yeas to 27 nays. Somewhat belatedly, North Carolina ratified the constitution in November 1789. Rhode Island, which had refused to participate in the Constitutional Convention, ratified the document by a close vote in 1790 only after the United States threatened to sever commercial ties.

Conclusion

In 1776 those radical revolutionaries who believed in a virtuous citizenry had sought to expand popular participation in government. By and large they succeeded. This first constitutional settlement proved to be unsatisfactory, however, largely because the weak central government under the

*C*hronology of Key Events

1775	Daniel Boone blazes the "Wilderness Road" to Kentucky; Lord Dunmore calls for the emancipation of Virginia's slaves
1775–1777	Several states adopt new state constitutions
1776–1777	Congress drafts the Articles of Confederation
1780	Pennsylvania becomes the first state to provide for the emancipation of slaves
1781	Articles of Confederation ratified by all the states
1783	Newburgh Conspiracy fails to produce a military coup
1784	Land Ordinance of 1784 guarantees western settlers territorial government
1785	Land Ordinance of 1785 provides for the survey and sale of western lands
1786	Virginia adopts Jefferson's Statute of Religious Freedom separating church and state; Shays's Rebellion; Annapolis Convention calls for a national constitutional convention
1787	Northwest Ordinance bars slavery north of the Ohio River; Constitutional Convention convenes in Philadelphia
1787–1788	Constitution ratified by eleven states

Articles of Confederation lacked the authority to support even the minimal needs of the new nation. Blaming the states and the people, the nationalist leaders produced a second constitutional settlement in 1787 by drafting a plan for a more powerful central government. It was to be above the people and the states, strong enough to establish and preserve national unity and stability.

The new republic began functioning in 1789. Yet the full potential of republican ideals had yet to be realized. Notions regarding each American's right to enjoy life, liberty, happiness, and property in an equalitarian society fell far short of full implementation. Women remained second-class citizens, and the bonds of slavery still manacled most African Americans. Even with the opening of the trans-Appalachian West, which came at the expense of thousands of Native Americans, poorer citizens found it difficult to gain access to farmland on which they could provide for themselves and secure their personal prosperity. Nonetheless, the years between 1776 and 1789 had witnessed a revolution in human expectations. The foundations of what would one day be a system of political democracy had been laid.

Suggestions for Further Reading

Valuable overviews of the early national period include Merrill Jensen, *The New Nation, 1781–1789* (1950); Forrest McDonald, *E Pluribus Unum: The Formation of the American Republic, 1776–1790* (1965); and Gordon S. Wood, *The Creation of the American Republic, 1776–1787* (1969).

On the crises that beset the Confederation see E. James Ferguson, *The Power of the Purse* (1961); David Szatmary, *Shays's Rebellion* (1980).

On the social impact of the American Revolution consult David Brion Davis, *The Problem of Slavery in the Age of Revolution* (1975); Philip S. Foner, *Labor and the American Revolution* (1977); Sylvia R. Frey, *Water from the Rock: Black Resistance in a Revolutionary Age* (1991); J. Franklin Jameson, *The American Revolution Considered as a Social Movement* (1926); Linda Kerber, *Women of the Republic* (1980); Mary Beth Norton, *Liberty's Daughters: The Revolutionary Experience of American Women, 1750–1800* (1980); and Laurel Thatcher Ulrich, *A Midwife's Tale: The Life of Martha Ballard* (1990).

For important studies of the Philadelphia convention, see Charles A. Beard, *An Economic Interpretation of the Constitution of the United States* (1913); Forrest McDonald, *We the People: The Economic Origins of the Constitution* (1958), and *Novus Ordo Seclorum: The Intellectual Origins of the Constitution* (1985). For insights into the opponents of the Constitution, see Jackson T. Main, *The Antifederalists* (1961). See also Robert Rutland, *James Madison, the Founding Father* (1987); Jack N. Rakove, *James Madison and the Creation of the American Republic* (1990).

Chapter 7

Shaping the New Nation, 1789–1800

The United States was the first nation in history to institute a periodic national census. Since 1790, the country has tried to count each man, woman, and child every ten years. The first census asked just six simple questions, yet when supplemented with other statistical information, it provides a treasure chest of information about the social and economic life of the American people.

Taking the nation's first census was an extraordinarily difficult challenge. The nation's sheer physical size—stretching across 867,980 square miles—made it impossible to conduct an accurate count. Many people refused to speak to census takers; some because they feared that this was a step toward enactment of new taxes, others because they felt that the Bible prohibited census taking. To make matters worse, census takers were abysmally paid, receiving just $1 for every 150 rural residents and $1 for every 300 city dwellers counted. Indeed, the pay was so low that one judge found it difficult to find "any person whatever" to take the census.

What was the United States like in 1790? According to the first census, the United States contained just 3,929,214 people, about half living in the northern states, half in the South. At first glance, the population seems quite small (it was only about a quarter the size of England's and a sixth the size of France's). But it was growing extraordinarily rapidly. Just 1.17 million in 1750, the population would pass five million by 1800.

The 1790 census revealed a nation still overwhelmingly rural in character. In a population of nearly four million, only two cities had more than 25,000 people. Yet the urban population, while small, was growing extremely rapidly, especially in the West, where frontier towns like Louisville started to sprout.

In 1790, most Americans still lived on the Atlantic coast. Nevertheless, the West was the most rapidly growing part of the nation. During the 1790s, the population of Kentucky and Tennessee increased nearly 300 percent, and by 1800, Kentucky had more people than five of the original 13 states.

The first census also revealed an extraordinarily youthful population, with half the people under the age of 16. Exceptionally diverse, three-fifths of the white population was English in ancestry and another fifth was Scottish or Irish. The remainder was of German, Dutch, French, Swedish, or other background. A fifth of the entire population was African-American.

Records indicate that the American economy was still quite undeveloped. There were fewer than 100 newspapers in the entire country; three banks (with total capital of less than $5 million); three insurance companies; and 75 post offices. And yet the United States was perched on the edge of an extraordinary decade of growth.

Over the next ten years, American society made tremendous economic advances. During the 1790s, states chartered almost ten times more corporations, banks, and transportation companies than during the 1780s. Exports climbed from $29 million to $107 million; cotton production rose from 3,000 bales to 73,000 bales. The number of patents issued increased from just three in 1790 to 44 in 1800. Altogether, 11 mechanized mills were built in the country during the 1790s, laying the foundations of future economic growth.

In 1800, as in 1790, the United States remained a nation of farms, plantations, and small towns, of yeomen, slaves, and artisans. Nevertheless, the nation was undergoing far-reaching social and economic transformations. Improvements in education and culture were particularly striking. Between 1783 and 1800, Americans founded 17 new colleges and a large number of female academies.

For the young United States, the last years of the eighteenth century were a period of rapid demographic and economic growth. They were also years of crucial political developments. During this period the United States adopted a bill of rights protecting individual liberties, enacted a financial program securing the nation's credit, and created its first political parties. It was during this dramatic era that the United States established a strong and vigorous national government.

Putting the New National Government into Operation

The United States was the first modern nation to achieve independence through a successful revolution against colonial rule. Although many colonies in the nineteenth and twentieth centuries followed the example of the United States in winning independence through revolution, few were as successful in subsequently developing politically and economically. Even the United States, however, struggled to establish itself in its first decade under the Constitution.

The new nation faced severe economic and foreign policy problems. A huge debt remained from the Revolutionary War, and paper money issued during the war was virtually worthless. Along with these pressing economic problems were foreign threats to the new nation's independence. In violation of the peace treaty of 1783 ending the Revolutionary War, Britain continued to occupy forts in the Old Northwest, and Spain refused to recognize the new nation's southern and western boundaries. In 1790, economic problems, domestic political conflict, and foreign policy issues challenged the new nation in its efforts to establish a stable republic.

Setting Up a New Government

The first task facing American leaders was to establish the machinery of government. The new United States government consisted of nothing more than 75 post offices, a large debt, a small number of unpaid clerks, and an army of just 46 officers and 672 soldiers. There was no federal court system, no navy, and no system for collecting taxes.

It fell to Congress to take the initial steps toward putting the new national government into operation. To raise revenue, it passed a tariff on imported goods and an excise tax on liquor. To encourage American shipping, it imposed duties on foreign vessels. To provide a structure for the executive branch of government, it created departments of State, Treasury, and War. By the Judiciary Act of 1789, Congress organized a federal judiciary, which consisted of a Supreme Court with six justices, a district court in each state, and three appeals courts.

To strengthen popular support for the new government, Congress also approved a Bill of Rights for the Constitution. These first ten amendments guaranteed the rights of free press, free speech, and religion; the right to peaceful assembly; and the right to petition government. The Bill of Rights also ensured that the national government could not infringe on the right to trial by jury. In an effort to reassure Antifederalists that the powers of the new government were limited, the tenth amendment "reserved to the States respectively, or to the people" all powers not specified in the Constitution.

Defining the Presidency

The Constitution provided only a broad outline of the office and powers of the president. Important issues that would profoundly affect future generations of Americans remained unsettled. It would be up to George Washington, as the first president, to define the office, and to establish many precedents regarding the president's relationship with the other branches of government. It was unclear, for example, whether the president was to personally run the executive branch or, instead, act like a constitutional monarch and delegate responsibility to the vice president and executive officers, called the "cabinet." Washington favored a strong and active role for the president. Modeling the executive branch along the lines of a general's staff, Washington consulted his cabinet officers and listened to them carefully, but he made the final decisions, just as he had done while serving as commander-in-chief.

The relationship between the executive and legislative branches was also uncertain. Should a president, like Britain's prime minister, personally appear before Congress to defend administration policies? Should the Senate have sole power to dismiss executive officials? The answers to such questions were not clear. Washington insisted that the president could dismiss presidential appointees without the Senate's permission. A bitterly divided Senate approved this principle by a single vote.

With regard to foreign policy, Washington tried to follow the literal words of the Constitution, which stated that the president should negotiate treaties with the advice and consent of the Senate. He appeared before the Senate in person to discuss a pending Indian treaty. The senators, however, refused to provide immediate answers and referred the matter to a committee. "This defeats every purpose of my coming here," Washington declared. In the future he negotiated treaties first and then sent them to the Senate for ratification.

The most difficult task that the president faced was deciding whom to nominate for public office. For secretary of war, Washington nominated Henry Knox, an old military comrade, who had held a similar position under the Articles of Confederation. As postmaster general, he named Samuel Osgood of Massachusetts, who carried out his tasks in a single room with the help of two clerks. For attorney general, he tapped fellow Virginian Edmund Randolph, and John Jay as chief justice of the Supreme Court. He nominated a fellow Virginian, Thomas Jefferson, to the State Department. He named his former aide-de-camp, the 34-year-old Alexander Hamilton, to head the Treasury Department.

Alexander Hamilton's Financial Program

The most pressing problems facing the new government were economic. As a result of the Revolution, the federal government had acquired a huge debt: $54 million including interest. The states owed another $25 million. Paper money issued under the Continental Congresses and the Articles of Confederation was worthless. Foreign credit was unavailable.

Ten days after Alexander Hamilton became treasury secretary, Congress asked him to report on ways to solve the nation's financial problems. Hamilton, a man of strong political convictions, immediately realized that he had an opportunity to create a financial program that would embody his political principles.

Hamilton believed that the nation's stability depended on an alliance between the government and citizens of wealth and influence. No society could succeed, he maintained, "which did not unite the interest and credit of rich individuals with those of the state." Unlike Thomas Jefferson, Hamilton doubted the capacity of common people to govern themselves. "The people are turbulent and changing," he maintained, "they seldom judge or determine right."

To keep the masses in check, Hamilton favored a strong national government. Born in the British West Indies, Hamilton never developed the

George Washington's first cabinet consisted of Secretary of War Henry Knox, Secretary of the Treasury Alexander Hamilton, Secretary of State Thomas Jefferson, and Attorney General Edmund Randolph.

intense loyalty to a state that was common among many Americans of the time. He wanted to create a unified nation and a powerful federal government, intending to use government fiscal policies to strengthen federal power at the expense of the states and "make it in the immediate interest of the moneyed men to co-operate with government in its support."

The paramount problem facing Hamilton was the huge national debt. In 1790, the national debt totaled about $79 million. Hamilton argued that it was vital for the nation to fund these debts in order to establish the credit of the federal government. He proposed in his "Report on the Public Credit" (1790) that the government assume the entire indebtedness—principal and interest—of the federal government and the states.

This proposal ignited a firestorm of controversy, since states like Maryland, Pennsylvania, North Carolina, and Virginia had already paid off their war debts. They saw no reason why they should be taxed by the federal government to pay off the debts of states like Massachusetts and South Carolina. Others opposed the scheme because it would provide enormous profits to speculators who had bought bonds from Revolutionary War veterans for as little as 10 or 15 cents on the dollar. Many of these financial speculators were associates of Hamilton or members of Congress who knew that Hamilton's report would recommend full payment of the debt.

For six months a bitter debate raged in Congress. The nation's future seemed in jeopardy until a compromise orchestrated by James Madison and Thomas Jefferson secured passage of Hamilton's plan. In exchange for southern votes in Congress, Hamilton promised his support for locating the future national capital on the banks of the Potomac River, the border between two southern states, Virginia and Maryland.

Hamilton's debt program was a remarkable success. Funding and assumption of the debt created pools of capital for business investment and firmly established the credit of the United States abroad. By demonstrating Americans' willingness to repay their debts, he made America a good credit risk attractive to foreign investors. European investment capital started pouring into the new nation in large amounts.

Hamilton's next objective was to create a Bank of the United States, modeled after the Bank of England, to issue currency, collect taxes, hold government funds, regulate the nation's financial system, and make loans to the government and private borrowers. This proposal, like his debt scheme, unleashed a storm of protest.

One criticism directed against the bank was that it threatened to undermine the nation's republican values. Banks—and the paper money they issued—would simply encourage speculation, stock-jobbing and corruption. The bank was also opposed on constitutional grounds. Adopting a position known as "strict constructionism," Thomas Jefferson and James Madison charged that a national bank was unconstitutional since the Constitution did not specifically give Congress the power to create a bank. Other grounds for criticism were that the bank would subject America to foreign influences (because foreigners would have to purchase a high percentage of the bank's stock) and give a propertied elite disproportionate influence over the nation's fiscal policies (since private investors would control the bank's board of directors). Worse yet, the bank would increase the public debt, which, in turn, would add to the nation's tax burden. Under Hamilton's plan, the bank would raise capital by selling stock to private investors. Investors could pay for up to three-quarters of the bank stock they purchased with government bonds of indebtedness. The burden of financing the bank, therefore, would ultimately rest on the public treasury.

Hamilton responded to the charge that a bank was unconstitutional by formulating the doctrine of "implied powers." He argued that Congress did have the power to create a bank since the Constitution granted the federal government authority to do anything "necessary and proper" to carry out its constitutional functions (in this case its fiscal duties). This represented the first attempt to defend a "loose" interpretation of the Constitution.

In 1791 Congress passed a bill creating a national bank for a term of 20 years. The first Bank of the United States, like Hamilton's debt plan, was a great success. It helped regulate the currency of private banks. It provided a reserve of capital on which the government and private investors drew. It helped attract foreign investment to the credit-short new nation. In 1811, however, the jealousy of private commercial banks convinced Congress to allow the bank, which was chartered for a maximum of 20 years, to expire.

The final step in Hamilton's economic program was a proposal to aid the nation's infant industries. In his *Report on Manufactures* (1791), Hamilton argued that the nation's long-term interests "will be advanced, rather than injured, by the due encouragement of manufactures." Through high tariffs designed to protect American industry from foreign

The National Bank of the United States, which opened in Philadelphia in 1791, was a key part of Alexander Hamilton's economic plan for a strong central government.

competition, government bounties and subsidies, and internal improvements of transportation, he hoped to break Britain's manufacturing hold on America.

Opposition to Hamilton's proposal came from many quarters. Many Americans feared that the proposal would excessively cut federal revenues by discouraging imports. Shippers worried that the plan would reduce foreign trade. Farmers feared the proposal would lead foreign countries to impose retaliatory tariffs on American agricultural products.

The most eloquent opposition came from Thomas Jefferson, who believed that the growth of manufacturing threatened the values of an agrarian way of life. Hamilton's industrial vision of America's future directly challenged Jefferson's ideal of a nation of freehold farmers, tilling the fields, communing with nature, and maintaining personal freedom by virtue of land ownership. Manufacturing, Jefferson believed, should be left to European cities, which were cesspools of human corruption. Like slaves, factory workers would be manipulated by their masters, who not only would deny them satisfying lives but also would make it impossible for them to think and act as independent citizens.

Congress rejected most of Hamilton's proposals to aid industry. Nevertheless, the debate over Hamilton's plan carried with it fateful consequences. Fundamental disagreements had arisen between Hamiltonians and Jeffersonians over the federal government's role, constitutional interpretation, and distinct visions of how the republic should develop. To resolve these fundamental differences, Americans would create modern political parties—parties the writers of the Constitution neither wanted nor planned for.

The Birth of Political Parties

When George Washington assembled his first cabinet, there were no national political parties in the United States. In selecting cabinet members, he paid no attention to partisan labels and simply chose the individuals he believed were best qualified to run the new nation. Similarly, the new Congress had no party divisions. In all the states except Pennsylvania, politics was not waged between parties but, rather, between impermanent factions built around leading families, political managers, ethnic groups, or such interest groups as debtors and creditors.

By the time Washington retired from the presidency in 1797, the nature of the American political system had radically changed. The first president devoted part of his "Farewell Address" to denouncing "the baneful effects of the Spirit of Party," which had come to dominate American politics. Local and state factions had given way to two competing national parties, known as the Federalists and the Republicans. They nominated political candidates, managed electoral campaigns, and represented distinctive outlooks or ideologies. By 1796, the United States had produced its first modern party system. These political parties breathed new life into the concept of popular sovereignty, by making the people the ultimate arbiters in American political life.

The framers of the Constitution had not prepared their plan of government with political parties in mind. They associated parties with the interest groups that dominated the British government and hoped that in the United States the "better sort of citizens," rising above popular self-interest, would debate key issues and reach a harmonious consensus regarding how best to legislate for the nation's future.

Yet despite a belief that parties were evil and posed a threat to enlightened government, political factions gradually coalesced into political parties during Washington's first administration. To build support for his financial programs, Alexander Hamilton relied heavily on government patronage. Of 2,000 federal officeholders appointed between 1789 and 1801, two-thirds were Federalist party activists, who used positions as postmasters, tax collectors, judges, and customs house officials to favor the interests of the Federalists. By 1794 Hamilton's faction and its opponents had evolved into the first national political parties in history capable of nominating candidates, coordinating votes in Congress, staging public meetings, organizing petition campaigns, and disseminating propaganda.

Hamilton's opponents struck back. Madison and his ally Thomas Jefferson saw in Hamilton's program an effort to establish the kind of corrupt patronage society that existed in Britain, with a huge public debt, a standing army, high taxes, and government-subsidized monopolies. Hamilton's aim, declared Jefferson, was to assimilate "the American government to the form and spirit of the British monarchy."

World Events and Political Polarization

World events intensified partisan divisions. On July 14, 1789, 20,000 French men and women stormed the Bastille, a hated royal fortress, marking the beginning of the French Revolution. For three years France experimented with a constitutional monarchy. Then in 1792, the revolution took a violent turn. In August, Austrian and Prussian troops invaded France to put an end to the revolution. French revolutionaries responded by deposing King Louis XVI and placing him on trial. He was found guilty and, in January 1793, beheaded. France declared itself a republic and launched a reign of terror against counterrevolutionary elements in the population. A general war erupted in Europe pitting revolutionary France against a coalition of European monarchies, led by Britain. With two brief interruptions, this war would last 23 years.

Many Americans reacted enthusiastically to the overthrow of the king and the creation of a French republic. The French people appeared to have joined America in a historic struggle against royal absolutism and aristocratic privilege. More cautious men of privilege expressed horror at the cataclysm sweeping France. The French Revolution, they feared, was not merely a rebellion against royal authority, but a mass assault against property and Christianity. Conservatives urged President Washington to support England in its war against France.

Washington believed that involvement in the European war would weaken the new nation before it had firmly established its own independence. He proposed to keep the country "free from political connections with every other country, to see them independent of all, and under the influence of none." The president, however, faced a problem. During the War for American Independence, the United States had signed an alliance with France. Washington took the position that while the United States should continue to make payments on its war debts to France, it should refrain from directly supporting the new French Republic. In April 1793 he issued a proclamation of neutrality, stating that the "conduct" of the United States would be "friendly and impartial toward the belligerent powers."

1793 and 1794: Years of Crisis

During 1793 and 1794 a series of explosive new controversies further divided the followers of Hamilton and Jefferson. Washington's administration confronted a French effort to entangle America in its war with England, armed rebellion in western Pennsylvania, Indian uprisings, and the threat of war with Britain. These controversies intensified party spirit and promoted an increase in voting along party lines in Congress.

In April 1793, "Citizen" Edmond Charles Genêt, minister of the French Republic, arrived in the United States. His mission was to persuade American citizens to join in France's "war of all peoples against all kings." Genêt proceeded to pass out military commissions as part of a plan to attack Spanish New Orleans, and letters authorizing Americans to attack British commercial vessels. Washington regarded these activities as clear violations of U.S. neutrality, and demanded that France recall its hot headed minister. Fearful of continued political turmoil at home, Genêt requested and was granted political asylum, bringing his ill-fated mission to an end. However, the Genêt affair did have an important effect—it intensified party feeling. From Vermont to South Carolina, citizens organized Democratic-Republican clubs to celebrate the triumphs of the French Revolution. Hamilton suspected that these societies really existed to stir up grass-roots opposition to the Washington administration. Jefferson hotly denied these accusations, but the practical consequence was to further divide followers of Hamilton and Jefferson.

Political polarization was further intensified by the outbreak of popular protests in western Pennsylvania against Hamilton's financial program. To help fund the nation's war debt, Congress in 1791 passed Hamilton's proposal for a whiskey excise tax. Frontier farmers objected to the tax on whiskey as unfair. On the frontier, because of high transportation costs, the only practical way to sell surplus corn was to distill it into whiskey. Thus, frontier farmers regarded a tax on whiskey in the same way as American colonists had regarded Britain's stamp tax.

By 1794 western Pennsylvanians had had enough. Like the Shaysites of 1786, they rose up in defense of their property and the fundamental right to earn a decent living. Some 7,000 frontiersmen marched on Pittsburgh to stop collection of the tax. Determined to set a precedent for the federal government's authority, Washington gathered an army of 15,000 militiamen to disperse the rebels. In the face of this overwhelming force, the uprising collapsed. Two men were convicted of treason, but later pardoned by the president. The new government had proved that it would enforce laws enacted by Congress.

Thomas Jefferson viewed the Whiskey Rebellion from quite a different perspective. He saw the fiendish hand of Hamilton in putting down what he called a rebellion that "could never be found." Further, Jefferson claimed, Hamilton had used the army to stifle legitimate opposition to unfair government policies.

The year 1794 also brought a crisis in America's relations with Britain. For a decade, Britain had refused to evacuate forts in the Old Northwest as promised in the treaty ending the Revolution. Control of those forts impeded white settlement of the Great Lakes region and allowed the British to monopolize the fur trade. Frontiersmen believed that British officials at those posts sold firearms to the Indians and incited uprisings against white settlers. War appeared imminent when British warships stopped 300 American ships carrying food supplies to France and to France's overseas possessions, seized their cargoes, and forced seamen suspected of deserting from British ships into the British navy.

Washington acted decisively to end the crisis. He first moved to end the Indian threat. He called upon Revolutionary War veteran Anthony Wayne to clear the Ohio country of Indians. On August 20, 1794, Wayne's soldiers overwhelmed the resisting Indians at the Battle of Fallen Timbers in northwestern Ohio. Wayne later met with representatives of the Miami Confederacy and negotiated the Treaty of Greenville. Under

President Washington is reviewing the troops at Fort Cumberland, Maryland. These troops formed part of the force of 15,000 militiamen Washington assembled to disperse the Whiskey Rebellion in western Pennsylvania, a protest against the whiskey excise tax.

this agreement, Native Americans ceded much of the present state of Ohio in return for cash, presents, and a promise that the federal government would treat the Indian nations fairly in land dealings.

The president next sent Chief Justice John Jay to London to seek a negotiated settlement with the British. The United States's strongest bargaining chip was a threat to join an alliance of European trading nations to resist British trade restrictions. Alexander Hamilton may have undercut Jay by secretly informing the British minister that the United States would not join the alliance.

Jay secured the best agreement he could under the circumstances. Britain agreed to evacuate its forts on American soil, and promised to cease harassing American shipping (provided the ships did not carry contraband to Britain's enemies). Britain additionally agreed to pay damages for the ships it had seized and to permit the United States to trade with India and to carry on restricted trade with the British West Indies. But Jay failed to win concessions on a host of other American grievances, such as British incitement of the Indians, and Britain's routine searching of American ships for escaping deserters.

As a result of the debate over Jay's Treaty, the first party system fully emerged. Publication of the terms of the treaty unleashed a storm of protest from the emerging Jeffersonian Republicans. Republican newspapers and pamphlets denounced the treaty as craven submission to British imperial power and wealthy commercial, shipping, and trading interests. In Philadelphia a mob hanged Jay in effigy; in New York angry crowds pelted Alexander Hamilton with stones.

Washington never anticipated the wave of outrage that greeted his decision to sign the treaty. Republicans accused him of forming an Anglo-American alliance, and they made his last years in office miserable by attacking him for conducting himself like a "tyrant." They sought to kill the treaty in the House of Representatives by refusing to appropriate the funds necessary to carry out the treaty's terms unless the president submitted all documents relating to the treaty negotiations. Washington refused to comply with the House's request for information, thereby establishing the principle of executive privilege. This precedent gives the chief executive authority to withhold information from Congress on grounds of national security. In the end, fear that rejection of the Jay Treaty would result in disunion or war convinced the House to approve the needed appropriations.

Washington's popularity returned within a few months when he was able to announce that a treaty had been negotiated with Spain opening up the Mississippi River to American trade. Spain, fearing joint British and American action against its American colonies, recognized the Mississippi River as the new nation's western boundary and the 31st parallel (the northern border of Florida) as America's southern boundary. Pinckney's Treaty (1795)—also known as the Treaty of San Lorenzo—also granted Americans the right to navigate the Mississippi River as well as the right to export goods, duty free, through New Orleans, which was still a Spanish city.

Washington Decides to Retire

President Washington was now in a position to retire gracefully. He had avoided war, crushed the Indians, pushed the British out of western forts, established trade with selected parts of Asia, and opened the Northwest Territory to settlement. In his Farewell Address, published in a Philadelphia newspaper in 1796, Washington warned his countrymen against the growth of partisan divisions. In foreign affairs, he warned against long-term alliances. Declaring the "primary interests" of America and Europe to be fundamentally different, he argued that "it is our true policy to steer clear of permanent alliance with any portion of the foreign world."

A New President and New Challenges

Washington's decision to retire set the stage for one of the most critical presidential elections in American history. The election of 1796 was the first in which voters could choose between competing political parties; it was also the first election in which candidates were nominated for the vice presidency. It was a critical test of whether the nation could transfer power through a contested election.

The Federalists chose John Adams, the first vice president, as their presidential candidate, and the Republicans selected Thomas Jefferson. In an effort to attract southern support, the Federalists named Thomas Pinckney of South Carolina as Adams's running mate. The Republicans, hopeful of attracting votes in New York and New England, chose Aaron Burr of New York as their vice-presidential nominee.

Both parties turned directly to the people, rallying supporters through the use of posters, handbills, and rallies. For the first time in American history, the mass of people became directly involved in a presidential election. Republicans portrayed their candidate as "a firm Republican" while they depicted his opponent as "the champion of rank, titles, and hereditary distinctions." Federalists countered by condemning Jefferson as the leader of a "French faction" intent on undermining religion and morality.

In the popular voting, Federalists drew support from New England; commercial, shipping, manufacturing, and banking interests; Congregational and Episcopalian clergy; professionals; and farmers who produced for markets. Republicans attracted votes from the South and from smaller planters; backcountry Baptists, Methodists, and Roman Catholics; small merchants, tradesmen, and craftsmen; and subsistence farmers.

John Adams won the election, despite backstage maneuvering by Alexander Hamilton, who disliked Adams intensely. Hamilton developed a complicated scheme to elect Thomas Pinckney, the Federalist candidate for vice president. Under the electoral system originally set up by the Constitution, each presidential elector was allowed to vote twice, with the candidate who received the most votes becoming president, while the candidate who came in second was elected vice president. According to Hamilton's plan, southern electors would drop Adams's name from their ballots, while still voting for Pinckney. Thus Pinckney would receive more votes than Adams and be elected president. When New Englanders learned of this plan, they dropped Pinckney from their ballots, ensuring that Adams won the election. When the final votes were tallied, Adams received 71 votes, only three more than Jefferson. As a result, Jefferson became vice president.

The Presidency of John Adams

The new president was a 61-year-old Harvard-educated lawyer who had been an early leader in the struggle for independence. Short, bald, over-weight, and vain (he was known, behind his back, as "His Rotundity"), Adams had found the vice presidency extremely frustrating. He complained to his wife Abigail: "My country has contrived for me the most insignificant office that ever the invention of man contrived or his imagination conceived."

His presidency also proved frustrating. He had failed to win a decisive electoral mandate and was saddled with the opposition leader as his vice president. He faced intense opposition within his own party and continuing problems from France throughout his four years in office. He avoided outright war with France, but he destroyed his political career. He suggested for his epitaph: "Here lies John Adams, who took upon himself the responsibility of the peace with France, in the year 1800."

The Quasi-War with France

A decade after the Constitution was written, the United States faced its most serious international crisis: an undeclared naval war with France. In the Jay Treaty, France perceived an American tilt toward Britain, especially in the provision permitting the British to seize French goods from American ships in exchange for financial compensation. France retaliated by launching an aggressive campaign against American shipping, particularly in the West Indies, capturing hundreds of vessels flying the United States flag.

Adams attempted to negotiate with France, but the French government refused to receive the American envoy and suspended commercial relations. Adams then called Congress into special session. Determined not to permit the United States to be "humiliated," he recommended that Congress arm American merchant ships, purchase new naval vessels, fortify harbors, and expand the artillery and cavalry. To pay for it all, Adams recommended a series of new taxes. By a single vote, a bitterly divided House of Representatives authorized the president to arm American merchant ships, but it postponed consideration of the other defense measures.

Adams then sent three commissioners to France to try to negotiate a settlement. Charles Maurice de Talleyrand, the French foreign minister, continually postponed official negotiations. In the meantime, three emissaries of the French minister (known later simply as X, Y, and Z) said that the only way the Americans could see the minister was to pay a bribe of

$250,000 and provide France with a $10 million loan. The indignant American commissioners refused. When word of the "XYZ affair" became known in the United States, it aroused a popular demand for war. The popular slogan was "millions for defense, but not one cent for tribute." The Federalist-controlled Congress authorized a standing army of 20,000 troops, a 30,000 man reserve army, and created the nation's first navy department. It also unilaterally abrogated America's 1778 treaty with France.

Adams named George Washington commanding general of the United States army, and, at Washington's insistence, designated Alexander Hamilton second in command. During the winter of 1798, 14 American warships backed by some 200 armed merchant ships captured some 80 French vessels and forced French warships out of American waters and back to bases in the West Indies. But the president refused to ask Congress for an official declaration of war. This is why this conflict is known as the quasi-war.

Despite intense pressure to declare war against France or to seize territory belonging to France's ally Spain, President Adams succeeded in averting full-scale war and achieving a peaceful settlement. Early in 1799, with the backing of moderate Federalists and Republicans, Adams proposed reestablishing diplomatic relations with France. When more extreme Federalists refused to go along with the plan, Adams threatened to resign and leave the presidency in the hands of Vice-President Jefferson.

In 1800, after seven months of wearisome negotiations, diplomats worked out an agreement known as the Convention of 1800. The agreement freed the United States from its alliance with France; in exchange, America forgave $20 million in damages caused by the illegal seizure of American merchant ships during the 1790s.

Adams kept the peace, but at the cost of a second term as president. The more extreme Federalists reacted furiously to the negotiated settlement. Hamilton vowed to destroy Adams: "If we must have an enemy at the head of Government, let it be one whom we can oppose, and for whom we are not responsible."

The Alien and Sedition Acts

During the quasi war the Federalist-controlled Congress attempted to suppress political opposition and stamp out sympathy for revolutionary France by enacting four laws in 1798 known as the Alien and Sedition acts. The Naturalization Act lengthened the period necessary before immigrants could receive citizenship from 5 to 14 years. The Alien Act gave the president the power to imprison or deport any foreigner believed to be dangerous to the United States. The Alien Enemies Act allowed the president to deport enemy aliens in time of war. Finally, the Sedition Act made it a crime to attack the government with "false, scandalous, or malicious" statements or writings. Adams, bitterly unhappy with the "spirit of falsehood and malignity" that threatened to undermine loyalty to the government, signed the measures.

The Alien acts were so broadly written that hundreds of foreign refugees fled to Europe fearing detention. But it was the Sedition Act that produced the greatest fear within the Republican opposition. Federalist prosecutors and judges used the Sedition Act to attack leading Republican newspapers, securing indictments against 25 people, mainly Republican editors and printers. Ten people were eventually convicted, one a Republican Congressman from Vermont.

Republicans accused the Federalists of conspiring to subvert fundamental liberties. In Virginia the state legislature adopted a resolution written by James Madison that advanced the idea that states have the right to determine the constitutionality of federal law, and pronounced the Alien and Sedition acts unconstitutional. Kentucky's state legislature went even further, adopting a resolution written by Thomas Jefferson that declared the Alien and Sedition acts "void and of no force." The Kentucky resolution raised an issue that would grow increasingly important in American politics in the years before the Civil War: Did states have the power to declare acts of Congress null and void? In 1799, however, no other states were willing to go as far as Kentucky and Virginia.

With the Union in danger, violence erupted. In the spring of 1799, German settlers in eastern Pennsylvania rose up in defiance of federal tax collectors. President Adams called out federal troops to suppress the so-called Fries Rebellion. The leader of the rebellion, an auctioneer named John Fries, was captured, convicted of treason, and sentenced to be hanged. Adams followed Washington's example in the Whiskey Rebellion and pardoned Fries, but Republicans feared that the Federalists were prepared to use the nation's army to suppress dissent.

The Revolution of 1800

In 1800 the young republic faced another critical test: Could national leadership pass peacefully from one political party to another? Once again, the nation had a choice between John Adams and Thomas Jefferson. But this election was more than a contest between two men; it was also a real party contest for control of the national government. Deep substantive and ideological issues divided the two parties. Federalists feared that Jefferson would reverse all the accomplishments of the preceding 12 years. A Republican president, they thought, would overthrow the Constitution by returning power to the states, dismantling the army and navy, and overturning Hamilton's financial system.

The Republicans charged that the Federalists, by creating a large standing army, imposing heavy taxes, and using federal troops and the federal courts to suppress dissent, had shown contempt for the liberties of the American people. They worried that the Federalists' ultimate goal was to centralize power in the national government and involve the United States in the European war on the side of Britain.

The contest was one of the most vigorous in American history and emotions ran high. Jefferson's Federalist opponents called him an "atheist in religion, and a fanatic in politics." They claimed he was a drunkard, an enemy of religion, and the father of numerous mulatto children. Jefferson's supporters responded by charging that President Adams was a warmonger, a spendthrift, and a monarchist who longed to reunite Britain with its former colonies.

The election was extremely close. The Federalists won all of New England's electoral votes, while the Republicans dominated the South and West. The final outcome hinged on the results in New York. Rural New York supported the Federalists, and Republican fortunes therefore depended on the voting in New York City. There, Jefferson's running mate, Aaron Burr, had created the most successful political organization the country had yet seen. Burr organized rallies, established ward committees, and promoted loyal supporters for public office. Burr's efforts paid off; Republicans won a majority in New York's legislature, which gave the state's 12 electoral votes to Jefferson and Burr.

Jefferson appeared to have won by a margin of eight electoral votes. But a complication soon arose. Because each Republican elector had cast one ballot for Jefferson and one for Burr, the two men received exactly the same number of electoral votes. Under the Constitution, the election was now thrown into the Federalist-controlled House of Representatives. Instead of emphatically declaring that he would not accept the presidency, Burr refused to say anything. So the Federalists faced a choice: they could help elect the hated Jefferson, or they could throw their support to the opportunistic Burr. Hamilton disliked Jefferson, but he believed he was a far more honorable man than Burr, whose "public principles have no other spring or aim than his own aggrandizement."

On February 17, 1801, after six days of balloting and 36 ballots, the House of Representatives finally elected Thomas Jefferson the third president of the United States. And as a result of the election, Congress adopted the Twelfth Amendment to the Constitution, which provides for separate ballots for president and for vice president.

Conclusion

In 1789 it was an open question whether the Constitution was a workable plan of government. It was still unclear if the new nation could establish a strong and vigorous national government or win the respect of foreign nations. For a decade, the new nation battled threats to its existence. It faced bitter party conflict, threats of secession, and foreign interference with American shipping and commerce.

*C*hronology of Key Events

1789	First session of Congress meets; Electoral College names George Washington the first president; Washington selects the first cabinet; Federal Judiciary Act establishes federal court system; French Revolution begins
1790	Congress adopts Hamilton's proposal to fund the national debt at full value and to assume all state debts
1791	Bank of the United States established; Congress adopts excise tax on distilled liquors; Bill of Rights becomes part of the Constitution
1793	Washington issues Neutrality Proclamation; Citizen Genêt affair
1794	Jay's Treaty; Whiskey Rebellion; Battle of Fallen Timbers
1795	Treaty of Greenville opens Ohio to white settlement; Pinckney Treaty negotiated with Spain
1796	Washington's Farewell Address
1797	John Adams inaugurated as second president
1798	XYZ Affair; undeclared naval war with France begins; Alien and Sedition acts; Virginia and Kentucky resolutions declare Alien and Sedition acts unconstitutional
1800	Washington, D.C. becomes nation's capital; Convention of 1800
1801	House of Representatives elects Thomas Jefferson as third president

By any standard, the new nation's achievements were impressive. During the first decade under the Constitution, the country adopted a bill of rights, protecting the rights of the individual against the power of the central and state governments; enacted a financial program that secured the government's credit and stimulated the economy; and created the first political parties that directly involved the enfranchised segment of the population in national politics. In the face of intense partisan conflict, the United States became the first nation to transfer political power peacefully from one party to another as a result of an election. A nation, strong and viable, had emerged from its baptism by fire.

Suggestions for Further Reading

For an overview of the Federalist period consult Stanley M. Elkins and Eric McKitrick, *The Age of Federalism* (1993); John C. Miller, *The Federalist Era* (1960). See also Leonard D. White, *The Federalists* (1948).

Important biographies of George Washington include Marcus Cunliffe, *George Washington: Man and Monument* (1958); James Thomas Flexner, *George Washington,* 4 vols. (1965–1972). For further information on the Washington administration consult Harry Ammon, *The Genêt Mission* (1973); Thomas P. Slaughter, *The Whiskey Rebellion* (1986). See also Jacob E. Cooke, *Alexander Hamilton* (1982). On John Adams see Ralph Adams Brown, *The Presidency of John Adams* (1975).

The rise of the two-party system is examined in John F. Hoadley, *Origins of American Political Parties* (1986). For more on the Jeffersonian ideology see Joyce Appleby, *Capitalism and a New Social Order: The Republican Vision of the 1790s* (1984); Lance Banning, *The Jeffersonian Persuasion* (1978); Daniel Sisson, *The American Revolution of 1800* (1974).

Chapter **8**

The Jeffersonians in Power, 1800–1815

On the morning of June 18, 1804, a visitor handed a package to the former Treasury secretary Alexander Hamilton. Inside was a newspaper clipping and a terse three-sentence letter. The clipping said that Hamilton had called Vice President Aaron Burr "a dangerous man, and one who ought not to be trusted with the reins of government." It went on to say that Hamilton had "expressed" a "still more despicable opinion" of Burr—apparently a bitter personal attack on Burr's public and private morality, not merely a political criticism. The letter, signed by Burr, demanded a "prompt and unqualified" denial or an immediate apology.

Hamilton and Burr had sparred verbally for decades. Hamilton regarded Burr as an unscrupulous man, and had worked to defeat him in Burr's race for governor of New York earlier in the year. When, after three weeks, Hamilton had failed to respond to his letter satisfactorily, Burr insisted that they settle the dispute according to the code of honor.

Shortly after 7 o'clock on the morning of July 11, 1804, Burr and Hamilton met on the wooded heights of Weehawken, New Jersey, a customary dueling ground directly across the Hudson River from New York. Hamilton's son Philip had died there in a duel in 1801.

Hamilton's second handed Burr one of two pistols equipped with hairspring triggers. After he and Burr took their positions ten paces apart, Hamilton raised his pistol on the command to "Present!" and fired. His shot struck a tree a few feet to Burr's side. Then Burr fired. His shot struck Hamilton in the right side and passed through his liver. Hamilton died the following day.

The states of New York and New Jersey wanted to try Burr for murder; New Jersey actually indicted him. The vice president fled through New Jersey by foot and wagon to Philadelphia, then took refuge in Georgia and South Carolina, until the indictments were quashed and he could finish his term in office.

The Jeffersonian era—the period stretching from 1800 to 1815—was rife with conflict, partisan passion, and larger-than-life personalities. On the domestic front, a new political party, the Republicans, came to office for the first time and a former vice president was charged with treason against his country. The era was also marked by foreign policy challenges. Pirates, operating from bases on the coast of North Africa, harassed American shipping and enslaved American sailors. Britain and France interfered with American shipping. Finally, the United States once again waged war with Britain, the world's strongest power. These developments raised profound questions: Could the country peacefully transfer political power from one party to another? Could the country preserve political stability? And most important of all, could the nation preserve its neutral rights and national honor in the face of grave threats from Britain and France?

In 1800, Aaron Burr ran as Jefferson's vice-presidential candidate. Burr's effective campaigning tactics and efficient political machine in New York helped bring victory to the Republican party.

Jefferson Takes Command

Thomas Jefferson's goal as president was to restore the principles of the American Revolution. In his view, a decade of Federalist party rule had threatened republican government. Not only had the Federalists levied oppressive taxes, stretched the provisions of the Constitution, and established a bastion of wealth and special privilege in the creation of a national bank, they also had subverted civil liberties and expanded the powers of the central government at the expense of the states. A new revolution was necessary, "as real a revolution in the principles of our government as that of 1776 was in its form." What was needed was a return to basic republican principles.

Beginning with his very first day in office Jefferson sought to demonstrate his administration's commitment to republican principles. At noon, March 4, 1801, Jefferson, clad in clothes of plain cloth, walked from a nearby boarding house to the new United States Capitol in Washington. Without ceremony, he entered the Senate chamber and took the presidential oath of office. In his inaugural address Jefferson sought to allay fear that he planned a Republican reign of terror. "We are all Republicans," he said, "we are all Federalists." Echoing George Washington's

Farewell Address, he asked his listeners to set aside partisan and sectional differences. He also laid out the principles that would guide his presidency: a frugal, limited government; reduction of the public debt; respect for states' rights; encouragement of agriculture; and a limited role for government in peoples' lives. He committed his administration to repealing oppressive taxes, slashing government expenses, cutting military expenditures, and paying off the public debt.

Restoring Republican Government

Thomas Jefferson, the nation's third president, was a man of many talents. Though best known for his political accomplishments, he was also an architect, inventor, philosopher, planter, scientist, and talented violinist. Jefferson was an extremely complex man, and his life was filled with apparent inconsistencies. An idealist who repeatedly denounced slavery, the "Apostle of Liberty" owned 200 slaves when he wrote the Declaration of Independence and freed only five slaves at the time of his death. A vigorous opponent of all forms of human tyranny and staunch defender of human equality, he adopted a patronizing attitude toward women, declaring that their proper role was to "soothe and calm the minds of their husbands." And yet Jefferson remains this country's most eloquent exponent of democratic principles. A product of the Enlightenment, Jefferson was a stalwart defender of political freedom, equality, religious freedom, and intellectual freedom. He was convinced that the yeoman farmer, who worked the land, provided the backbone of democracy. He popularized the idea that a democratic republic required an enlightened and educated citizenry and that government had a duty to assist in the education of a meritocracy based on talent and ability.

As president, Jefferson strove to return the nation to republican values. Through his personal conduct and public policies he sought to return the country to the principles of democratic simplicity, economy, and limited government. He took a number of steps designed to rid the White House of aristocratic customs that had prevailed during the administrations of Washington and Adams. He introduced the custom of having guests shake hands instead of bowing stiffly; he also placed dinner guests at a round table, so that no individual would have to sit in a more important place than any other. In an effort to discourage a "cult of personality," he refused to sanction public celebrations of his birthday declaring, "The only birthday I ever commemorate is that of our Independence, the Fourth of July." Jefferson refused to ride in an elegant coach or host formal dinner parties and balls. Instead, he invited small groups of senators and representatives to dinner and wore clothes made of homespun cloth.

Jefferson believed that presidents should not try to impose their will on Congress, and consequently he refused to initiate legislation or to veto congressional bills on policy grounds. Convinced that presidents Washington and Adams had acted like British monarchs by personally appearing before Congress and requesting legislation, Jefferson simply sent Congress written messages. It would not be until the presidency of Woodrow Wilson that another president would publicly address Congress and call for legislation.

Jefferson's commitment to republican simplicity was matched by his stress on economy in government. His ideal was "a wise and frugal Government, which shall . . . leave [Americans] free to regulate their own pursuits of industry and improvement." He slashed army and navy expenditures, cut the budget, eliminated taxes on whiskey, houses, and slaves, and fired all federal tax collectors. He reduced the army to 3,000 soldiers and 172 officers, the navy to 6 frigates, and foreign embassies to 3—in Britain, France, and Spain. His budget cuts allowed him to cut the federal debt by a third, despite the elimination of all internal taxes.

Jefferson did not conceive of government in entirely negative terms. Convinced that ownership of land and honest labor were the firmest bases of political stability, Jefferson convinced Congress to cut the price of public lands and to extend credit to purchasers in order to encourage landownership and rapid western settlement. A firm believer in the idea that America should be the "asylum" for "oppressed humanity," he persuaded Congress to reduce the residence requirement for citizenship from 14 to 5 years. In the interest of protecting civil liberties, he allowed the Sedition Act to expire in 1801, freed all people imprisoned under the act, and refunded their fines.

In one area Jefferson felt his hands were tied. He considered the Bank of the United States "the most deadly" institution to republican government. But Hamilton's bank had been legally chartered for 20 years and Jefferson's secretary of the Treasury, Albert Gallatin, said that the bank was needed to provide credit for the nation's growing economy. So Jefferson allowed the bank to continue to operate, but he weakened its influence by distributing the federal government's deposits among 21 state banks.

Contemporaries were astonished by the sight of a president who had renounced all the practical tools of government: an army, a navy, and taxes. Jefferson's actions promised, said a British observer, "a sort of Millennium in government." Jefferson's goal was, indeed, to create a new kind of government, a republican government wholly unlike the centralized, corrupt, patronage-ridden one against which Americans had rebelled in 1776.

Reforming the Federal Government

Jefferson thought that one of the major obstacles to restoring republican government was the 3,000 Federalist officeholders. Of the first 600 political appointees named to federal office by presidents Washington and Adams, all but six were Federalists. Even after learning of his defeat, Adams appointed Federalists to every vacant government position. The most dramatic postelection appointment was naming John Marshall, a Federalist, chief justice of the Supreme Court.

Jefferson was committed in principle to the idea that government office should be filled on the basis of merit, not political connections. Only government officeholders guilty of malfeasance or incompetence should be fired. Nothing more should be asked of government officials, he felt, than that they be honest, able, and loyal to the Constitution. Jefferson wholly rejected the idea that a victorious political party had a right to fill public offices with loyal party supporters.

Although many Republicans felt that Federalists should be replaced by loyal Republicans, Jefferson declared that he would remove only "midnight" appointees who had been named to office by President Adams after he learned of his electoral defeat. Nevertheless, Jefferson fired relatively few Federalists. During his first two years in office, he replaced just one-third of all government officials.

War on the Judiciary

When Thomas Jefferson took office, not a single Republican served as a federal judge. In Jefferson's view, the Federalists had turned the federal judiciary into a branch of their political party and intended to use the courts to frustrate Republican plans. The first major political battle of Jefferson's presidency involved his effort to weaken Federalist control of the federal judiciary.

The specific issue that provoked Republican anger was the Judiciary Act of 1801, which was passed by Congress five days before Adams's term expired. The law created 16 new federal judgeships, positions which President Adams promptly filled with Federalists. Even more damaging, from a Republican perspective, the act strengthened the power of the central government by extending the jurisdiction of the federal courts over such issues as bankruptcy and land disputes, which were previously the exclusive domain of state courts. Finally, the act reduced the number of Supreme Court justices effective with the next vacancy, delaying Jefferson's opportunity to name a new Supreme Court justice.

Jefferson's supporters in Congress repealed the Judiciary Act of 1801, but the war over control of the federal courts continued. One of Adams's "midnight appointments" to a judgeship was William Marbury, a loyal Federalist. Although approved by the Senate, Marbury never received his letter of appointment from Adams. When Jefferson became president, Marbury demanded that the new secretary of state, James Madison, issue the commission. Madison refused and Marbury sued, claiming that under section 13 of the Judiciary Act of 1789, the Supreme Court had the power to issue a court order that would compel Madison to give him his judgeship.

The case threatened to provoke a direct confrontation between the judiciary on the one hand and the executive and legislative branches of the federal government on the other. If the Supreme Court ordered Madison to give Marbury his judgeship, the secretary of state was likely to ignore the Court, and Jeffersonians in Congress might try to limit the high court's power.

In his opinion in *Marbury* v. *Madison* John Marshall, the new chief justice of the Supreme Court, ingeniously expanded the court's power without directly provoking the Jeffersonians. Marshall conceded that Mar-

John Marshall, the fourth chief justice of the United States, expanded the Court's power in *Marbury v. Madison* by establishing the right of judicial review. He thus gave the federal courts the power to determine the constitutionality of federal laws and congressional acts.

bury had a right to his appointment but ruled the Court had no authority to order the secretary of state to act, since the section of the Judiciary Act that gave the Court the power to issue an order was unconstitutional.

Marbury v. *Madison* was a landmark in American constitutional history. The decision firmly established the power of the federal courts to review the constitutionality of federal laws and to invalidate acts of Congress when they are found to conflict with the Constitution. This power, known as *judicial review,* provides the basis for the important place that the Supreme Court occupies in American life today.

Marshall's decision in *Marbury* v. *Madison* intensified Republican party distrust of the courts. Impeachment, Jefferson and his followers believed, was the only way to be rid of federal judges they considered unfit or overly partisan, and make the courts responsive to the public will. Federalists responded by accusing the administration of endangering the independence of the federal judiciary.

Three weeks before the Court handed down its decision in *Marbury* v. *Madison,* congressional Republicans launched impeachment proceedings against Federal District Judge John Pickering of New Hampshire. An alcoholic who may have been insane, Pickering was convicted and removed from office.

On the day of Pickering's conviction, the House voted to impeach Supreme Court Justice Samuel Chase, a staunch Federalist. From the bench, he had openly denounced equal rights and universal suffrage and accused the Jeffersonians of atheism and being power hungry. Undoubtedly, Chase was guilty of unrestrained partisanship and injudicious statements. An irate President Jefferson called for Chase's impeachment.

Chase was put on trial for holding opinions "hurtful to the welfare of the country." But the real issue was whether Chase had committed an impeachable offense, since the Constitution specified that a judge could only be removed from office for "treason, bribery, or other high crimes" and not for partisanship or judicial misconduct. In a historic decision that helped to guarantee the independence of the judiciary, the Senate voted to acquit Chase. Although a majority of the Senate found him guilty, seven Republicans broke ranks and denied Jefferson the two-thirds majority needed for a conviction.

Chase's acquittal had momentous consequences for the future. If the Jeffersonians had succeeded in removing Chase, they would probably have removed other Federalist judges from the federal bench. However, since Chase's acquittal, no further attempts have ever been made to remove federal judges solely on the grounds of partisanship or to reshape the federal courts through impeachment. Despite the Republicans' active hostility toward an independent judiciary, the Supreme Court had emerged as a vigorous third branch of government.

International Conflict

In his inaugural address Thomas Jefferson declared that his fondest wish was for peace. "Peace is my passion," he repeatedly insisted. As president, however, he was unable to realize his wish. Like Washington and Adams before him, Jefferson faced the difficult task of preserving American independence and neutrality in a world torn by war and revolution.

The Barbary Pirates

Jefferson's first major foreign policy crisis came from the "Barbary pirates" who preyed on American shipping off the coast of North Africa. The conflict began in 1785, when Algerian pirates boarded an American merchant schooner sailing off the coast of Portugal, took its 21-member crew to Algeria, and enslaved them. During the next eight years, 100 more hostages were seized from American ships. Congress agreed to pay a ransom for their release, and by 1800 one-fifth of all federal revenues went to the North African states as tribute.

Early in Jefferson's first term, he refused to pay additional tribute demanded by the North African states. Determined to end the humiliating demands, he sent warships to the Mediterranean to enforce a blockade of Tripoli. The result was a protracted conflict with Tripoli, which lasted until 1805. Tripoli eventually agreed to make peace, though the United States continued to pay other Barbary states until 1816.

The Louisiana Purchase

At the same time that conflict raged with the Barbary pirates, a more serious crisis loomed on the Mississippi River. In 1795, Spain granted western farmers the right to ship their produce down the Mississippi River to New Orleans, where their cargoes of corn, whiskey, and pork were loaded aboard ships bound for the east coast and foreign ports. In 1800, Spain secretly ceded the Louisiana territory to France, and closed the port of New

Barbary States

Thomas Jefferson's first foreign policy crisis occurred when he refused to pay tribute to the Barbary States for the release of hostages captured by Algerian pirates. Instead, he sent eight ships to enforce a blockade of Tripoli.

Orleans to American farmers. Westerners, left without a port from which to export their goods, exploded with anger. Many demanded war.

The prospect of French control of the Mississippi alarmed Jefferson. Spain had held only a weak and tenuous grip on the Mississippi, but France was a much stronger power. Jefferson feared the establishment of a French colonial empire in North America blocking American expansion. The United States appeared to have only two options: diplomacy or war.

The president sent James Monroe to join Robert Livingston, the American minister to France, with instructions to purchase New Orleans and as much of the Gulf Coast as they could for $2 million. Circumstances played into American hands when 100,000 slaves rose up in revolt in the French colony of Haiti. In 1800, France sent troops to crush the insurrection, but they met a determined resistance led by a former slave named Toussaint L'Ouverture. Then, they were wiped out by mosquitoes carrying yellow fever. Without Haiti, which he regarded as the centerpiece of an American empire, French ruler Napoleon Bonaparte had little interest in keeping Louisiana.

Two days after Monroe's arrival, the French finance minister unexpectedly announced that France was willing to sell not just New Orleans but all of Louisiana Province, a territory extending from Canada to the Gulf of Mexico and westward as far as the Rocky Mountains. The American negotiators agreed on a price of $15 million, or about 4 cents an acre.

Since the Constitution did not give the president specific authorization to purchase land, Jefferson considered asking for a constitutional amendment empowering the government to acquire territory. In Congress Federalists bitterly denounced the purchase, fearing that the creation of new western states would weaken the influence of their party. In the end Jefferson, fearing that Napoleon might change his mind, simply sent the agreement to the Senate, which ratified it. "The less said about any constitutional difficulty, the better," he stated. In a single stroke, Jefferson had doubled the size of the country.

To gather information about the geography, natural resources, wildlife, and peoples of Louisiana, President Jefferson dispatched an expedition led by his private secretary Meriwether Lewis and William Clark, a Virginia-born military officer. For two years Lewis and Clark led some 30 soldiers and ten civilians up the Missouri River as far as present-day central North Dakota and then west to the Pacific.

Disunionist Conspiracies

Anger over the acquisition of Louisiana led some Federalists to consider secession as a last resort to restore their party's former dominance. One group of Federalist congressmen plotted to establish a "Northern Confederacy," which would consist of New Jersey, New York, the New England

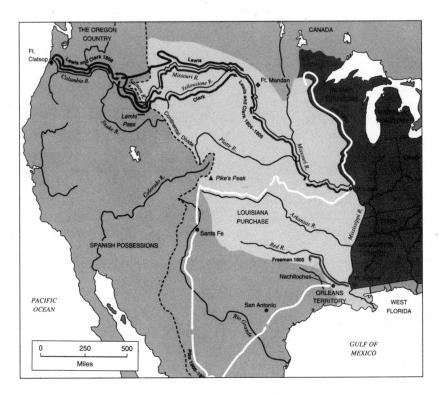

The Louisiana Purchase and Route of Lewis and Clark

No one realized how much territory Jefferson had acquired through the
Louisiana Purchase until Lewis and Clark explored the far West.

states, and Canada. Alexander Hamilton repudiated this scheme, and the
conspirators turned to Vice President Aaron Burr. In return for Federalist
support in his campaign for the governorship of New York, Burr was to
swing New York into the Northern Confederacy. Burr was badly beaten,
in part because of Hamilton's opposition. Incensed and irate, Burr challenged Hamilton to the duel described at the beginning of this chapter.

Because of the duel, Burr was now a ruined politician and a fugitive
from the law. The Republican party stripped away his control over political patronage in New York. His fortunes at their lowest point, the desperate Burr became involved in a conspiracy for which he would be put on
trial for treason.

During the spring of 1805 Burr traveled to the West, where he and
James Wilkinson, military governor of Louisiana, hatched an adventurous
scheme. It is still uncertain what the conspirators' goal was, since Burr, in
his efforts to attract support, told different stories to different people.

Spain's minister believed that Burr planned to set up an independent nation in the Mississippi Valley. Others reported that he planned to seize Spanish territory in what is now Texas, California, and New Mexico. The British minister was told that for $500,000 and British naval support, Burr would separate the states and territories west of the Appalachians from the rest of the Union and create an empire with himself as its head.

In the fall of 1806 Burr and some 60 conspirators traveled down the Ohio River toward New Orleans to assess possibilities and perhaps to incite disgruntled French settlers to revolt. Wilkinson, recognizing that the scheme was doomed to failure, decided to betray Burr. He wrote a letter to Jefferson describing a "deep, dark, wicked, and widespread conspiracy, . . . to seize on New Orleans, revolutionize the territory, and carry an expedition against Mexico."

Burr fled, but was finally apprehended in the Mississippi Territory. He was then taken to the Richmond, Virginia, circuit court, where, in 1807, he was tried for treason. Jefferson, convinced that Burr was a dangerous man, wanted a conviction regardless of the evidence. Chief Justice Marshall, who presided over the trial, was equally eager to discredit Jefferson. Ultimately, Burr was acquitted. The reason for the acquittal was the Constitution's very strict definition of treason as "levying war against the United States" or "giving . . . aid and comfort" to the nation's enemies. In addition, each overt act of treason had to be attested to by two witnesses. The prosecution was unable to meet this strict standard, and as a result of Burr's acquittal, few future cases of treason have ever been tried in the United States.

Was Burr guilty of conspiring to destabilize the United States and separate the West by force? Probably not. The prosecution's case rested largely on the unreliable testimony of coconspirator James Wilkinson, who was a spy in the pay of Spain while also a U.S. army commander and governor of Louisiana. What, then, was the purpose of Burr's mysterious scheming? It appears likely that the former vice president was planning a filibuster expedition—an unauthorized military attack—on Mexico, which was then controlled by Spain. The dream of creating a western republic appealed to many early nineteenth-century Americans—especially to those who feared that a European power might seize Spain's New World colonies unless America launched a preemptive strike. To the end of his life, Burr denied that he had plotted treason against the United States.

The Eagle, the Tiger, and the Shark

In 1804 Jefferson was easily reelected, carrying every state except Connecticut and Delaware. He received 162 electoral votes to only 14 for his Federalist opponent, Charles C. Pinckney. Although his second term began, he later wrote, "without a cloud on the horizon," storm clouds soon gathered as a result of renewed war in Europe. Jefferson faced the difficult challenge of keeping the United States out of the European war, while defending the nation's rights as a neutral.

In May 1803, just two weeks after Napoleon sold Louisiana to the United States, France declared war on Britain. As part of his overall strategy to bring Britain to its knees, Napoleon instituted the "Continental System," a policy of economic warfare which closed European ports to British goods and ordered the seizure of any neutral vessel that carried British goods or stopped in a British port. Britain retaliated in 1807 by issuing Orders in Council, which required all neutral ships to land at a British port to obtain a trading license and pay a tariff. Britain threatened to seize any ship that failed to obey the Orders in Council. By 1807, France had seized 500 ships and Britain nearly 1,000.

United States shipping was caught in the crossfire. The most outrageous violation of America's neutral rights was the British practice of impressment. The British navy desperately needed sailors. Unable to procure sufficient volunteers, the British navy resorted to seizing—impressing—men on streets, in taverns, and on British merchant ships. When these efforts failed to muster sufficient men, the British began to stop foreign ships and remove seamen alleged to be British subjects. By 1811, nearly 10,000 American sailors had been forced into the British Navy, although an undetermined number were actually deserters from British ships who made more money sailing on U.S. ships.

Outrage over impressment reached a fever pitch in 1807 when the British man-of-war *Leopard* fired three broadsides at the American naval frigate *Chesapeake,* which had refused to allow British officers to search the American ship for Royal Navy deserters. The blasts killed three American sailors. British authorities then boarded the American ship and removed four seamen, only one of whom was really a British subject.

"Dambargo"

In a desperate attempt to stave off war, for which it was ill prepared, and win respect for America's neutral rights, the United States imposed an embargo on foreign trade. Convinced that American trade was vital to European industry, Jefferson persuaded Congress in late 1807 to adopt a policy of "peaceable coercion": a ban on all foreign shipping and exports.

Jefferson regarded the embargo as an idealistic experiment—a moral alternative to war. Jefferson was not a doctrinaire pacifist, but he had long advocated economic coercion as an instrument of diplomacy. Now he had a chance to put his ideas into practice.

The embargo was an unpopular and costly failure. It hurt the American economy far more than the British or French, and resulted in widespread smuggling. Without the European export market, warehouses were crammed with huge stockpiles of unsold grain and cotton. Farm prices fell sharply. Shippers also suffered. Without the lucrative wartime trade, harbors filled with idle ships and nearly 30,000 sailors found themselves jobless. The embargo resuscitated the Federalist party, which regained power in several New England states and made substantial gains in the congressional elections of 1808.

Jefferson believed that Americans would cooperate with the embargo out of a sense of patriotism. Instead, evasions of the act were widespread, and smuggling flourished, particularly through Canada. Pressure to abandon the embargo mounted, and early in 1809, just three days before Jefferson left office, Congress repealed the embargo. In effect for 15 months, the embargo exacted no political concessions from either France or Britain. But it had produced economic hardship, evasion of the law, and political dissension at home.

The problem of American neutrality now fell to Jefferson's handpicked successor, James Madison. "The Father of the Constitution" was small in stature and frail in health. A quiet and scholarly man, who secretly suffered from epilepsy, Madison brought a keen intellect and a wealth of experience to the presidency. As Jefferson's secretary of state, he had kept the United States out of the Napoleonic wars, and was committed to using economic coercion to force Britain and France to respect America's neutral rights.

In 1809, Congress replaced the failed embargo with the Non-Intercourse Act, which reopened trade with all nations except Britain and France. Violations of American neutrality continued, and a year later Congress replaced the Non-Intercourse Act with a new measure, Macon's Bill No. 2. This policy reopened trade with France and Britain. It stated, however, that if either Britain or France agreed to respect America's neutral rights, the United States would immediately stop trade with the other nation. Napoleon seized on this new policy in an effort to entangle the United States in his war with Britain. In the summer of 1810 he announced repeal of all French restrictions on American trade. Even though France continued to seize American ships and cargoes, President Madison snapped at the bait. In early 1811, he cut off trade with Britain and recalled the American minister.

For 19 months, the British went without American trade, but gradually economic coercion worked. Food shortages, mounting unemployment, and increasing inventories of unsold manufactured goods led the British to end its trade restrictions (though not the British Navy's policy of impressment). But it was too late; President Madison had already asked Congress for a declaration of war. A divided House and Senate concurred. The House voted to declare war on Britain by a vote of 79 to 49; the Senate by a vote of 19 to 13.

A Second War of Independence

Why did the United States declare war on Britain in 1812? Resentment at British interference with American rights on the high seas was certainly the most loudly voiced grievance. British trade restrictions, impressment of thousands of American seamen, and British blockades humiliated the country and undercut America's national honor and neutral rights.

But if British harassment of American shipping was the primary motivation for war, why then did the pro-war majority in Congress come largely from the South, the West, and the frontier, and not from northeastern shipowners and sailors? The vote to declare war on Britain divided along sharp regional lines. Representatives from western, southern, and frontier states voted 65 to 15 for war, while representatives from New England, New York, and New Jersey, states with strong shipping interests, voted 34 to 14 against war.

Northeastern Federalists and a handful of Republicans from coastal regions of the South regarded war with Britain as a grave mistake. The United States, they insisted, could not hope to challenge British supremacy on the seas and the government could not finance a war without bankrupting the country. Southerners and westerners, in contrast, were eager to avenge British actions that mocked American sovereignty on land and sea. Many southerners and westerners blamed British trade policies for depressing agricultural prices and producing an economic depression. War with Britain also offered another incentive: the possibility of clearing western lands of Indians by removing the Indians' strongest ally—the British. And finally, many westerners and southerners had their eye on expansion, viewing war as an opportunity to add Canada and Spanish-held Florida to the United States.

Weary of Jefferson and Madison's patient and pacifistic policy of economic coercion, voters swept 63 out of 142 representatives from Congress in 1810 and replaced them with young Republicans that Federalists dubbed "War Hawks." These second-generation Republicans avidly supported national expansion and national honor. These young Republicans elected Henry Clay, a representative from frontier Kentucky, Speaker of the House on his very first day in Congress. Clay then assigned other young Republicans, such as John C. Calhoun, a freshman representative from South Carolina, to key House committees.

Staunchly nationalist and rabidly anti-British, eager for territorial expansion and economic growth, the young Republicans regarded the Napoleonic Wars in Europe as an unparalleled opportunity to defend national honor, assert American interests, and conquer Canada and Florida.

Further contributing to their pro-war fervor was the belief that the British incited frontier Indian attacks. Anti-British feeling soared in November 1811, when General William Henry Harrison precipitated a fight with an Indian alliance led by the Shawnee Prophet, Tenskwatawa, at Tippecanoe Creek in Indiana. More than 60 American soldiers were killed and 100 were wounded. Since British guns were found on the battlefield, young Republicans concluded that the British were responsible for the incident.

Early Defeats

Although Congress voted strongly in favor of war, the country entered the conflict deeply divided. Not only would many New Englanders refuse to subscribe to war loans, some merchants would actually ship provisions that Britain needed to support its army, which was fighting Napoleon in

At the Battle of Tippecanoe, U.S. troops led by General William Henry Harrison routed the smaller force of Native Americans under the Shawnee prophet, Tenskwatawa.

Europe. Moreover, the United States was woefully unprepared for war. The army consisted of fewer than 7,000 soldiers and the navy was grotesquely overmatched.

The American strategy called for a three-pronged invasion of Canada and heavy harassment of British shipping. The attack on Canada, however, was a disastrous failure. At Detroit, 2,000 American troops surrendered to a much smaller British and Indian force. An attack across the Niagara River, near Buffalo, resulted in 900 American prisoners of war when the New York State militia refused to provide support. Along Lake Champlain a third army retreated into American territory after failing to cut undefended British supply lines. By the end of 1812, British forces controlled key forts in the Old Northwest, including Detroit and Fort Dearborn, the future site of Chicago. The only consolation for the Americans was a string of naval victories in single-ship encounters.

In 1813 America suffered new failures. In January, an American army advancing toward Detroit was defeated and captured in the swamps west of Lake Erie. Then, in April, Americans staged a raid across Lake Ontario to York (now Toronto). American soldiers set fire to the two houses of the provincial parliament, an act that brought retaliation in the burning of Washington, D.C., by the British. A plan to capture Montreal in the fall of 1813 also ended without an attack.

Only a series of unexpected victories at the end of the year raised American spirits. On September 10, 1813, America won a major naval victory at the Battle of Lake Erie. There, Oliver Hazard Perry successfully engaged six British ships. Though Perry's flagship, the *Lawrence,* was disabled in the fighting, he went on to capture the British fleet. He reported his victory with the stirring words, "We have met the enemy and they are ours."

The Battle of Lake Erie was America's first major victory of the war. It forced the British to abandon Detroit and retreat toward Niagara. On October 5, 1813, Major General William Henry Harrison overtook the retreating British army and their Indian allies at the Thames River. He won a decisive victory in which the Indian leader Tecumseh was killed, thereby ending the fighting strength of the northwestern Indians.

The Tide Turns

In early 1814, prospects for an American victory dimmed. In the spring, Britain defeated Napoleon in Europe, freeing 18,000 veteran British troops to participate in an invasion of the United States. The British planned to invade the United States at three points: upstate New York across the Niagara River and Lake Champlain, the Chesapeake Bay, and New Orleans.

At Niagara, however, a small American army stopped the British advance, and on Lake Champlain American naval forces commanded by Thomas Macdonough placed British supply lines in jeopardy, forcing 11,000 British troops to retreat into Canada. Outnumbered more than three to one, American forces had halted Britain's invasion from the north.

In a second attempt to invade the United States, Britain landed 4,000 soldiers on the Chesapeake Bay coast. But no one knew if the British planned to march first on Baltimore or on Washington, D.C. The answer was Washington, where untrained soldiers lacking uniforms and standard equipment were protecting the capital.

The result was utter chaos. On August 24, 1814, the British humiliated the nation by capturing and burning Washington, D.C. President Madison and his wife Dolly were forced to flee the capital, carrying with them many of the nation's treasures, including the Declaration of Independence and Gilbert Stuart's portrait of George Washington. For 72 hours, the president was forced to hide in the Virginia and Maryland countryside. The British arrived so soon after the president fled that the officers dined on a White House meal that had been prepared for the Madisons and 40 invited guests.

Britain's next objective was Baltimore. To reach the city, British warships had to pass the guns of Fort McHenry, which was manned by 1,000 American soldiers. On September 13, 1814, British warships began a 25-hour bombardment of the fort.

All through the night British cannons fired on Fort McHenry. At dawn on September 14, Francis Scott Key, a young lawyer detained on a British ship, saw the flag still waving over the fort's ramparts. The Americans had repulsed the British attack, with only four soldiers killed and 24 wounded. Key was so moved by the American victory that he wrote the words to "The Star-Spangled Banner" on the back of an envelope. The song was destined to become the young nation's national anthem.

The country still faced grave threats in the South. In 1813, the Creek Indians, encouraged by the British, had attacked American settlements in what are now Alabama and Mississippi. Frontiersmen from Georgia, Mississippi, and Tennessee, led by Major General Andrew Jackson, retaliated and succeeded in defeating the Creeks in March 1814, at the battle of Horseshoe Bend in Alabama. When the Creek War ended, Jackson proceeded to cut British supply lines in the South. He knew that Spain, supposedly neutral, had allowed Britain to use the Florida port of Pensacola as a base of operations for a planned invasion of New Orleans. In a week Jackson marched from Mobile, Alabama, to Pensacola and seized the city, forcing the British to delay their invasion.

But, on January 8, 1815, the British fleet and a battle-tested 10,000-man army finally attacked New Orleans in an attempt to seize control of the mouth of the Mississippi River. To defend the city, Jackson assembled a ragtag army, including French pirates, Choctaw Indians, western militia, and freed slaves. Although British forces outnumbered Americans by more than two to one, American artillery and sharpshooters stopped the invasion. American losses totaled only 8 dead and 13 wounded, while British casualties were 2,036, with almost 400 soldiers killed.

Ironically, American and British negotiators in Ghent, Belgium, had signed the peace treaty ending the War of 1812 two weeks earlier. Britain, convinced that the American war was so difficult and costly that nothing would be gained from further fighting, agreed to return to the conditions that existed before the war. Left unmentioned in the peace treaty were the issues over which Americans had fought the war—impressment, naval blockades, or the British Orders in Council.

The War's Significance

Although often treated as unimportant, a minor footnote to the bloody European war between France and Britain, the War of 1812 was crucial for the United States. First, it effectively destroyed the Indians' ability to resist American expansion east of the Mississippi. Native Americans were crushed in the North by General William Henry Harrison and in the South by General Andrew Jackson. Abandoned by their British allies, the Indians made the best treaties they could. Reluctantly, they ceded most of their lands north of the Ohio River and in southern and western Alabama to the U.S. government.

Second, the war strengthened America's position relative to Spain in the South and Southwest. It allowed the United States to rewrite its boundaries with Spain and solidify control over the lower Mississippi River and the Gulf of Mexico. Although the United States did not succeed in conquering Canada or defeating the British empire, it had fought the world's strongest power to a stalemate. Spain recognized the significance of this fact, and in 1819 Spanish leaders abandoned Florida and agreed to an American boundary running clear to the Pacific Ocean.

Third, the Federalist party never recovered from its opposition to the war. Many Federalists believed that the War of 1812 was really fought to help Napoleon in his struggle against Britain, and they had opposed the war by refusing to pay taxes, boycotting war loans, and refusing to furnish troops. In December 1814, delegates from New England gathered in Hartford, Connecticut, where they recommended a series of constitutional amendments to restrict the power of Congress to wage war, regulate commerce, and admit new states. The delegates also supported a one-term presidency (in order to break the grip of Virginians on the office) and abolition of the three-fifths compromise (which increased the political clout of the South), and talked of seceding if they did not get their way. The proposals of the Hartford Convention became public knowledge at the same time as the terms of the Treaty of Ghent and the American victory in the Battle of New Orleans. Euphoria over the war's end led many people to brand the Federalists as traitors. The party never recovered from this stigma and disappeared from national politics.

*C*hronology of Key Events

1801	John Marshall becomes chief justice; House of Representatives elects Thomas Jefferson as the third president; Jefferson sends eight ships to enforce a blockade of Tripoli
1802	Judiciary Act of 1801 repealed
1803	*Marbury* v. *Madison* upholds principle of judicial review; Jefferson purchases Louisiana from France
1804	Lewis and Clark expedition in Louisiana; Aaron Burr kills Alexander Hamilton in a duel; impeachment of federal district Judge John Pickering and Supreme Court Justice Samuel Chase
1807	Aaron Burr charged with treason; U.S. frigate *Chesapeake* attacked by British; Embargo Act
1809	Embargo Act repealed; James Madison sworn in as fourth president; Non-Intercourse Act prohibits trade with Britian and France
1810	Macon's Bill No. 2 reopens trade with Britian and France
1811	William Henry Harrison routs Indians led by Tenskwatawa in Battle of Tippecanoe
1812	War against Britain declared; Americans surrender Detroit to British
1813	Battle of Lake Erie; Battle of the Thames
1814	Battle of Horseshoe Bend; British burn Washington, D.C.; British fleet defeated on Lake Champlain; Hartford Convention; Treaty of Ghent ends war of 1812
1815	Jackson defeats British at Battle of New Orleans

Conclusion

Between 1800 and 1815 the Jeffersonian Republicans increased the nation's size, opened new lands to western settlement, and won international respect for American independence. In a climate of war and revolution, the new nation acquired Louisiana and the Southeast, defeated powerful Indian confederations in the Northwest and South, and evicted British troops from American soil. What emerged from this period was a strong, confident, and united nation.

Suggestions for Further Reading

For an overview of the Jeffersonian era consult Merrill Peterson, *Thomas Jefferson and the New Nation* (1970). Other valuable biographies of Thomas Jefferson include Fawn M. Brodie, *Thomas Jefferson: An Intimate History* (1974); Noble E. Cunningham, Jr., *In Pursuit of Reason: The Life of Thomas Jefferson* (1987); Dumas Malone, *Jefferson and His Time,* 6 vols. (1948–1981); Forrest McDonald, *The Presidency of Thomas Jefferson* (1976); Robert W. Tucker and David C. Hendrickson, *Empire of Liberty: The Statecraft of Thomas Jefferson* (1990); Robert M. Johnstone, Jr., *Jefferson and the Presidency* (1978);

For more on Jeffersonian republicanism consult Drew McCoy, *The Elusive Republic: Political Economy in Jeffersonian America* (1980), and *The Last of the Fathers: James Madison and the Republican Legacy* (1989); Merrill Peterson, *The Jefferson Image in the American Mind* (1960); Leonard D. White, *The Jeffersonians* (1951); James S. Young, *The Washington Community, 1800–1828* (1966).

For information on the Federalists during the Jeffersonian period see David H. Fischer, *The Revolution of American Conservatism* (1965); Linda K. Kerber, *Federalists in Dissent* (1970); Shaw Livermore, *The Twilight of Federalism* (1962).

The War of 1812 is examined in R. David Edmunds, *Tecumseh and the Quest for Indian Leadership* (1984); Donald R. Hickey, *The War of 1812* (1989); Regionald Horsman, *The Causes of the War of 1812* (1962); Ralph Ketcham, *James Madison* (1971); J. C. A. Stagg, *Mr. Madison's War* (1983).

Chapter **9**

Nationalism, Economic Growth, and the Roots of Sectional Conflict, 1815–1824

As the year 1810 began, Francis Cabot Lowell, a 36-year-old Boston importer, was bitterly discouraged. His health was failing and, as a result of war between Britain and France, his importing business was in ruins. Uncertain about which way to turn, he decided to travel abroad. While overseas, he discovered his life's calling. In Britain, he marveled at textile factories at Manchester. Although it was illegal to export textile machinery or plans, Lowell carefully studied the power looms and secretly made sketches of the designs.

Upon his return to Boston in 1813, Lowell constructed textile machinery superior to any he had seen in England. The next year, in Waltham, Massachusetts, he and two associates built the world's first factory able to convert raw cotton into cloth by power machinery under one roof.

To staff his new textile mill, Lowell chose a labor force different from that found in any previous factory. Determined to avoid the misery of England's textile mills, Lowell recruited his labor force from among the daughters of New England farmers, who agreed to work in Lowell's mill for two or three years as a way of earning a dowry or an independent income. Because spinning and weaving had long been performed by women in the home, and because young women were willing to work for half or a third of the wages of young men, they seemed to offer a perfect solution to the factory's labor needs.

To break down the prejudice against factory work as degrading and immoral, the company announced that it would employ only women of good moral character. It threatened to fire any employee guilty of smoking, drinking, lying, swearing, or any other immoral conduct. The company required employees to attend church and provided boardinghouses where mill girls lived under the careful supervision of housekeepers of impeccable character. Within a few years, the new factory was overwhelmed with job applicants.

The opening of the Boston Manufacturing Company's textile mill in 1814 marked a symbolic beginning to a new era in the nation's history. For Americans, the end of the War of 1812 unleashed a surge of nationalism, dramatic industrial growth, and rapid expansion to the West. In the years ahead, the United States would undergo an economic transformation, symbolized by improvements in transportation and agriculture, rapid urban growth, and many technological innovations.

Paradoxically, it was during these years of nationalism and growth that sectional and political conflicts were exacerbated. Westward expansion, the rapid growth of industry in the North, and the strengthening of the federal government created problems that dominated American political life for the next 40 years.

The Growth of American Nationalism

Early in the summer of 1817, as a conciliatory gesture toward the Federalists who had opposed the War of 1812, James Monroe, the nation's fifth president, embarked on a goodwill tour through the Northeast and Midwest. Everywhere Monroe went, citizens greeted him warmly, holding parades and banquets in his honor. In Federalist Boston, a crowd of 40,000 welcomed the Republican president. John Quincy Adams expressed amazement at the acclaim with which the president was greeted: "Party spirit has indeed subsided throughout the Union to a degree that I should have thought scarcely possible."

A Federalist newspaper, reflecting on the end of party warfare and the renewal of national unity, called the times the "Era of Good Feelings." The phrase accurately describes the period of James Monroe's presidency, which, at least in its early years, was marked by a relative absence of political strife and opposition. With the collapse of the Federalist party, the Jeffersonian Republicans dominated national politics. Reflecting a new spirit of political unity, the Republicans adopted many of the nationalistic policies of their former opponents, establishing a second national bank, a protective tariff, and improvements in transportation.

To the American people, James Monroe was the popular symbol of the Era of Good Feelings. A dignified and formal man, Monroe was the last president to don the fashions of the eighteenth century. He wore his hair in a powdered wig and favored knee breeches, long white stockings, and buckled shoes. His political values, too, were those of an earlier day. Like George Washington, Monroe worked to eliminate party and sectional rivalries by his attitudes and behavior. He hoped for a country without political parties, governed by leaders chosen on their merits. So great was his popularity that he won a second presidential term by an electoral college vote of 231 to 1. A new era of national unity appeared to have dawned.

Neo-Hamiltonianism

Traditionally, the Republican party stood for limited government, states' rights, and a strict interpretation of the Constitution. By 1815, however, the party had adopted former Federalist positions on a national bank, protective tariffs, a standing army, and national roads.

In a series of policy recommendations to Congress at the end of the War of 1812, President Madison revealed the extent to which Republicans had adopted Federalist policies. He called for a program of national economic development directed by the central government, which included the creation of a second Bank of the United States to provide for a stable currency, a protective tariff to encourage industry, a program of internal improvements to facilitate transportation, and a permanent 20,000-man army. In subsequent messages, he recommended an extensive system of roads and canals, new military academies, and establishment of a national university in Washington.

Old-style Republicans, who clung to the Jeffersonian ideal of limited government, dismissed Madison's proposals, but his nationalistic program found enthusiastic support among the new generation of political leaders. Convinced that inadequate roads, the lack of a national bank, and dependence on foreign imports had nearly resulted in a British victory in the war, these young leaders were eager to use the federal government to promote national economic development. Henry Clay, John C. Calhoun, and Daniel Webster were the principal leaders of the second generation of American political life—the period stretching from the War of 1812 to almost the eve of the Civil War. Each was destined to become the preeminent spokesman of his region—Clay of the West, Calhoun of the South, Webster of the North.

The leader of this group of younger politicians was Henry Clay, a Republican from Kentucky. Clay was one of the "War Hawks" who had urged President Madison to wage war against Britain. After the war, Clay became one of the strongest proponents of an active federal role in national economic development. He used his position as Speaker of the House to advance an economic program that he later called the "American System." According to this plan, the federal government would erect a high protective tariff to keep out foreign goods, stimulate the growth of industry, and create a large urban market for western and southern farmers. Revenue from the tariff, in turn, would be used to finance internal improvements of roads and canals to stimulate the growth of the South and West.

Another leader of postwar nationalism was John C. Calhoun, a Republican from South Carolina. Calhoun, like Clay, entered Congress in 1811, and later served with distinction as secretary of war under Monroe and as vice president under both John Quincy Adams and Andrew Jackson. Later, Calhoun became the nation's leading exponent of states' rights, but at this point he seemed to John Quincy Adams "above all sectional and factious prejudices more than any other statesman of this Union with whom I have ever acted."

The other dominant political figure of the era was Daniel Webster. Nicknamed "the Godlike Daniel" for his magnificent speaking style, Webster argued 168 cases before the Supreme Court. When he entered Congress as a Massachusetts Federalist, he opposed the War of 1812, the

Eager to use the federal government to promote economic development, young politicians like Henry Clay of Kentucky (left) and John C. Calhoun of South Carolina (right) supported a protective tariff to stimulate industry, a national bank to promote economic growth, and federally funded aid for transportation.

creation of a second national bank, and a protectionist tariff. But, later in his career, after industrial interests supplanted shipping and importing interests in the Northeast, Webster became a staunch defender of the national bank and a high tariff, and perhaps the nation's strongest exponent of nationalism and most vigorous critic of states' rights. His argument that the United States was not only a union of states but a union of people would later be developed by Abraham Lincoln.

The severe financial problems created by the War of 1812 led to a wave of support for the creation of a second national bank. The demise of the first Bank of the United States just before the war had left the nation ill equipped to deal with the war's financial demands. To finance the war effort, the government borrowed from private banks at high interest rates. As demand for credit rose, the private banks issued bank notes greatly exceeding the amount of gold or silver that they held. One Rhode Island bank issued $580,000 in notes backed up by only $86.48 in gold and silver. The result was high inflation. Prices jumped 40 percent in just two years.

In 1816 Congress voted by a narrow margin to charter a second Bank of the United States for 20 years and give it the privilege of holding government funds without paying interest for their use. Supporters of a second national bank argued that it would provide a safe place to deposit government funds and a convenient mechanism for transferring money between states. Supporters also claimed that a national bank would promote monetary stability by regulating private banks. A national bank would strengthen the banking system by refusing to accept the notes issued by overspeculative private banks and ensuring that bank notes were readily exchangeable for gold or silver. Opposition to a national bank came largely from private banking interests and traditional Jeffersonians, who considered a national bank to be unconstitutional and a threat to republican government.

The War of 1812 provided tremendous stimulus to American manufacturing. It encouraged American manufacturers to produce goods previously imported from overseas. By 1816, 100,000 factory workers, two-thirds of them women and children, produced more than $40 million worth of manufactured goods a year. Capital investment in textile manufacturing, sugar refining, and other industries totaled $100 million.

Following the war, however, cheap British imports flooded the nation, threatening to undermine local industries. Congress responded to the flood of imports by continuing a tariff to protect America's infant industries from low-cost competition. With import duties ranging from 15 to 30 percent on cotton, textiles, leather, paper, pig iron, wool, and other goods, the tariff promised to protect America's growing industries from foreign competition. Shipping and farming interests, on the other hand, opposed the tariff on the grounds that it would make foreign goods more expensive to buy and would provoke foreign retaliation.

Conquering Space

Prior to 1812 westward expansion had proceeded slowly. Most Americans were nestled along the Atlantic coastline. In 1800 more than two-thirds of the new nation's population still lived within 50 miles of the Atlantic seaboard, and the center of population rested within 18 miles of Baltimore. Only two roads cut across the Allegheny Mountains, and no more than half a million pioneers had moved as far west as Kentucky, Tennessee, Ohio, or the western portion of Pennsylvania. Cincinnati was a town of 15,000 people; Buffalo and Rochester, New York did not yet exist. Thomas Jefferson estimated in 1803 that it would be a thousand years before settlers occupied the region east of the Mississippi.

The end of the War of 1812 unleashed a rush of pioneers to Indiana, Illinois, Ohio, northern Georgia, western North Carolina, Alabama, Mississippi, Louisiana, and Tennessee. Congress quickly admitted five states to the Union: Louisiana in 1812, Indiana in 1816, Mississippi in 1817, Illinois in 1818, and Alabama in 1819. Pioneers demanded cheaper land and clamored for better transportation to move goods to eastern markets.

Farmers demanded that Congress revise legislation to make it easier to obtain land. Originally, Congress viewed federal lands as a source of revenue, and public land policies reflected that view. Under a policy adopted in 1785 and reaffirmed in 1796, the federal government only sold land in blocks of at least 640 acres. Although the minimum allotment was reduced to 320 acres in 1800, federal land policy continued to retard sales and concentrate ownership in the hands of a few large land companies and wealthy speculators.

In 1820 Congress sought to make it easier for farmers to purchase homesteads in the West by selling land in small lots suitable for operation by a family. Congress reduced the minimum allotment offered for sale from 320 to 80 acres. The minimum price per acre fell from $2 to $1.25. The second Bank of the United States encouraged land purchases by liberally extending credit. The result was a boom in land sales. For a decade, the government sold approximately a million acres of land annually.

Westward expansion also created a demand to expand and improve the nation's roads and canals. In 1808, Albert Gallatin, Thomas Jefferson's Treasury secretary, proposed a $20 million program of canal and road construction. As a result of state and sectional jealousies and charges that federal aid to transportation was unconstitutional, the federal government funded only a single turnpike, the National Road, at this time stretching from Cumberland, Maryland, to Wheeling, Virginia (later West Virginia), but much later extending westward from Baltimore through Ohio and Indiana to Vandalia, Illinois.

In 1816 John C. Calhoun introduced a new proposal for federal aid for road and canal construction. "Let us," he exclaimed, "bind the republic together with a perfect system of roads and canals. Let us conquer space." Narrowly, Calhoun's proposal passed. But on the day before he left office, Madison vetoed the bill on constitutional grounds.

Despite this setback, Congress did adopt major parts of the nationalist neo-Hamiltonian economic program. It had established a second Bank of the United States to provide a stable means of issuing money and a safe depository for federal funds. It had enacted a tariff to raise duties on foreign imports and guard American industries from low-cost competition. It had also instituted a new public land policy to encourage western settlement. In short, Congress had translated the spirit of national pride and unity that the nation felt after the War of 1812 into a legislative program that placed the national interest above narrow sectional interests.

Judicial Nationalism

The decisions of the Supreme Court also reflected the nationalism of the postwar period. With John Marshall as chief justice, the Supreme Court acquired greater prestige and independence. When Marshall took office, in the last days of John Adams's administration in 1801, the Court met in the basement of the Capitol and was rarely in session for more than six weeks a year. Since its creation in 1789, the Court had only decided 100 cases.

In a series of critical decisions, the Supreme Court greatly expanded its authority. As previously noted, *Marbury* v. *Madison* established the Supreme Court as the final arbiter of the Constitution and its power to declare acts of Congress unconstitutional. *Fletcher* v. *Peck* (1810) declared the Court's power to void state laws. *Martin* v. *Hunter's Lessee* (1816) gave the Court the power to review decisions by state courts.

After the War of 1812, Marshall wrote a series of decisions that further strengthened the powers of the national government. *McCulloch* v. *Maryland* (1819) established the constitutionality of the second Bank of the United States and denied to states the right to exert independent checks on federal authority. The case involved a direct attack on the second Bank of the United States by the state of Maryland, which had placed a tax on the bank notes of all banks not chartered by the state.

In his decision, Marshall dealt with two fundamental questions. The first was whether the federal government had the power to incorporate a bank. The answer to this question, the Court ruled, was yes because the Constitution granted Congress implied powers to do whatever was "necessary and proper" to carry out its constitutional powers—in this case, the power to manage a currency. The second question raised was whether a state had the power to tax a branch of the Bank of the United States. In answer to this question, the Court said no. The Constitution, the Court asserted, created a new government with sovereign power over the states. "The power to tax involves the power to destroy," the Court declared, and the states do not have the right to exert an independent check on the authority of the federal government.

During this period the Supreme Court also encouraged economic competition and development. In *Dartmouth* v. *Woodward* (1819), the Court served to promote business growth by denying states the right to alter or impair contracts unilaterally. The case involved the efforts of the New Hampshire legislature to alter the charter of Dartmouth College, which had been granted by George III in 1769. The Court held that a charter was a valid contract protected by the Constitution and that states do not have the power to alter contracts unilaterally. In *Gibbons* v. *Ogden* (1824), the Court broadened federal power over interstate commerce. The Court overturned a New York law that had awarded a monopoly over steamboat traffic on the Hudson River, ruling that the Constitution had specifically given Congress the power to regulate commerce.

Under John Marshall, the Supreme Court became the final arbiter of the constitutionality of federal and state laws. The Court's role in shifting sovereign power from the states to the federal government was an important development. It would become increasingly difficult in the future to argue that the union was a creation of the states, that states could exert an independent check on federal government authority, or that Congress's powers were limited to those specifically conferred by the Constitution.

Defending American Interests in Foreign Affairs

The War of 1812 stirred a new nationalistic spirit in foreign affairs. This spirit resulted in a decision to end the raids by the Barbary pirates on American commercial shipping in the Mediterranean. For 17 years the United States had paid tribute to the ruler of Algiers. In March 1815 Captain Stephen Decatur and a fleet of ten ships sailed into the Mediterranean, where they captured two Algerian gunboats, towed the ships into Algiers harbor, and threatened to bombard the city. As a result, all the North African states agreed to treaties releasing American prisoners without ransom, ending all demands for American tribute, guaranteeing that American commerce would not be interfered with, and providing compensation for American vessels that had been seized.

After successfully defending American interests in North Africa, Monroe acted to settle old grievances with the British. Britain and the United States had left a host of issues unresolved in the peace treaty ending the War of 1812, including disputes over boundaries, trading and fishing rights, and rival claims to the Oregon region. The two governments moved quickly to settle these issues. The Rush-Bagot Agreement, signed with Great Britain in 1817, removed most military ships from the Great Lakes. In 1818, Britain granted American fishermen the right to fish in eastern Canadian waters, agreed to the 49th parallel as the boundary between the United States and Canada from Minnesota to the Rocky Mountains, and consented to joint occupation of the Oregon region.

The critical foreign policy issue facing the United States after the War of 1812 was the fate of Spain's crumbling New World empire. Many of Spain's colonies had taken advantage of the turmoil in Europe during the Napoleonic Wars to fight for their independence. Florida, however, was still under Spanish control. Pirates, fugitive slaves, and Native Americans used Florida as a sanctuary and as a jumping-off point for raids on settlements in Georgia. In December 1817, to end these incursions, Monroe authorized General Andrew Jackson to lead a punitive expedition against the Seminole Indians in Florida. Jackson attacked the Seminoles, destroyed their villages, and overthrew the Spanish governor. He also court-martialed and executed two British citizens whom he accused of inciting the Seminoles to commit atrocities against Americans.

Jackson's actions provoked a furor in Washington. Secretary of War John C. Calhoun and other members of Monroe's cabinet urged the president to reprimand Jackson for acting without specific authorization. In Congress, Henry Clay called for Jackson's censure. Secretary of State Adams, however, saw in Jackson's actions an opportunity to wrest Florida from Spain.

Instead of apologizing for Jackson's conduct, Adams declared that the Florida raid was a legitimate act of self-defense. Adams informed the Spanish government that it would either have to police Florida effectively or cede it to the United States. Convinced that American annexation was inevitable, Spain ceded Florida to the United States in the Adams-Onis Treaty of 1819. In return, the United States agreed to honor $5 million in damage claims by Americans against Spain, and renounced, at least temporarily, its claims to Texas.

At the same time, European intervention in the Pacific Northwest and Latin America threatened to become a new source of anxiety for American leaders. In 1821, Russia claimed control of the entire Pacific coast from Alaska to Oregon and closed the area to foreign shipping. This development coincided with rumors that Spain, with the help of its European allies, was planning to reconquer its former colonies in Latin America. European intervention threatened British as well as American interests. Not only did Britain have a flourishing trade with Latin America, which would decline if Spain regained its New World colonies, but it also occupied the Oregon region jointly with the United States. In 1823, British Foreign Minister George Canning proposed that the United States and Britain jointly announce their opposition to further European intervention in the Americas.

Monroe initially regarded the British proposal favorably. But his secretary of state, John Quincy Adams, opposed a joint Anglo-American declaration. Secure in the knowledge that the British would use their fleet to support the American position, Adams convinced President Monroe to make an independent declaration of American policy. In his annual message to Congress in 1823, Monroe outlined the principles that have become known as the Monroe Doctrine. He announced that the Western

Hemisphere was henceforth closed to any further European colonization, declaring that the United States would regard any attempt by European nations "to extend their system to any portion of this hemisphere as dangerous to our peace and safety." European countries with possessions in the hemisphere—Britain, France, the Netherlands, and Spain—were warned not to attempt expansion. Monroe also said that the United States would not interfere in internal European affairs.

For the American people, the Monroe Doctrine was the proud symbol of American hegemony in the Western Hemisphere. Unilaterally, the United States had defined its rights and interests in the New World. During the first half of the nineteenth century the United States lacked the military power to enforce the Monroe Doctrine and depended on the British navy to deter European intervention in the Americas, but the nation had clearly warned the European powers that any threat to American security would provoke American retaliation.

The Roots of American Economic Growth

At the beginning of the nineteenth century the United States was an overwhelmingly rural and agricultural nation. Most Americans lived on farms or in villages with fewer than 2,500 inhabitants. The nation's population was small and scattered over a vast geographical area—just 5.3 million in 1800, compared to Britain's 15 million and France's 27 million. Transportation and communications had changed little over the previous half century. A coach ride between Boston and New York took three days. South of the Mason-Dixon line, except for a single stagecoach that traveled between Charleston and Savannah, there was no public transportation of any kind.

American houses, clothing, and agricultural methods were surprisingly primitive. Fifty miles inland, half the houses were log cabins, lacking even glass windows. Farmers planted their crops in much the same way as their parents and grandparents. Few farmers practiced crop rotation or used fertilizers or drained fields. They made plows out of wood, allowed their swine to run loose, and left their cattle outside except on the coldest nights.

Manufacturing was also still quite backward. In rural areas, farm families grew their own food, produced their own soap and candles, wove their own blankets, and constructed their own furniture. The leading manufacturing industries—iron-making, textiles, and clothes-making—employed only about 15,000 people in mills or factories.

After the War of 1812, however, the American economy grew at an astonishing rate. The twenty-five years that followed Andrew Jackson's victory at New Orleans represented a critical period for the nation's future economic growth, during which the United States overcame a series of obstacles that had stood in the way of sustained economic expansion. Improved transportation, rapid urbanization, increased farm productivity, and technological innovation transformed a rural, agricultural nation into one of the world's industrial leaders.

Accelerating Transportation

At the outset of the nineteenth century the lack of reliable, low-cost transportation was a major barrier to American industrial development. The stagecoach, slow and cumbersome, was the main form of transportation. Twelve passengers, crowded along with their bags and parcels, traveled at just four miles an hour. In Connecticut and Massachusetts, Sunday travel was still forbidden by law.

Wretched roads plagued travelers. Larger towns had streets paved with cobblestones, but most roads were simply dirt paths left muddy and rutted by rain. The presence of tree stumps in the middle of many roads posed a serious obstacle to carriages. Charles Dickens aptly described American roads as a "series of alternate swamps and gravel pits."

In 1791 builders first inaugurated a new era in transportation with the construction of a 66-mile-long turnpike between Philadelphia and Lancaster, Pennsylvania. This stimulated a craze for toll road construction. By 1811, 135 private companies in New York had invested $7.5 million in 1,500 miles of road. By 1838, Pennsylvania had invested $37 million to build 2,200 miles of turnpikes.

Despite the construction of turnpikes, the cost of transporting freight over land remained high. Because water transportation was cheaper, farmers often shipped their produce down the Mississippi, Potomac, or Hudson rivers by flatboat or raft. Unfortunately, water transportation was slow and few vessels were capable of going very far upstream. The trip downstream from Pittsburgh to New Orleans took a month; the trip upstream against the current took four months. Steam power offered the obvious solution, and inventors built at least 16 steamships before Robert Fulton successfully demonstrated the commercial practicality of steam navigation. In 1807, he sailed a 160-ton side-wheeler, the *Clermont,* 150 miles from New York City to Albany in only 32 hours. "Fulton's folly," as critics called it, opened a new era of faster and cheaper water transportation.

Water transportation was further revolutionized by the building of canals. In 1825 the state of New York opened the Erie Canal, which connected the Great Lakes to the Atlantic Ocean. The canal was a stupendous engineering achievement. Three thousand workers, using hand

In 1807, Robert Fulton demonstrated the feasibility of steam travel by launching his 160-ton-side-wheeler, the *Clermont,* on the Hudson River.

labor, toiled for eight years to build the canal. They built 84 locks, each 15 feet wide and 90 feet long, to raise or lower barges 10 feet at a time.

Built almost entirely with state and local funding, "Clinton's Ditch"—named after the Erie canal's chief backer, Governor DeWitt Clinton—sparked an economic revolution. Before the canal was built, it cost $100 and took 20 days to transport a ton of freight from Buffalo to New York City. After the canal was opened, the cost fell to $5 a ton and transit time was reduced to 6 days.

The success of the Erie Canal led other states to embark on expensive programs of canal building. Pennsylvania spent $10 million to build a canal between Philadelphia and Pittsburgh. The states of Illinois, Indiana, and Ohio launched projects to connect the Ohio and Mississippi rivers to the Great Lakes. By 1840, 3,326 miles of canals had been dug at a cost of $125 million.

Cities like Baltimore and Boston, which were unable to reach the West with canals experimented with the railroad, a novel form of transportation. Early railroads suffered from nagging engineering problems and vociferous opposition. Brakes were wholly inadequate, consisting of wooden blocks operated by a foot pedal. Boilers exploded so frequently that passengers had to be protected by bales of cotton. Engine sparks set fire to fields and burned unprotected passengers. Vested interests, including turnpike and bridge companies, stagecoaches, ferries, and canals, sought laws to prohibit trains from carrying freight.

Nonetheless, it quickly became clear after 1830 that railroads were destined to become the nation's chief means of moving freight. During the

1830s, construction companies laid down 3,328 miles of track, roughly equal to all the miles of canals in the country. With an average speed of ten miles an hour, railroads were faster than stagecoaches, canalboats, and steamboats, and, unlike water-going vessels, could travel in any season.

The transportation revolution sharply reduced the cost of shipping goods to market and stimulated agriculture and industry. New roads, canals, and railroads speeded the pace of commerce and strengthened ties between the East and West.

Transforming American Law

The growth of an industrial economy in the United States required a shift in American law. At the beginning of the nineteenth century, American law was rooted in concepts that reflected the values of a slowly changing, agricultural society. The law presumed that goods and services had a just price, independent of supply and demand. Courts forbade many forms of competition and innovation in the name of a stable society. Courts and judges legally protected monopolies and prevented lenders from charging high rates of interest. The law allowed property owners to sue for damages if a mill built upstream flooded their land or impeded their water supply. After 1815, however, the American legal system favored economic growth, profit, and entrepreneurial enterprise.

By the 1820s courts, particularly in the Northeast, had begun to abandon many traditional legal doctrines that stood in the way of a competitive market economy. Courts dropped older doctrines that assumed that goods and services had an objective price, independent of supply and demand. Courts also rejected many usury laws, and increasingly held that only the market could determine interest rates or prices or the equity of a contract.

To promote rapid economic growth, courts and state legislatures gave new powers and privileges to private firms. Companies building roads, bridges, canals, and other public works were given the power to appropriate land; private firms were allowed to avoid legal penalties for fires, floods, or noise they caused on the grounds that the companies served a public purpose. Courts also reduced the liability of companies for injuries to their own employees, ruling that an injured party had to prove negligence or carelessness on the part of an employer in order to collect damages. The legal barriers to economic expansion had been struck down.

Early Industrialization

The United States lagged far behind Europe in the practical application of science and technology. There was probably just one steam engine in regular operation in the United States in 1800, one hundred years after simple engines had first been used in Europe. Inventors often failed because they were unable to finance their projects or persuade the public to use their inventions. The inadequate state of higher education also slowed technological innovation. At the beginning of the nineteenth century, Harvard, the nation's most famous college, graduated just 39 men a year, no more than it had graduated in 1720. All the nation's libraries put together contained barely 50,000 volumes.

By the 1820s, however, the United States had largely overcome resistance to technological innovation, with literally hundreds of inventors and amateur scientists transforming European ideas into practical technologies. Their inventions inspired in Americans a boundless faith in technology. Early American technology was pioneered largely by self-taught amateurs, whose zeal led them to create inventions that trained European scientists did not attempt. As early as the 1720s it was known that electricity could be conducted along a wire to convey messages, but it was not until 1844 that an American named Samuel F. B. Morse demonstrated the practicality of the telegraph and devised a workable code for sending messages. A Frenchman built the first working steamship in 1783, but it was 24 years later that Robert Fulton produced the first commercially successful steamship. The first real steam engine was invented by an Englishman in 1699, but it was an American named Oliver Evans who in 1805 produced a light and powerful steam engine with high-pressure cylinders.

In the 1820s and 1830s America became the world's leader in adopting mechanization, standardization, and mass production. Manufacturers began to adopt labor-saving machinery that allowed workers to produce more goods at lower costs. The single most important figure in the development of this system was Eli Whitney, the inventor of the cotton gin. In 1798, Whitney persuaded the U.S. government to award him a contract for 10,000 muskets. Until then, rifles had been manufactured by skilled artisans, who made individual parts by hand and then carefully fitted the pieces together. At the time Whitney made his offer, the federal arsenal at Springfield, Massachusetts, was capable of producing only 245 muskets in two years. Whitney's idea was to develop precision machinery that would allow a worker with little manual skill to manufacture identical gun parts that would be interchangeable from one gun to another.

Other industries soon adopted the system. As early as 1800 manufacturers of wooden clocks began to use interchangeable parts. Makers of sewing machines used mass production techniques as early as 1846, and the next year manufacturers mechanized the production of farm machinery.

Innovation was not confined to manufacturing. During the years following the War of 1812, American agriculture underwent a transformation nearly as profound and far-reaching as the revolution taking place in industry. No longer cut off from markets by the high cost of transportation, farmers began to grow larger crop surpluses and to specialize in cash crops. A growing demand for cotton for England's textile mills led to the introduction of long-staple cotton from the West Indies into the islands and lowlands of Georgia and South Carolina. Eli Whitney's invention of the cotton gin in 1793—which permitted an individual to clean 50 pounds of short-staple cotton in a single day, 50 times more than could be cleaned by hand—made it practical to produce the crop in the South. Other cash crops raised by southern farmers included rice, sugar, flax for linen, and hemp for rope fibers. In the Northeast, the growth of mill towns and urban centers created a growing demand for hogs, cattle, sheep, corn, wheat, wool, butter, milk, cheese, fruit, vegetables, and hay to feed horses.

As production for the market increased, farmers began to demand improved farm technology. An improved cast-iron plow replaced the conventional wooden plow, allowing a farmer to double the acreage he could put into cultivation. Prior to the introduction in 1803 of the cradle scythe—a rake used to cut and gather up grain and deposit it in even piles—a farmer could not harvest more than half an acre a day. The horse rake—a device introduced in 1820 to mow hay—allowed a single farmer to perform the work of eight to ten men. The invention in 1836 of a mechanical thresher, used to separate the wheat from the chaff, helped to cut in half the man-hours required to produce an acre of wheat.

By 1830 the roots of America's future industrial growth had been firmly planted. Back in 1807, the nation had just 15 or 20 cotton mills, containing approximately 8,000 spindles. By 1831 the number of spindles in use totaled nearly a million and a quarter. Factory production had made household manufacture of shoes, clothing, textiles, and farm implements obsolete. The United States was well on its way to becoming one of the world's leading manufacturing nations.

The Growth of Cities

At the beginning of the nineteenth century the United States was a nation of farms and rural villages. Only four cities had populations with more than 10,000 inhabitants. Boston, which in 1800 contained just 25,000 inhabitants, looked much as it had prior to the Revolution. Its streets, still paved with cobblestones, were unlighted at night. New York City's entire police force, which only patrolled the city at night, consisted of two captains, two deputies, and 72 assistants.

During the 1820s and 1830s the nation's cities grew at an extraordinary rate. The urban population increased sixty percent a decade, five times as fast as that of the country as a whole. In 1810, New York City's population was less than 100,000. Two decades later it was more than 200,000.

The chief cause of the increase was the migration of sons and daughters away from farms and villages. The growth of commerce drew thousands of farm children to the cities to work as bookkeepers, clerks, and salespeople. The expansion of factories demanded thousands of laborers, mechanics, teamsters, and operatives. The need of rural areas for services available only in urban centers also promoted the growth of cities, particularly in the West. Farmers needed their grain milled and their livestock butchered; tobacco growers needed their crop cured and marketed.

Pittsburgh's growth illustrates these processes at work. Frontier farmers needed products made of iron, such as nails, horseshoes, and farm implements. Pittsburgh lay near western Pennsylvania's coal fields. Because it was cheaper to bring the iron ore to the coal supply for smelting than to transport the coal to the side of the iron mine, Pittsburgh became a major iron producer. Iron foundries and blacksmith shops proliferated. So did glass factories, which required large amounts of fuel to provide heat for glassblowing. As a result, Pittsburgh's population tripled between 1810 and 1830.

As urban areas grew, many problems were exacerbated, including the absence of clean drinking water, the pressing need for cheap public transportation, and, most important, poor sanitation. Sanitation problems led to heavy urban mortality rates and frequent typhoid, dysentery, typhus, cholera, and yellow fever epidemics.

Most city dwellers used outdoor privies, which emptied into vaults and cesspools that sometimes leaked into the soil and contaminated the water supply. Kitchen wastes were thrown into ditches; refuse was thrown into trash piles by the side of the streets. Every horse deposited as much as 20 pounds of manure and urine on city streets each day. To help remove the garbage and refuse, many cities allowed packs of dogs, goats, and pigs to scavenge freely.

Although elite urbanites were beginning to enjoy some amenities, such as indoor toilets, which began to appear around 1815, many of the cities' poorest inhabitants lived in slums. On New York's lower east side, men, women, and children were crowded into damp, unlighted, ill-ventilated cellars with 6 to 20 persons living in a single room. Despite growing public awareness of the problems of slums and urban poverty, conditions remained unchanged for several generations.

The Growth of Political Factionalism and Sectionalism

The Era of Good Feelings began with a burst of nationalistic fervor. The economic program adopted by Congress, including a national bank and a protective tariff, reflected the growing feeling of national unity. The Supreme Court promoted the spirit of nationalism by establishing the principle of federal supremacy. Industrialization and improvements in transportation also added to the sense of national unity by contributing to the nation's economic strength and independence and by linking the West and the East together.

But this same period also witnessed the emergence of growing factional divisions in politics, including a deepening sectional split between the North and South. A severe economic depression between 1819 and 1822 provoked bitter division over questions of banking and tariffs. Geographic expansion exposed latent tensions over the morality of slavery and the balance of economic power. It was during the Era of Good Feelings that the political issues arose that would dominate American politics for the next 40 years.

The Panic of 1819

In 1819 a financial panic swept across the country. The growth in trade that followed the War of 1812 came to an abrupt halt. Unemployment mounted, banks failed, mortgages were foreclosed, and agricultural prices fell by half. Investment in western lands collapsed. The downswing spread like a plague across the country. In Cincinnati bankruptcy sales occurred almost daily. In Lexington, Kentucky, factories worth half a million dollars were idle. One economist estimated that 3 million people, one-third of the nation's population, were adversely affected by the panic.

The panic had several causes, including a dramatic decline in cotton prices, a contraction of credit by the Bank of the United States designed to curb inflation, an 1817 congressional order requiring hard-currency payments for land purchases, and the closing of many factories due to foreign competition.

The panic unleashed a storm of popular protest. Many debtors agitated for "stay laws" to provide relief from debts as well as the abolition of debtors' prisons. Manufacturing interests called for increased protection from foreign imports, but a growing number of southerners believed that high protective tariffs, which raised the cost of imported goods and reduced the flow of international trade, were the root of their troubles. Many people clamored for a reduction in the cost of government and pressed for sharp reductions in federal and state budgets. Others, particularly in the South and West, blamed the panic on the nation's banks and particularly the tight-money policies of the Bank of the United States.

By 1823 the panic was over, but it had made a lasting imprint on American politics. The panic led to demands for the democratization of state constitutions, an end to restrictions on voting and officeholding, and heightened hostility toward banks and other "privileged" corporations and monopolies. The panic also exacerbated tensions within the Republican party and aggravated sectional tensions as northerners pressed for higher tariffs while southerners abandoned their support of nationalistic economic programs.

The Missouri Crisis

In the midst of the panic a crisis over slavery erupted with stunning suddenness. It was, Thomas Jefferson wrote, like "a firebell in the night." The crisis was ignited by the application of Missouri for statehood, and it involved the status of slavery west of the Mississippi River.

East of the Mississippi, the Mason-Dixon line and the Ohio River formed a boundary between the North and South. States south of this line were slave states; states north of this line had either abolished slavery or adopted gradual emancipation policies. West of the Mississippi, however, no clear line demarcated the boundary between free and slave territory.

Representative James Tallmadge, a New York Republican, provoked the crisis in February 1819 by introducing an amendment to restrict slavery in Missouri as a condition of statehood. The amendment prohibited the further introduction of slaves into Missouri and provided for emancipation of all children of slaves at the age of 25. Voting along ominously sectional lines, the House approved the Tallmadge Amendment, but the amendment was defeated in the Senate.

Southern and northern politicians alike responded with fury. Southerners condemned the Tallmadge proposal as part of a northeastern plot to dominate the government. They declared the United States to be a union of equals, claiming that Congress had no power to place special restrictions upon a state. Talk of disunion and civil war was rife. Northern politicians responded with equal vehemence. Northern leaders argued that national policy, enshrined in the Northwest Ordinance, committed the government to halt the expansion of the institution of slavery. They warned that the extension of slavery into the West would inevitably increase the pressures to reopen the African slave trade. Mass meetings convened in a number of cities in the Northeast. Never before had passions over the issue of slavery been so heated or sectional antagonisms so overt.

Compromise ultimately resolved the crisis. In 1820, the Senate narrowly voted to admit Missouri as a slave state. To preserve the sectional balance, it also voted to admit Maine, which had previously been a part of Massachusetts, as a free state, and to prohibit the formation of any further slave states from the territory of the Louisiana Purchase north of the 36° 30' north latitude. Henry Clay then skillfully steered the Missouri compromise through the House, where a handful of antislavery representatives, fearful of the threat to the Union, threw their support behind the proposals.

Although compromise had been achieved, it was clear that sectional conflict had not been resolved, only postponed. Southerners won a victory in 1820, but they paid a high price. While many states would eventually be organized from the Louisiana Purchase area north of the compromise line, only two (Arkansas and part of Oklahoma) would be formed from the southern portion. If the South was to defend its political power against an antislavery majority, it had but two options in the future. It would ei-

Missouri Compromise

The agreement reached in the Missouri Compromise temporarily settled the argument over slavery in the territories.

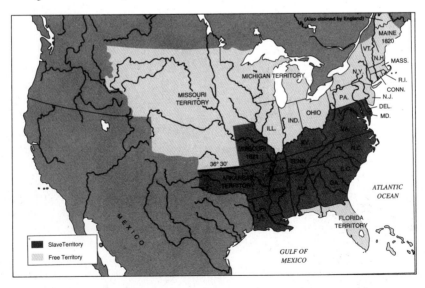

ther have to forge new political alliances with the North and West, or it would have to acquire new territory in the Southwest. The latter would inevitably reignite northern opposition to the further expansion of slavery. Thus the Era of Good Feelings ended on a note of foreboding.

Conclusion

The Era of Good Feelings came to a formal close on March 4, 1825, the day that John Quincy Adams was inaugurated as the nation's sixth president. Adams, who had served eight years as his predecessor's secretary of state, believed that James Monroe's terms in office would be regarded by future generations of Americans as a "golden age." In his inaugural address he spoke with pride of the nation's achievements since the War of 1812. A strong spirit of nationalism pervaded the nation and the country stood united under a single political party, the Republicans. The nation had settled its most serious disputes with England and Spain, extended its boundaries to the Pacific, asserted its diplomatic independence, encour-

*C*hronology of Key Events

1807	Robert Fulton's *Clermont* demonstrates practicality of steam-powered navigation
1814	Boston Manufacturing Company's textile mill opens
1815	Congress declares war on Algiers
1816	Congress charters Second Bank of the United States; James Monroe elected fifth president
1818	General Andrew Jackson invades Florida; Rush-Bagot Agreement establishes U.S.–Canadian boundary
1819	Panic of 1819; Adams-Onis Treaty; *Dartmouth* v. *Woodward*; *McCulloch* v. *Maryland*
1820	Missouri Compromise prohibits slavery in the northern half of Louisiana Purchase; Monroe reelected
1823	Monroe Doctrine issued, opposes European colonization or interference in the Americas
1825	Erie Canal opens

aged the wars for national independence in Latin America, developed a strong manufacturing system, and had begun to create a system of transportation adequate to a great nation.

The Era of Good Feelings marked a period of dramatic growth and intense nationalism, but it also witnessed the emergence of new political divisions as well as growing sectional animosities. The period following the War of 1812 brought rapid growth to cities, manufacturing, and the factory system in the North, while the South's economy remained centered around slavery and cotton. These two great sections were developing along diverging lines. Whether the spirit of nationalism or the spirit of sectionalism would triumph was the great question that would dominate American politics over the next four decades.

Suggestions for Further Reading

For an overview of the period see William Barney, *The Passage of the Republic* (1987); John R. Howe, *From the Revolution Through the Age of Jackson* (1973); John Mustfield, *The New Nation, 1800–1845* rev. ed. (1982).

For American economic development after 1815 consult Alfred D. Chandler, Jr., *The Visible Hand* (1977); Paul W. Gates, *The Farmer's Age* (1960); Carter Goodrich, *Government Promotion of American Canals and Railroads* (1960); David Hamer, *New Towns in the New World* (1990); David A. Hounshell, *From the American System to Mass Production* (1984); Glenn Porter and Harold C. Livesay, *Merchants and Manufacturers* (1971); Peter Temin, *Causal Factors in American Economic Growth in the Nineteenth Century* (1975).

On American foreign policy during this period see Samuel F. Bemis, *John Quincy Adams and the Foundations of American Foreign Policy* (1949); Ernest R. May, *The Making of the Monroe Doctrine* (1975); Frederick W. Merk, *The Monroe Doctrine and American Expansionism* (1966).

Significant biographies include Harry Ammon, *James Monroe: The Quest for National Identity* (1971); Leonard Baker, *John Marshall: A Life in Law* (1974); Richard Current, *Daniel Webster and the Rise of National Conservatism* (1955); Mary W. M. Hargreaves, *The Presidency of John Quincy Adams* (1985); *John Marshall: Defender of the Constitution* (1981); Barbara M. Tucker, *Samuel Slater and the Origins of the American Textile Industry* (1984).

Chapter *10*

Power and Politics in Jackson's America

It was, without a doubt, one of the most exciting, colorful, and dirty presidential campaigns in American history. In 1840 William Henry Harrison, a military hero best known for fighting an alliance of Indians at the Battle of Tippecanoe in 1811, challenged the Democratic incumbent, Martin Van Buren, for the presidency.

Harrison's campaign began on May 4 when a huge procession, made up of an estimated 75,000 people, marched through the streets of Baltimore to celebrate Harrison's nomination by the Whig party convention. Although Harrison was college-educated and brought up on a plantation with a work force of some 200 slaves, his Democratic opponents had already dubbed him the "log cabin" candidate, who was happiest on his backwoods farm sipping hard cider. In response, Harrison's supporters enthusiastically seized on this image and promoted it in a number of colorful ways. They distributed barrels of hard cider, passed out campaign hats and placards, and mounted eight log cabins on floats.

Harrison's campaign brought many innovations to the art of electioneering. For the first time a presidential candidate spoke out on his own behalf. Previous candidates had chosen to let others speak for them. Harrison's backers also coined the first campaign slogans: "Tippecanoe and Tyler Too," and "Van, Van is a used up man." They staged log cabin raisings, including the erection of a 50-by-100-foot cabin on Broadway in New York City. They sponsored barbecues and mass rallies attended by thousands of people.

While defending their man as the "people's" candidate, Harrison's backers heaped an unprecedented avalanche of personal abuse on his Democratic opponent. The Whigs accused President Van Buren of eating off of golden plates and lace tablecloths, and drinking French wines. Whigs in Congress denied Van Buren an appropriation of $3,665 to repair the White House lest he turn the executive mansion into a "palace as splendid as that of the Caesars." The object of this rough and colorful kind of campaigning was to convince voters that the Democratic candidate harbored aristocratic leanings, while Harrison truly represented the people.

The Harrison campaign provided a number of effective lessons for future politicians, most notably an emphasis on symbols and imagery over ideas and substance. Fearful of alienating voters and dividing the Whig party, the political convention that nominated Harrison agreed to adopt no party platform. Harrison himself said nothing during the campaign about his principles or proposals. He closely followed the suggestion of one of his advisers that he run on his military record and offer no indication "about what he thinks now, or what he will do hereafter."

The new campaign techniques produced an overwhelming victory. In 1840 voter turnout was the highest it had ever been in a presidential election: nearly 80 percent of eligible voters cast ballots. The log cabin candidate for president won 53 percent of the popular vote and a landslide victory in the electoral college.

Political Democratization

In 1821 American politics was still largely dominated by deference. Competing political parties were nonexistent and voters generally deferred to the leadership of local elites or leading families. Political campaigns tended to be relatively staid affairs. Direct appeals by candidates for support were considered in poor taste. Election procedures were, by later standards, quite undemocratic. Most states imposed property and taxpaying requirements on the white adult males who alone had the vote, and conducted voting by voice. Presidential electors were generally chosen by state legislatures. Given the fact that citizens had only the most indirect say in the election of the president, it is not surprising that voting participation was generally extremely low, amounting to less than 30 percent of adult white males.

Between 1820 and 1840 a revolution took place in American politics. In most states, property qualifications for voting and officeholding were repealed, and voting by voice was largely eliminated. Direct methods of selecting presidential electors, county officials, state judges, and governors replaced indirect methods. Because of these and other political innovations, voter participation skyrocketed. By 1840 voting participation had reached unprecedented levels. Nearly 80 percent of adult white males went to the polls.

A new two-party system, made possible by an expanded electorate, replaced the politics of deference to and leadership by elites. By the mid-1830s two national political parties with marked philosophical differences, strong organizations, and wide popular appeal competed in virtually every state. Professional party managers used partisan newspapers, speeches, parades, rallies, and barbecues to mobilize popular support. Our modern political system had been born.

The Expansion of Voting Rights

The most significant political innovation of the early nineteenth century was the abolition of property qualifications for voting and officeholding. Hard times resulting from the panic of 1819 led many people to demand an end to these restrictions. In New York, for example, fewer than two adult males in five could legally vote for senator or governor. Under a state constitution approved in 1821 all adult white males were allowed to vote, so long as they paid taxes or had served in the militia. Five years later, an amendment to the state's constitution eliminated the taxpaying and militia qualifications, thereby establishing universal white manhood suffrage. By 1840 universal white manhood suffrage had largely become a reality. Only three states—Louisiana, Rhode Island, and Virginia—still restricted the suffrage to white male property owners and taxpayers.

In order to encourage popular participation in politics, most states also instituted statewide nominating conventions, opened polling places in more convenient locations, extended the hours that polls were open, and eliminated the earlier practice of voting by voice. This last reform did not truly institute the secret ballot, which was only adopted beginning in the 1880s, since voters during the mid-nineteenth century usually voted with

Extension of Male Suffrage

Some states and territories reserved the suffrage to white male property holders and taxpayers, while other permitted an alternative such as a period of residence.

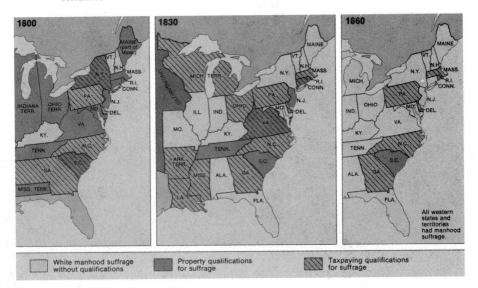

straight-ticket paper ballots prepared by the political parties themselves. Each party had a different colored ballot, which voters deposited in a publicly viewed ballot box, so that those present knew who had voted for which party. By 1824 only six of the nation's 24 states still chose presidential electors in the state legislature, and eight years later the only state still to do so was South Carolina, which continued this practice until the Civil War.

In addition to removing property and tax qualifications for voting and officeholding, states also reduced residency requirements for voting. Immigrant males were permitted to vote in most states if they had declared their intention to become citizens. During the nineteenth century 22 states and territories permitted immigrants who were not yet naturalized citizens to vote. States also allowed voters to choose presidential electors, governors, and county officials.

While universal white manhood suffrage was becoming a reality, restrictions on voting by blacks and women remained in force. Only one state, New Jersey, had given unmarried women property holders the right to vote following the Revolution, but the state rescinded this right at the same time it extended suffrage to all adult white men. Most states also explicitly denied the right to vote to free blacks. By 1858 free blacks were eligible to vote in just four northern states: New Hampshire, Maine, Massachusetts, and Vermont.

Popular Attacks on Privilege

The democratic impulse that swept the country in the 1820s was also apparent in widespread attacks on special privilege and aristocratic pretension. Established churches, the courts, and the legal and medical professions all saw their elitist status diminished.

The judiciary was made more responsive to public opinion through the election, rather than the appointment, of judges. To open up the legal profession, many states dropped formal training requirements to practice law. Some states also abolished training and licensing requirements for physicians, allowing unorthodox "herb and root" doctors, including many women, to compete freely with established physicians.

The surge of democratic sentiment had an important political consequence: the breakdown of deferential politics. During the first quarter of the nineteenth century local elites lost much of their influence. They were replaced by professional politicians. In the 1820s political innovators such as Martin Van Buren, the son of a tavernkeeper, and Thurlow Weed, a newspaper editor in Albany, New York, devised new campaign tools, such as torchlight parades, subsidized partisan newspapers, and nominating conventions. These political bosses and manipulators soon discovered that the most successful technique for arousing popular interest in politics was to attack a privileged group or institution that had used political influence to attain power or profit.

The "Anti-Masonic party" was the first political movement to win a widespread popular following using this technique. In the mid-1820s a growing number of people in New York and surrounding states had come to believe that members of the fraternal order of Freemasons, who seemed to monopolize many of the region's most prestigious political offices and business positions, had used their connections to enrich themselves. They noted, for instance, that Masons held 22 of the nation's 24 governorships. By 1830 the Anti-Mason movement had succeeded in capturing half the vote in New York state and had gained substantial support throughout New England.

The Rebirth of Parties

The first years of the new republic had given rise to two competing political parties, the Federalists and the Republicans. The first party system, unlike the kinds of political parties Americans are familiar with today, tended to have a strong sectional character, with the Federalists dominant in New England and the Republicans dominant elsewhere.

After the War of 1812 the nation reverted to a period of one-party government in national politics. The decline of the Federalist party created the illusion of national political unity, but appearances were deceptive. Without the discipline imposed by competition with a strong opposition party, the Republican party began to fragment into cliques and factions.

During James Monroe's presidency the Republican party disintegrated as a stable national organization. Following his overwhelming victory in 1816, Monroe sought to promote the ideal expressed by George Washington in his Farewell Address: a nation free of partisan divisions. Like Washington, he appointed rival factional leaders, such as John Quincy Adams and John C. Calhoun, to his cabinet. He refused to use federal patronage to strengthen the Republican party. He also took the position that Congress, not the president, was the best representative of the public will, and therefore should define public policy.

The absence of a strong leader, however, led to the fragmentation of the Republican party during Monroe's administration. Factional and sectional rivalries grew increasingly bitter and party machinery fell into disuse.

Birth of the Second Party System

Over time, local and personal factions began to coalesce into a new political party system. Three critical factors contributed to the creation of the second party system. The first was the financial panic of 1819 and the subsequent depression. The panic resulted in significant political differences over such issues as debt relief, banking and monetary policy, and tariffs. Farmers, particularly in the South and West, demanded enactment of stay laws to postpone repayment of debts. Many artisans and farmers blamed banks for causing the panic by printing an excess of worthless paper money. They demanded that bank notes be replaced by hard money, gold and silver coinage. These groups often disagreed with pro-business interests, which called for the extension of credit, higher tariffs to protect infant industries, and government-financed transportation improvements to reduce the cost of trade.

A second source of political division was southern alarm over the slavery debates in Congress in 1819 and 1820. Many southern leaders feared that the Missouri crisis might spark a realignment in national politics along sectional lines. Anxiety over the slavery debates induced many southerners to seek political alliances with the North. As early as 1821, Old Republicans in the South—those who opposed high tariffs, a national bank, and federally funded internal improvements—had begun to form a loose alliance with Senator Martin Van Buren of New York and the Republican party faction he commanded, the Albany Regency.

The third major source of political division was the selection of presidential candidates. The "Virginia dynasty" of presidents, a chain that had begun with George Washington and included Thomas Jefferson, James Madison, and James Monroe, was at its end by 1824. Traditionally, the Republican party's candidate was selected by a caucus of the party's members in Congress. At the 1824 caucus the members met in closed session and chose William Crawford, Monroe's secretary of the Treasury, as the party's choice. Not all Republicans, however, supported this method of nominating candidates, and therefore refused to participate.

When Crawford suffered a stroke and was left partially disabled, four other candidates emerged: Secretary of State John Quincy Adams, the son of the nation's second president and the only candidate from the North; John C. Calhoun, who had little support outside of his native South Carolina; Henry Clay, the Speaker of the House; and General Andrew Jackson, the hero of the Battle of New Orleans and victor over the Creek and Seminole Indians.

In the election of 1824 Jackson received the greatest number of votes both at the polls and in the electoral college, followed (in electoral votes) by Adams, Crawford, and then Clay. But he failed to receive the constitutionally required majority of the electoral votes. As provided by the Twelfth Amendment of the Constitution, the election was therefore thrown into the House of Representatives, which was required to choose from among the top three vote-getters in the electoral college. There, Henry Clay persuaded his supporters to vote for Adams, commenting acidly that he did not believe "that killing two thousand five hundred Englishmen at New Orleans" was a proper qualification for the presidency. Adams was elected on the first ballot.

The Philadelphia *Observer* charged that Adams had made a secret deal to obtain Clay's support. Three days later, Adams's nomination of Clay as secretary of state seemed to confirm the charges of a "corrupt bargain." Jackson was outraged, since he could legitimately argue that he was the popular favorite. The general exclaimed, "The Judas of the West has closed the contract and will receive the thirty pieces of silver."

The Presidency of John Quincy Adams

John Quincy Adams was one of the most brilliant and well-qualified men ever to occupy the White House. A deeply religious, intensely scholarly man, he read biblical passages at least three times a day—once in English, once in German, and once in French. He was fluent in seven foreign languages, including Greek and Latin. During his brilliant career as a diplomat and secretary of state, he negotiated the treaty that ended the War of 1812, acquired the Floridas, and conceived the Monroe Doctrine.

But Adams lacked the political skills and personality necessary to create support for his program. Like his father, Adams lacked personal warmth. His adversaries mockingly described him as a "chip off the old iceberg."

Adams's problems as president did not arise exclusively from his temperament. His misfortune was to serve as president at a time of growing partisan divisions. The Republican party had now split into two distinct camps. Adams and his supporters, known as National Republicans, favored a vigorous role for the central government in promoting national economic growth, while the Jacksonian Democrats demanded a limited government and strict adherence to laissez-faire principles.

As the only president to lose both the popular vote and the electoral vote, Adams faced hostility from the start. Jackson and his supporters accused the new president of "corruptions and intrigues" to gain Henry Clay's support. Acutely aware of the fact that "two-thirds of the whole people [were] averse" to his election as president, Adams promised in his inaugural address to make up for this with "intentions upright and pure, a heart devoted to the welfare of our country." A staunch nationalist,

Adams proposed an extraordinary program of federal support for science and economic development that included a national university, astronomical observatories ("lighthouses of the skies"), federal funding of roads and canals, and exploration of the country's territory—all to be financed by a high tariff.

Adams's advocacy of a strong federal government and a high tariff enraged defenders of slavery and states' rights advocates who clung to traditional Jeffersonian principles of limited government and strict construction of the Constitution. They feared that any expansion of federal authority might set a precedent for interference with slavery. Adams met with further frustration because he was unwilling to adapt to the practical demands of politics. Adams made no effort to use his patronage powers to build support for his proposals, and refused to fire federal officeholders who openly opposed his policies. During his entire term in office he removed just 12 incumbents, and these only for gross incompetence. He justified his actions by saying that he did not want to make "government a perpetual and intermitting scramble for office."

Adams's Indian policies also cost him supporters. Although he, like his predecessor Monroe, wanted to remove the southern Indians to the area west of the Mississippi River, he believed that the state and federal governments had a duty to abide by Indian treaties and to purchase, not merely annex, Indian lands. Adams's decision to repudiate and renegotiate a fraudulent treaty that stripped the Georgia Creek Indians of their land outraged land-hungry southerners and westerners.

Even in the realm of foreign policy, his strong suit prior to the presidency, Adams encountered difficulties. To strengthen ties with Latin America, he sent delegates to a Pan-American conference in Central America, but his representatives arrived too late to take part. His attempts to peacefully acquire Texas from Mexico failed, as did his efforts to persuade Britain to permit more American trade with the British West Indies.

The "American System" and the "Tariff of Abominations"

President Adams was committed to using the federal government to promote national economic development. His program included a high protective tariff to promote industry, the sale of public lands at low prices to encourage western settlement, federally financed transportation improvements, expanded markets for western grain and southern cotton, and a strong national bank to regulate the economy.

Adams's secretary of state, Henry Clay, called this economic program the "American system" because it was supposed to promote growth in all parts of the country. But the program infuriated southerners who believed that it favored northeastern industrial interests at their region's expense. Southerners particularly disliked a protective tariff, since it raised the cost of manufactured goods, which they did not produce.

Andrew Jackson's supporters in Congress sought to exploit the tariff question in order to embarrass Adams and help Jackson win the presidency in 1828. They framed a bill, which became known as the Tariff of Abominations, to win support for Jackson in Kentucky, Missouri, New York, Ohio, and Pennsylvania while weakening the Adams administration in New England. The bill raised duties on iron, hemp, and flax (which would benefit westerners), while lowering the tariff on woolen goods (to the detriment of New England textile manufacturers).

The Tariff of Abominations created a political uproar in the South, where it was denounced as unconstitutional and discriminatory. The tariff, southerners insisted, was essentially a tax on their region to assist northern manufacturers. South Carolina expressed the loudest outcry against the tariff. At a public meeting in Charleston, protesters declared that a tariff was designed to benefit "one class of citizens [manufacturers] at the expense of every other class." Some South Carolinians called for revolutionary defiance of the national government.

Vice President John C. Calhoun, a skilled logician well versed in political philosophy, offered a theoretical framework for southern discontent. Retreating from his early nationalistic position, Calhoun anonymously published the "South Carolina Exposition," an essay that advanced the principle of "nullification." A single state, Calhoun maintained, might overrule or "nullify" a federal law within its own territory, until three-quarters of the states had upheld the law as constitutional. In 1828 the state of South Carolina decided not to implement this doctrine but rather to wait and see what attitude the next president would adopt toward the tariff.

The Election of 1828

"J. Q. Adams who can write" squared off against "Andy Jackson who can fight" in the election of 1828, one of the most bitter campaigns in American history. Jackson's followers repeated the charge that Adams was an "aristocrat" who had obtained office as a result of a "corrupt bargain." The Jackson forces also alleged that the president had used public funds to buy personal luxuries and had installed gaming tables in the White House.

Adams's supporters countered by digging up an old story that Jackson had begun living with his wife before she was legally divorced from her first husband (which was technically true, although neither Jackson nor his wife Rachel knew her first husband was still living). They called the general a slave trader, a gambler, and a backwoods buffoon who could not spell more than one word out of four correctly.

The Jackson campaign in 1828 was the first to appeal directly for voter support through a professional political organization. Skilled political leaders, like Martin Van Buren of New York, Amos Kendall of Kentucky, and Thomas Ritchie of Virginia, created a vast network of pro-Jackson newspapers, which pictured the general as the "candidate of the people." Jackson supporters set up an extensive network of campaign committees and subcommittees to organize mass rallies, parades, and barbecues, and to erect hickory poles, Jackson's symbol.

For the first time in American history a presidential election was the focus of public attention, and voter participation increased dramatically. Twice as many voters cast ballots in the election of 1828 as in 1824, four times as many as in 1820. As in most previous elections, the vote divided along sectional lines. Jackson swept every state in the South and West and Adams won the electoral votes of every state in the North except Pennsylvania and part of New York.

Contemporaries interpreted Jackson's resounding victory as a triumph for political democracy. Jackson supporters called the vote a victory for the "farmers and mechanics of the country" over the "rich and well born." Even Jackson's opponents agreed that the election marked a watershed in the nation's political history, signaling the beginning of a new democratic age. One Adams supporter said bluntly, "a great revolution has taken place."

Andrew Jackson: The Politics of Egalitarianism

Supporters of Adams regarded Jackson's victory with deep pessimism. A justice of the Supreme Court declared, "The reign of King 'Mob' seems triumphant." But enthusiasts greeted Jackson's victory as a great triumph for the people. At the inaugural, a cable that was stretched in front of the east portico of the Capitol to keep back the throngs snapped under the

Table 10.1

Election of 1828			
Candidate	Party	Popular Vote	Electoral Vote
Andrew Jackson	Democratic	642,553	178
John Q. Adams	National Republican	500,897	83

pressure of the surging crowd. As many as 20,000 well-wishers attended a White House reception to honor the new president, muddying rugs, breaking furniture, and damaging china and glassware.

In certain respects, Jackson was truly a self-made man. Born in 1767 in a frontier region along the North and South Carolina border known as the Waxhaws, he was the first president to be born in a log cabin. Orphaned at an early age, he had volunteered to fight in the American Revolution when he was 13.

Jackson soon rose from poverty to a career in law and politics. Although he would later gain a reputation as the champion of the common people, in Tennessee he was allied by marriage, business, and political ties to the state's elite and against the yeomanry. As a land speculator, cotton planter, and attorney, he accumulated a large personal fortune and acquired more than 100 slaves. His candidacy for the presidency was initially promoted by speculators, creditors, and elite leaders in Tennessee who hoped to exploit Jackson's popularity in order to combat antibanking sentiment and fend off challenges to their dominance of state politics.

Twenty thousand people attended a reception for President Jackson at the White House, trampling rugs, breaking furniture, and damaging china.

Rotation in Office

Few presidents have aroused as much controversy as Andrew Jackson. In office, Jackson greatly enhanced the power and prestige of the presidency. Whereas each member of Congress represented a specific regional constituency, only the president, Jackson declared, represented all the people of the United States. Jackson convinced many Americans that their votes mattered. He espoused a political ideology of "democratic republicanism" that stressed the common people's virtue, intelligence, and capacity for self-government. He also expressed a deep disdain for the "better classes," which claimed a "more enlightened wisdom" than common men and women.

Endorsing the view that a fundamental conflict existed between working people and the "nonproducing" classes of society, Jackson and his supporters promised to remove any impediments to the ordinary citizen's opportunities for economic improvement. According to the Jacksonians, inequalities of wealth and power were the direct result of monopoly, favoritism, and special privileges, which made "the rich richer and the powerful more potent." Only free competition in an open marketplace would ensure that wealth would be distributed in accordance with each person's "industry, economy, enterprise, and prudence." The goal of the Jacksonians was to remove all obstacles that prevented farmers, artisans, and small shopkeepers from earning a greater share of the nation's wealth.

Nowhere was the Jacksonian ideal of openness made more concrete than in Jackson's theory of rotation in office, known as the "spoils system." In his first annual message to Congress, Jackson defended the principle that public offices should be rotated among party supporters in

Known as a champion of the common people, President Jackson greatly expanded the powers of the presidency.

order to help the nation achieve its republican ideals. Performance in public office, Jackson maintained, required no special intelligence or training, and rotation in office would ensure that the federal government did not develop a class of corrupt civil servants set apart from the people. His supporters advocated the spoils system on practical political grounds, viewing it as a way to reward political party loyalists and build a stronger party organization. As Jacksonian Senator William Marcy of New York proclaimed, "To the victor belongs the spoils."

The spoils system opened government positions to many of Jackson's supporters, but it was neither as new nor as democratic as it appeared. During his first 18 months in office, Jackson replaced fewer than 1,000 of the nation's 10,000 civil servants on political grounds, and fewer than 20 percent of federal officeholders were removed during his administration. Moreover, many of the men Jackson appointed to office had backgrounds of wealth and social eminence. Further, Jackson did not originate the spoils system. By the time he took office, a number of states, including New York and Pennsylvania, practiced political patronage.

Clearing the Land of Indians

The first major political controversy of Jackson's presidency involved Indian policy. At the time Jackson took office, 125,000 Native Americans still lived east of the Mississippi River. The key issues were whether these Indian tribes would be permitted to block white expansion and whether the U.S. government and its citizens would abide by previously made treaties.

Since Jefferson's presidency, two conflicting Indian policies, assimilation and removal, had governed the treatment of Native Americans. The assimilation policy encouraged Indians to adopt white American customs and economic practices. The government provided financial assistance to missionaries in order to Christianize and educate Native Americans and convince them to adopt single-family farms. Proponents defended assimilation as the only way Native Americans would be able to survive in a white-dominated society. By the 1820s the Cherokees had demonstrated an ability to adapt to changing conditions while maintaining their tribal heritage. Sequoyah, a leader of these people, had developed a written alphabet. Soon the Cherokees opened schools, established churches, built roads, operated printing presses, and even adopted a constitution.

The other policy—removal—was first suggested by Thomas Jefferson as the only way to ensure the survival of Indian cultures. The goal of this policy was to encourage the voluntary migration of Indians westward to tracts of land where they could live free from white harassment. As early as 1817 James Monroe declared that the nation's security depended on rapid settlement along the southern coast, and that it was in the best interests of Native Americans to move westward. In 1825 he set before Congress a plan to resettle all eastern Indians on tracts in the West where whites would not be allowed to live.

After initially supporting both policies, Jackson favored removal as the solution to the controversy. This shift in federal Indian policy came partly as a result of a dispute between the Cherokee nation and the state of Georgia. The Cherokee people had adopted a constitution asserting sovereignty over their land. The state responded by abolishing tribal rule and claiming that the Cherokees fell under its jurisdiction. The discovery of gold on Cherokee land triggered a land rush, and the Cherokee nation sued to keep white settlers from encroaching on its territory. In two important cases, *Cherokee Nation* v. *Georgia* in 1831 and *Worcester* v. *Georgia* in 1832, the Supreme Court ruled that states could not pass laws conflicting with federal Indian treaties and that the federal government had an obligation to exclude white intruders from Indian lands. Angered, Jackson is said to have exclaimed: "John Marshall has made his decision; now let him enforce it."

The primary thrust of Jackson's removal policy was to encourage Indian tribes to sell all tribal lands in exchange for new lands in Oklahoma and Arkansas. Such a policy, the president maintained, would open new farm land to whites while offering Indians a haven where they would be free to develop at their own pace.

During the winter of 1831 the Choctaw became the first tribe to walk the "Trail of Tears" westward. Promised government assistance failed to arrive, and malnutrition, exposure, and a cholera epidemic killed many members of the Indian nation. Then, in 1836, the Creek suffered the hardships of removal. About 3,500 of the tribe's 15,000 members died along the westward trek. Those who resisted removal were bound in chains and marched in double file.

Emboldened by the Supreme Court decisions declaring that Georgia law had no force on Indian territory, the Cherokees resisted removal. The federal government bribed a faction of the tribe to leave the land in exchange for transportation costs and $5 million, but most Cherokees held out until 1838, when the army evicted them from their land. All told, 4,000 of the 15,000 tribal members died along the trail to Indian territory in what is now Oklahoma.

A number of other tribes also organized resistance against removal. In the Old Northwest, the Sauk and Fox Indians fought the Black Hawk War to recover ceded tribal lands in Illinois and Wisconsin. The Indians claimed that when they had signed the treaty transferring title to their land, they had not understood the implications of the action. The United

States army and the Illinois state militia ended the resistance by wantonly killing nearly 500 Sauk and Fox men, women, and children who were trying to retreat across the Mississippi River. In Florida the military spent seven years putting down Seminole resistance at a cost of $20 million and 1,500 casualties, and even then succeeding only after kidnapping a Seminole leader during peace talks.

By twentieth-century standards Jackson's Indian policy was both callous and inhumane. Despite the semblance of legality—94 treaties were signed with Indians during Jackson's presidency—Indian migrations to the West almost always occurred under the threat of government coercion. The federal government probably lacked the resources and military means necessary to protect the eastern Indians from encroaching whites, even had it wanted to do so. By the 1830s a growing number of missionaries and humanitarians agreed with Jackson that Indians needed to be resettled westward for their own protection. Removal failed in large part because of the nation's commitment to limited government and its lack of experience with social welfare programs. Contracts for food, clothing, and transportation were awarded to the lowest bidders, many of whom failed to fulfill their contractual responsibilities. The tragic outcome was readily foreseeable.

The problem of preserving native cultures in the face of an expanding nation was not confined to the United States. Jackson's removal policy can only be properly understood when seen as part of a broader process: the political and economic conquest of frontier regions by expanding nation states. During the early decades of the nineteenth century European nations were penetrating into many frontier areas, including the steppes of Russia, the plains of Argentina, the veldt of South Africa, the outback of Australia, and the American West. In each of these regions national expansion was justified on the grounds of strategic interest (to preempt settlement by other powers) or in the name of opening valuable land to white settlement and development. And in each case expansion was accompanied by the removal or wholesale killing of native peoples.

Sectional Disputes over Public Lands and Nullification

Bitter sectional disputes arose during Jackson's presidency over public lands and the tariff. After the Revolutionary War the federal government owned one-quarter billion acres of public land; the Louisiana Purchase added another half billion acres to the public domain. These public lands constituted the federal government's single greatest source of public revenue.

In 1820, to promote the establishment of farms, Congress encouraged the rapid sale of public land by reducing the minimum land purchase from 160 to just 80 acres, at a price of $1.25 per acre. Still, a variety of groups favored even easier terms for land sales. Squatters, for example, who violated federal laws that forbade settlement prior to the completion of public surveys, pressured Congress to adopt preemption acts that would permit them to buy the land they occupied at the minimum price of $1.25 when it came up for sale. Urban workingmen demanded free homesteads for any American who would settle the public domain. Transportation companies, which built roads, canals, and later railroads, called for grants of public land to help fund their projects.

In Congress two proposals—"distribution" and "graduation"—competed for support. Under the distribution proposal, which was identified with Henry Clay, Congress would distribute the proceeds from the sale of public lands to the states, which would use the funds to finance transportation improvements. Senator Thomas Hart Benton of Missouri offered an alternative proposal, graduation. He proposed that Congress gradually reduce the price of unsold government land and, finally, give away land that remained unpurchased.

At the end of 1829 a Connecticut senator proposed a cessation of public land sales. This transformed the debate over public lands into a sectional battle over the nature of the union. Senator Benton denounced the proposal as a brazen attempt by manufacturers to keep laborers from settling the West, fearing that westward migration would reduce the size of the urban work force and therefore raise their wage costs.

Benton's speech prompted Robert Y. Hayne, a supporter of John C. Calhoun, to propose an alliance of southern and western interests based on a low tariff and cheap land. Affirming the principle of nullification, he called on the two sections to unite against attempts by the northeast to strengthen the powers of the federal government.

Daniel Webster of Massachusetts answered Hayne in one of the most famous speeches in American history. The United States, Webster proclaimed, was not simply a compact of the states. It was a creation of the people, who had invested the Constitution and the national government with ultimate sovereignty. If a state disagreed with an action of the federal government, it had a right to sue in federal court or seek to amend the Constitution, but it had no right to nullify a federal law. Such action would inevitably lead to anarchy and civil war. It was delusion and folly to think that Americans could have "Liberty first and Union afterwards," Webster declared. "Liberty and Union, now and forever, one and inseparable."

Jackson revealed his position on the questions of states' rights and nullification at a Jefferson Day dinner on April 13, 1830. Fixing his eyes on Vice President John C. Calhoun, the president expressed his sentiments with this toast: "Our Union: It must be preserved." Calhoun responded to Jackson's challenge and offered the next toast: "The Union, next to our liberty, most dear. May we always remember that it can only be preserved by distributing equally the benefits and burdens of the Union."

Relations between Jackson and Calhoun had grown increasingly strained. Jackson had learned that when Calhoun was secretary of war under Monroe he had called for Jackson's court-martial for his conduct during the military occupation of Florida in 1818. Jackson was also angry because Mrs. Calhoun had snubbed the wife of Secretary of War John H. Eaton, because Mrs. Eaton was the twice-married daughter of a tavern-keeper. Because Jackson's own late wife Rachel had been snubbed by society, the president had empathy for young Peggy Eaton. In 1831 Jackson reorganized his cabinet and forced Calhoun's supporters out. The next year Calhoun became the first vice president to resign his office, when he became a senator from South Carolina.

In 1832, in an effort to conciliate the South, Jackson proposed a lower tariff. Revenue from the existing tariff (together with the sale of public lands) was so high that the federal debt was quickly being paid off; in fact on January 1, 1835, the United States Treasury had a $440,000 surplus. The new tariff adopted in 1832 was somewhat lower than the Tariff of 1828 but still maintained the principle of protection. In protest, South Carolina's fiery "states' righters" declared both the Tariff of 1832 and the Tariff of 1828 null and void. To defend nullification, the state legislature voted to raise an army.

Jackson responded by declaring nullification illegal, and then asked Congress to empower him to use force to execute federal law. Congress promptly enacted a Force Act. Privately, Jackson threatened to "hang every leader . . . of that infatuated people, sir, by martial law, irrespective of his name, or political or social position." He also dispatched a fleet of eight ships and a shipment of 5,000 muskets to Fort Pinckney, a federal installation in Charleston harbor.

In Congress, Henry Clay, the "great compromiser" who had engineered the Missouri Compromise of 1820, worked feverishly to reduce South Carolina's sense of grievance. "He who loves the Union must desire to see this agitating question brought to a termination," he said. In less than a month he persuaded Congress to enact a compromise tariff with lower levels of protection. South Carolinians backed down, rescinding the ordinance nullifying the federal tariff.

South Carolina's anxiety had many causes. By 1831 declining cotton prices and growing concern about the future of slavery had turned the state from a staunch supporter of economic nationalism into the nation's most aggressive advocate of states' rights. Increasingly, economic grievances fused with concerns over slavery. In 1832 the Palmetto State was one of just two states whose population was made up of a majority of slaves. By that year events throughout the hemisphere made South Carolinians desperately uneasy about the future of slavery. In 1831 and 1832 militant abolitionism had erupted in the North, slave insurrections had occurred in Southampton County, Virginia, and Jamaica, and Britain was moving to emancipate all slaves in the British Caribbean.

By using the federal tariff as the focus of their grievances, South Carolinians found an ideal way of debating the question of state sovereignty without debating the morality of slavery. Following the Missouri Compromise debates, a slave insurrection led by Denmark Vesey had been uncovered in Charleston in 1822. By 1832 South Carolinians did not want to stage debates in Congress that might bring the explosive slavery issue to the fore and possibly incite another slave revolt.

The Bank War

Although the tariff was important, the major political issue of Jackson's presidency was his war against the second Bank of the United States. To understand this battle, the nature of the banking system at the time Jackson assumed the presidency must be understood. It was completely different than it is today. At that time, the federal government coined only a limited supply of hard money and printed no paper money at all. The principal source of circulating currency—of paper bank notes—was private commercial banks (of which there were 329 in 1829), chartered by the various states. These private, state-chartered banks supplied the credit necessary to finance land purchases, business operations, and economic growth. The notes they issued were promises to pay gold or silver, but they were backed by a limited amount of precious metal and they fluctuated greatly in value.

In 1816 the federal government had chartered the second Bank of the United States partly in an effort to control the notes issued by state banks. By demanding payment in gold or silver, the national bank could discipline overspeculative private banks. But the very idea of a national bank was unpopular for various reasons. Many people blamed it for causing the Panic of 1819. Others resented its political influence. For example, Senator Daniel Webster was both the bank's chief lobbyist and a director of the bank's Boston branch. Wage earners and small businesspeople blamed it for economic fluctuations and loan restrictions. Private banks resented its privileged position in the banking industry.

In 1832 Henry Clay, Daniel Webster, and other Jackson opponents in Congress, seeking an issue for that year's presidential election, passed a bill rechartering the second Bank of the United States. The bank's charter was not due to expire until 1836, but Clay and Webster wanted to force

Jackson to take a clear pro-bank or antibank position. Jackson had frequently attacked the bank as an agency through which speculators, monopolists, and other seekers of economic privilege cheated honest farmers and mechanics. Now his adversaries wanted to force him either to sign the bill for recharter, alienating voters hostile to the bank, or veto it, antagonizing conservative voters who favored a sound banking system.

Jackson vetoed the bill in a forceful message that condemned the bank as a privileged "monopoly" created to make "rich men . . . richer by act of Congress." The bank, he declared, was "unauthorized by the Constitution, subversive of the rights of the States, and dangerous to the liberties of the people." In the presidential campaign of 1832 Henry Clay tried to make an issue of Jackson's bank veto, but Jackson swept to an easy second-term victory, defeating Clay by 219 electoral votes to 49.

Jackson interpreted his reelection as a mandate to undermine the bank still further. In September 1833 he ordered his Treasury secretary to divert federal revenues from the Bank of the United States to selected state banks, which came to be known as "pet" banks. The secretary of the Treasury and his successor resigned rather than carry out the president's order. It was only after Jackson appointed a second new secretary that his order was implemented. Jackson's decision to divert federal deposits from the national bank prompted his adversaries in the Senate to formally censure the president's actions as arbitrary and unconstitutional. The bank's president, Nicholas Biddle, responded to Jackson's actions by reducing loans and calling in debts. Over the span of six months the bank reduced loans by nearly $10 million in an attempt to pressure Jackson to approve a new charter. "The Bank . . . is trying to kill me," Jackson declared, "but I will kill it."

Jackson's decision to divert funds drew strong support from many conservative businesspeople who believed that the bank's destruction would increase the availability of credit and open up new business opportunities. Jackson, however, hated all banks, and believed that the only sound currencies were gold and silver. Having crippled the Bank of the United States, he promptly launched a crusade to replace all bank notes with hard money. In the Specie Circular of 1836 Jackson prohibited payment for public lands with anything but gold or silver. That same year, in another antibanking measure, Congress voted to deprive pet banks of federal deposits. Instead, nearly $35 million in surplus federal funds to the states was distributed to help finance internal improvements.

To Jackson's supporters, the presidential veto of the bank bill was a principled assault on a bastion of wealth and special privilege. His efforts to curtail the circulation of bank notes was an attempt to rid the country of a tool used by commercial interests to exploit farmers and working men and women. To his critics, the veto was an act of economic igno-

rance that destroyed a valuable institution that promoted monetary stability, eased the long-distance transfer of funds, provided a reserve of capital
on which other banks drew, and helped regulate the bank notes issued by
private banks. Jackson's effort to limit the circulation of bank notes was a
misguided act of a president who failed to understand the role of a banking system in a modern economy.

The effect of Jackson's banking policies remains a subject of debate.
Initially, land sales, canal construction, cotton production, and manufacturing boomed following Jackson's decision to divert federal funds from
the bank. At the same time, however, state debts rose sharply and inflation
increased dramatically. Prices climbed 28 percent in just three years. Then
in 1837, just after the election of Jackson's successor Democrat Martin
Van Buren, a deep financial depression struck the nation. Cotton prices
fell by half. In New York City 50,000 people were thrown out of work
and 200,000 lacked adequate means of support. Mobs in New York broke
into the city's flour warehouse. From across the country came "rumor
after rumor of riot, insurrection, and tumult." Not until the mid-1840s
would the country fully pull out of the depression.

Who was to blame for the Panic of 1837? One school of thought
holds Jackson responsible, arguing that his banking policies removed a
vital check on the activities of state-chartered banks. Freed from the regulation of the second Bank of the United States, private banks rapidly expanded the volume of bank notes in circulation, contributing to the rapid
increase in inflation. Jackson's Specie Circular of 1836, which sought to
curb inflation by requiring that public land payments be made in hard
currency, forced many Americans to exchange paper bills for gold and silver. Many private banks lacked sufficient reserves of hard currency and
were forced to close their doors, triggering a financial crisis.

Another school of thought blames the panic on factors outside of Jackson's control. A surplus of cotton on the world market caused the price of
cotton to drop sharply, throwing many southern and western cotton farmers into bankruptcy. Meanwhile, in 1836, Britain suddenly raised interest
rates, which drastically reduced investment in the American economy and
forced a number of states to default on loans from foreign investors.

If Jackson's policies did not necessarily cause the panic, they certainly
made recovery more difficult. Jackson's handpicked successor, Martin Van
Buren, responded to the economic depression in an extremely doctrinaire
way. A firm believer in the Jeffersonian principle of limited government,
Van Buren refused to provide government aid to business. Fearful that the
federal government might lose funds it had deposited in private banks, Van
Buren convinced Congress in 1840 to adopt an independent treasury system. Under this proposal federal funds were locked up in subtreasuries, depriving the banking system of hard currency that might have aided recovery.

The Jacksonian Court

Presidents' judicial appointments represent one of their most enduring legacies. In his two terms as president Andrew Jackson appointed five of the seven justices on the Supreme Court. To replace Chief Justice John Marshall, who died in 1835, Jackson selected his Treasury secretary, Roger B. Taney, who would lead the court for nearly three decades. Under Taney, the Court broke with tradition, and sought to extend Jacksonian principles of promoting individual opportunity by removing traditional restraints on competition in the marketplace. The Taney Court upheld the doctrine of limited liability for corporations and provided legal sanction to state subsidies for canals, turnpikes, and railroads. Taken together, the decisions of the Taney Court played a vital role in the emergence of the American system of free enterprise.

One case in particular, that of *Charles River Bridge* v. *Warren Bridge,* raised an issue fundamental to the nation's future economic growth: whether state-granted monopolies would be allowed to block competition from new enterprises. In 1828 the state of Massachusetts chartered a company to build a toll-free bridge connecting Boston and neighboring Charlestown. The owners of an existing toll bridge sued, claiming that their 1785 charter included an implied right to a monopoly.

In its decision, the Court ensured that monopolistic privileges granted in the past would not be allowed to interfere with public welfare. The Court held that contracts conferred only explicitly stated rights. The decision epitomized the ideals of Jacksonian democracy: a commitment to removing artificial barriers to opportunity and an emphasis upon free competition in an open marketplace.

Jackson's Legacy

Andrew Jackson was one of the nation's most resourceful and effective presidents. In the face of hostile majorities in Congress, he carried out his most important policies, affecting banking, internal improvements, Native Americans, and tariffs. As president, Jackson used the veto power more often than all previous presidents combined during the preceding 40 years, and used it in such a way that he succeeded in representing himself as the champion of the people against special interests in Congress. In addition, his skillful use of patronage and party organization and his successful manipulation of public symbols helped create the nation's first modern political party with truly national appeal.

And yet, despite his popular appeal, Jackson's legacy is a matter of great dispute among historians. His Indian policies continue to arouse passionate criticism, while his economic policies, contrary to his reputation as the president of the common man, did little to help small farmers, artisans, and working people. In fact, his policies actually weakened the ability of the federal government to regulate the nation's economy. Indeed, many historians now believe that slaveholders—not small farmers or working people—benefited most. His Indian policies helped to open new lands for slaveowners, and his view of limited government forestalled federal interference with slavery.

Rise of a Political Opposition

Although it took a number of years for Jackson's opponents to coalesce into an effective national political organization, by the mid-1830s the Whig party, as the opposition came to be known, was able to battle the Democratic party on almost equal terms throughout the country. The party was formed in 1834 as a coalition of National Republicans, Anti-Masons, and disgruntled Democrats, who were united by their hatred of "King Andrew" Jackson and his "usurpations" of congressional and judicial authority. The party took its name from the seventeenth-century British Whigs, who had defended English liberties against the usurpations of pro-Catholic Stuart Kings.

In 1836 the Whigs mounted their first presidential campaign. The party ran three regional candidates against Martin Van Buren: Daniel Webster, the senator from Massachusetts; Hugh Lawson White, who had appeal in the South; and William Henry Harrison, who fought an Indian alliance at the Battle of Tippecanoe and appealed to the West. The party strategy was to throw the election into the House of Representatives, where the Whigs would unite behind a single candidate. Van Buren easily defeated all his Whig opponents, winning 170 electoral votes to just 73 for his closest rival.

The emergence of Martin Van Buren as Jackson's successor resulted in a major defection of southerners and conservative Democrats to the Whig party. Unlike the southern slave-owning Jackson, Van Buren was a "Yankee" from New York, and many southerners feared that he could not be trusted to protect slavery. As a result, the Whigs carried Georgia, Kentucky, Maryland, and Tennessee.

Ironically, as president, Van Buren supported a congressional rule—known as the Gag Rule—which quashed debate over antislavery petitions in the House of Representatives. His independent treasury scheme combined with his staunch opposition to any federal interference in the economy lured Calhoun and the southern nullifiers back to the Democratic party. Conversely, his attacks on paper money and his scheme to remove federal funds from the private banking system alienated many conservative Democrats who threw their support to the Whigs.

Following his strong showing in the election of 1836, William Henry Harrison received the united support of the Whig party in 1840. Benefiting from the Panic of 1837 and from a host of colorful campaign innovations, Harrison easily defeated Van Buren by a vote of 234 to 60 in the electoral college.

Unfortunately, the 68-year-old Harrison caught cold while delivering a two-hour inaugural address in the freezing rain. Barely a month later, he died of pneumonia, the first president to die in office. His successor, John Tyler of Virginia, was an ardent defender of slavery, a staunch advocate of states' rights, and a former Democrat, whom the Whigs had nominated in order to attract Democratic support to the Whig ticket.

A firm believer in the principle that the federal government should exercise no powers other than those expressly enumerated in the Constitution, Tyler rejected the entire Whig legislative program, which called for the reestablishment of a national bank, an increased tariff, and federally funded internal improvements.

The Whig party was furious. To protest Tyler's rejection of the Whig political agenda, all members of the cabinet but one resigned. Tyler had become a president without a party. "His Accidency" vetoed nine bills during his four years in office, frustrating Whig plans to recharter the national bank and raise the tariff, while simultaneously distributing proceeds of land sales to the states. In 1843 Whigs in the House of Representatives made Tyler the subject of the first serious impeachment attempt, but the resolutions were defeated by a vote of 127 to 83.

Curiously, it was during Tyler's administration that the nation's new two-party system achieved full maturity. Prior to Tyler's ascension to office, the Whig party had been a loose conglomeration of diverse political factions unable to agree on a party platform. Tyler's presidency increased unity among Whigs who found common cause in their opposition to his policies. On important issues four-fifths of all Whig members of Congress regularly voted together. At the same time, the Whigs created an elaborate network of party newspapers in all parts of the country. Never before had party identity been so high or partisan sentiment so strong.

Who Were the Whigs?

The Jacksonians made a great effort to to persuade voters to identify their own cause with Thomas Jefferson and their Whig opponents with Alexander Hamilton. In spite of Democratic charges to the contrary, however, the Whigs were not simply a continuation of the Federalist party. Like the Democrats, the Whigs drew support from all parts of the nation. Indeed, the Whigs often formed the majority of the South's representatives in Congress. Like the Democrats, the Whigs were a coalition of sectional interests, class and economic interests, and ethnic and religious interests.

Democratic voters tended to be small farmers, residents of less-prosperous towns, and the Scots-Irish and Catholic Irish. Whigs tended to be educators and professionals, manufacturers, business-oriented farmers, British and German Protestant immigrants, upwardly aspiring manual laborers, free blacks, and active members of Presbyterian, Unitarian, and Congregational churches. The Whig coalition included supporters of Henry Clay's American System, states' righters, religious groups alienated by Jackson's Indian removal policies, and bankers and businesspeople frightened by the Democrats' antimonopoly and antibank rhetoric.

Whereas the Democrats stressed class conflict, Whigs emphasized the harmony of interests between labor and capital, the need for humanitarian reform, and leadership by men of talent. The Whigs also idealized the "self-made man," who starts "from an humble origin, and from small beginnings rise[s] gradually in the world, as a result of merit and industry." Finally, the Whigs viewed technology and factory enterprise as forces for increasing national wealth and improving living conditions.

In 1848 and 1852 the Whigs tried to repeat their successful 1840 presidential campaign by nominating military heroes for the presidency. The party won the 1848 election with General Zachary Taylor, an Indian fighter and hero of the Mexican War, who had never cast a vote in a presidential election. Like Harrison, Taylor confined his campaign speeches to uncontroversial platitudes. "Old Rough and Ready," as he was known, died after just sixteen months in office. Then, in 1852, the Whigs nominated another Indian fighter and Mexican War hero, General Winfield Scott, who carried just four states for his dying party. Scott was the last Whig nominee to play an important role in a presidential election.

Conclusion

A political revolution occurred in the United States between 1820 and 1840. Property qualifications for voting and officeholding were abolished, voting by voice was eliminated, voter participation increased, and a new party system emerged. Unlike America's first political parties, the Federalists and Republicans, the Jacksonian Democrats and the Whigs were parties with grass-roots organization and support in all parts of the nation.

Andrew Jackson, the dominant political figure of the period, spelled out the new democratic approach to politics. In the name of eliminating special privilege and promoting equality of opportunity, he helped institute the national political nominating convention, defended the spoils system, destroyed the second Bank of the United States, and opened

*C*hronology of Key Events

1820	Land Act reduces price of public land to $1.25 an acre
1825	House of Representatives elects John Quincy Adams as sixth president
1828	South Carolina Exposition; Congress passes Tariff of Abominations; Andrew Jackson elected seventh president
1830	Indian Removal Act; Webster-Hayne debate
1832	Jackson vetoes second Bank of the United States recharter bill;
1833	Congress adopts "Compromise Tariff" lowering tariff rates and "Force Bill" authorizing Jackson to enforce federal law in South Carolina
1835	Roger B. Taney succeeds John Marshall as Chief Justice
1836	Specie Circular; Martin Van Buren elected eighth president
1837	Panic of 1837; *Charles River Bridge* v. *Warren Bridge*
1840	Independent Treasury Act; William Henry Harrison elected ninth president
1841	John Tyler becomes tenth president on death of Harrison

millions of acres of Indian lands to white settlement. A strong and determined leader, Jackson greatly expanded the power of the presidency. No matter how one evaluates his eight years in the White House, there can be no doubt that he left an indelible stamp on the nation's highest office; indeed, on a whole epoch in American history.

Suggestions for Further Reading

General surveys of the Jacksonian era include Edward Pessen, *Jacksonian America: Society, Personality, and Politics,* rev. ed. (1978); Arthur M. Schlesinger, Jr., *The Age of Jackson* (1945); Harry L. Watson, *Liberty and Power* (1990).

Biographies of Andrew Jackson include James C. Curtis, *Andrew Jackson and the Search for Vindication* (1976); Robert Remini, *Andrew Jackson and the Course of American Freedom* (1981), and *Andrew Jackson and the Course of American Democracy* (1984). See also Marvin Meyers, *The Jacksonian Persuasion* (1957); John W. Ward, *Andrew Jackson: Symbol for an Age* (1955).

On Jackson's banking and economic policies, see Bray Hammond, *Banks and Politics in America: From the Revolution to the Civil War* (1957); Peter Temin, *The Jacksonian Economy* (1969). Other aspects of Jackson's presidency are examined in Daniel Feller, *Public Lands in Jacksonian Politics* (1984); Ronald Satz, *American Indian Policy in the Jacksonian Era* (1975).

Significant biographies of Jackson's opponents are Irving H. Bartlett, *Daniel Webster* (1978); John Niven, *John C. Calhoun and the Price of Union* (1988); Robert Remini, *Henry Clay* (1991).

On the emergence of the second party system, see Richard Hofstadter, *The Idea of a Party System* (1969); Richard P. McCormick, *The Second American Party System* (1966). The political ideologies of the two parties are examined in Lee Benson, *The Concept of Jacksonian Democracy* (1961); Daniel Walker Howe, *The Political Culture of the American Whigs* (1979). See also W. P. Vaughn, *The Antimasonic Party in the United States* (1983).

Chapter II

Reforming American Society

The Reform Impulse
Sources of the Reform Impulse
Second Great Awakening

Moral Reform

Social Reform
The Problem of Crime in a Free Society
The Struggle for Educational Opportunity
Asylums for Society's Outcasts

Radical Reform
The Rise of the Antislavery Movement
Division in the Antislavery Movement
The Birth of Feminism
Catalyst for Women's Rights
Utopian Communities

Artistic and Cultural Ferment
American Transcendentalism
A Literary and Artistic Renaissance
Popular Culture

Many early nineteenth-century New Yorkers feared that their city was being overwhelmed by crime. In one highly publicized incident a little girl was stabbed to death over a penny she had begged. In another incident in 1849, 30 people died and another 100 were injured in a riot outside the city's Astor Place Opera House. Declared the city's mayor: "This city is infested by gangs of hardened wretches" who "patrol the streets making night hideous and insulting all who are not strong enough to defend themselves." Between 1814 and 1835 New York City's population doubled, but reports of crime increased fivefold.

Poverty and crime appeared to be epidemic. Young girls, dressed in rags, tried to support themselves by selling toothpicks. An estimated 10,000 prostitutes plied their trade, brazenly standing outside of fashionable hotels or strolling through theaters. Gangs, bearing such names as the Plug Uglies, Dead Rabbits, and the Bowery B'hoys, prowled the city streets, stealing from warehouses, junk shops, and private residences.

Critics decried a "carnival of murder." In 1857 six men were shot or stabbed in barroom brawls in a single night. In response to the apparent upsurge in crime, fearful citizens armed themselves, carrying guns and night sticks for their defense when they went outside at night. For added protection, many homeowners installed iron bars over their ground-floor windows.

During the decades before the Civil War, newspapers were filled with reports of crime, vice, and violence in the growing cities of the North, in the slave South, and on the frontier. Incidents of crime and violence led many Americans to ask how a free society could maintain stability and moral order. Americans sought to answer this question through religion, education, and social reform.

The Reform Impulse

The first half of the nineteenth century witnessed an enormous effort to improve society through reform. Reformers launched unprecedented campaigns to assist the handicapped, rehabilitate criminals and prostitutes, outlaw alcohol, guarantee women's rights, and abolish slavery. Our modern systems of free public schools, prisons, and hospitals for the infirm and the mentally ill are all legacies of this first generation of American reform. What factors gave rise to the reform impulse and why was it unleashed with such vigor in pre–Civil War America?

Sources of the Reform Impulse

The reformers had many different reasons for wanting to change American society. Some people turned to reform as a way of imposing order;

others were motivated by a religious vision of creating a godly society on earth. Still others viewed reform as a way of spreading the values associated with the Protestant ethic: sobriety, punctuality, self-discipline, and personal responsibility.

During the first decades of the nineteenth century America's revolutionary heritage, Enlightenment philosophy, and religious zeal all contributed to a spirit of optimism, a sensitivity to human suffering, and a boundless faith in humankind's capacity to improve social institutions. The Declaration of Independence, with its emphasis on natural rights, liberty, and equality, led reformers to view their efforts as a continuation of political struggles begun during the Revolution. The philosophy of the Enlightenment, with its belief in the people's innate goodness and its rejection of the inevitability of poverty and ignorance, was another important source of reform. By providing a more favorable moral and physical environment through the application of reason, reform could overcome social problems and antisocial behavior.

Religion further strengthened the reform impulse. Almost all the leading reformers were devoutly religious men and women, who wanted to deepen the nation's commitment to Christian principles. Two trends in religious thought—religious liberalism and evangelical revivalism—strengthened reformers' zeal. Religious liberalism was an emerging form of humanitarianism that rejected the harsh Calvinist doctrines of original sin and predestination. Its preachers stressed the basic goodness of human nature and each individual's capacity to follow the example of Christ.

William Ellery Channing was America's leading exponent of religious liberalism. In 1815 Channing's beliefs became the basis for American Unitarianism. The new religious denomination stressed individual freedom of belief, and a united world under a single God. Channing's beliefs stimulated many reformers to work toward improving the conditions of the physically handicapped, the criminal, the pauper, and the enslaved.

Second Great Awakening

The evangelical revivalism that swept the country in the early nineteenth century was also a source of the reform impulse. This great religious fervor came to be called the Second Great Awakening. Evangelical leaders urged their followers to repent their sins and reject selfishness and materialism. To the revivalists, sin was not a metaphysical abstraction. Luxury, high living, indifference to religion, preoccupation with worldly and commercial matters—all these were denounced as sinful. If men and women did not seek God through Christ, the nation would face divine retribution. Evangelical revivals helped instill a belief that Americans had been chosen by God to lead the world toward "a millennium of republicanism."

Charles Grandison Finney, the "father of modern revivalism," led revivals throughout the Northeast. Despite his lack of formal theological training, Finney was remarkably successful in converting souls to Christ. He prayed for sinners by name; he held meetings that lasted night after night for a week or more; he set up an "anxious bench" at the front of the meeting, where the almost-saved could receive special prayers. He also encouraged women to actively participate in revivals. Finney's message was that anyone could experience a redemptive change of heart and a resurgence of religious feeling. If only enough people converted to Christ, Finney told his listeners, the millennium would arrive within three years.

Revival meetings attracted both frontier settlers and city folk, slaves and masters, farmers and shopkeepers. The revivals had their greatest appeal among isolated farming families on the western and southern frontier, among upwardly mobile merchants, shopkeepers, artisans, and skilled laborers in the expanding commercial and industrial towns of the North. They drew support from social conservatives who feared that America would disintegrate into a state of anarchy without the influence of evangelical religion, and also enlisted followers among poorer whites and slaves in the South. Above all, revivals attracted large numbers of young women, who took an active role in organizing meetings, establishing church organizations, and editing religious publications.

Moral Reform

The earliest reformers wanted to persuade Americans to adopt more godly personal habits. They set up associations to battle profanity and Sabbath breaking, to place a Bible in every American home, to provide religious education for the children of the poor, and to curb the widespread heavy use of hard liquor. By discouraging drinking, gambling, and encouraging observance of the Sabbath, reformers hoped to "restore the government of God."

The most extensive moral reform campaign was against drinking, which had long been an integral part of American life. Many people believed that downing a glass of whiskey before breakfast was conducive to good health. Easily affordable to even the poorest Americans—a gallon of whiskey cost 25 cents in the 1820s—consumption had risen markedly since the beginning of the century.

Reformers sought to alter the cultural norms that encouraged alcohol consumption by identifying liquor as the cause of a wide range of social, family, and personal problems. Many middle-class women blamed alcohol for the abuse of wives and children and the squandering of family resources. Many businesspeople identified drinking with crime, poverty, and inefficient, unproductive employees.

Americans turned to revival meetings in times of social and economic upheaval. These meetings, which stressed new birth conversions, could last for days.

The stage was clearly set for the appearance of an organized movement against liquor. In 1826 the nation's first formal national temperance organization was born: the American Society for the Promotion of Temperance. Led by socially prominent clergy and laypeople, the new organization called for total abstinence from distilled liquor.

By 1835 an estimated 2 million Americans had taken the "pledge" to abstain from hard liquor. Temperance reform drew support from many southerners and westerners who were otherwise indifferent or hostile to reform. Their efforts helped reduce annual per capita consumption of alcohol from seven gallons in 1830 to just three gallons a decade later. In addition, a campaign to restrict the manufacture and sale of alcohol culminated in the nation's first statewide prohibition law in Maine in 1851.

The sudden arrival of hundreds of thousands of immigrants heightened the concerns of temperance reformers. Between 1830 and 1860 nearly two million Irish arrived in the United States along with an additional 893,000 Germans. Increasingly, the alleged heavy drinking of immigrants was regarded as a problem demanding government action.

Social Reform

The nation's first reformers tried to improve the nation's moral and spiritual values by distributing Bibles and religious tracts, promoting observance of the Sabbath, and curbing drinking. Beginning in the 1820s a new phase of reform—social reform—spread across the country, directed at such problems as crime, illiteracy, poverty, and disease. Reformers sought to solve these problems by creating new institutions to deal with them—including prisons, public schools, and asylums for the deaf, the blind, and the mentally ill.

The Problem of Crime in a Free Society

Prior to the American Revolution punishment for crimes generally involved some form of corporal punishment, ranging from the death

As early as the 1820s, urban slums like New York City's Five Points began to appear. These areas of poverty, crime, filth, and violence attracted beggars, pimps, prostitutes, and hoodlums.

penalty for serious crimes to public whipping, confinement in stocks, and branding for lesser offenses. Jails were used as temporary confinement for criminal defendants awaiting trial or punishment. Conditions in these early jails were abominable. Debtors were confined with hardened criminals, and offenders of both sexes and of all ages were confined in large groups in cramped cells.

During the pre–Civil War decades reformers began to view crime as a social problem—a product of environment and parental neglect—rather than the result of original sin or human depravity. Revulsion over the spectacle of public punishment led to the rapid construction of penal institutions in which the "disease" of crime could be quarantined and inmates could be gradually rehabilitated in a controlled environment. Two rival prison systems competed for public support. After constructing Auburn Prison, New York State authorities adopted a system in which inmates worked in large workshops during the day and slept in separate cells at night. Convicts had to march in lockstep and refrain from speaking or even looking at each other. In Pennsylvania's Eastern State Penitentiary, constructed in 1829, authorities placed even greater stress on the physical isolation of prisoners. Every prison cell had its own exercise yard, work space, and toilet facilities. Under the Pennsylvania plan prisoners lived and worked in complete isolation from each other. Called "penitentiaries" or "reformatories," these new prisons reflected the belief that hard physical labor and solitary confinement might encourage introspection and instill habits of discipline that would rehabilitate criminals.

The legal principle that a criminal act should only be legally punished if the offender was fully capable of distinguishing between right and wrong opened the way to one of the most controversial aspects of American jurisprudence—the insanity defense. The question arose dramatically in 1835 when a deranged Englishman named Richard Lawrence walked up to President Andrew Jackson and fired two pistols at him at a distance of six feet. Incredibly, both guns misfired, and Jackson was unhurt. The court found Lawrence insane and not subject to criminal prosecution; instead, he was confined for treatment of his mental condition.

Another major effort was a movement to outlaw capital punishment. Prior to the 1830s most states reduced the number of crimes punishable by death and began to perform executions outside of public view, lest the public be stimulated to acts of violence by the spectacle of hangings. In 1847 Michigan became the first modern jurisdiction to outlaw the death penalty and was soon followed by Rhode Island and Wisconsin.

Imprisonment for debt also came under attack. As late as 1816 an average of 600 residents of New York City were in prison at any one time for failure to pay debts. More than half owed less than $50. Imprisoned debtors were, of course, unable to work and therefore unable to pay off their debts. Increasingly, reformers regarded imprisonment as irrational. Beginning with New York State in 1817, states eliminated the practice of jailing people for trifling debts. Subsequently other states forbade the jailing of women for debt.

The Struggle for Educational Opportunity

Of all the ideas advanced by antebellum reformers, none was more original than the principle that all American children should be educated to their fullest capacity at public expense. Prior to the 1840s apprenticeship had been a major form of education, and formal schooling was largely limited to those who could afford to pay. Reformers viewed education as the key to individual opportunity and the creation of an enlightened and responsible citizenry. They also believed that public schooling could be an effective weapon in the fight against juvenile delinquency and an essential ingredient in the education and assimilation of immigrants.

Horace Mann of Massachusetts, the nation's leading educational reformer, led the fight for government support for public schools. As a state legislator, Mann took the lead in establishing a board of education, and his efforts resulted in a doubling of state expenditures on education. He was also successful in winning state support for teacher training, an improved curriculum in schools, grading of pupils by age and ability, and a lengthened school year. He was also partially successful in curtailing the use of corporal punishment. In 1852 Massachusetts adopted the first compulsory school attendance law in American history. By 1860 almost one third of the high schools in the United States were located in Massachusetts.

Support for public schools transcended class lines. It came not only from conservatives but also from working people. Public schools were largely the result of local efforts around the country and were most successful in the Northeast and later in the Midwest.

Such educational opportunities, however, were not available to all. Most northern cities specifically excluded blacks from their public school systems; cities like New York and Boston consigned black children to inferior segregated schools. Women and religious minorities also experienced discrimination. Many public school teachers showed an anti-Catholic bias by using texts that portrayed the Catholic church as a threat to republican values and by reading biblical passages from the Protestant version of the scriptures. Beginning in New York City in 1840, Catholics decided to establish a separate system of parochial schools in which children would receive a religious education as well as training in the arts and sciences. For women, education beyond the level of handicrafts and basic reading and writing was largely confined to separate female academies and seminaries for the affluent.

In higher education a few institutions opened their doors to blacks and women. In 1833 Oberlin College became the nation's first coeducational college. Three colleges for blacks were established before the Civil War, and a few other institutions began to admit small numbers of black students. In 1837 Mount Holyoke, the first women's college, was established to train teachers and missionaries. A number of western universities also admitted women.

The reform impulse was evident in other changes in higher education. At the beginning of the nineteenth century most colleges offered their students, who usually enrolled between the ages of 12 and 15, only a narrow training in the classics designed to prepare them for the ministry. During the 1820s and 1830s colleges broadened their curricula to include the study of history, literature, geography, modern languages, and the sciences. The entrance age was also raised and the requirements demanded of students were broadened.

The number of colleges also increased. Most of the new colleges, particularly in the South and West, were church-affiliated, but several states established state universities. Prior to the Civil War 16 states provided some financial support to higher education, and in New York City by the 1850s an education, from elementary school to college, was available tuition free.

Asylums for Society's Outcasts

A number of reformers devoted their attention to the problems of the mentally ill, the deaf, and the blind. In 1841 Dorothea Dix, a 39-year-old former schoolteacher, volunteered to give religious instruction to women incarcerated in the East Cambridge, Massachusetts, House of Correction. She was horrified to find mentally ill inmates dressed in rags and confined to a single dreary room without any source of heat. Shocked by what she saw, she embarked on a lifelong crusade to reform the treatment of the mentally ill. After a two-year secret investigation of every jail and almshouse in Massachusetts, Dix issued a report to the state legislature. The mentally ill, she found, were brutally treated and mixed indiscriminately with paupers and hardened criminals. Dix then carried her campaign for state-supported asylums nationwide, persuading more than a dozen state legislatures to improve institutional care for the insane.

Through the efforts of such reformers as Thomas Gallaudet and Samuel Howe, institutions to care for the deaf and blind began to appear. Thomas Hopkins Gallaudet established in 1817 the nation's first school in Hartford, Connecticut, to teach deaf-mutes to read and write, read lips, and communicate through hand signals. Samuel Gridley Howe accomplished for the blind what Gallaudet achieved for the deaf. He founded the country's first school for the blind in Boston and produced printed materials with raised type.

Radical Reform

The initial thrust of reform—moral reform—was to rescue the nation from infidelity and intemperance. A second line of reform, social or humanitarian reform, sought to alleviate such sources of human misery as crime, cruelty, disease, and ignorance. A third line of reform, radical reform, sought national regeneration by eliminating slavery and racial and sexual discrimination.

The Rise of the Antislavery Movement

In the early nineteenth century the emancipation of slaves in the northern states and the prohibition against the African slave trade generated optimism that slavery was dying. Congress in 1787 had barred slavery from the Old Northwest, the region north of the Ohio River to the Mississippi River. The number of slaves freed by their masters had risen dramatically in the upper South during the 1780s and 1790s, and more antislavery societies had been formed in the South than in the North. At the present rate of progress, predicted one religious leader in 1791, within 50 years it will "be as shameful for a man to hold a Negro slave, as to be guilty of common robbery or theft."

By the early 1830s, however, the development of the Cotton Kingdom proved that slavery was not on the road to extinction. Despite the end of the African slave trade, the slave population had continued to grow, climbing from 1.5 million in 1820 to over 2 million a decade later.

A widespread belief that blacks and whites could not coexist and that racial separation was necessary encouraged futile efforts at deportation and overseas colonization. In 1816 a group of prominent ministers and politicians formed the American Colonization Society to resettle free blacks in West Africa, encourage planters voluntarily to emancipate their slaves, and create a group of black missionaries who would spread Christianity in Africa. During the 1820s Congress helped fund the cost of transporting free blacks to Africa—first to Sierra Leone and then, beginning in 1822, to Liberia. It soon became apparent that colonization was a wholly impractical solution to the nation's slavery problem. Each year the nation's slave population rose by roughly 50,000, but in 1830 the American Colonization Society succeeded in persuading just 259 free blacks to migrate to Liberia, bringing the total number of blacks colonized in Africa to just 1,400.

The movement condemning colonization and northern discrimination against African Americans was initially led by free blacks. As early as 1817 more than 3,000 members of Philadelphia's black community staged a protest against colonization. In 1829 David Walker, a free black owner of a secondhand clothing store in Boston, issued the militant pamphlet *Appeal to the Colored Citizens of the World.* The appeal threatened insurrection and violence if calls for the abolition of slavery and improved conditions for free blacks were not realized. The next year some 40 black delegates from eight states held the first of a series of annual conventions that denounced slavery and called for an end to discriminatory laws in the northern states.

The idea of abolition received impetus from William Lloyd Garrison. In 1829 the 25-year-old white Bostonian added his voice to the outcry against colonization, denouncing it as a cruel hoax designed to promote the racial purity of the northern population while doing nothing to end slavery in the South. Instead, he called for "immediate emancipation." By "immediate" he meant the immediate and unconditional release of slaves from bondage without compensation to slaveowners.

Garrison founded *The Liberator,* a militant abolitionist newspaper that was the country's first publication to demand an immediate end to slavery. On the front page of the first issue he defiantly declared: "I will not equivocate—I will not excuse—I will not retreat a single inch—AND I WILL BE HEARD."

Within four years 200 antislavery societies had appeared in the North. They had mounted a massive propaganda campaign to proclaim

The Liberator sought immediate freedom for slaves, without compensation to their owners.

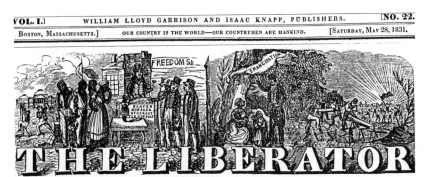

William Lloyd Garrison, the symbol of radical abolitionism, sought immediate freedom for slaves, without compensation to their owners.

the sinfulness of slavery. These societies distributed a million pieces of abolitionist literature and sent 20,000 tracts directly to the South. They avoided concrete proposals for emancipation, however, fearful of becoming embroiled in debates over the details of specific plans.

Abolitionists attacked slavery on several grounds. Slavery was illegal because it violated the principles of natural rights to life and liberty embodied in the Declaration of Independence. Justice, said Garrison, required that the nation "secure to the colored population . . . all the rights and privileges that belong to them as men and as Americans." Slavery was sinful because slaveholders, in the words of abolitionist Theodore Weld, had usurped "the prerogative of God." Slavery also encouraged sexual immorality and undermined the institutions of marriage and the family. Not only did slave masters sexually abuse and exploit slave women, abolitionists charged, but in some older southern states, such as Virginia and Maryland, they bred slaves for sale to the more recently settled parts of the Deep South.

Antislavery agitation provoked a harsh public reaction in both the North and the South. Mobs led by "gentlemen of property and standing" attacked the homes and businesses of abolitionist merchants, destroyed abolitionist printing presses, disrupted antislavery meetings, and attacked black neighborhoods. During antiabolitionist rioting in Philadelphia in October 1834, a white mob destroyed 45 homes in the city's black community. A year later a Boston mob dragged Garrison through the streets and almost lynched him before authorities removed him to a city jail for his own safety. In 1837 the abolitionist movement acquired its first martyr when an antiabolitionist mob in Illinois set fire to the printing business of the Reverend Elijah P. Lovejoy, then shot him as he fled the building.

Division in the Antislavery Movement

The violent response produced division within the antislavery movement. At the 1840 annual meeting of the American Anti-Slavery Society in New York, abolitionists split over such questions as women's right to participate in the administration of the organization and the advisability of nominating abolitionists as independent political candidates. Garrison won control of the organization, and his opponents promptly walked out. From this point on, no single organization could speak for abolitionism.

One group of abolitionists looked to politics as the answer to ending slavery and founded political parties, such as the Liberty party, for that purpose. The Liberty party, founded in 1840 under the leadership of Arthur and Lewis Tappan, wealthy New York City businessmen, and James G. Birney, a former slaveholder, called on Congress to abolish slavery in the District of Columbia, end the interstate slave trade, and cease admitting new slave states to the Union. The party also sought the repeal of local and state laws in the North, which discriminated against free blacks. The Liberty party nominated Birney for president in 1840 and again in 1844, and although it gathered less than 7,100 votes in its first campaign, it polled some 62,000 votes four years later and captured enough votes in Michigan and New York to deny Henry Clay the presidency.

In 1848 antislavery Democrats and Whigs merged with the Liberty party to form the Free Soil party. Unlike the Liberty party, which was dedicated to the abolition of slavery and equal rights for blacks, the Free Soil party narrowed its demands to the abolition of slavery in the District of Columbia and exclusion of slavery from the federal territories. The Free Soilers also wanted a homestead law to provide free land for western settlers, high tariffs to protect American industry, and federally sponsored internal improvements.

Other abolitionists, led by Garrison, took a more radical direction, advocating civil disobedience and linking abolitionism to such other reforms as women's rights, world government, and international peace. Garrison and his supporters established the New England Non-Resistance Society in 1838. Members refused to vote or hold public office. In 1854 Garrison attracted notoriety by publicly burning a copy of the Constitution, which he called "a covenant with death and an agreement with Hell" because it acknowledged the legality of slavery.

African Americans played a vital role in the abolitionist movement, staging protests against segregated churches, schools, and public transportation. In New York and Pennsylvania free blacks launched petition drives for equal voting rights. Northern blacks also had a pivotal role in the "underground railroad," which provided escape routes for southern slaves through the northern states and into Canada. African-American churches offered sanctuary to runaways, and black "vigilance" groups in cities like New York and Detroit offered physical resistance to slave catchers.

Fugitive slaves, such as Harriet Tubman, advanced abolitionism by publicizing the horrors of slavery. Their firsthand tales of whippings and separation from spouses and children combated the notion that slaves were content under slavery and undermined belief in racial inferiority. Tubman risked her life by making 19 trips into slave territory in order to free as many as 300 slaves. Slaveholders posted a reward of $40,000 for the capture of the "Black Moses."

Frederick Douglass was the most famous fugitive slave and black abolitionist. The son of a Maryland slave woman and an unknown white father, Douglass was separated from his mother and sent to work on a plantation when he was six years old. At the age of 20 he escaped from slavery by borrowing the papers of a free black sailor. In the North, Douglass became the first runaway slave to speak out on behalf of the antislavery cause. Although he initially allied himself with William Lloyd Garrison, Douglass later started his own newspaper, *The North Star,* and supported political action against slavery.

By the 1850s many blacks had become pessimistic about defeating slavery. Colonizationist sentiment appeared among African Americans. In the 15 months following passage of the federal Fugitive Slave Law in 1850, some 13,000 free blacks fled the North for Canada. In 1854 the National Emigration Convention was created to investigate possible sites for black colonization in Haiti, Central America, and West Africa.

Other blacks argued in favor of violence. Black abolitionists in Ohio adopted resolutions encouraging slaves to escape and called on their fellow citizens to violate any law that "conflicts with reason, liberty and justice, North or South." By the late 1850s a growing number of free blacks had concluded that it was just as legitimate to use violence to secure the freedom of the slaves as it had been to establish the independence of the American colonies.

Over the long run, the fragmentation of the antislavery movement worked to the advantage of the cause. Henceforth, northerners could support whichever form of antislavery best reflected their views. Moderates could vote for political candidates with abolitionist sentiments without

Harriet Tubman, a fugitive slave who led 19 raids into slave territory, was a strong proponent of abolitionism. In 1841 Frederick Douglass gained public notice by giving a powerful speech against slavery. He opposed not only slavery but all forms of racial discrimination.

being accused of radical Garrisonian views or of advocating violence for redress of grievances.

The Birth of Feminism

The women's rights movement was a major legacy of radical reform. At the outset of the century women experienced political, social, and legal discrimination. Women were prohibited from voting or holding office in every state; they had no access to higher education and were excluded from professional occupations. American law was guided by the principle that a wife had no legal identity apart from her husband. She could not be sued, nor could she bring a legal suit, make a contract, or own property. She was not permitted to control her own wages or gain custody of her children in case of separation or divorce, and under many circumstances she was even deemed incapable of committing crimes.

Broad social and economic changes, such as the development of a market economy and a decline in the birthrate, opened employment opportunities for women. Instead of bearing children at two-year intervals after marriage, as was the general case throughout the colonial era, early nineteenth-century women bore fewer children and ceased childbearing at younger ages. More women were postponing marriage or not marrying at all; unmarried women gained new employment opportunities as "mill girls" and elementary school teachers; and a growing number of women achieved prominence as novelists, editors, teachers, and leaders of church and philanthropic societies.

While there were many improvements in the status of women during the first half of the century, women still lost political and economic status when compared with men. As the franchise was extended to larger and larger numbers of white males, including large groups of recent immigrants, the gap in political power between women and men widened. Even though women made up a core of supporters for many reform movements, men excluded them from positions of decision making and relegated them to separate female auxiliaries. Women also lost economic status as production shifted away from the household to the factory and workshop. During the late eighteenth century the need for a cash income led women and older children to engage in a variety of household industries, such as weaving and spinning. Increasingly, in the nineteenth century these tasks were performed in factories and mills.

The fact that changes in the economy tended to confine women to a sphere separate from men had important implications for reform. Since women were believed to be uncontaminated by the competitive struggle for wealth and power, many argued that they had a duty—and the capacity—to exert an uplifting moral influence on American society.

Catharine Beecher and Sarah J. Hale helped lead the effort to expand women's roles through moral influence. Beecher, the eldest sister of Harriet Beecher Stowe, was one of the nation's most prominent educators before the Civil War. A woman of many talents and strong leadership, she spearheaded the campaign to convince school boards that women were suited to serve as schoolteachers. Hale edited the nation's most popular women's magazines, the *Ladies' Magazine* and *Godey's Lady's Book.*

Both Beecher and Hale worked tirelessly for women's education (Hale helped found Vassar College). They gave voice to the grievances of women: the abysmally low wages paid in the needle trades, the physical hardships endured in the nation's shops and mills (where women worked 14 hours a day), and the minimizing of women's intellectual aspirations. Even though neither woman supported full equal rights, they were important transitional figures in the emergence of feminism. Each significantly broadened society's definition of "women's sphere" and assigned women vital social responsibilities: to shape the character of children, to morally uplift husbands, and to promote causes of "practical benevolence."

Catalyst for Women's Rights

A public debate over the proper role of women in the antislavery movement, especially their right to lecture to audiences composed of both sexes, led to the first organized movement for women's rights. By the mid-1830s more than a hundred female antislavery societies had been created, and women abolitionists were circulating petitions, editing abolitionist tracts, and organizing antislavery conventions. A key question was whether women abolitionists would be permitted to lecture to "mixed" audiences of men and women.

Angelina Grimké and her sister Sarah—two sisters from a wealthy Charleston, South Carolina, slaveholding family—were the first women to break the restrictions and widen women's sphere through their writings and lectures. In 1837 Angelina gained national notoriety by lecturing against slavery to audiences that included men as well as women. Sarah Grimké followed with a pamphlet entitled *Letters on the Equality of the Sexes and the Condition of Women,* one of the first modern statements of feminist principles. She denounced the injustice of lower pay and denial of equal educational opportunities for women. Her pamphlet expressed outrage that women were "regarded by men, as pretty toys or as mere instruments of pleasure," and taught to aspire to no higher goal than marriage. Men and women, she concluded, should not be treated differently, since both were endowed with inherent natural rights.

In 1848 Lucretia Mott and Elizabeth Cady Stanton organized the first women's rights convention in history. The convention was held in July 1848 at Seneca Falls, New York. Participants drew up a Declaration of Sentiments, modeled on the Declaration of Independence, that opened with the phrase "All men and women are created equal." Among the resolutions adopted by the convention, only one was not ratified unanimously—that women be granted the right to vote.

By midcentury women's rights conventions had been held in every northern state. Despite public ridicule, female reformers contributed to important, if limited, advances against discrimination. They succeeded in gaining adoption of Married Women's Property Laws in a number of states, granting married women full control over their own income and property. A New York law passed in 1860 gave women joint custody over children and the right to sue and be sued, and several states adopted permissive divorce laws.

Utopian Communities

Between the 1820s and 1840s hundreds of "utopian communities" were founded by individuals who believed in the perfectability of the social and political order. The characteristics of these communities varied widely. Although most were short-lived, these communities sought to provide blueprints for a perfectionist vision of an ideal society.

One group, popularly known as the Shakers, believed that the millennium was at hand and that the time had come for people to totally renounce sin. By 1800 there were 12 Shaker colonies. These communities placed Shaker men and women on a level of sexual equality and both sexes served as elders and deacons. Aspiring to live like the early Christians, the Shakers adopted communal ownership of property and a way of life emphasizing simplicity. The two most striking characteristics of the Shaker communities were their dances and abstinence from sexual relations. The Shakers believed that religious fervor should be expressed through the head, heart, and mind, and their ritual religious practices included shaking, shouting, and dancing. Viewing sexual intercourse as the basic cause of human sin, the Shakers also adopted strict rules concerning celibacy. They attempted to replenish their membership by admitting volunteers and taking in orphans.

Another utopian effort was Robert Owen's experimental community at New Harmony, Indiana, which reflected the influence of Enlightenment ideas. Owen, a paternalistic Scottish industrialist, was deeply troubled by the social consequences of the industrial revolution. Inspired by the idea that people are shaped by their environment, Owen purchased a site in Indiana where he sought to establish common ownership of property and abolish religion. At New Harmony the marriage ceremony was reduced to a single sentence and children were raised outside of their natural parents' home. The community lasted just three years, from 1825 to 1828.

Some 40 utopian communities were inspired by the French theorist Charles Fourier, who hoped to eliminate poverty through the establishment of scientifically organized cooperative communities called "phalanxes." In each phalanx profits were divided according to the amount of money members had invested, their skill, and their labor. Women received equal job opportunities and equal pay, equal participation in decision making, and the right to speak in public assemblies. Although one Fourier community lasted for 18 years, most were unsuccessful.

In 1841 George Ripley, a former Unitarian clergyman, established the Brook Farm community near Boston in an attempt to substitute ideals of "brotherly cooperation," harmony, and spiritual fulfillment for the "selfish competition," class division, and alienation that increasingly characterized the larger society. "Our ulterior aim is nothing less than Heaven on Earth," declared one community member. Brook Farm's residents, who never numbered more than 200, supported themselves by farming, teaching, and manufacturing clothing.

Perhaps the most notorious and successful experimental colony was John Humphrey Noyes's Oneida Community in New York. Noyes believed that the final millennium would only occur when people strove to become perfect through an "immediate and total cessation from sin." In 1848 he established a perfectionist community that practiced communal ownership of property and "complex marriage." Complex marriage involved the marriage of each member of the community to every member of the opposite sex. Exclusive emotional or sexual attachments were forbidden, and sexual relations were arranged through an intermediary in order to protect a woman's individuality and give her a choice in the matter. After the Civil War the community conducted experiments in eugenics, the selective control of mating in order to improve the hereditary qualities of children. Oneida flourished in its original form until 1880.

Artistic and Cultural Ferment

During the early nineteenth century Europeans treated American culture with contempt. They charged that America was too commercial and materialistic, too preoccupied with money and technology, to produce great art and literature. "In the four quarters of the globe," asked one English critic, "who reads an American book? or goes to an American play? or looks at an American picture or statue?"

In fact, the decades preceding the American Civil War are among the most creative in all of American cultural and intellectual history, producing some of this nation's greatest poets, novelists, and philosophers.

At the beginning of the nineteenth century many Americans wondered whether their country's infant democracy was capable of producing great works of art. The United States had few professional writers or artists. In part, the United States lacked a large class of patrons to subsidize the arts. It possessed few magazines and only a single art museum. Above all, America seemed to lack the traditions out of which artists and writers could create great works. In 1837 Ralph Waldo Emerson urged Americans to cast off their "long apprenticeship to the learning of other lands," abandon subservience to English models, and create distinctly American forms of art rooted in the facts of American life.

Even before Emerson's call for a distinctly American culture, a number of authors had already begun to create literature emphasizing native scenes and characters. Washington Irving (1783–1859), who was probably the first American to support himself as a man of letters, demonstrated the possibility of creating art out of native elements in his classic tales "Rip Van Winkle" (1819) and "The Legend of Sleepy Hollow" (1820).

The poet Henry Wadsworth Longfellow was even more successful in transforming American legends into the stuff of art and reaching a broad popular audience. His narrative poems dramatizing scenes from America's past made such figures as Paul Revere, Miles Standish, John Alden, Priscilla Mullins, and Hiawatha household names.

James Fenimore Cooper was another successful mythmaker. In *The Spy* (1821) and *The Pioneers* (1823) Cooper created one of the most enduring archetypes in American culture. His hero, the frontiersman Natty Bumppo (also known as Hawkeye, Leather stocking, and the Pathfinder) was an American knight errant at home in the wilderness. He became the prototype not only for future trappers and scouts, but also for countless cowboys, detectives, and superheroes found in popular American fiction and film. Part of Natty Bumppo's appeal was that he gave expression to many of the misgivings early nineteenth-century Americans felt about the cost of progress. An acute social critic, Cooper railed against the destruction of the natural environment, the violence directed at American Indians, and the rapaciousness and materialism of an expansive American society.

American Transcendentalism

Some intellectuals, many of them young New Englanders of Unitarian background, found liberal religion too formal and rationalistic to meet their spiritual and emotional needs. Known as Transcendentalists, they believed that logic and reason were incapable of explaining the fundamental mysteries of human existence. Where, then, could people find answers to life's fundamental problems? The deepest insights, the Transcendentalists believed, were to be found within the human individual, through intuition.

The Transcendentalists shared a common outlook: a belief that each person contains infinite and godlike potentialities; an emphasis on emotion and the senses over reason and intellect; and a glorification of nature as a creative, dynamic force in which people could discover their true selves and commune with the supernatural. Like the romantic artists and poets of Europe, they emphasized the individual, the subjective, the imaginative, the personal, the emotional, and the visionary.

The central figure in Transcendentalism was Ralph Waldo Emerson. Trained, like his father, to be a liberal Unitarian minister, Emerson found his parents' faith unsatisfying. Unitarian theology and ritual, he wrote, was "corpse-cold"; it was the "thin porridge or cold tea" of genteel Bostonians. Emerson's life was marked by personal tragedy and illness—his father died when he was a boy; his first wife died after less than two years of marriage; his firstborn son died at the age of five; a brother went insane. Consequently, Emerson could never believe that logic and reason offered answers to life's mysteries.

Appalled by the complacency, provinciality, and materialism of Boston's elite, the 29-year-old Emerson resigned as minister of the prestigious Second Church of Boston in 1832. Convinced that no external answers existed to the fundamental problems of life, he decided to look inward.

In his essays and public lectures Emerson distilled the essence of the new philosophy: All people contain seeds of divinity, but society, traditionalism, and lifeless religious institutions thwart the fulfillment of these potentialities. In his essay "Nature" (1836) Emerson asserted that God's presence is immanent within both humanity and nature and can best be sensed through intuition rather than through reason. In his essay "Self-Reliance" (1841) he called on his readers to strive for true individuality in the face of intense social pressures for conformity.

Although Emerson himself was not an active reformer, his philosophy inspired many reformers far more radical than he. His stress on the individual, his defense of nonconformity, and his vocal critique of the alienation and social fragmentation that had accompanied the growth of cities and industry led others to try to apply the principles of Transcendentalism to their personal lives and to society at large.

Henry David Thoreau was one of the Transcendentalists who strove to realize Emersonian ideals in his personal life. Thoreau, like Emerson, felt nothing but contempt for social conventions. In March 1845 the 28-year-old Thoreau, convinced that his life was being frittered away by details, walked into the woods near Concord, Massachusetts, to live alone. He put up a cabin near Walden Pond as an experiment—to see if it was possible for a person to live truly free and uncommitted:

> I went into the woods because I wished to live deliberately, to front only the essential facts of life, and see if I could not learn what it had to teach, and not, when I came to die, discover that I had not lived.

The aim of his experiment was to break free from the distractions and artificialities of life, to shed himself of needless obligations and possessions, and to establish an original relationship with nature. His motto was "simplify, simplify."

During his 26 months at Walden Pond he constructed his own cabin, raised his own food, observed nature, explored his inner self, and kept a 6,000-page journal. He also spent a night in jail for refusing to pay taxes as a protest against the Mexican War. This incident led him to write the classic defense of nonviolent direct action, "Civil Disobedience."

A Literary and Artistic Renaissance

Emerson's 1837 plea for Americans to cease imitating Europeans, speak with their own voices, and create art drawn from their own experiences coincided with an extraordinary burst of literary creativity. Nathaniel Hawthorne,

Herman Melville, Edgar Allan Poe, Harriet Beecher Stowe, and Walt Whitman, like Emerson and Thoreau, produced literary works of the highest magnitude, yet in their own time many of their greatest works were greeted with derision, abuse, or indifference. It is a tragic fact that with the sole exception of Harriet Beecher Stowe, none of pre–Civil War America's greatest writers was able to earn more than a modest income from his or her books.

During his lifetime Edgar Allan Poe received far more notoriety from his legendary dissipation—he died an alcoholic at age 40—than from his poetry or short stories. Sorely underappreciated by contemporaries, Poe invented the detective novel; edited the *Southern Literary Messenger,* one of the country's leading literary journals; wrote incisive essays on literary criticism; and produced some of the most masterful poems and frightening tales of horror ever written. Poe said that his writing style consisted of "the ludicrous heightened into the grotesque; the fearful coloured into the horrible; the witty exaggerated into the burlesque; the singular wrought into the strange and mystical."

Nathaniel Hawthorne, the author of *The Scarlet Letter* (1850), more than any other early nineteenth-century American writer, challenged society's faith in science, technology, progress, and humanity's essential goodness. Many of his greatest works project nineteenth-century concerns—about women's roles, sexuality, and religion—on to seventeenth-century Puritan settings. Some of his stories examine the hubris of scientists and social reformers who dare to tamper with the natural environment and human nature.

Herman Melville, author of *Moby Dick* (1851), had little formal education and claimed that his intellectual development did not begin until he was 25. Part of a New York literary circle called Young America, Melville dreamed of creating a novel as vast and energetic as the nation itself. In *Moby Dick* he produced such a masterwork. Based on the tale of a gigantic white whale that sank a whaling ship, *Moby Dick* combined whaling lore and sea adventure into an epic drama of human hubris, producing an allegory that explores what happens to a people who defy divine limits. Tragically, neither *Moby Dick* nor Melville's later works found an audience. Melville died in utter obscurity, and his literary genius was only rediscovered in the 1920s.

Walt Whitman was a carpenter's son with only five years of schooling. Emerson considered him to be the very ideal of the native American poet, but most reviewers reacted scornfully to his collection of poems, *Leaves of Grass,* deeming it "trashy, profane & obscene" for its sexual frankness. Unconventional in style—Whitman invented "free verse" rather than use conventionally rhymed or regularly metered verse—the volume stands out as a landmark in the history of American literature for its celebration of the diversity, the energy, and the expansiveness of pre–Civil War America.

If Americans could produce literary masterpieces, were they also capable of creating visual art that would rival that of Europe? Although the last half of the eighteenth century witnessed the appearance of a number of talented portrait painters, most were simply skilled craftspeople who devoted most of their time to painting houses, furniture, or signs. Perhaps the biggest obstacle to the development of the visual arts was the fact that the revolutionary generation associated art with luxury, corruption, sensual appetite, and aristocracy. Commented one person: "When a people get a taste for the fine arts, they are ruined."

During the early nineteenth century, however, artists succeeded in overcoming public hostility toward the visual arts. One way artists gained a degree of respectability was through historical painting. The American public hungered for visual representations of the great events of the American Revolution, and works such as John Trumbull's Revolutionary War battle scenes and his painting of the Declaration of Independence (1818) fed the public's appetite. Romantic landscape paintings also attracted a large popular audience. Portrayals of the American landscape by such artists as Thomas Cole and the Hudson River school, Albert Bierstadt, and Frederick Church evoked a sense of the immensity, power, and grandeur of nature, which had not yet been completely tamed by an expansive American civilization.

Popular Culture

Existing alongside these literary and artistic achievements was a vibrant popular culture. One important aspect of a common culture was the mass-circulation newspaper. After the Revolution most newspapers were subsidized by political parties, which used them as mouthpieces to promote their views. But with the development in the 1830s of the steam printing press, which dramatically cut printing costs and speeded production, the modern mass-circulation newspaper emerged. Journalistic pioneers, like James Gordon Bennett of the New York *Herald,* introduced features that we still associate with the daily newspaper, including crime stories, gossip columns, and sports pages. To increase circulation, the New York *Sun* relied on sensationalism and even hoaxes, practices that were soon copied by its rivals. Along with the modern newspaper came magazines. By 1850 magazines began to appeal to almost every imaginable audience, with the proliferation of children's magazines, scientific journals, literary reviews, women's magazines, religious periodicals, and comics.

American literary tastes were extremely varied. The middle class tended to read sentimental domestic tales, like Susan Warner's *The Wide, Wide World,* one of the most popular mid-nineteenth century novels; sentimental love poetry by authors like Lydia Sigourney, or morally high-minded adventure tales, like Richard Henry Dana, Jr.'s *Two Years Before the Mast* (1840) or historian Francis Parkman's *The Oregon Trail* (1847). Less well educated Americans favored dime novels (which usually sold for a nickel), which often dealt with such topics as frontier adventure, pirate tales, and urban crime.

Pseudoscience also captured the popular fancy during the decades before the Civil War. During the early nineteenth century science was advancing so rapidly that it was difficult to distinguish authentic scientific discoveries from hoaxes. Before the Civil War Americans were fascinated by a variety of pseudosciences, including phrenology (which linked human character to the shape and bumps of a person's head), animal magnetism (the belief in a universal electrical fluid influencing physics and even human psychology), mesmerism (the control of a hypnotized person by a medium), and spiritualism (direct communication with spirits of the deceased through trance visions or seances).

Another distinctive feature of pre–Civil War popular culture was the minstrel show. The first uniquely American entertainment form, the minstrel show provided comedy, music, dance, and novelty acts to audiences hungry for entertainment. Offering humor that ranged from comedy skits to slapstick and one-liners—often mocking pompous politicians and pretentious professionals—the minstrel shows also introduced many of America's most enduring popular songs, including "Turkey in the Straw" and "Dixie."

Minstrel shows popularized the songs of Stephen Foster, the most popular American composer of the mid-nineteenth century. Foster wrote more than 200 songs during his lifetime, mainly sentimental ballads and love songs (such as "Old Folks at Home," "My Old Kentucky Home," and "Beautiful Dreamer") and uptempo, rhythmic comic songs (such as "Camptown Races" and "Oh! Susanna").

Reflecting the racism of the broader society, minstrel shows presented a denigrating portrayal of black Americans. Racial stereotypes were the minstrel shows' stock in trade. Actors wore grotesque makeup, spoke in ludicrous dialects, and presented plantation life in a highly romanticized manner.

Conclusion

The first half of the nineteenth century witnessed the rise of the first secular movements in history to educate the deaf and blind, care for the mentally ill, extend equal rights to women, and abolish slavery. Inspired by the revolutionary ideals of the Declaration of Independence and the Bill of Rights, the Enlightenment faith in reason, and liberal and evangelical religious principles, educational reformers created a system of free public education, prison reformers constructed specialized institutions to reform criminals, temperance reformers sought to end the drinking of liquor, and utopian socialists established ideal communities to serve as models of a better world.

*C*hronology of Key Events

1776 First Shaker community in America founded near Albany, New York

1817 American Colonization Society founded

1818 Washington Irving publishes *Rip Van Winkle*

1825 Charles Finney leads his first religious revivals; Robert Owen founds New Harmony community in Indiana

1826 American Society for the Promotion of Temperance founded

1829 David Walker issues *Appeal to the Colored Citizens of the World*

1831 William Lloyd Garrison begins publishing *The Liberator,* militant abolistionist newspaper

1833 American Anti-Slavery Society formed; New York *Sun,* the first penny newspaper, published

1837 Emerson presents his address on the "American Scholar"; abolitionist Elijah P. Lovejoy killed by a proslavery mob in Illinois

1840 James G. Birney runs for president as Liberty party candidate; Sarah Grimké publishes *Letters on the Equality of the Sexes and the Condition of Women*

1841 Dorothea Dix begins crusade on behalf of the mentally ill; Brook Farm founded

1848 Seneca Falls convention on women's rights held in New York; Free Soil party receives ten percent of presidential vote

1850 Nathaniel Hawthorne publishes *The Scarlet Letter*

1851 Herman Melville publishes *Moby Dick*

1852 Massachusetts adopts the first compulsory education law

1854 Henry David Thoreau publishes *Walden*

1855 Walt Whitman publishes *Leaves of Grass*

The Civil War largely brought an end to the era of optimistic, perfectionist reform. The grim violence of the war shattered the pre–Civil War reformers' confidence in the "perfectability of man" and sparked a reaction against the emotionalism and utopian idealism of pre–Civil War reform. Although a large number of abolitionists continued to fight for black equality and many feminists moved from women's rights to the fight for women's suffrage, a period of retrenchment set in during the 1870s and 1880s, when counterreformers reversed many of the accomplishments of prewar reformers by restoring capital punishment and making divorce laws more stringent.

Still, many of the goals of the antebellum reformers would live on. The pre–Civil War reformers' spirit of hope and their willingness to question established customs and institutions would survive as a source of inspiration for later proponents of penal reform, women's rights, labor unions, and racial justice.

Suggestions for Further Reading

Valuable overviews of the reform impulse in the antebellum period are Robert H. Abzug, *Cosmos* (*rumbling; American Reform and the Religious Imagination* (1994); and Ronald Walters, *American Reformers* (1978). For more on the Second Great Awakening see Whitney R. Cross, *The Burned Over District* (1950); Keith J. Hardman, *Charles Grandison Finney* (1987); Paul Johnson, *A Shopkeeper's Millennium* (1978).

Moral reform issues are examined in Clifford S. Griffin, *Their Brothers' Keepers* (1960); Mark E. Lender and James Kirby Martin, *Drinking in America,* rev. ed. (1987); W. J. Rorabaugh, *The Alcoholic Republic* (1979); Ian R. Tyrell, *Sobering Up: From Temperance to Prohibition in Antebellum America* (1979). On social reform see Jonathan Messerli, *Horace Mann* (1972); Raymond A. Mohl, *Poverty in New York* (1971); David Rothman, *The Discovery of the Asylum* (1971).

On the early feminist movement consult Lois Banner, *Elizabeth Cady Stanton* (1980); Nancy F. Cott, *The Bonds of Womanhood* (1977); Carl N. Degler, *At Odds* (1980); Sara Evans, *Born for Liberty* (1989); Mary P. Ryan, *Womanhood in America,* 3d ed. (1983); Nancy Woloch, *Women and the American Experience* (1984).

The antislavery movement is examined in Benjamin Quarles, *Black Abolitionists* (1969); P. J. Staudenraus, *The African Colonization Movement* (1961); James B. Stewart, *Holy Warriors: The Abolitionists and American Slavery* (1976).

On American intellectuals and literary achievements during the antebellum period see Paul F. Boller, Jr., *American Transcendentalism* (1974); Lawrence Buell, *New England Literary Culture* (1986). On popular culture see Lawrence Levine, *Highbrow/Lowbrow: The Emergence of Cultural Hierarchy in America* (1988).

Chapter *12*

The Divided North, the Divided South

In the early 1790s slavery appeared to be a dying institution. Slave imports into the New World were declining and slave prices were falling because the crops grown by slaves—tobacco, rice, and indigo—did not generate enough income to pay for their upkeep. In Maryland and Virginia planters were replacing tobacco, a crop grown by a slave labor force, with wheat and corn, which was not. At the same time, leading Southerners, including Thomas Jefferson, denounced slavery as a source of debt, economic stagnation, and moral dissipation. A French traveler reported that people throughout the South "are constantly talking of abolishing slavery, of contriving some other means of cultivating their estates."

Then Eli Whitney of Massachusetts gave slavery a new lease on life. In 1792, just after graduating from Yale, Whitney traveled south in search of employment as a schoolteacher. While visiting a plantation near Savannah, Georgia, Whitney became intrigued with the problems encountered by southern planters in successfully producing green seed, short-staple cotton. The booming textile industry had created a high demand for the crop, but it could not be marketed until the seeds had been extracted from the cotton boll, a laborious and time-consuming process.

From a slave known only as Sam, Whitney learned that a comb could be used to remove seeds from cotton. In just ten days Whitney devised a way of mechanizing the comb. Within a month Whitney's cotton engine (gin for short) could separate fiber from seeds faster than 50 people working by hand.

Whitney's invention revitalized slavery in the South. In two years the price of slaves doubled. By 1825 field hands, who brought $500 apiece in 1794, were worth $1,500. As the price of slaves rose, so too did the number of slaves. During the first decade of the nineteenth century the number of slaves in the United States increased by 33 percent.

As the institution of slavery expanded in the South, it declined in the North. In 1780 Pennsylvania adopted the first emancipation law in the New World. Judicial decisions freed slaves in Massachusetts and New Hampshire, and other northern states passed gradual emancipation acts. By the early nineteenth century the new republic was fatefully divided into a slave section and a free section.

A Divided Culture

By 1860 most Americans believed that the Mason-Dixon line divided the nation into two distinctive cultures: a commercial North and an agrarian South. Many factors contributed to this sense of sectional difference. Diction, work habits, diet, and labor systems distinguished the two regions. One section depended on slave-based agriculture; the other emphasized

While seeking employment in the South, Yankee schoolteacher Eli Whitney developed a simple machine for separating cotton from its seeds. The "cotton gin" met the increasing demand for cotton and breathed new life into the institution of slavery.

commercial agriculture based on family farms and a developing industrial sector resting on wage labor.

The population of the North was more than 50 percent greater than in the South. Urbanization was far more advanced, as thousands of European immigrants flocked to northern cities. In addition, commerce, financial institutions, manufacturing, and transportation were more developed. In contrast, the South had more primitive transportation facilities. Cities were smaller and fewer in number. Most important of all, a third of the South's population lived in slavery.

Despite these differences, the pre–Civil War North and the South were in certain respects strikingly similar. Both sections were predominantly rural. Both had booming economies and were engaged in speculation and trade. Both were rapidly expanding westward. Both enacted democratic political reforms and voted for the same national political parties. Nevertheless, most Americans thought of their nation as divided into two halves, a commercial civilization and an agrarian civilization, each operating according to entirely different sets of values.

The Emergence of a New Industrial Order in the North

By 1860, even though the North remained predominantly a rural agricultural society, profound and far-reaching changes had taken place. Commercial agriculture had replaced subsistence agriculture. Household production had been supplanted by centralized manufacturing outside the home. And nonagricultural employment had begun to overtake agricultural employment. By 1860, nearly half of the North's population made a living outside of the agricultural sector.

These economic transformations were all aspects of the industrial revolution, a revolution that affected every aspect of life. It raised living standards, transformed the work process, and relocated hundreds of thousands of people across oceans and from rural farms and villages to fast-growing industrial cities.

The most obvious consequence of this revolution was an impressive increase in wealth, per capita income, and commercial, middle-class job opportunities. Between 1800 and 1860 output increased 12-fold, and purchasing power doubled. New middle-class jobs proliferated. Increasing numbers of men found work as agents, bankers, brokers, clerks, merchants, professionals, and traders. Living standards rose sharply, at least for the rapidly expanding middle class. By 1860 many urban middle-class families had central heating, indoor plumbing, and wall-to-wall carpeting.

Although the industrial revolution brought many material benefits, critics decried its negative consequences. Labor leaders deplored the bitter suffering of factory and sweatshop workers, the breakdown of craft skills, the vulnerability of urban workers to layoffs and economic crises, and the maldistribution of wealth and property. Conservatives lamented the disintegration of an older household-centered economy in which husbands, wives, and children had labored together. Southern writers argued that the North's growing class of free laborers were slaves of the marketplace, suffering even more insecurity than the South's chattel slaves, who were provided for in sickness and old age.

During the early nineteenth century the industrial revolution transformed northern society, altering the way people worked and lived and contributing to growing sectional differences between the North and South. How and why did the industrial revolution occur when it did? What were its consequences? How did it fuel sectional antagonisms?

The Transformation of the Rural Countryside

In 1790 most families in the rural North produced most of what they needed to live. Instead of using money to purchase necessities, families entered into complex exchange relationships with relatives and neighbors and used barter to acquire the goods they needed. To supplement their meager incomes, farm families often did piecework for shopkeepers and craftsmen. In the late eighteenth century these "household industries" provided work for thousands of men, women, and children in rural areas. Shopkeepers or master craftspeople supplied farm families with raw materials and paid them piece rates to produce such items as linens and farm utensils.

Between 1790 and the 1820s a new pattern emerged. Subsistence farming gave way to commercial agriculture as farmers increasingly began to grow cash crops for sale, using the proceeds to buy goods produced by others. In New Hampshire farmers raised sheep for wool; in western Massachusetts they began to fatten cattle and pigs for sale to Boston; in eastern Pennsylvania they specialized in dairy products.

The household industries that had once employed thousands of rural women and children also began to decline during this period. They were replaced by manufacturing in city shops and factories. New England farm families began to buy their shoes, furniture, and sometimes even their clothes ready-made. Small rural factories closed their doors, and village artisans who produced for local markets found themselves unable to compete against cheaper city-made goods. As local opportunities declined, many long-settled farm areas suffered sharp population losses, as thousands of young people left the fields for cities.

The Disruption of the Artisan System of Labor

In the late eighteenth century the North's few industries were small. Skilled craftspeople, known as *artisans* or *mechanics,* performed most manufacturing in small towns and larger cities. Such crafts as blacksmithing, bootmaking, carriage building, and leather working were performed by hand in a small shop or home.

The artisan class was divided into three subgroups. At the highest level were self-employed master craftspeople. They were assisted by skilled journeymen, who owned their own tools but lacked the capital to set up their own shops, and by apprentices, teenaged boys who typically served a three-year term in exchange for training in a craft.

The first half of the nineteenth century witnessed the decline of the artisan system of labor. The independent artisans of earlier years gave way to an increasingly industrial economy of wage laborers and salaried employees. Skilled tasks, previously performed by artisans, were divided and subcontracted out to less expensive unskilled laborers. Small shops were replaced by factories, which made the relationship between employer and employee increasingly impersonal. Many masters abandoned their supervisory role to foremen and contractors and substituted unskilled teenaged boys for journeymen. Words like *employer, employee, boss,* and *foreman*—descriptive of the new relationships—began to be widely used.

Between 1790 and 1850 the work process, especially in the building trades, printing, and such rapidly expanding consumer manufacturing industries as tailoring and shoemaking, was radically reorganized. The older household-based economy, in which assistants lived in the homes of their employers, gradually disappeared. Young men moved out of rooms in their master's home into hotels and boardinghouses in distinct working-class neighborhoods. The older view that each worker should be attached to a particular master, who would supervise his behavior and assume responsibility for his welfare, declined. The older paternalistic view was replaced by a new conception of labor as a commodity, like cotton, that could be acquired or disposed of according to the laws of supply and demand.

The Introduction of the Factory System

In 1789 Samuel Slater, who had just finished an apprenticeship in a Derbyshire textile mill, emigrated to the United States. He obtained a job as manager of a mill in Pawtucket, Rhode Island, which opened a year later. Although the little factory had only 19 empoyees, it was among the first to consolidate manufacturing operations under a single roof, thus marking the beginning of the modern factory system.

For an inexpensive and reliable work force Slater and other factory owners turned to child labor. During the early phases of industrialization textile mills and other factories had a ravenous appetite for cheap teenage laborers. In many mechanized industries, from a quarter to over half of the work force was made up of young men or women under the age of 20.

During the first half of the nineteenth century unmarried women made up a majority of the work force in cotton textile mills and a substantial minority of workers in factories manufacturing ready-made clothing, hats, and shoes. Unlike farmwork or domestic service, employment in a mill offered female companionship and an independent income. Wages were twice what a woman could make as a seamstress, tailor, or schoolteacher. Furthermore, most mill girls viewed the work as only temporary before marriage. Most worked in the mills fewer than four years, and frequently interrupted their stints in the mill for several months at a time with trips back home.

By the 1830s increasing competition among textile manufacturers caused deteriorating working conditions that drove native-born women out of the mills. Employers cut wages, lengthened the workday, and required mill workers to tend four looms instead of just two. Hannah Borden, textile worker from Fall River, Massachusetts, was required to have her loom running at 5 A.M. She was given an hour for breakfast and a half hour for lunch. Her workday ended at 7:30 P.M. For a 6-day work week she received between $2.50 and $3.50.

The mill girls militantly protested these conditions. In 1834 and again in 1836 they went out on strike. During the 1840s fewer and fewer native-born women were willing to work in the mills. Increasingly, employers replaced them with a new class of permanent factory operatives: immigrant women from Ireland.

The Rise of Organized Labor

By the 1820s a growing number of journeymen were organizing to protest employer practices. Unlike their counterparts in Britain, American journeymen did not protest against the introduction of machinery into the workplace. Instead, they vehemently protested wage reductions, declining standards of workmanship, and the increased use of unskilled and semiskilled workers. Journeymen charged that manufacturers had reduced "them to degradation and the loss of that self-respect which had made the mechanics and laborers the pride of the world." They insisted that they were the true producers of wealth and that manufacturers, who did not engage in manual labor, were unjust expropriators of wealth.

In an attempt to raise wages, restrict hours, and reduce competition from unskilled workers, skilled journeymen formed the nation's first labor unions. In larger eastern cities like Boston, New York, and Philadelphia, as well as in smaller western cities like Cincinnati, Louisville, and Pittsburgh, they formed local trade unions and city trades' assemblies. House carpenters, handloom weavers, combmakers, shoemakers, and printers formed national societies to uphold uniform wage standards. In 1834 journeymen established the National Trades' Union, the first organization of American wage earners on a national scale. By 1836 union membership had climbed to 300,000.

Despite bitter employer opposition, some gains were made. In 1842, in the landmark case *Commonwealth* v. *Hunt*, the Massachusetts supreme court established a new precedent by recognizing the right of unions to exist. In addition to establishing the nation's first labor unions, journeymen also formed political organizations, known as Working Men's parties. Working men and women published at least 68 labor papers, and they agitated for

During the 1830s, rapid inflation and mounting competition for jobs encouraged growth of unions. By the late 1830s, an estimated 300,000 American workers were union members.

free public education, reduction of the workday, and abolition of capital punishment, state militias, and imprisonment for debt. Following the Panic of 1837, land reform was one of labor's chief demands. One hundred sixty acres of free public land for those who would actually settle the land was the demand, and "Vote Yourself a Farm" became the popular slogan.

Labor's greatest success was a campaign to establish a ten-hour work-day in most major northeastern cities. In 1835 carpenters, masons, and stonecutters in Boston staged a seven-month strike in favor of a ten-hour day. Quickly, the movement spread to Philadelphia, where carpenters, bricklayers, and blacksmiths went on strike. Textile workers in Paterson, New Jersey, were the first factory operatives to strike for a reduction in work hours. Soon, women textile operatives in Lowell added their voices to the call for a ten-hour day, contending that such a law would "lengthen the lives of those employed, by giving them a greater opportunity to breathe the pure air of heaven" as well as provide "more time for mental and moral cultivation."

In 1840 the federal government introduced a ten-hour workday on public works projects. In 1847 New Hampshire became the first state to adopt a ten-hour day law. It was followed by Pennsylvania in 1848. Both states' laws, however, included a clause that allowed workers to agree voluntarily to work more than a ten-hour day. Despite the limitations of these state laws, agitation for a ten-hour day did result in a reduction in the average number of hours worked, to approximately 11.5 by 1850.

At the same time, however, the quickening pace of commerce dramatically increased demand for unskilled workers, who earned extremely low incomes and led difficult lives. Frequent unemployment compounded the problems of the unskilled. In Massachusetts upward of 40 percent of all workers were out of a job for part of a year, usually for four months or more. Fluctuations in demand, inclement weather, interruptions in transportation, technological displacement, fire, injury, and illness all could leave workers jobless.

Typically, a male laborer earned just two-thirds of his family's income. The other third was earned by wives and children. Many married women performed work in the home, such as embroidery and making artificial flowers, tailoring garments, or doing laundry. The wages of children were critical for a family's standard of living. Children under the age of 15 contributed 20 percent of the income of many working-class families.

Immigrants: The New Working Class

At the beginning of the nineteenth century only about 5,000 immigrants arrived in the United States each year. During the 1830s, however, immigration climbed sharply as 600,000 immigrants poured into the country. This figure jumped to 1.7 million in the 1840s, when harvests all across Europe failed, and reached 2.6 million in the 1850s. Most of these immigrants came from Germany, Ireland, and Scandinavia, pushed from their homelands by famine, eviction from farm lands by landlords, political unrest, and the destruction of traditional handicrafts by factory enterprises. Attracted to the United States by the prospects of economic opportunity and political and religious freedom, many dispossessed Europeans braved the voyage across the Atlantic.

During the summer of 1845 a "blight of unusual character" devastated Ireland's potato crop, the basic staple in the Irish diet. Famine and disease soon spread through the Irish countryside. Observers reported seeing children crying with pain and looking "like skeletons, their features sharpened with hunger and their limbs wasted, so that there was little left but bones, their hands and arms." Masses of bodies were buried without coffins, a few inches below the soil. Over the next ten years 750,000 Irish

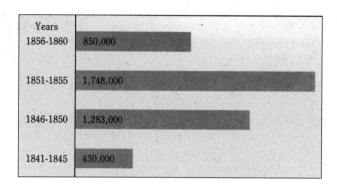

Total immigration, 1840–1860

died and another 2 million left their homeland for Great Britain, Canada, and the United States.

By the 1850s the Irish comprised half the population of Boston and New York, and German immigrants made up a significant proportion of the populations in Cincinnati, Milwaukee, and St. Louis. The new immigrants found employment in construction work, domestic service, factories, foundries, and mining. As early as 1855 German and Irish immigrants constituted 96 percent of New York City's shoemakers and tailors.

The Divided North

During the decades preceding the Civil War it was an article of faith among Northerners that their society offered unprecedented economic equality and opportunity, free of rigid class divisions and glaring extremes of wealth and poverty.

In fact, the percentage of wealth held by those at the top of the economic hierarchy appears to have increased substantially before the Civil War. The first stages of industrialization and urbanization in the North, far from diminishing social inequality, actually widened class distinctions and intensified social stratification. At the top of the social and economic hierarchy was an elite class of families, linked together by intermarriage, membership in exclusive social clubs, and residence in exclusive neighborhoods, as rich as the wealthiest families of Europe. At the bottom were the working poor—immigrants, casual laborers, free blacks, widows, and orphans—who might be thrown out of work at any time. These poor, propertyless, unskilled laborers comprised a vast floating population, which trekked from city to city in search of work.

Between these two extremes were family farmers and a rapidly expanding urban middle class. This was a highly mixed group which ranged from prosperous entrepreneurs and professionals to hard-pressed journeymen, who found their skills increasingly obsolete.

Does this mean that the pre–Civil War North was not the fluid, "egalitarian" society that Jacksonians claimed? The answer is a qualified no. In the first place, the North's richest individuals, unlike Europe's aristocracy, were not ostentatiously rich; they were a working class, engaged in commerce, finance, manufacturing, real estate, and the professions. Even more important, wealthy Northerners publicly rejected the older Hamiltonian notion that the rich and well-born were superior to the masses of people. During the early decades of the nineteenth century wealthy Northerners shed the wigs, knee breeches, ruffled shirts, and white-topped boots that had symbolized high social status in colonial America and began to dress like other men, signaling their acceptance of an ideal of social equality.

Above all, it was the North's relatively high rates of economic and social mobility that gave substance to a widespread belief in equality of opportunity. Although few rich men were truly "self-made," there were many dramatic examples of upward mobility and countless instances of more modest climbs up the ladder of success. Even at the bottom of the economic hierarchy, prospects for advancement increased markedly after 1850. During the 1830s and 1840s less than one unskilled worker in ten managed in the course of a decade to advance to a white-collar job. After 1850 the percentage doubled. The sons of unskilled laborers were even more likely to advance to skilled or white-collar employment. Even the poorest unskilled laborers often were able to acquire a house and a savings account.

It was the reality of economic mobility that convinced the overwhelming majority of Northerners that they lived in a uniquely open society, in which differences in wealth or status were the result of hard work and ambition.

Southern Distinctiveness

Pre–Civil War Americans regarded Southerners as a distinct people, who possessed their own values and way of life. It was widely though mistakenly believed that the North and South had originally been settled by two distinct groups of immigrants, each with its own ethos. Northerners were said to be the descendants of seventeenth-century English Puritans, while Southerners were the descendants of England's country gentry. In the eyes of many pre–Civil War Americans this contributed to two distinct kinds of Americans: the aggressive, individualistic, money-grubbing Yankee and the southern cavalier. According to the popular stereotype, the cavalier, unlike the Yankee, was violently sensitive to insult, indifferent to money, and preoccupied with honor.

The Old South: Images and Realities

During the three decades before the Civil War popular writers created a stereotype, now known as the "plantation legend," that described the South as a land of aristocratic planters, beautiful southern belles, poor white trash, faithful black household servants, and superstitious field-hands. In the eyes of many Northerners, uneasy with their increasingly urban, individualistic commercial society, the culture of the South seemed to have many things absent from the North—a leisurely pace of life, a clear social hierarchy, and an indifference to money.

Despite the strength of the plantation stereotype, the South was, in reality, a diverse and complex region. Though Americans today often associate the Old South with cotton plantations, large parts of the South were unsuitable for plantation life. In the mountainous regions of eastern Tennessee and western Virginia few plantations and few slaves were to be found. Nor did southern farms and plantations devote their efforts exclusively to growing cotton or other cash crops, such as rice and tobacco. Unlike the slave societies of the Caribbean, which produced crops exclusively for export, the South devoted much of its energy to raising food and livestock.

The white South's social structure was much more complex than the popular stereotype of proud aristocrats disdainful of honest work and ignorant, vicious, exploited poor whites. The Old South's intricate social hierarchy included many small slave owners and relatively few large ones.

Actually, large slaveholders were extremely rare. In 1860 just 11,000 Southerners—three-quarters of one percent of the white population—owned more than 50 slaves; just 2,358 owned as many as 100 slaves. However, although large slaveholders were few in number, they owned most of the South's slaves. Over half of all slaves lived on plantations with 20 or more slaves and a quarter lived on plantations with more than 50 slaves.

Slave ownership was relatively widespread. In the first half of the nineteenth century one-third of all southern white families owned slaves, and a majority of white southern families either owned slaves, had owned them, or expected to own them. Few slave owners led lives of leisure or refinement. The average slave owner lived in a log cabin rather than a mansion and was a farmer rather than a planter. The average holding varied between four and six slaves, and most slaveholders possessed no more than five.

White women in the South, despite the image of the hoop-skirted southern belle, suffered under heavier burdens than their northern counterparts. They married earlier, bore more children, and were more likely to die young. They lived in greater isolation and had less access to the company of other women. Their education was briefer and much less likely to result in opportunities for independent careers.

The plantation legend was misleading in still other respects. Slavery was neither dying nor was it unprofitable. In 1860 the South was richer than any country in Europe except England. The southern economy generated enormous wealth and was critical to the economic growth of the entire United States. Prior to the Civil War the South grew 60 percent of the world's cotton, provided over half of all U.S. export earnings, and furnished 70 percent of the cotton consumed by the British textile industry. Cotton exports paid for a substantial share of the capital and technology that laid the basis for America's industrial revolution. In addition, precisely because the South specialized in agricultural production, the North developed a variety of business that provided services for the southern states, including textile and meat processing factories, and financial and commercial facilities.

Impact of Slavery on the Southern Economy

Although slavery was highly profitable, it had a negative impact on the southern economy. It impeded the development of industry and cities and contributed to high debts, soil exhaustion, and a lack of technological innovation.

The South, like other slave societies, did not develop urban centers for commerce, finance, and industry on a scale equal to those found in the North. Southern cities were small because they failed to develop diversified economies. Unlike the cities of the North, southern cities rarely became processing or finishing centers and southern ports rarely engaged in international trade. Their primary functions were to market and transport cotton or other agricultural crops, supply local planters and farmers with such necessities as agricultural implements, and produce the small number of manufactured goods, such as cotton gins, needed by farmers.

An overemphasis on slave-based agriculture led Southerners to neglect industry and transportation improvements. As a result, manufacturing and transportation lagged far behind the North's. In 1860 the North had approximately 1.3 million industrial workers compared to the South's 110,000, and northern factories manufactured nine-tenths of the industrial goods produced in the United States.

The South's transportation network was primitive by northern standards. Most southern railroads served primarily to transport cotton to southern ports, where the crop could be shipped on northern vessels to northern or British factories for processing.

Southern states kept taxation and government spending at much lower levels than in the North. As a result, Southerners lagged far behind Northerners in their support for public education. Illiteracy was widespread. In 1850 20 percent of all southern white adults could not read or write, while the illiteracy rate in New England was less than half of one percent during the same period.

Because large slaveholders owned most of the region's slaves, wealth was more stratified than in the North. In the deep South the middle class held a relatively small proportion of the region's property, but wealthy planters owned a very significant portion of the productive lands and slave labor.

There are indications that during the last decade before the Civil War slave ownership was increasingly concentrated in fewer and fewer hands. As soil erosion and exhaustion diminished the availability of cotton land, scarcity and heavy demand forced the price of land and slaves to rise beyond the reach of most, and in newer cotton-growing regions yeomen farmers were pushed off the land as planters expanded their holdings. During the 1850s the percentage of the total white population owning slaves declined significantly. By 1860 the proportion of white slaveholders had fallen from about one-third to one-fourth. As slave and land ownership grew more concentrated, a growing number of whites were forced by economic pressure to leave the land and move to urban centers.

Growth of a Distinctive Southern Identity

Beginning in the 1830s the South developed a new and aggressive "nationalism" that was rooted in its sense of distinctiveness and its perception that it was ringed by enemies. The South began to conceive of itself more and more as the true custodian of America's revolutionary heritage. Southern travelers who ventured into the North regarded it as a "strange and distant land" and expressed disgust with its vice-ridden cities and its grasping materialism.

At the same time, southern intellectuals began to defend slavery as a positive good. After 1830 white Southerners stopped referring to slavery as a necessary evil. Instead, they argued that it was a beneficial institution that created a hierarchical society superior to the leveling democracy of the North. By the late 1840s a new, more explicitly racist rationale for slavery had emerged.

With the emergence of militant abolitionism in the North, sharpened by slave uprisings in Jamaica and Virginia, the South began to see itself as surrounded by enemies. Southern leaders responded aggressively. Prior to the 1830s southern statements on slavery had been defensive; afterward, they were defiant.

In the 1840s a growing number of southern ministers, journalists, and politicians began to denounce the North's form of capitalism as exploitative. Southern writers like George Fitzhugh argued that slavery was a beneficent institution that permitted the development of an upper class devoted to high intellectual pursuits. The champions of slavery maintained that the South's hierarchical society was superior to the individualistic, materialistic civilization of the North in which abolitionism, feminism, and labor unrest indicated that the social order was disintegrating.

During the 1840s a growing number of Southerners defended slavery on explicitly racial grounds. In doing so, they drew on new pseudoscientific theories of racial inferiority. Some of these theories came from Europe, which was seeking justification for imperial expansion over nonwhite peoples in Africa and Asia. Other racist ideas were drawn from northern scientists, who claimed that blacks and whites were separate species.

The Decline of Antislavery Sentiment in the South

During the eighteenth century the South was unique among slave societies in its openness to antislavery ideas. In Delaware, Maryland, and North Carolina Quakers freed more than 1,500 slaves and sent them out of state. Scattered Presbyterian, Baptist, and Methodist ministers condemned slavery as a sin "contrary to the word of God." As late as 1827, the number of antislavery organizations in the South actually outnumbered those in the free states by at least four to one.

The South's historical openness to antislavery ideas ended in the 1830s. Southern religious sects that had expressed opposition to slavery in the late eighteenth century modified their antislavery beliefs. State law and public opinion stifled debate and forced conformity to proslavery arguments. Southern state legislatures adopted a series of laws suppressing criticism of the institution. Louisiana in 1830 made it a crime to make any statement that might produce discontent or insubordination among free blacks. Six years later Virginia made it a felony for any member of an abolition society to come into the state and for any citizen to deny the legality of slavery. The silent pressure of public opinion limited public discussion of the slavery question. An "iron curtain" against the invasion of antislavery propaganda was erected.

Nonetheless, many white Southerners felt genuine moral doubts about slavery. For the most part, however, these doubts were directed into efforts to reform the institution by converting slaves to Christianity, revising slave codes to make them less harsh, and making slavery conform to the ideal depicted in the Old Testament.

During the early nineteenth century the southern states enacted new codes regulating the punishment of slaves and setting minimum standards for maintenance. State legislatures defined killing a slave with malice as murder and made dismemberment and some other cruel punishments illegal. Three states forbade the sale of young slave children from their parents, and four states permitted slaves to be taught to read and write.

Many of the new laws went unenforced, but they suggest that a new code of values and behavior was emerging. Paternalism was the defining characteristic of this new code. According to this new ideal, slaveholding was "a duty and a burden" carrying strict moral obligations. A humane master of a plantation was supposed to show concern for the spiritual and physical well-being of his slaves.

These minimal efforts to reform slavery were, however, accompanied by tighter restrictions on other aspects of slave life. Private manumissions were made illegal. Southern states instituted the death penalty for any slaves involved in plotting a rebellion. Most states prohibited slaves from owning firearms, placed tight restrictions on slave funerals, and barred black preachers from conducting religious services unless a white person was present. In order to restrict contact between free blacks and slaves, a number of southern states required manumitted slaves to leave the state. Other restrictive laws quarantined vessels containing black sailors and imprisoned those who stepped on shore.

Southern Nationalism

Seeking to free their region from cultural and economic dependence on the North, southern "nationalists" sought to insulate the South from the corrupting commercial and industrial values of the North. This desire for regional independence took many forms, all of which stressed the distinctiveness of southern culture.

The 1830s and 1840s saw attempts to promote southern economic self-sufficiency, to create southern-oriented educational and religious institutions, and to develop a distinctive southern literature. Beginning in 1837 southern leaders held the first of a series of commercial conventions in an attempt to diversify their economy. Other southern nationalists strove to create educational institutions, arguing that the South had to create its own institutions of higher learning in order to protect the young from antislavery ideas. Regional independence was also called for in religion. Due in large part to a fear of antislavery agitation, southern Baptists,

Methodists and Presbyterians sought to sever their denominational affiliations with northern churches. Southerners also called for a distinctive and peculiarly southern literature. More than 30 periodicals were founded with the word "Southern" in their title, all intended to "breathe a Southern spirit, and sustain a strictly Southern character."

By the early 1850s a growing number of aggressive Southerners had moved beyond earlier calls for cultural and economic separatism. Militant nationalists called for the reopening of the slave trade and the annexation of new slave territories in Latin America and the Caribbean.

In a bid to acquire new lands for slavery a filibustering expedition was launched from New Orleans in 1851 to secure Cuba for the South. After this failed, extreme southern nationalists supported the efforts of William Walker, "the gray-eyed man of destiny," to extend slave labor into Latin America. In 1853, with considerable southern support, Walker raised a private army and unsuccessfully invaded Mexico. Two years later he launched the first of three invasions of Nicaragua. On his final foray in 1860 he was taken prisoner by a British officer, handed over to Honduran authorities, and, at the age of 36, executed by a firing squad. The only practical effect of these schemes was to arouse northern opinion against an aggressive southern slaveocracy.

Slavery

The primary distinguishing characteristic of the South was its dependence on slave labor. During the decades before the Civil War 4 million black Americans, one-third of the South's population, labored as slaves.

In general, slaves were overworked, poorly clad, inadequately housed, and received the minimum of medical care. Debt, the death of a master, or merely the prospect of economic gain frequently tore slave husbands from wives and slave parents from children. And yet, as brutal and destructive as the institution of slavery was, slaves were not defenseless or emasculated victims. Slaves were able to sustain ties to their African past and to maintain a separate life. Through religion, folklore, music, and family life as well as more direct forms of resistance, slaves were able to sustain a vital culture supportive of human dignity.

The Legal Status of Slaves

Every southern state enacted a slave code that defined the slave owners' power and the slaves' status as property. The codes stated that a slave, like a domestic animal, could be bought, sold, and leased. A master also had the right to compel a slave to work. The codes prohibited slaves from owning property, testifying against whites in court, or making contracts. Slave marriages were not recognized by law. Under the slave codes, slavery was lifelong and hereditary, and any child born to a slave woman was the property of her master.

The slave codes gave slaves limited legal rights, but their primary purpose was to enforce discipline. In order to refute abolitionist contentions that slavery was unjust and inhumane, southern legislators adopted statutes regulating slaves' hours of labor and establishing certain minimal standards for slave upkeep. Most states also defined the wanton killing of a slave as murder, prohibited cruel and unusual punishments, and extended to slaves accused of capital offenses the right to trial by jury and legal counsel. Whipping, however, was not regarded by southern legislatures as a cruel punishment, and slaves were prohibited from bringing suit to seek legal redress for violations of their rights.

The main goal of the slave codes, however, was to regulate slaves' lives. Slaves were forbidden to strike whites or use insulting language toward white people, hold a meeting without a white person present, visit whites or free blacks, or leave plantations without permission. The laws prohibited whites and free blacks from teaching slaves to read and write, gambling with slaves, or supplying them with liquor, guns, or poisonous

Slavery's worst evil was that it reduced people to the status of property. Under slavery, slaves could be bought, sold, leased, and traded from their families.

Handbill (*reduced size*) of sale of livestock and other property

drugs. Most of the time, authorities loosely enforced these legal restrictions, but whenever fears of slave uprisings spread, enforcement tightened.

Slave Labor

Slaves performed all kinds of work. During the 1850s half a million slaves lived in southern towns and cities, where they were hired out by their owners as skilled artisans or laborers. Many other slaves were engaged in construction of roads and railroads. Most slaves, to be sure, were field hands, but even on plantations not all slaves were menial laborers. Some worked as blacksmiths or carpenters; others were domestic servants; and still others held managerial posts. At least two-thirds of the slaves worked under the supervision of black foremen of gangs, called drivers. Not infrequently they managed the whole plantation in the absence of their masters.

For most slaves, slavery meant backbreaking field work on small farms or larger plantations. Solomon Northrup, a free black who was kidnapped and enslaved for 12 years on a Louisiana cotton plantation, wrote a graphic description of the work regimen imposed on slaves: "The hands are required to be in the cotton field as soon as it is light in the morning, and, with the exception of ten or fifteen minutes, which is given them at noon to swallow their allowance of cold bacon, they are not permitted to be a moment idle until it is too dark to see, and when the moon is full, they often times labor till the middle of the night." Even then, the slaves' work was not over; it was still necessary to feed swine and mules, cut wood, and pack the cotton. At planting time or harvest time work was even more exacting, as planters required slaves to stay in the fields 15 or 16 hours a day.

To maximize productivity, slave owners assigned each hand a specific set of tasks throughout the year. During the winter field slaves ginned and pressed cotton, cut wood, repaired buildings and fences, and cleared fields. In the spring and summer field hands plowed and hoed the land, killed weeds, and planted and cultivated crops. In the fall slaves picked, ginned, and packed cotton, shucked corn, and gathered peas. Elderly slaves cared for children, made clothes, and prepared food.

Labor on large plantations was as rigidly organized as in a factory. Under the gang system, which was widely used on cotton plantations, field hands were divided into plow gangs and hoe gangs, each commanded by a driver. Under the task system, mainly used on rice plantations, each hand was given a specific daily work assignment.

Because slaves had little direct incentive to work hard, slave owners combined a variety of harsh penalties with positive incentives. Some masters denied disobedient slaves passes or forced them to work on Sundays

or holidays. Other planters confined disobedient hands to private or public jails. Chains and shackles were widely used to control runaways.
Whipping was a key part of the system of discipline and motivation. On
one Louisiana plantation at least one slave was lashed every four-and-a-
half days. In his diary Bennet H. Barrow, a Louisiana planter, recorded
flogging "every hand in the field," breaking his sword on the head of one
slave, shooting another in the thigh, and cutting another with a club "in 3
places very bad."

But physical pain alone was not enough to elicit hard work. To stimulate productivity, some masters gave slaves small garden plots and permitted them to sell their produce. Others distributed gifts of food or
money at the end of the year. Still other planters awarded prizes, holidays,
and year-end bonuses to particularly productive slaves. One Alabama
master permitted his slaves to share in the profits of the crops.

Material Conditions of Slave Life

Deprivation and physical hardship were the hallmarks of life under slavery. It now seems clear that the material conditions of slave life may have
been even worse than those of the poorest, most downtrodden free laborers in the North and in Europe. Although the slaves' material conditions
improved greatly in the nineteenth century, slaves were still much more
likely than southern or northern whites to die prematurely, suffer malnutrition or dietary deficiencies, or lose a child in infancy.

The slaves' diet was monotonous and unvaried, consisting largely of
cornmeal, salt pork, and bacon. Only rarely did slaves drink milk or eat
fresh meat or vegetables. This diet provided enough bulk calories to ensure that slaves had sufficient strength and energy to work as productive
field hands, but it did not provide adequate nutrition. As a result, slaves
were small for their age, suffered from vitamin and protein deficiencies,
and were victims of such ailments as beriberi, kwashiorkor, and pellagra.

Plantation records reveal that over half of all slave babies died during
their first year of life—a rate twice that of white babies. Although slave
children's death rate declined after the first year of life, it remained twice
the white rate. Poor nutrition and high rates of infant and child mortality
contributed to a short average life expectancy—just 21 or 22 years compared to 40 to 43 years for whites.

The physical conditions in which slaves lived were appalling. Lacking
privies, slaves had to urinate and defecate in the cover of nearby bushes. Lacking any sanitary disposal of garbage, they were surrounded by decaying food.
Chickens, dogs, and pigs lived next to the slave quarters, and in consequence
animal feces contaminated the area. Such squalor contributed to high rates of
dysentery, typhus, diarrhea, hepatitis, typhoid fever, and intestinal worms.

Slave quarters were cramped and crowded. The typical cabin—a single, windowless room, with a chimney constructed of clay and twigs and a floor made up of dirt or planks resting on the ground—ranged in size from 10×10 feet to 21×21 feet. These small cabins were often quite crowded, containing five, six, or more occupants. On some plantations slaves lived in single-family cabins; on others, two or more shared the same room. On the largest plantations unmarried men and women were sometimes lodged together in barracks-like structures.

Slave Family Life

Slavery severely strained black family life. Slave sales frequently broke up slave families. During the Civil War nearly 20 percent of ex-slaves reported that an earlier marriage had been terminated by "force." The sale of children from parents was even more common. Over the course of a lifetime, the average slave had a fifty-fifty chance of being sold at least once and was likely to witness the sale of several members of his immediate family.

Even in instances in which marriages were not broken by sale, slave husbands and wives often resided on separate farms or plantations and were owned by different individuals. On large plantations one slave father in three had a different owner than his wife and could visit his family only at his master's discretion. On smaller holdings divided ownership occurred even more frequently. The typical farm and plantation were so small that it was difficult for many slaves to find a spouse at all. As one ex-slave put it, men "had a hell of a time getting a wife during slavery."

Other obstacles stood in the way of an independent family life. Living accommodations undermined privacy. Many slaves had to share their single-room cabins with relatives and other slaves who were not related to them. On larger plantations food was cooked in a common kitchen and young children were cared for in a communal nursery while their parents worked in the fields. Even on model plantations children between the ages of seven and ten were taken from their parents and sent to live in separate cabins.

Slavery imposed rigid limits on the authority of slave parents. Nearly every slave child went through an experience similar to one recalled by a young South Carolina slave named Jacob Stroyer. Jacob was being trained as a jockey. His trainer beat him regularly, for no apparent reason. Jacob appealed to his father for help, but his father simply said to work harder, "for I cannot do anything for you." When Jacob's mother argued with the trainer, she was whipped for her efforts. From this episode, Jacob learned a critical lesson: The ability of slave parents to protect their own children was sharply limited.

Of all the evils associated with slavery, abolitionists most bitterly denounced the sexual abuse suffered by slave women. Abolitionists claimed that slaveholders adopted deliberate policies to breed slaves for sale in the lower South and sexually exploited slave women. Some masters did indeed take slave mistresses and concubines. One slave, Henry Bibb, said that a slave trader forced Bibb's wife to become a prostitute.

Planters also sought to increase slave birthrates through a variety of economic incentives. Many slaveholders gave bounties in the form of cash or household goods to mothers who bore healthy children and increased rations and lightened the workload of pregnant and nursing women.

And yet, despite the constant threat of sale and family breakup, African Americans managed to forge strong family ties and personal relationships. Although southern law provided no legal sanction for slave marriages, most slaves established de facto arrangements that were often stable over long periods of time. In spite of frequent family disruption, a majority of slaves grew up in families headed by a father and a mother. Nuclear family ties stretched outward to an involved network of extended kin. In large measure because of the strength and flexibility of kinship ties, black Americans were able to resist the psychologically debilitating effects of slavery.

Contrary to what early nineteenth-century abolitionists charged, the sexual life of slaves was not casual or promiscuous nor did slave women become mothers at a particularly early age. Some slave women, like some white women, engaged in premarital intercourse and bore children outside of marriage. But most slave women settled into a long-lasting monogamous relationship in their early twenties, which lasted, unless broken by sale, until the wife or her husband died.

Slave Cultural Expression

Notwithstanding the harshness and misery of slave life, slaves developed a distinctive culture. Even under the weight of slavery blacks developed a vital religion, music, and folklore. Through their families, their religion, and their cultural traditions, they were able to fashion an autonomous culture and community, beyond the direct control of their masters.

During the late eighteenth and early nineteenth centuries slaves embraced Christianity, but they molded and transformed it to meet their own needs. Their religious beliefs were a mixture of African traditions and Christianity. From their African heritage they brought a hopeful and optimistic view of life, which contrasted sharply with evangelical Protestantism's emphasis on human sinfulness. In Protestant Christianity the slaves found an emphasis on love and the spiritual equality of all people that strengthened their ties to other blacks. Many slaves fused the concepts of Moses, who led his people to freedom, and Jesus, who suffered on behalf of all humankind, into a promise of deliverance in this world.

A major form of black religious expression was the spiritual. Slave spirituals, like "Go Down Moses" with its refrain "let my people go," indicated that slaves identified with the history of the Hebrew people, who had been oppressed and enslaved, but achieved eventual deliverance.

In addition to the spiritual, another major form of slave cultural expression was folklore. Slave folktales were much more than amusing stories; slaves used them to comment on the whites around them and to convey everyday lessons for living. Among the most popular slave folktales were the Brer Rabbit tales, derived from similar African stories, which told of powerless animals who achieve their will through wit and guile rather than power and authority. These tales taught slave children how they had to function in a white-dominated world and held out the promise that the powerless would eventually triumph over the strong.

Slave Resistance

It was a basic tenet of the proslavery argument that slaves were docile, contented, faithful, and loyal. In fact, there is no evidence that the majority of slaves were contented. One scholar has identified more than 200 instances of attempted insurrection or rumors of slave resistance between the seventeenth century and the Civil War. And many slaves who did not directly rebel made their masters' lives miserable through a variety of indirect protests against slavery, including sabotage, stealing, malingering, murder, arson, and infanticide.

Four times during the first 31 years of the nineteenth century slaves attempted major insurrections. In 1800 a 24-year-old Virginia slave named Gabriel Prosser, who was a blacksmith, led a march of perhaps 50 armed slaves on Richmond. The plot failed when a storm washed out the road to Richmond, giving the Virginia militia time to arrest the rebels. White authorities executed Prosser and 25 other conspirators.

In 1811 in southern Louisiana, between 180 and 500 slaves, led by Charles Deslondes, a free mulatto from Haiti, marched on New Orleans, armed with axes and other weapons. Slave owners retaliated by killing 82 blacks and placing the heads of 16 leaders on pikes.

In 1822 Denmark Vesey, a former West Indian slave who had been born in Africa, bought his freedom and moved to Charleston, South Carolina. There he devised a conspiracy to take over the city on a summer Sunday when many whites would be vacationing outside the city. Using his connections as a leader in the African Church of Charleston, Vesey drew support from skilled black artisans, as well as from field slaves. Before the revolt could take place, however, a domestic slave of a prominent Charlestonian informed his master. The authorities proceeded to arrest 131 blacks and hang 37.

The most famous slave revolt took place nine years later in Southampton County in southern Virginia. On August 22, 1831, Nat Turner, a Baptist preacher, led a small group of fellow slaves into the home of his master Joseph Travis and killed the entire Travis household. By August 23 Turner's force had increased to between 60 and 80 slaves and had killed more than 50 whites. The local militia counterattacked and killed about 100 blacks. Twenty more slaves, including Turner, were later executed. Turner's revolt sparked a panic that spread as far south as Alabama and Louisiana.

Slave uprisings were much less frequent and less extensive in the American South than in the West Indies or Brazil. Outright revolts did not occur more often because the chances of success were minimal and the consequences of defeat catastrophic.

The conditions that favored revolts elsewhere were absent in the South. In Jamaica, blacks outnumbered whites ten to one, whereas in the South whites were a majority in every state except Mississippi and South Carolina. In addition, slaveholding units in the South were much smaller than in other slave societies in the Western Hemisphere. Half of all U.S. slaves worked in units of 20 or less; in contrast, many sugar plantations in Jamaica had more than 500 slaves. Finally, southern slaves had few havens to which to escape. The major exception was the swamp country in Florida where black "maroons" joined with Seminole Indians in resisting the U.S. army.

Recognizing that open resistance would be futile or even counterproductive, many plantation slaves expressed their opposition to slavery in a variety of subtle ways. Most day-to-day resistance took the form of breaking tools, feigning illness, doing shoddy work, stealing, and running away. These acts of resistance were apt to occur when a master or overseer overstepped customary bounds. Through these acts, slaves tried to establish a right to proper treatment.

Free Blacks

In 1860 488,000 black Americans were *not* slaves. After the American Revolution, slave owners freed thousands of slaves, and countless others emancipated themselves by running away. In Louisiana a large free black Creole population had emerged under Spanish and French rule, and in

South Carolina a Creole population had arrived from Barbados. The number of free blacks in the Deep South increased rapidly with the arrival of thousands of light-colored refugees from the black revolt in Haiti.

Free blacks varied greatly in status. Most lived in poverty, but in a few cities, such as New Orleans, Baltimore, and Charleston, free blacks worked as skilled craftsmen. In the lower South a few free blacks achieved high occupational status and actually bought slaves of their own. One of the wealthiest free blacks was William Ellison, the son of a slave mother and a white planter. As a slave apprenticed to a skilled artisan, Ellison had learned how to make cotton gins, and at the age of 26 bought his freedom with his overtime earnings. At his death in 1861 he had acquired the home of a former South Carolina governor, a shop, lands, and 63 slaves worth more than $100,000.

Free people of color occupied an uneasy middle ground between the dominant whites and the masses of slaves. Legally, courts denied them the right to serve on juries or to testify against whites. Some, like William Ellison, distanced themselves from those black people who remained in slavery and even bought and sold slaves. Others identified with slaves and poor free blacks and took the lead in establishing separate black churches.

In addition to the more than 250,000 free blacks who lived in the South, another 200,000 free blacks lived in the North. Although free blacks comprised no more than 3.8 percent of the population of any northern state, they faced intense legal, economic, and social discrimination, which kept them desperately poor. All but four states—New Hampshire, Maine, Massachusetts, and Vermont—denied them the right to vote.

In the North as well as the South most free blacks faced economic hardship and substandard living conditions. Free blacks in both regions suffered from heightened discrimination and competition from white immigrants in both the skilled trades and such traditional occupations as domestic service. On the eve of the Civil War the plight of free blacks worsened. South Carolina debated the reenslavement of free blacks, prompting almost 3,000 to emigrate to the North.

Conclusion

In the late 1850s the North and South had become in the eyes of many Americans two distinct civilizations, each having its own distinctive set of values and ideals: one increasingly urban and industrial, the other committed to slave labor. Although the two sections shared many of the same ideals, ambitions, and prejudices, they had developed along diverging lines. In increasing numbers, Northerners identified their society with

Chronology of Key Events

1790	Samuel Slater opens the nation's first textile mill in Pawtucket, Rhode Island
1793	Eli Whitney obtains a patent for the cotton gin
1801	Gabriel Prosser's slave insurrection uncovered
1806	Journeymen shoemakers in New York stage one of the nation's first labor strikes
1811	Charles Deslondes's slave insurrection in southern Louisiana suppressed
1822	Denmark Vesey's slave rebellion uncovered in South Carolina
1831	Nat Turner rebellion
1832	Virginia legislature defeats proposal to abolish slavery
1834	National Trades' Union organized; Massachusetts mill girls stage their first strike
1837	Panic of 1837
1840	Ten-hour day established for federal employees
1842	Massachusetts supreme court, in *Commonwealth* v. *Hunt,* recognizes unions' right to exist
1845	Irish Potato Famine

progress and believed that slavery was an intolerable obstacle to innovation, self-improvement, and commercial and economic growth. A growing number of Southerners, in turn, regarded their rural and agricultural society as the true embodiment of republican values. The great question before the nation was whether it could continue to exist half slave, half free.

Suggestions for Further Reading

For information on the antebellum North and the rise of industrialization see Thomas Dublin, *Women at Work: The Transformation of Work and Community in Lowell, Massachusetts,* (1979); Philip Taylor, *The Distant Magnet: European*

Emigration to the U.S.A. (1971); Stephan Thernstrom, *Poverty and Progress, Social Mobility in a Nineteenth Century City* (1964); Anthony F. C. Wallace, *Rockdale: The Growth of an American Village in the Early Industrial Revolution* (1978); Sean Wilentz, *Chants Democratic* (1984).

Studies focusing on the southern slaveocracy include William J. Cooper, Jr., *South and the Politics of Slavery* (1978); William J. Cooper, Jr. and Thomas E. Terrill, *The American South* (1990); Eugene D. Genovese, *The Political Economy of Slavery* (1965), and *The World the Slaveholders Made* (1969); Robert E. May, *The Southern Dream of a Caribbean Empire* (1973).

Valuable studies on the culture of slaves and free blacks are Ira Berlin, *Slaves Without Masters: The Free Negro in the Antebellum South* (1974); John W. Blassingame, *The Slave Community: Plantation Life in the Antebellum South,* rev. ed. (1979); John B. Boles, *Black Southerners* (1983); Eugene D. Genovese, *From Rebellion to Revolution: Afro-American Slave Revolts in the Making of the Modern World* (1979), and *Roll, Jordan, Roll: The World the Slaves Made* (1974); Leon Litwack, *North of Slavery: The Negro in the Free States* (1961); Stephen B. Oates, *The Fires of Jubilee: Nat Turner's Fierce Rebellion* (1975).

Chapter **I3**

Surge to the Pacific

Early in April 1846, 87 pioneers led by George Donner, a well-to-do 62 year-old farmer, set out from Illinois, for California. As this group of pioneers headed westward, they never imagined the hardship and tragedy that awaited them. Like many emigrants, they were ill prepared for the dangerous trek. The pioneers' 27 wagons were loaded not only with necessities but with fancy foods and liquor and such luxuries as built-in beds and stoves.

In Wyoming the party decided to take a shortcut, having read in a guidebook that pioneers could save 400 miles by cutting south of the Great Salt Lake. At first the trail was "all that could be desired," but soon huge boulders, arid desert, and dangerous mountain passes slowed the expedition to a crawl. During one stretch, the party traveled only 36 miles in 21 days. In late October the Donner party reached the eastern Sierra Nevada Mountains and prepared to cross Truckee Pass, the last remaining barrier before they arrived in California's Sacramento Valley. They climbed the high Sierra ridges in an attempt to cross the pass, but early snows blocked their path.

Trapped, the party built crude tents covered with clothing, blankets, and animal hides, which were soon buried under 14 feet of snow. The pioneers intended to slaughter their livestock for food, but many of the animals perished in 40-foot snowdrifts. To survive, the Donner party was forced to eat mice, their rugs, and even their shoes. In the end, surviving members of the party escaped starvation only by eating the flesh of those who died.

Finally, in mid-December, 17 men and women made a last-ditch effort to cross the pass to find help. They took only a six-day supply of rations, consisting of finger-sized pieces of dried beef—two pieces a person per day. During a severe storm two of the group died. The surviving members of the party "stripped the flesh from their bones, roasted and ate it, averting their eyes from each other, and weeping." More than a month passed before seven frostbitten survivors reached an American settlement. By then, the rest had died and two Indian guides had been shot and eaten.

Relief teams immediately sought to rescue the pioneers still trapped near Truckee Pass. The situation that the rescuers found was unspeakably gruesome. Thirteen were dead. Surviving members of the Donner party were delirious from hunger and overexposure. One survivor was found in a small cabin next to a cannibalized body of a young boy. Of the original 87 members of the party, only 47 survived.

It took Americans a century and a half to expand as far west as the Appalachian Mountains, a few hundred miles from the Atlantic coast. It took another 50 years to push the frontier to the Mississippi River. By 1830 fewer than 100,000 pioneers had crossed the Mississippi.

Margaret Reed was one of only 47 survivors of the original party of 87 pioneers to reach California.

Only a small number of explorers, fur trappers, traders, and missionaries had ventured far beyond the Mississippi River. These trailblazers drew a picture of the American West as a land of promise, a paradise of plenty, filled with fertile valleys and rich land. During the 1840s tens of thousands of Americans began the process of settling the West beyond the Mississippi River. Thousands of families chalked GTT ("Gone to Texas") on their gates or painted "California or Bust" on their wagons and joined the trek westward. By 1850 pioneers had pushed the edge of settlement all the way to Texas, the Rocky Mountains, and the Pacific Ocean.

Opening the West

Before the nineteenth century, mystery shrouded the Far West. Mapmakers knew very little about the shape, size, or topography of the land west of the Mississippi River. French, British, and Spanish trappers, traders, and missionaries had traveled the Upper and Lower Missouri River and the British and Spanish had explored the Pacific coast, but most of western North America was an unknown.

The popular conception of the West was largely a mixture of legend and guesswork. Even educated people like Thomas Jefferson, believed that the West was populated by primeval beasts and that only a single ridge of mountains, known as the "Stony Mountains," needed to be crossed before one could see the Pacific Ocean.

Pathfinders

In 1803 President Thomas Jefferson appointed Meriwether Lewis and William Clark to explore the Missouri and Columbia rivers as far as the Pacific. As a politician interested in the rapid settlement and commercial development of the West, Jefferson wanted Lewis and Clark to establish American claims to the region west of the Rocky Mountains, gather information about furs and minerals in the region, and identify sites for trading posts and settlements. The president also instructed the expedition to collect information covering the diversity of life in the West, ranging from climate, geology, and plant growth to fossils of extinct animals and Indian religions, laws, and customs.

In 1806 the year that Lewis and Clark returned from their 8,000-mile expedition, a young army lieutenant named Zebulon Pike left St. Louis to explore the southern border of the Louisiana Territory, just as Lewis and Clark had explored the territory's northern portion. Traveling along the Arkansas River, Pike saw the towering peak that bears his name. He and his party then traveled into Spanish territory along the Rio Grande and Red River. Pike's description of the wealth of Spanish towns, primarily Chihuahua and Santa Fe, in the Southwest brought some American traders to the region.

Pike's report of his expedition, published in 1810, helped to create one of the most influential myths about the Great Plains: This region was nothing more than a "Great American Desert," a treeless and waterless land of dust storms and starvation. "Here," wrote Pike, is "barren soil, parched and dried up for eight months of the year . . . [without] a speck of vegetation." This image of the West as a region of savages, wild beasts, and deserts received added support from another government-sponsored expedition, one led by Major Stephen H. Long in 1820 in search of the source of the Red River. Long's report described the West as "wholly unfit for cultivation, and . . . uninhabitable by a people depending upon agriculture for their subsistence." This report helped implant the image of the

"Great American Desert" even more deeply in the American mind, retarding western settlement for a generation.

The view of the West as a dry, barren wasteland was not fully offset until the 1840s when another government-sponsored explorer, John C. Frémont, nicknamed "The Pathfinder," mapped much of the territory between the Mississippi Valley and the Pacific Ocean. His glowing descriptions of the West as a paradise of plenty captivated the imagination of many midwestern families who, by the 1840s, were eager for new lands to settle.

Mountain Men

Traders and trappers were more important than government explorers in opening the West to white settlement. Trappers and traders were the first U.S. citizens to exploit the West economically. They trapped beaver and bartered with Indians for pelts. They blazed the great westward trails through the Rockies and Sierra Nevada and stirred the popular imagination with stories of redwood forests, geysers, and fertile valleys in California, Oregon, and other areas west of the Rocky Mountains. The men also undermined the ability of the western Indians to resist white incursions by encouraging intertribal warfare and making Indians dependent on American manufactured goods. They killed off animals that provided a major part of the Indian hunting and gathering economy, distributed alcohol, and spread disease.

When Lewis and Clark completed their expedition, they brought back reports of rivers and streams in the northern Rockies teeming with beaver and otter. Fur traders and trappers quickly followed in their footsteps. Starting in 1807, keelboats ferried fur trappers up the Missouri River. By the mid-1830s these "mountain men" had marked out the overland trails that would lead pioneers to Oregon and California.

The Rocky Mountain Fur Company played a central role in the opening of the western fur trade. Instead of buying skins from the Indians, the company inserted ads in St. Louis newspapers asking for white trappers willing to go to the wilderness. In 1822 it sent a hundred trappers out along the upper Missouri River. Three years later the company introduced the "rendezvous" system, under which trappers met once a year at an agreed-upon meeting place to barter pelts for supplies. "The rendezvous," wrote one participant, "is one continued scene of drunkenness, gambling, and brawling and fighting, as long as the money and the credit of the trappers last."

At the same time that mountain men searched for beaver in the Rockies and along the Columbia River, other groups trapped furs in the Southwest, then part of Mexico. In 1827 Jedediah Smith and a party of 15 trappers, after nearly dying of thirst, discovered a westward route to California.

It led across the burning Mojave Desert and the San Bernardino Mountains to the Pacific Coast. Jim Beckwourth, a black mountain man who was the son of a Virginia slave, also discovered a pass through the Sierra Nevada that became part of the overland trail to California.

The western fur trade lasted only until 1840, when the last annual rendezvous was held. Beaver hats for gentlemen went out of style in favor of silk hats, bringing the romantic era of the mountain man, dressed in a fringed buckskin suit, to an end. Fur-bearing animals had been trapped out, and profits from trading, which amounted to as much as 2,000 percent during the early years, fell steeply. Instead of hunting furs, some trappers became scouts for the United States Army or pilots for the wagon trains that were beginning to carry pioneers to Oregon and California.

Trailblazing

The Santa Fe and Oregon trails were the two principal routes to the Far West. William Becknell, an American trader, opened the Santa Fe Trail in 1821. Ultimately, the trail tied the New Mexican Southwest economically to the rest of the United States and hastened American penetration of the region.

Western Trails

The Santa Fe Trail served primarily commercial functions. From the early 1820s until the 1840s an average of 80 wagons and 150 traders used the Santa Fe Trail each year. Mexican settlers in Santa Fe purchased cloth, hardware, glass, and books. On their return east, American traders carried Mexican blankets, beaver pelts, wool, mules, and silver. By the 1830s traders had extended the trail into California, with branches reaching Los Angeles and San Diego. By the 1850s and 1860s more than 5,000 wagons a year took the trail across long stretches of desert, dangerous water crossings, and treacherous mountain passes. The Santa Fe Trail made the Spanish southwest economically dependent on the United States and first brought Americans into the areas that became Arizona, California, and New Mexico.

In 1811 and 1812 fur trappers marked out the Oregon Trail, the longest and most famous pioneer route in American history. This trail crossed about 2,000 miles from Independence, Missouri, to the Columbia River country of Oregon. During the 1840s 12,000 pioneers traveled the trail's entire length to Oregon.

Travel on the Oregon Trail was a tremendous test of human endurance. The journey by wagon train took six months. Settlers encountered prairie fires, sudden blizzards, and impassable mountains. Cholera and other diseases were common; food, water, and wood were scarce. Only the stalwart dared brave the physical hardship of the westward trek.

Spanish and Indian America

When Americans ventured westward, they did not enter virgin land. Large parts of the Far West were already occupied by Indians and Mexicans, who had lived in the region for hundreds of years and established their own distinctive ways of life.

Hispanic America

Between 1528 and 1800 Spain established imperial claims and isolated outposts in an area extending from present-day Montana to Mexico and from California to the Mississippi River. Half a century before the first English colonists arrived at Jamestown, Spain had permanent settlements in the Far West, founded partly as a way to keep out other European powers. Then, in the late sixteenth century, Spain planted a colony in New Mexico and a century later built the first settlements in what is now Arizona and Texas. In the late eighteenth century fears of British and Russian occupation of the Pacific Coast led Spain also to establish outposts in California.

The Spanish clergy, particularly Jesuits and Franciscans, played a critical role in settling the Southwest, using the mission system. Their missions were designed to spread Christianity among, and establish control over, native populations. In some areas, they forced Indians to live in mission communities where the priests taught them weaving, blacksmithing, candle-making, and leather-working, and forced them to work in workshops, orchards, and fields for long hours. The missions were most successful in New Mexico (despite an Indian revolt in 1680) and California, and far less successful in Arizona and Texas.

Mission life reached its peak in California, an area that Spain did not begin to colonize until 1769. In the mid-eighteenth century Spain learned that Russian seal hunters and traders were moving south from Alaska into California. Determined to halt the Russian advance, Spanish authorities established a string of missions and presidios (military forts) along the Pacific coast. Between 1769 and 1823 Spain established 21 missions in California, extending from San Diego northward to Sonoma.

By the early nineteenth century, however, resistance to colonial rule in Spanish America was growing. In 1810 Miguel Hidalgo y Costilla, a Mexican priest, led a revolt which, although short-lived, represented the beginning of Mexico's struggle for independence. Mexican independence was finally achieved in 1821. The War of Independence marked the beginning of a period of far-reaching change in the Southwest. Among the most important consequences of the collapse of Spanish rule was the opening of the region to American economic penetration. Mexican authorities in New Mexico and Arizona allowed American traders to bring American goods into the area and trappers to hunt for beaver. Texas and California were also opened up to American commerce and settlement. By 1848 Americans made up about half of California's non-Indian population.

Mexican independence also led to the demise of the mission system in California. After the revolution the missions were "secularized"—broken up and their property sold or given away to private citizens. In 1833–1834 the Mexican government confiscated California mission properties and exiled the Franciscan friars. As a result, mission properties fell into private hands. By 1846 mission land and cattle had largely passed into the hands of 800 private landowners called rancheros, who controlled 8 million acres of land in units (ranchos) ranging in size from 4,500 to 50,000 acres. The ranchos were run like feudal estates, and the Indians who worked on the estates had a status similar to that of slaves. Indeed, the death rate of Indians who worked on ranchos was twice as high as the rate among southern slaves, and by 1848 one-fifth of California's Indian population had died.

After it won its independence from Spain, Mexico secularized the missions and divided land into ranchos. This painting shows a Mexican *ranchero*.

Western Indians

In 1840, before large numbers of pioneers and farmers crossed the Mississippi, at least 300,000 Indians lived in the Southwest, on the Great Plains, in California, and on the northwest Pacific Coast. The Native American population was divided into more than 200 tribes. Their life-styles ranged from nomadic hunting and gathering to sedentary farming. Their social organization was equally diverse, each tribe having its own language, religious beliefs, kinship patterns, and system of government.

The best-known of the western Indians are the 23 Indian tribes—including the Cheyenne and Sioux—who lived on the Great Plains and hunted buffalo, antelope, deer, and elk for subsistence. For many present-day Americans, the Plains Indians, riding on horseback, wearing a war-bonnet, and living in a tepee, are regarded as the typical American Indians. In fact, however, the Plains Indians first acquired the horse from the Spanish in the sixteenth century. Not until the middle of the eighteenth century did these tribes have a large supply of horses and not until the early to mid-nineteenth century did most Plains Indians have firearms.

South and west of the Plains, in the huge arid region that is now Arizona and New Mexico, sophisticated farmers, like the Hopi, Zuni, and other Pueblo groups, coexisted with nomadic hunters and gatherers, like the Apache and Navajo. In the Great Basin, the harsh barren region between the Sierra Nevada and the Rocky Mountains, food was so scarce that nations like the Paiutes and the Gosiutes subsisted on berries, nuts, roots, insects, and reptiles.

More than 100,000 Indians still lived in California when the area was acquired by the United States in 1848. Most of these people occupied small villages during the winter but moved during the rest of the year gathering wild plants and seeds, hunting small game, and fishing in the rivers.

The large number of tribes living along the northwest Pacific Coast developed an elaborate social hierarchy based on wealth and descent. These people found an abundant food supply in the sea, coastal rivers, and forests. They took salmon, seal, whale, and otter from the coastal waters and hunted deer, moose, and elk in the forests.

Contact with white traders, trappers, and settlers caused a dramatic decline in Indian populations. In California, disease and deliberate campaigns of extermination killed 70,000 Indians between 1849 and 1859. In the Great Basin, impoverished Gosiutes and Paiutes were shot by trappers for sport. In Texas, the Karankawas and many of the other original tribes of the area largely disappeared. Further west, Comanche, Kiowa, and Apache warriors bitterly resisted white encroachment on their land. Tribes in the Pacific Northwest and the northern Plains struggled desperately to slow the arrival of whites along the Oregon Trail. The Nez Percé and Flathead Indians expelled American missionaries from their tribal lands, and the Snake, Cheyenne, Shasta, and Rogue River Indians tried futilely to cut emigrant routes. The federal government employed the army to protect settlers and attack the western Indians and forced the cession of 147 million acres of tribal lands to the United States between 1853 and 1857.

Settling the Far West

During the early 1840s thousands of pioneers headed westward toward California and Oregon. In 1841 the first party of 69 pioneers left Missouri for California, led by an Ohio schoolteacher named John Bidwell. The members of the party knew little about western travel: "We only knew that California lay to the west." The hardships the party endured were nearly unbearable. They were forced to abandon their wagons and eat their pack animals. American pioneering of the Far West had begun. During the next 25 years some 350,000 more made the trek along the overland trails.

The rugged pioneer life was not a new experience for most of these early western settlers. Most of the pioneers who migrated to the Far West came from the states that border the Mississippi River—Missouri, Arkansas, Louisiana, and Illinois—which had only recently acquired statehood. Either they or their parents had already moved several times before reaching the Mississippi Valley.

Life on the Trail

For many families, the great spur for emigration was economic; the financial depression of the late 1830s, accompanied by floods and epidemics in the Mississippi Valley, forced many to pull up stakes and head west. Said one woman: "We had nothing to lose, and we might gain a fortune." Most settlers traveled in family units. Even single men attached themselves to family groups.

At first, pioneers tried to maintain the rigid sexual division of labor that characterized early nineteenth-century America. Men drove the wagons and livestock, stood guard duty, and hunted buffalo and antelope for extra meat. Women got up before dawn, collected wood and "buffalo chips" (animal dung used for fuel), hauled water, kindled campfires, kneaded dough, and milked cows. The demands of the journey forced a blurring of gender-role distinctions for women who, in addition to domestic chores, performed many duties previously reserved for men. They drove wagons, yoked cattle, and loaded wagons. Some men even did things such as cooking, previously regarded as women's work.

Accidents, disease, and sudden disaster were ever-present dangers. Diseases such as typhoid, dysentery, and mountain fever killed many pioneers. Emigrant parties also suffered devastation from buffalo stampedes, prairie fires, and floods. Pioneers buried at least 20,000 emigrants along the Oregon Trail.

Still, despite the hardships of the experience, few emigrants ever regretted their decision to move west. As one pioneer put it: "Those who crossed the plains . . . never forgot the ungratified thirst, the intense heat and bitter cold, the craving hunger and utter physical exhaustion of the trail. . . . But there was another side. True they had suffered, but the satisfaction of deeds accomplished and difficulties overcome more than compensated and made the overland passage a thing never to be forgotten."

Manifest Destiny

In 1845 John L. O'Sullivan, editor of the *Democratic Review,* referred in his magazine to America's "manifest destiny to overspread the continent allotted by Providence for the free development of our yearly multiplying millions." One of the most influential slogans ever coined, *manifest destiny* expressed the romantic emotion that led Americans to risk their lives to settle the Far West.

The idea that America had a special destiny to stretch across the continent motivated many people to migrate west and encouraged men and women to dream big dreams. "We Americans," wrote Herman Melville, one of this country's greatest novelists, "are the peculiar, chosen people—the Israel of our time." Aggressive nationalists invoked the idea to justify Indian removal, war with Mexico, and American expansion into Cuba and Central America. More positively, the idea of manifest destiny inspired missionaries, farmers, and pioneers, who dreamed only of transforming plains and fertile valleys into farms and small towns.

Gone to Texas

In 1822, when the first caravan of American traders traversed the Santa Fe Trail and the first hundred fur trappers searched the Rocky Mountains for beaver, a small number of Americans followed trails to another frontier—Texas.

American settlement in Texas began with the encouragement of first the Spanish, and then Mexican, governments. In the summer of 1820 Moses Austin, a bankrupt 59-year-old Missourian, asked Spanish authorities for a large Texas land tract that he would promote and sell to American pioneers. The following year the Spanish government gave him permission to settle 300 families in Texas. Spain welcomed the Americans for two reasons—to provide a buffer against illegal U.S. settlers, who were creating problems in east Texas even before the grant was made to Austin, and to help develop the land, since only 3,500 native Mexicans had settled in Texas (which was part of the Mexican state of Coahuila y Tejas).

Moses Austin soon died, but his son Stephen carried out his dream to colonize Texas. By 1824 he had attracted 272 colonists to Texas and persuaded the new government of Mexico that encouragement of American immigration was the best way to develop the area. To promote colonization, Mexico in 1825 gave land agents (called *empresarios*) 67,000 acres of land for every 200 families they brought to Texas. Mexico imposed two conditions on land ownership: Settlers had to become Mexican citizens and they had to convert to Roman Catholicism. By 1830 there were 16,000 Americans in Texas.

As the Anglo population swelled, Mexican authorities grew increasingly suspicious of the growing American presence in Texas, and in 1827 the government sent General Manuel de Mier y Terán to investigate the situation. In his report Terán warned that unless the Mexican government took timely measures, American settlers in Texas were certain to rebel. Differences in language and culture, Terán believed, had produced bitter enmity between the colonists and native Mexicans. The colonists, he noted, refused to learn the Spanish language, maintained their own separate schools, and conducted most of their trade with the United States. They complained bitterly that they had to travel more than 500 miles to reach a Mexican court and resented the efforts of Mexican authorities to deprive them of the right to vote.

To reassert its authority over Texas, the Mexican government reaffirmed its constitutional prohibition against slavery throughout Mexico, established a chain of military posts occupied by convict soldiers, levied customs duties, restricted trade with the United States, and decreed an end to further American immigration. These actions might have provoked Texans to revolution. But in 1832 General Antonio López de Santa Anna became Mexico's president. Colonists hoped that he would make Texas a self-governing state within the Mexican republic, separate from the much more populous Coahuila, thereby eliminating any reason for rebellion. Once in power, however, Santa Anna proved to be far less liberal than many Americans had believed. In 1834 he overthrew Mexico's constitutional government, abolished state governments, and made himself dictator. When Stephen Austin went to Mexico City to try to settle the Texans' grievances, Santa Anna imprisoned him in a Mexican jail for a year.

On November 3, 1835, American colonists adopted a constitution and organized a temporary government but voted overwhelmingly against declaring independence. A majority of colonists hoped to attract the support of Mexican liberals in a joint effort to depose Santa Anna and to restore power to the state governments, hopefully including a separate state of Texas.

While holding out the possibility of compromise, the Texans prepared for war. The provisional government elected Sam Houston, a former Tennessee governor and close friend of Andrew Jackson, to lead whatever military forces he could muster. In the middle of 1835 scattered local outbursts erupted against Mexican rule. Then a band of 300 to 500 Texans captured Mexico's military headquarters in San Antonio. The Texas Revolution was underway.

Soon the ominous news reached Texas that Santa Anna himself was marching north with 7,000 soldiers to crush the revolt. In actuality, Santa

Anna's army was not particularly impressive; it was filled with raw recruits and included many Indian troops who spoke and understood little Spanish. When Houston learned that Santa Anna's initial goal was to recapture San Antonio, he ordered San Antonio abandoned. But Texas rebels decided to defend the town and made their stand at an abandoned Spanish mission, the Alamo. The Texans were led by William Travis and Jim Bowie and included the frontier hero David Crockett.

For 12 days Mexican forces laid siege to the Alamo. At 5 A.M., March 6, Mexican troops scaled the mission's walls. By 8 A.M., the fighting was over. One hundred eighty-three defenders lay dead, including several Mexicans who had fought for Texas independence.

Two weeks after the defeat at the Alamo, James Fannin and his men surrendered to Mexican forces near Goliad with the understanding that they would be treated as prisoners of war. Instead, Santa Anna ordered more than 350 Texans shot.

These defeats, however, had an unexpected side effect. They gave Sam Houston time to raise and train an army. Volunteers from the American South flocked to his banner. On April 21 his army of less than 800 men surprised and utterly defeated Santa Anna's army as it camped out on the San Jacinto River, east of present-day Houston. The next day Houston's army captured Santa Anna himself and forced him to sign a treaty granting Texas its independence, a treaty that was never ratified by the Mexican government because it was acquired under duress.

For most Mexican settlers in Texas, defeat meant that they would be relegated to second-class social, political, and economic positions. The new Texas constitution denied citizenship and property rights to those who failed to support the revolution. All persons of Hispanic ancestry were considered in the "denial" category unless they could prove otherwise. Consequently, many Mexican landowners fled the region.

Texas grew rapidly, following independence. In 1836 5,000 immigrants arrived in Texas, boosting its population to 30,000. By 1847 its population had reached 140,000. The region also grew economically. Although cotton farming dominated the Texas economy, cattle were becoming an increasingly important industry. Many Mexican landowners abandoned cattle after the Texas Revolution, and, by the 1840s, large numbers of wild cattle roamed the range. By 1850 the first American cowboys were driving 60,000 cattle a year to New Orleans and California.

The Texas Question

Texas had barely won its independence when it decided to become a part of the United States. A referendum held soon after the Battle of San Jacinto showed Texans favoring annexation by a vote of 3,277 to 93.

The annexation question became one of the most controversial issues in American politics in the late 1830s and early 1840s. The issue was not Texas but slavery. The admission of Texas to the Union would upset the sectional balance of power in the U.S. Senate, just as the admission of Missouri had threatened 15 years earlier. President Andrew Jackson, acutely conscious of the opposition to admitting Texas as a slave state, agreed only to recognize Texan independence. In 1838 John Quincy Adams, now a member of the House of Representatives, staged a 22-day filibuster that successfully blocked annexation. It appeared that Congress had settled the Texas question. For the time being, Texas would remain an independent republic.

At this point, proslavery Southerners began to popularize a conspiracy theory that would eventually bring Texas into the Union as a slave state. In 1841 John Tyler, an ardent defender of slavery, succeeded to the presidency on the death of William Henry Harrison. Tyler and his secretary of state, John C. Calhoun, argued that Great Britain was scheming to annex Texas and transform it into a haven for runaway slaves. According to this theory, British slave emancipation in the West Indies had been a total economic disaster, and the British now hoped to undermine slavery in the American South by turning Texas into a British satellite state. In fact, British abolitionists, but not the British government, were working to convince Texas to outlaw slavery in exchange for British foreign aid. Sam Houston did his part to excite the fears of Americans by conducting highly visible negotiations with the British government. If the United States would not annex Texas, Houston warned, Texas would seek the support of "some other friend." In the spring of 1844 Calhoun hammered out an annexation treaty with Texas diplomats, but the agreement failed to gain the required two-thirds majority for Senate ratification.

The Texas question became the major political issue in the presidential campaign of 1844. James K. Polk, the Democratic candidate, was a strong supporter of annexation, and his victory encouraged Tyler to attempt to annex Texas again in the waning months of his administration. This time Tyler submitted the measure in the form of a resolution, which required only a simple majority of both houses. Congress narrowly approved the resolution in 1845, making Texas the twenty-eighth state.

Webster-Ashburton Treaty

During the decades before the Civil War the border between the United States and British America was the scene of constant tensions. In 1837 many Americans viewed an insurrection in eastern Canada as an opportunity to annex the country. Americans who lived near the Canadian border aided the rebels, and in one incident several hundred western New Yorkers crossed into Canada and staged an abortive attack on a band of British soldiers. After British forces suppressed the uprising, New Yorkers provided safe haven for the insurrection's leaders. When the rebels began to launch raids into Canada from western New York State, Canadian officials crossed the U.S. border, killed a Canadian rebel, and burned an American ship, the *Caroline,* which had supplied the rebels. When Americans demanded an apology and reparations, Canadian officials refused. Almost immediately, another dispute erupted over the Maine boundary as American and Canadian lumberjacks and farmers battled for possession of northern Maine and western New Brunswick.

The Webster-Ashburton Treaty of 1842 settled these controversies. The treaty awarded the United States most of the disputed territory in Maine and New Brunswick, and adjusted the Canadian-United States boundary between Lake Superior and Lake of the Woods. The Webster-Ashburton Treaty left one major border controversy unresolved: the Canadian-American boundary in the Pacific Northwest.

Oregon

Disputes between the United States and Britain over the "Oregon" country emerged early in the nineteenth century. In 1810 John Jacob Astor, an American who had made a fortune in the Great Lakes fur trade, decided to open a trading post, named Astoria, at the mouth of the Columbia River. He hoped the post would secure a monopoly over the western fur trade, and then ship the furs to eager customers in China. The venture proved unsuccessful, however, and for nearly two decades the fur trade was dominated by the British Hudson's Bay Company.

As British fur traders expanded their activities in the Pacific Northwest, American politicians grew alarmed that Britain would gain sovereignty over the region. American diplomats moved quickly to try to solidify American claims to Oregon. Spain, Russia, Britain, and the United States all claimed rights to the Pacific Northwest. In 1818 British and American negotiators agreed that nationals of both countries could trade in the region; this agreement was renewed in 1827. In 1819 the United States persuaded Spain to cede its claims to Oregon to the United States, and two years later Secretary of State John Quincy Adams warned Russia that the United States would oppose any Russian attempts to occupy the territory.

The rapid influx of a large number of land-hungry Americans into Oregon in the mid-1840s forced Britain and the United States to decide the status of Oregon. In the presidential election of 1844 the Democratic party demanded the "re-occupation" of Oregon and annexation of the entire Pacific Northwest coast up to the edge of Russian-held Alaska, which was fixed at 54° 40'. This demand helped James K. Polk win the presidency in 1844.

In truth, Polk had little desire to go to war with Britain. Furthermore, he believed that the northernmost portions of the Oregon country were unsuitable for agriculture. Therefore, in 1846—despite the expansionist slogan "54° 40' or fight"—he readily accepted a British compromise on the boundary dispute to extend the existing United States-British American boundary along the 49th parallel from the Rocky Mountains to the Pacific Ocean.

The Mormon Frontier

Pioneers migrated to the West for a variety of reasons. Some were driven westward by the hope of economic and social betterment, others by a restless curiosity and an urge for adventure. The Mormons moved west for an entirely different reason—to escape religious persecution.

Oregon Country, Pacific Northwest Boundary Dispute

The United States and Great Britain nearly came to blows over the disputed boundary in Oregon.

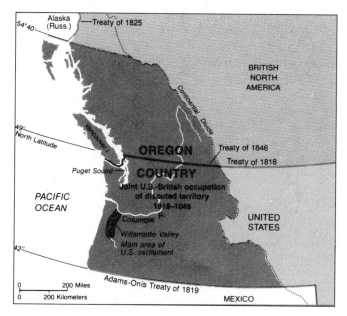

The Mormon church had its beginnings in upstate New York in 1823. Joseph Smith, the son of a farmer, claimed to have received divine revelations that told him of the existence of a set of buried golden plates that contained a lost section from the Bible describing a tribe of Israelites that had lived in America. Smith also claimed to have unearthed the golden plates, and four years later, with the aid of magic stones, translated them into English. The messages on the plates were later published as the *Book of Mormon*.

By the 1830s Smith had attracted several thousand followers from rural areas of the North and the frontier Midwest. The converts to Mormonism were usually small farmers and tradesmen who had been displaced by the growing commercial economy and who were repelled by the rising tide of liberal religion and individualism in early nineteenth-century America.

Because Joseph Smith said that he conversed with angels and received direct revelations from the Lord, local authorities threatened to indict him for blasphemy. He and his followers responded by moving to Ohio, then to Missouri. There, proslavery mobs attacked the Mormons, accusing them of inciting slave insurrection. They burned several Mormon settlements and seized Mormon farms and houses. Fifteen thousand Mormons fled Missouri after the governor proclaimed them enemies who "had to be exterminated, or driven from the state."

In 1839 the Mormons resettled along the east bank of the Mississippi River in Nauvoo, Illinois, which soon grew into the second largest city in the state. Both Illinois Whigs and Democrats eagerly sought support among the Mormons. In exchange for their votes the state legislature awarded Nauvoo a special charter that made the town an autonomous city-state, complete with its own 2,000-man militia.

But trouble arose again. In 1844 a dissident group within the church published a newspaper denouncing the practice of polygamy and attacking Joseph Smith for trying to become "king or lawgiver to the church." On Smith's orders, city officials destroyed the dissidents' printing press. Under the protection of the Illinois governor, Smith and his brother were then confined to a jail cell in Carthage. A mob of citizens broke into Smith's cell, shot him and his brother, and threw their bodies out of a second-story window.

Why did the Mormons seem so menacing? Many individualistic Americans felt threatened by the communalism of the Mormon church. By voting as their elders told them to and controlling land as a bloc, the Mormons seemed to have an unfair advantage in the struggle for wealth and power. Mormonism was also denounced as a threat to fundamental social values. Protestant ministers railed against it as a threat to Christianity since Mormons insisted that the *Book of Mormon* was Holy Scripture, equal in importance to the Bible. The Mormons were also accused of corrupt moral values. Before the church changed its rules in 1890, the Mormons practiced polygamy, which they saw as an effort to reestablish the patriarchal Old Testament family. Polygamy also served an important social function by absorbing single or widowed women into Mormon communities. Contrary to popular belief, it was not widely practiced. Altogether, only 10 to 20 percent of Mormon families were polygamous and nearly two-thirds involved a man and two wives.

After the murder of Joseph Smith, the Mormons decided to migrate across a thousand miles of unsettled prairie, plains, and arid desert in search of a new refuge. In 1846 a new leader, Brigham Young, led the Mormons to the Great Salt Lake. As governor of the Mormon state of Deseret and later as governor of Utah, Young oversaw the building of Salt Lake City and 186 other Mormon communities, developed church-owned businesses, and established the first cooperative irrigation projects.

Early nineteenth-century American society attached enormous importance to individualism, secularism, monogamous marriage, and private property, and the Mormons were believed to threaten each of these values. But, in a larger sense, the Mormons' aspirations were truly American. They sought nothing less than the establishment of the Kingdom of God on earth—a dream that was, of course, not new in this country. In seeking to build God's kingdom the Mormons were carrying on a quest that had been begun by their Puritan ancestors two centuries before.

The Mexican War

When Brigham Young led the Mormons west, he was seeking a homeland outside the boundaries of the United States. But even before he arrived at the Great Salt Lake during the summer of 1847, Utah as well as California, Nevada, and parts of Arizona, Colorado, New Mexico, and Wyoming, became part of the United States as a result of the war with Mexico.

Why War?

Fifteen years before the United States was plunged into Civil War, it fought a war against Mexico that added half a million square miles of territory to the United States. Not only was it the first American war fought almost entirely outside the United States, it was also the first American war to be reported, while it happened, by daily newspapers. It was also a controversial war that bitterly divided American public opinion. Finally, it was the war that gave young officers such as Ulysses S. Grant, Robert E. Lee, Thomas ("Stonewall") Jackson, William Tecumseh Sherman, and George McClellan their first experience in a major conflict.

The underlying cause of the Mexican War was the inexorable movement of American pioneers into the Far West. As Americans marched westward, they moved into land claimed by Mexico, and inevitably Mexican and American interests clashed.

The immediate reason for the conflict was the annexation of Texas in 1845. Despite its defeat at San Jacinto in 1836, Mexico refused to recognize Texan independence and warned the United States that annexation would be tantamount to a declaration of war. In early 1845 when Congress voted to annex Texas, Mexico cut diplomatic relations, but took no further action.

The Mexican War was the nation's first war to be reported in newspapers while it happened.

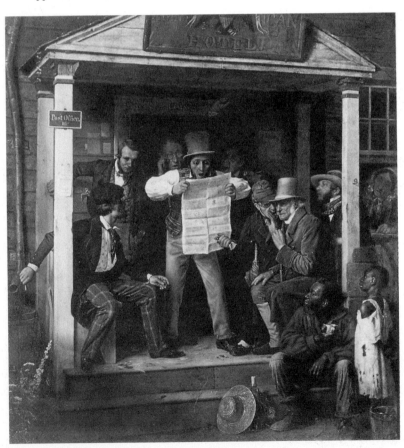

Polk told his commanders to prepare for the possibility of war. He ordered American naval vessels in the Gulf of Mexico to position themselves outside Mexican ports. Secretly, he warned the Pacific fleet to prepare to seize ports along the California coast in the event of war. Anticipating a possible Mexican invasion of Texas, he dispatched American forces in Louisiana to Corpus Christi.

Peaceful settlement of the two countries' differences still seemed possible. In the fall of 1845 the president sent John Slidell as "envoy extraordinary and minister plenipotentiary" to Mexico City with a proposal to resolve the disputes peacefully. The most significant controversies concerned Texas's boundary and the Mexican government's failure to compensate American citizens for losses incurred during Mexico's years of political turmoil. Slidell was authorized to cancel the damage claims and pay $5 million in reparations if the Mexicans agreed to recognize the Rio Grande as the southwestern boundary of Texas (earlier, the Spanish government had defined the Texas boundary as the Nueces River, 130 miles north of the Rio Grande). No Americans lived between the Nueces and the Rio Grande, although many Hispanics lived in the region.

Polk not only wanted to settle the boundary and claims disputes, he also wanted to acquire Mexico's two northwestern provinces, New Mexico and California. He directed Slidell to offer up to $5 million for the province of New Mexico—which included Nevada and Utah and parts of four other states—and up to $25 million for California.

Polk was anxious to acquire California because in mid-October 1845 he had been led to believe that Britain was on the verge of making California a protectorate. It was widely believed that Mexico had agreed to cede California to Britain as payment for outstanding debts. Immediate preventive action seemed necessary. Polk therefore instructed his consul in Monterey to encourage Californians to agitate for annexation by the United States. He also dispatched a young Marine Corps lieutenant, Archibald H. Gillespie, to California, apparently to foment revolt against Mexican authority.

The Mexican government, already incensed over the annexation of Texas, refused to negotiate. The Mexican president, José Herrera, refused to receive Slidell and ordered his leading commander, General Mariano Paredes y Arrillaga, to assemble an army and reconquer Texas. Paredes proceeded to topple Herrera's government and declared himself president. But he also refused to receive Slidell.

The failure of Slidell's mission led Polk to order Brigadier General Zachary Taylor to march 3,000 troops from Corpus Christi, Texas, to "defend the Rio Grande." Late in March of 1846 Taylor and his men set up camp along the Rio Grande, directly across from the Mexican city of Matamoros, on a stretch of land claimed by both Mexico and the United States.

On April 25 a Mexican cavalry force crossed the Rio Grande and clashed with a small American squadron, forcing the Americans to surrender after the loss of several lives. Polk used this episode as an excuse to declare war. "Hostilities may be considered to have commenced," Taylor wrote to President Polk.

Hours before he received word of the skirmish on May 9, Polk and his cabinet had already decided to press for war with Mexico. On May 11 Polk asked Congress to acknowledge that a state of war already existed. "Mexico," the president announced, "has passed the boundary of the United States, has invaded our territory and shed American blood upon the American soil." Congress responded with a declaration of war.

The Mexican War was extremely controversial. Its supporters blamed Mexico for the hostilities because it had severed relations with the United States, threatened war, refused to receive an American emissary, or to pay the damage claims of American citizens. Opposition leaders denounced the war as an immoral land grab by an expansionistic power against a weak neighbor that had been independent barely two decades. The war's critics claimed that Polk deliberately provoked Mexico into war by ordering American troops into disputed territory. A Delaware senator declared that ordering Taylor to the Rio Grande was "as much an act of aggression on our part as is a man's pointing a pistol at another's breast."

Critics argued that the war was an expansionist power play dictated by an aggressive southern slaveocracy intent on acquiring more land for cotton cultivation and more slave states to better balance the northern free states in the U.S. Senate. "Bigger pens to cram with slaves," was the way poet James Russell Lowell put it. Others blamed the war on expansion-minded Westerners who were hungry for land, and on eastern trading interests, which dreamed of establishing "an American Boston or New York" in San Francisco to increase trade with Asia. Mexicans denounced the war as a brazen attempt by the United States to seize Mexican territory.

The War

American strategy was based on a three-pronged attack. Colonel Stephen Kearny had the task of securing New Mexico, while naval forces under Commodore John D. Sloat blockaded the California coast and General Zachary Taylor invaded Mexico.

Kearny easily accomplished his mission. In less than two months he marched his 1,700-man army more than a thousand miles. On August 18, 1846, he occupied Santa Fe and declared New Mexico's 80,000 inhabitants American citizens. In California, American settlers in the Sacramento Valley, fearful that Mexican authorities were about to expel them, revolted even before reliable reports of the outbreak of war reached the area. The so-called Bear Flag Rebellion soon came to an end, and by January 1847 U.S. naval forces under Commodore Robert F. Stockton and an expeditionary force under Captain John C. Frémont had brought the region under American control. Meanwhile, the main U.S. army under Taylor's command had taken Matamoros, and by late September captured Monterrey, Mexico's largest northern city.

Although the American invasion of Mexico's northernmost provinces was completely successful, the Mexican government did not surrender. In June 1846 Colonel A. W. Doniphan led 856 Missouri cavalry volunteers 3,000 miles across mountains and desert into the northern Mexican province of Chihuahua. He occupied El Paso and then captured the capital city of Chihuahua. Further south, 6,000 volunteers under the command of Zachary Taylor held their ground against a Mexican force of 15,000 at the battle of Buena Vista on February 22 and 23, 1847.

Despite an impressive string of American victories, Mexico still refused to negotiate. Switching strategy, Polk ordered General Winfield Scott to invade central Mexico from the sea, march inland, and capture Mexico City. On March 9, 1847, the Mexicans allowed an American force of 10,000 men to land unopposed at Veracruz on the Gulf of Mexico. Scott's army then began to march on the Mexican capital. On April 18, at a mountain pass near Jalapa, a 9,000-man American force met 13,000 Mexican troops and in bitter hand-to-hand fighting, forced the Mexicans to flee. As Scott's army pushed on toward Mexico City, it stormed a Mexican fortress at Contreras and then routed a large Mexican force at Churubusco on August 19 and 20. For two weeks, from August 22 to September 7, Scott observed an armistice to allow the Mexicans to consider peace proposals. When the negotiations failed, Scott's 6,000 remaining men attacked El Molino del Rey and stormed Chapultepec, a fortified castle guarding Mexico City's gates.

Despite the capture of their capital, the Mexicans refused to surrender. Hostile crowds staged demonstrations in the streets, and snipers fired shots and hurled stones and broken bottles from the tops of flat-roofed Mexican houses. To quell the protests, General Scott ordered the streets "swept with grape and cannister" and artillery "turned upon the houses whence the fire proceeded." Outside the capital, belligerent civilians attacked army supply wagons, and guerrilla fighters harassed American troops.

War Fever and Antiwar Protests

During the first few weeks following the declaration of war a frenzy of pro-war hysteria swept the country. Two hundred thousand men responded

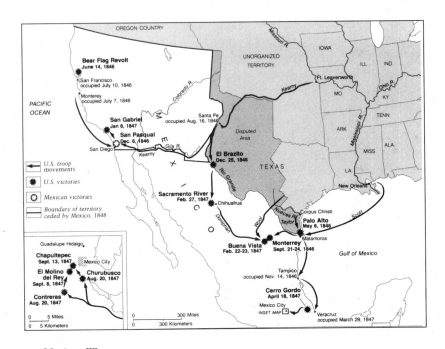

Mexican War

The Mexican War would increase the nation's size by one-third.

to a call for 50,000 volunteers. Novelist Herman Melville observed, "a military ardor pervades all ranks. . . . Nothing is talked about but the halls of the Montezumas." In New York placards bore the slogan "Mexico or Death." Many newspapers, especially in the North, declared that the war would benefit the Mexican people by bringing them the blessings of democracy and liberty. The *Boston Times* said that an American victory "must necessarily be a great blessing" because it would introduce "the reign of law where license has existed for a generation."

In Philadelphia 20,000 turned out for a pro-war rally, and in Cincinnati 12,000 celebrated Zachary Taylor's victories with cannon salutes, parades, and speeches. In Tennessee 30,000 men volunteered for 3,000 positions as soldiers, prompting one applicant to complain that it was "difficult even to purchase a place in the ranks." The war was particularly popular in the West. Of the 69,540 men who were accepted for service, more than 40,000 were from the western states.

But from the war's very beginning, a small but highly visible group of intellectuals, clergymen, pacifists, abolitionists, and Whig and Democratic politicians denounced the war as brutal aggression against a "poor, fee-ble, distracted country." Abolitionist William Lloyd Garrison's militant newspaper, the *Liberator,* expressed open support for the Mexican people: "Every lover of Freedom and humanity throughout the world must wish them the most triumphant success."

Most Whigs supported the war—in part because two of the leading American generals, Zachary Taylor and Winfield Scott, were Whigs, and in part because they remembered that opposition to the War of 1812 had destroyed the Federalist party. But many prominent Whigs, from the South as well as the North, openly expressed opposition. Thomas Corwin of Ohio denounced the war as merely the latest example of American in-justice to Mexico. Daniel Webster, a frequent Whig presidential candi-date, mockingly described the conflict as a "war of pretexts"—the pretext that Mexico had refused to receive an American emissary, had refused to pay Americans financial claims, and had invaded American territory.

A freshman Whig congressman from Illinois named Abraham Lin-coln lashed out against the war, calling it immoral, proslavery, and a threat to the nation's republican values. One of Lincoln's constituents branded him "the Benedict Arnold of our district," and he was denied renomina-tion by his own party.

As newspapers informed their readers about the hardships and savagery of life on the front, public enthusiasm for the war began to wane. The war did not turn out to be the romantic exploit that Americans envisioned. Troops complained that their food was "green with slime;" their meat, they said, would stick "if thrown against a smooth plank." Diarrhea, amoebic dysentery, measles, and yellow fever ravaged American soldiers. Seven times as many Americans died of disease and exposure as died of battlefield in-juries. Of the 90,000 Americans who served in the war, only 1,721 died in action. Another 11,155 died from disease and exposure to the elements.

Public support for the war was further eroded by reports of brutality against Mexican civilians. After one of their members was murdered, the Arkansas volunteer cavalry surrounded a group of Mexican peasants and began an "indiscriminate and bloody massacre of the poor creatures." A young lieutenant named George G. Meade reported that volunteers in Mata-moros robbed the citizens, stole their cattle, and killed innocent civilians "for no other object than their own amusement." If only a tenth of the horror sto-ries were true, General Winfield Scott wrote, it was enough "to make Heaven weep, & every American of Christian morals blush for his country."

During wartime the party in power has often lost support. The Mex-ican War was no exception. In the congressional election of 1846, which took place half a year after the outbreak of war, the Democrats lost control of the House of Representatives to the Whigs.

Peace

Difficult negotiations followed the war. After American troops entered the Mexican capital, Santa Anna, the Mexican president, resigned and the Mexican Congress retreated to a provincial capital to try to reorganize. Not until mid-November 1847 was a new civilian government able to gain control over the country and name a peace negotiator.

As Americans waited impatiently for a final peace settlement, they grew increasingly divided over their war aims. Ultra-expansionists, who drew support from such cities as Baltimore, New York, and Philadelphia as well as from the West, wanted the United States to annex all of Mexico. Many Southerners, led by John C. Calhoun, called for a withdrawal to the Rio Grande. They opposed annexation of any territory below the Rio Grande because they did not want to extend American citizenship to Mexicans. Most Democratic party leaders, however, wanted to annex at least the one-third of Mexico south and west of the Rio Grande.

Then suddenly on February 22, 1848, word reached Washington that a peace treaty had been signed. On February 2, 1848, Nicholas Trist, a Spanish-speaking State Department official, signed the Treaty of Guadalupe Hidalgo, ending the Mexican War. Trist had actually been ordered home two months earlier by Polk, but he had continued negotiating anyway, fearing that his recall would be "deadly to the cause of peace."

According to the treaty, Mexico ceded to the United States only those areas that Polk had originally sought to purchase. Mexico ceded California, Nevada, Utah, New Mexico, and parts of Arizona, Colorado, Kansas, and Wyoming to the United States for $15 million and the assumption of $3.25 million in debts owed to Americans by Mexico. The treaty also settled the Texas border dispute in favor of the United States, placing the Texas-Mexico boundary at the Rio Grande.

Ultra-expansionists called on Polk to throw out the treaty, but a war-weary public wanted peace. Polk quickly submitted the treaty to the Senate, which ratified it overwhelmingly. The war was over.

The War's Significance

The story of America's conflict with Mexico tends to be overshadowed by the story of the Civil War, which began only a decade and a half later. In fact, the conflict had far-reaching consequences for the nation's future. It increased the nation's size by a third, but it also created deep political divisions that threatened the country's future.

The most significant result of the Mexican War was to reignite the question of slavery in the western territories—the very question that had divided the country in 1819. Even before the war had begun, philosopher

Ralph Waldo Emerson had predicted that the United States would "conquer Mexico, but it will be as the man who swallows the arsenic which will bring him down in turn. Mexico will poison us." The war convinced a growing number of Northerners that southern slave owners had precipitated the war in order to open new lands to slavery and acquire new slave states. And most significant of all, the war weakened the party system and made it increasingly difficult for congressional leaders to prevent the issue of slavery from dominating congressional activity.

Political Crisis of the 1840s

Prior to the Mexican War, the major political issues that divided Americans were questions of tariffs, banking, internal improvements, and land. Political positions on these issues largely divided along party lines. After the outbreak of war with Mexico a new issue began to dominate American politics—the extension of slavery in the western territories. Public opinion began to polarize and party cohesion began to break down as party factional and sectional divisions grew more important than traditional party coalitions.

The question of slavery burst into the public spotlight one summer evening in 1846. Congressman David Wilmot, a Pennsylvania Democrat, introduced an amendment, known as the Wilmot Proviso, to a war appropriations bill. The proviso forbade slavery in any territory acquired from Mexico. Throughout the North, thousands of workingmen, mechanics, and farmers feared that free workers would be unable to compete successfully against slave labor. "If slavery is not excluded by law," said one northern congressman, "the presence of the slave will exclude the laboring white man."

Southerners denounced the Wilmot Proviso as "treason to the Constitution." Polk tried to quiet the debate between "Southern agitators and Northern fanatics" by assuring moderate Northerners that slavery could never take root in the arid southwest, but his efforts were to no avail. With the strong support of westerners, the amendment passed the House twice, but was defeated in the Senate. Although the Wilmot Proviso did not become law, the issue it raised—the extension of slavery into the western territories—continued to contribute to the growth of political factionalism.

Meanwhile, at the very moment that Congress was debating the Wilmot Proviso, another sectional dispute flared up over the tariff. In 1846 President Polk persuaded Congress to enact the Walker Tariff, a low tariff that delighted Southerners, but infuriated Northerners who favored tariff protection for industry.

Growing sectional tensions were also evident in the founding of the Free Soil party in 1848. This sectional party opposed the westward expansion of slavery and favored free land for western homesteaders. Much more popular than the Liberty party, an earlier antislavery political party, the Free Soil party drew support from dissident New England Whigs (known as "conscience" Whigs because of their opposition to slavery), antislavery New York Democrats, and former members of the Liberty party. Under the slogan "free soil, free speech, free labor, and free men," the party nominated Martin Van Buren as its presidential nominee in 1848 and polled 291,000 votes. This was enough to split the Democratic vote and throw the election to Whig candidate Zachary Taylor.

Up until the last month of 1848, the debate over slavery in the Mexican cession seemed academic. Most Americans thought of the newly acquired territory as a wasteland filled with "broken mountains and dreary desert." Then, in his farewell address, Polk electrified Congress with the news that gold had been discovered in California—and suddenly the question of slavery was inescapably important.

The Gold Rush

On January 24, 1848, less than ten days before the signing of the peace treaty ending the Mexican War, James W. Marshall, a 36-year-old carpenter and handyman, noticed several bright bits of yellow mineral near a sawmill in California's Sacramento Valley that he was building for John A. Sutter, a Swiss-born rancher. The yellow mineral was gold.

On March 15 a San Francisco newspaper, the *Californian,* printed the first account of Marshall's discovery. Within two weeks the paper had lost its staff and was forced to shut down its printing press. In its last edition it told its readers: "The whole country, from San Francisco to Los Angeles . . . resounds with the sordid cry of Gold! Gold! Gold! while the field is left half-planted, the house half-built, and everything neglected but the manufacture of picks and shovels."

In 1849 80,000 men arrived in California—half by land and half by ship around Cape Horn or across the Isthmus of Panama. Only half were Americans; the rest came from Europe, Latin America, and China. Soldiers deserted; sailors jumped ship; husbands left wives; apprentices ran away from their masters; farmers and businesspeople deserted their livelihoods. Within a year California's population had swollen from 14,000 to 100,000.

The gold rush transformed California from a sleepy society into one that was wild, unruly, ethnically diverse, and violent. In San Francisco alone there were more than 500 bars and 1,000 gambling dens. There were a thousand murders in San Francisco during the early 1850s, but only one conviction. "Forty-niners" slaughtered Indians for sport, drove Mexicans from the mines on penalty of death, and sought to restrict the immigration of foreigners, especially the Chinese. Since the military government was incapable of keeping order, leading merchants formed vigilance committees, which attempted to rule by lynch law and the establishment of "popular" courts.

The gold rush era in California lasted less than a decade. By the mid-1850s the lone miner who prospected for gold with a pick, a shovel, and a washpan was already an anachronism. Mining companies using heavy machinery replaced the individual prospector. Systems of dams exposed whole river bottoms. Drilling machines drove shafts 700 feet into the earth. Hydraulic mining machines blasted streams of water against mountainsides. The romantic era of California gold mining had come to a close.

Chronology of Key Events

1803	Louisiana Purchase
1804	Lewis and Clark Expedition
1810	Mexican War for Independence begins; John Jacob Astor attempts to plant a trading post in Oregon
1811–1812	Fur trappers mark out the Oregon Trail
1818	United States and Britain agree to joint occupation of Oregon
1821	Mexico gains independence from Spain; first American traders traverse the Santa Fe Trail; Stephen Austin founds American colony in Texas
1830	Joseph Smith, Jr., founds Church of Jesus Christ of Latter-Day Saints
1835–36	Texas Revolution
1838	John Quincy Adams's filibuster defeats move to annex Texas
1841	First party of pioneers leaves Missouri for California
1844	Joseph Smith, Jr., assassinated at Carthage, Illinois
1845	Texas admitted as twenty-eighth state
1846	The United States declares war on Mexico; Britain and the United States divide Oregon along 49th parallel; Donner party becomes trapped in Sierra Nevada; Brigham Young leads the Mormons to the Great Salt Lake Valley
1848	Gold discovered in California; Treaty of Guadalupe Hidalgo
1849	Gold Rush begins

Conclusion

By 1860 the gold rush was over. Prospectors had found more than $350 million worth of gold. Certainly, some fortunes were made, but few struck it rich. Even James W. Marshall, who discovered the first gold bits, and John A. Sutter, on whose ranch gold was discovered, died penniless.

By 1850 the American flag flew over an area that stretched from sea to sea. In the span of just five years, the United States had increased in size by a third and acquired an area that now includes the states of Arizona, California, Colorado, Idaho, Nevada, New Mexico, Oregon, Texas, Utah, Washington, and Wyoming.

The exploration and settlement of the Far West is one of the great epics of nineteenth-century history. But America's dramatic territorial expansion also created severe problems. In addition to providing the United States with its richest mines, greatest forests, and most fertile farm land, the Far West intensified the sectional conflict between the North and South and raised the fateful and ultimately divisive question of whether slavery would be permitted in the western territories. Could democratic political institutions resolve the question of slavery in the western territories? That question would dominate American politics in the 1850s.

Suggestions for Further Reading

For general overviews of the period, see Ray A. Billington, *Westward Expansion*, 5th ed. (1982); and Richard White, *"Its Your Misfortune and None of My Own"* (1991). Valuable studies focusing on various aspects of Manifest Destiny are Norman A. Graebner, *Empire on the Pacific* (1955); Thomas R. Hietala, *Manifest Design: Anxious Aggrandizement in Late Jacksonian America* (1985); Reginald Horsman, *Race and Manifest Destiny* (1981); Robert Johannsen, *To the Halls of the Montezumas* (1985); Albert K. Weinberg, *Manifest Destiny* (1935). Biographies of James K. Polk include Paul H. Bergeron, *The Presidency of James K. Polk* (1987); and Charles Sellers, *James K. Polk: Continentalist* (1966).

For studies of the settlement of the trans-Mississippi west during the antebellum period consult William Cronon, *Nature's Metropolis: Chicago and the Great West* (1991); Sandra L. Myres, *Westering Women and the Frontier Experience* (1982); John Unruh, *The Plains Across* (1979). On the borderlands see David J. Weber, *The Mexican Frontier* (1982). For studies on Texas, see Sam W. Haynes, *Soldiers of Misfortune* (1990); Paul D. Lack, *The Texas Revolutionary Experience* (1992).

Chapter *14*

The House Divided

Early in 1864 a New York economist named John Smith Dye published a book entitled *The Adder's Den or Secrets of the Great Conspiracy to Overthrow Liberty in America.* In his volume Dye set out to prove that for more than 30 years a ruthless Southern "slave power" had engaged in a deliberate, systematic plan to subvert civil liberties, undermine the Constitution, and extend slavery into the western territories.

In Dye's eyes, the entire history of the United States was the record of repeated Southern plots to expand slavery. An arrogant "slave power," he maintained, had entrenched slavery in the Constitution, caused financial panics to sabotage the Northern economy, dispossessed Indians from their native lands, and fomented revolution in Texas and war with Mexico in order to expand the South's slave empire. Most important of all, he insisted, the Southern slaveocracy had secretly assassinated two presidents by poison and unsuccessfully attempted to murder three others.

According to Dye, this campaign of assassination began in 1835 when John C. Calhoun, outraged by Andrew Jackson's opposition to states' rights, encouraged a deranged man named Richard Lawrence to kill Jackson. This plot failed when Lawrence's pistols misfired. Six years later, Dye argued, a successful attempt was made on William Henry Harrison's life. After he refused to cooperate in a Southern scheme to annex Texas, Harrison died of symptoms resembling arsenic poisoning. This left John Tyler, a strong defender of slavery, in the White House.

The next president to die at the hands of the slave power, according to Dye, was Zachary Taylor, who had opposed the extension of slavery into California. Just 16 months after taking office Taylor was stricken by acute gastroenteritis, caused, claimed Dye, by arsenic poisoning. He was succeeded by Vice President Millard Fillmore, who was more sympathetic to the Southern cause. Just three years later, Dye maintained, another attempt was made on a president's life. The slave power considered Franklin Pierce, a New Hampshire Democrat, unreliable. On the way to his inauguration Pierce's railroad car derailed and rolled down an embankment. The president and his wife escaped injury, but their 12-year-old son was killed. In the future, Pierce toed the Southern line.

In 1857, Dye claimed, yet another attempt was made to kill a president. James Buchanan, a Pennsylvania Democrat, had won his party's nomination in the face of fierce Southern opposition, and, in Dye's view, the slaveocracy wanted to remind Buchanan who was in charge. At a Washington banquet shortly before Buchanan's inauguration, Southern agents sprinkled arsenic on the lump sugar used by Northerners to sweeten their tea. Because Southerners drank coffee and used granulated sugar, no Southerners were injured. But, according to Dye, 60 Northerners were poisoned, including the president, and 38 died. Frightened by this near bout with death, Buchanan proved to be a reliable tool of the slave power.

No credible evidence supports any of Dye's sensational allegations. Yet even if his charges were without foundation, Dye was not alone in interpreting events in conspiratorial terms. His book *The Adder's Den* was only one of the most extreme examples of conspiratorial charges that had been made by abolitionists since the late 1830s. By the 1850s a growing number of Northerners had come to believe that an aggressive Southern slave power had seized control of the federal government and threatened to subvert republican ideals. At the same time, an increasing number of Southerners had begun to believe that antislavery radicals dominated Northern politics and would "rejoice" in the race war and racial amalgamation that would surely follow emancipation.

During the 1850s the American political system was incapable of containing the sectional disputes that had smoldered for more than half a century. One major political party—the Whigs—collapsed. Another—the Democrats—split into Northern and Southern factions. With the breakdown of the party system the issues raised by slavery exploded. The bonds that had bound the country for more than seven decades began to unravel.

The Crisis of 1850

In 1849 an expedition of Texas slave owners and their slaves arrived in the California gold fields. As curious prospectors looked on, the Texans staked out claims and put their slaves to work panning for gold. White miners, who considered it unfair that they should have to compete with slave labor, were outraged. They held a mass meeting and resolved "that no slave or Negro should own claims or even work in the mines." They ordered the Texans out of the gold fields within 24 hours.

Three days later the white miners elected a delegate to a convention that had been called to frame a state constitution and to apply for admission to the Union. At the convention, the miners' delegate proposed that "neither slavery nor involuntary servitude" should ever "be tolerated" in California. The convention adopted his proposal unanimously.

California's application for admission to the Union as a free state in 1849 raised the question that would dominate American politics during the 1850s: Would slavery be allowed to expand into the West or would the West remain free soil? It was the issue of slave expansion—and not the morality of slavery—that would make antislavery a respectable political position in the North, polarize public opinion, and initiate the chain of events that would lead the United States to civil war.

California's application for statehood made slavery's expansion an unavoidable political issue. Southerners feared that California's admission as a free state would upset the sectional balance of power. The free states already held a commanding majority in the House of Representatives because they had a much greater population than did the slave states. Therefore the political power of proslavery Southerners depended on maintaining a balance of power in the Senate. Since the Missouri Compromise, Congress had paired the admission of a free state and a slave state. If California was admitted as a free state, there would be 16 free states and only 15 slave states. The sectional balance of power in the Senate would be disrupted, and the South feared that it would lose its ability to influence political events.

The instability of the Democratic and Whig parties, and the growing political power of Northern opponents of slave expansion, further dimmed chances of a peaceful compromise. When the Thirty-first Congress convened in December 1849, neither the Democrats nor the Whigs had a stable majority. Southern Whigs were deserting their party in droves, and Northern and Southern Democrats were badly split.

In the North and Midwest opponents of the westward expansion of slavery made striking gains, particularly within the Democratic party. Coalitions of Democrats and Free Soilers elected congressmen determined to prevent Southern expansion. Every Northern state legislature except Iowa's asserted that Congress had the power and duty to exclude slavery from the territories.

Southern hotspurs talked openly of secession. Senator Robert Toombs of Georgia declared that if the North deprived the South of the right to take slaves into California and New Mexico, "I am for disunion." Such bold talk inched the South closer to secession.

The South's Dilemma

Why were the South's political leaders so worried about whether slavery would be permitted in the West when geography and climate made it unlikely that slavery would ever prosper in the area? The answer lies in the South's growing awareness of its minority status in the Union, of the elimination of slavery in many other areas of the Western Hemisphere, and of the decline of slavery in the upper South. For more and more Southerners, the region's future depended on whether the West was opened or closed to slavery.

By 1850 New World slavery was confined to Brazil, Cuba, Puerto Rico, a small number of Dutch colonies, and the American South. British slave emancipation in the Caribbean in 1833 had been followed by an intensified campaign to eradicate the international slave trade. In areas like

Brazil and Cuba, slavery could not long survive once the slave trade was cut off because the slave populations of these countries had a skewed sex ratio and were unable to naturally reproduce their numbers. Only in the American South could slavery survive without the Atlantic slave trade.

Exacerbating Southern fears about slavery's future was a sharp decline in slavery in the upper South. The South's leaders feared that in the future the upper South would soon become a region of free labor. By midcentury, the South's slave owners faced a further dilemma. Within the region itself, slave ownership was increasingly concentrated in fewer and fewer hands. The desire to ensure the support for slavery among poorer whites led some Southerners to agitate for reopening the African slave trade, believing that nonslaveholding Southerners would only support the institution if they had a chance to own slaves themselves. But most Southern leaders believed the best way to perpetuate slavery was through westward expansion, and they wanted concrete assurance that Congress would not infringe on the right to take slaves into the western territories. Without such a guarantee, declared an Alabama politician, "THIS UNION CANNOT STAND."

Slave Concentration, 1860/The Cotton Kingdom

As shown here, northern African Americans were providing escape routes for slaves along the Underground Railroad. Slave-owning Southerners feared that the end of slavery would reduce their economic and political status in the Union.

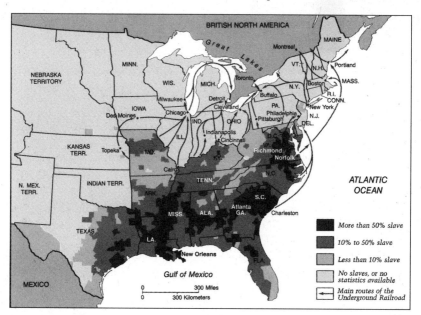

The Compromise of 1850: The Illusion of Sectional Peace

Ever since David Wilmot had proposed in 1846 that slavery be prohibited from any territory acquired from Mexico, opponents of slavery had argued that Congress possessed the power to regulate slavery in all of the territories. Ardent proslavery Southerners vigorously disagreed. Politicians had repeatedly but unsuccessfully tried to work out a compromise. One simple proposal had been to extend the Missouri Compromise line to the Pacific Ocean, excluding slavery north of 36° 30' latitude but permitting it south of that line. This proposal attracted the support of moderate Southerners but generated little support outside the region. Another proposal, supported by two key Democratic senators, Lewis Cass of Michigan and Stephen Douglas of Illinois, was known as "squatter sovereignty" or "popular sovereignty." It declared that the people actually living in a territory should decide whether or not to allow slavery.

Henry Clay, the aging statesman known as the "Great Compromiser" for his efforts on behalf of the Missouri Compromise and the Compromise Tariff of 1832 (which resolved the nullification crisis), once again appealed to Northerners and Southerners to place national patriotism ahead of sectional loyalties. He believed that compromise could only be effective if it addressed all the issues dividing the two regions. He proposed that California be admitted as a free state; that territorial governments be established in New Mexico and Utah without any restrictions on slavery; that Texas relinquish its claim to land in New Mexico in exchange for federal assumption of Texas's unpaid debts; that Congress enact a stringent and enforceable fugitive slave law; and that the slave trade—but not slavery—be abolished in the District of Columbia.

Clay's proposal ignited an eight-month debate in Congress and led John C. Calhoun to threaten Southern secession. On March 4, 1850, Calhoun offered his response to Clay's compromise proposal. Calhoun was dying of tuberculosis and was too ill to speak publicly, so his speech was read by a colleague. He warned the North that the only way to save the Union was to "cease the agitation of the slave question," concede "to the South an equal right" to the western territories, return runaway slaves, and accept a constitutional amendment that would protect the South against Northern violations of its rights. In the absence of such concessions, Calhoun argued, the South's only option was to secede.

Three days later Daniel Webster, the North's most spellbinding orator, abandoned his previous opposition to the expansion of slavery into the western territories and threw his support behind Clay's compromise. The 68-year-old Massachusetts Whig called on both sides to resolve their differences in the name of patriotism. The North, he insisted, could afford to be generous because climate and geography ensured that slavery would never be profitable in the western territories. He concluded by warning his listeners that "there can be no such thing as a peaceable secession." Webster's speech provoked a storm of outrage from Northern opponents of compromise, but it did have one important effect. It reassured moderate Southerners that powerful interests in the North were committed to compromise.

Still, opposition to compromise was fierce. Whig President Zachary Taylor argued that California, New Mexico, Oregon, Utah, and Minnesota should all be admitted to statehood before the question of slavery was addressed—a proposal that would have given the North a ten-vote majority in the Senate. William H. Seward, the New York senator, speaking for the opponents of slave expansion, denounced the compromise as conceding too much to the South and proclaimed that there was a "higher law" than the Constitution, a law that demanded an end to slavery. At the same time, many Southern extremists bristled at the idea of admitting California as a free state. In July, Northern and Southern senators opposed to the very idea of compromise joined ranks to defeat a bill that would have admitted California to the Union and organized New Mexico and Utah without reference to slavery.

Compromise appeared to be dead. A bitterly disappointed Henry Clay left Washington, his efforts apparently for nought. Then with unexpected suddenness the outlook abruptly changed. On the evening of July 9, 1850, President Taylor died of gastroenteritis. Taylor's successor was Millard Fillmore, a 50-year-old New Yorker, who was an ardent supporter of compromise.

In Congress leadership in the fight for a compromise passed to Stephen Douglas, a Democratic senator from Illinois. An arrogant and dynamic leader, 5 foot 4 inches in height, with a massive head, bushy eyebrows, and a booming voice, Douglas was known as the "Little Giant." Douglas abandoned Clay's strategy of gathering all issues dividing the sections into a single "omnibus" bill. Instead, he introduced Clay's proposals one at a time. In this way, he was able to gather support from varying coalitions of Whigs and Democrats and Northerners and Southerners on each issue.

As finally approved, the compromise admitted California as a free state, allowed the territorial legislatures of New Mexico and Utah to settle the question of slavery in those areas, provided for the return of runaway slaves, abolished the slave trade in the District of Columbia, and gave Texas $10 million to abandon its claims to territory in New Mexico east of the Rio Grande.

The Fugitive Slave Law

The most divisive element in the Compromise of 1850 was the Fugitive Slave Law, which permitted any black to be sent south solely on the affidavit of anyone claiming to be his or her owner. As a result, free blacks were in danger of being placed in slavery. The law also stripped runaway slaves of such basic legal rights as the right to a jury trial and the right to testify in one's own defense. The law further stipulated that accused runaways stand trial in front of special commissioners, not a judge or a jury, and that the commissioners be paid $10 if a fugitive was returned to slavery but only $5 if the fugitive was freed—a provision that many Northerners regarded as a bribe to ensure that any black accused of being a runaway would be found guilty. And finally, the law required all U.S. citizens and U.S. marshals to assist in the capture of escapees. Anyone who refused to aid in the capture of a fugitive, interfered with the arrest of a slave, or tried to free a slave already in custody was subject to a heavy fine and imprisonment.

The Fugitive Slave Law kindled widespread outrage in the North and converted thousands of Northerners to the free soil doctrine that slavery should be barred from the western territories. "We went to bed one night old-fashioned, conservative, compromise, Union Whigs," wrote a Massachusetts factory owner, "and waked up stark mad Abolitionists." Efforts to enforce the law resulted in abuses that repelled many Northern moderates. Riots directed against the law broke out in many cities. In Boston federal marshals and 22 companies of state troops were needed to prevent a crowd from storming a courthouse to free a fugitive named Anthony Burns.

Eight Northern states attempted to invalidate the law by enacting "personal liberty" laws that forbade state officials from assisting in the return of runaways and extended the right of jury trial to fugitives. Southerners regarded these attempts to obstruct the return of runaways as a violation of the Constitution and federal law.

The free black communities of the North responded defiantly to the 1850 law. Northern blacks provided about 1,500 fugitive slaves with sanctuary along the Underground Railroad to freedom. Others established vigilance committees to protect blacks from hired kidnappers who were searching the North for runaways. And 15,000 free blacks, convinced that they could never achieve equality in America, emigrated to Canada, the Caribbean, and Africa after the adoption of the federal law.

One Northern moderate who was repelled by the fugitive slave law was Harriet Beecher Stowe. In 1852 she published *Uncle Tom's Cabin,* the single most powerful attack on slavery ever written. Stowe had learned about slavery while living in Cincinnati, Ohio, across from slaveholding Kentucky. Her book awakened millions of Northerners to the moral evil of slavery. Southerners denounced Stowe as a "wretch in petticoats," but in the North the book sold a million copies in 16 months. No novel has ever exerted a stronger influence on American public opinion. Legend has it that when President Lincoln met Mrs. Stowe during the Civil War, he said, "So this is the little woman who made this big war."

Disintegration of the Party System

As late as 1850 the two-party system was, to all outward appearances, still healthy. Every state, except for South Carolina, had two effective political parties. Both the Democratic party and the Whigs were able to attract support in every section and in every state in the country. Voter participation was extremely high, and in presidential elections neither party was able to gain more than 53 percent of the popular vote. Then, in the space of just five years, the two-party system began to disintegrate in response to two issues: massive foreign immigration and the reemergence of the issue of the expansion of slavery.

The Know-Nothings

The most momentous shift in party sentiment in American history took place in the early 1850s following the rise of a party vigorously opposed to immigrants and Catholics. This party, which was known as the American party or Know-Nothing party, crippled the Whig party, weakened the Democratic party, and made the political system incapable of resolving the growing crisis over slavery.

Hostility toward immigrants and Catholics had deep roots in American culture. The Protestant religious revivals of the 1820s and 1830s stimulated a "No Popery" movement. Prominent Northern clergymen accused the Catholic Church of conspiring to overthrow democracy and subject the United States to Catholic despotism. Popular fiction offered graphic descriptions of priests seducing women during confession and nuns cutting unborn infants from their mothers' wombs and throwing them to dogs. Anti-Catholic sentiment culminated in mob rioting and in the burning of churches and convents. In 1834, for example, a Philadelphia mob rampaged through Irish neighborhoods, burning churches and houses.

A massive wave of immigration from Ireland and Germany after 1845 led to a renewed outburst of antiforeign and anti-Catholic sentiment. Between 1846 and 1855, more than three million foreigners arrived in America. In cities such as Chicago, Milwaukee, New York, and St. Louis immigrants actually outnumbered native-born citizens. Nativists—ardent opponents of immigration—capitalized on deep-seated Protestant antagonism toward Catholics, working-class fear of economic

competition from cheaper immigrant labor, and resentment among native-born Americans of the growing political power of foreigners. Nativists charged that Catholics were responsible for a sharp increase in
poverty, crime, and drunkenness and were subservient to a foreign
leader, the pope.

To native-born Protestant workers, the new immigrants posed a tan-
gible economic threat. Economic slumps in 1851 and 1854 resulted in severe unemployment and wage cuts. Native workers blamed Irish and German immigrants for their plight. The immigrants also posed a political
threat. Concentrated in the large cities of the eastern seaboard, Irish and
German immigrants voted as blocs and quickly built up strong political
organizations.

One example of anti-Catholic hostility was the formation of a secret fraternal society made up of native-born Protestant workingmen. Called "The
Order of the Star Spangled Banner," it soon formed the nucleus of a new political party known as the Know-Nothing or the American party. The party
received its name from the fact that when members were asked about the
workings of the party, they were supposed to reply, "I know nothing."

By 1855 the Know-Nothings had captured control of the legislatures
in New England except in Vermont and Maine and were the dominant
opposition party to the Democrats in New York, Pennsylvania, Maryland,
Virginia, Tennessee, Georgia, Alabama, Mississippi, and Louisiana. In the
presidential election of 1856 the party supported Millard Fillmore and
won more than 21 percent of the popular vote and 8 electoral votes. In
Congress the party had 5 senators and 43 representatives. Between 1853
and 1855 the Know-Nothings replaced the Whigs as the nation's second
largest party.

By 1856, however, the Know-Nothing party was already in decline.
Many Know-Nothing officeholders were relatively unknown men with
little political experience. In the states where they gained control, the
Know-Nothings proved unable to enact their legislative program, which
included a 21-year residency period before immigrants could become citizens and vote, a limitation on political officeholding to native-born
Americans, and restrictions on the sale of liquor.

After 1855 the Know-Nothing party was supplanted in the North by
a new and explosive sectional party, the Republicans. By 1856 Northern
workers felt more threatened by the Southern slave power than by the
pope and Catholic immigrants. At the same time, fewer and fewer Southerners were willing to support a party that ignored the question of the expansion of slavery. As a result, the Know-Nothing party rapidly dissolved.

Nevertheless, the Know-Nothings left an indelible mark on American
politics. The Know-Nothing movement eroded loyalty to the national

political parties, helped destroy the Whig party, and undermined the capacity of the political system to contain the divisive issue of slavery.

Young America

For nearly four years following the Compromise of 1850, agitation over the question of the expansion of slavery abated. Most Americans were weary of the continuing controversy and turned their attention away from politics to focus instead on railroads, cotton, and trade. The early 1850s were dominated by dreams of greater American influence abroad—in areas such as Asia, the Caribbean, and Central America. Majestic clipper ships raced from New York to China in as few as 104 days. Steamship and railroad promoters launched ambitious schemes to build transit routes across Central America to link California and the Atlantic Coast. In 1853 Commodore Matthew Perry sailed into Tokyo Bay with two steam frigates and two sailing ships, thereby ending Japan's era of isolation from the Western world. The whole world appeared to be opening up to American influence.

Franklin Pierce, a New Hampshire Democrat elected as the nation's fourteenth president in 1852, tried to unite the country with an aggressive program of foreign expansion called "Young America." He sought to annex Hawaii, expand American influence in Honduras and Nicaragua, and acquire new territory from Mexico and Spain. He announced that his administration would not be deterred "by any timid forebodings of evil" raised by the slavery question. But each effort to expand the country's boundaries only provoked new sectional disputes because any acquisition would have posed the question of its status with regard to slavery.

Pierce was the first "doughface" president. He was, in the popular phrase, "a Northern man with Southern principles." Many Northerners suspected that Pierce's real goal was the acquisition of new territory for slavery. This suspicion was first raised in 1853, when the president instructed James Gadsden, his minister to Mexico, to purchase Mexican territory to provide a route for a southern transcontinental railroad.

Cuba was the next object of Pierce's ambitions. Southern slaveholders coveted Cuba's 300,000 slaves. Other Americans wanted to free Cuba's white population from Spanish rule. In 1854 Pierce instructed his ambassador to Spain to offer $130 million for Cuba, but Spain refused the offer. That same year, at a meeting in Ostend, Belgium, three of Pierce's diplomatic ministers sent a dispatch, later titled the Ostend Manifesto, to the secretary of state, urging the seizure of Cuba if Spain continued to refuse to sell the island. The Ostend Manifesto outraged Northerners, who regarded it as a brazen attempt to expand U.S. slavery in defiance of Spain's sovereign rights.

The Kansas-Nebraska Act

In 1854, less than four years after the Compromise of 1850, a piece of legislation was introduced in Congress that revived the issue of the expansion of slavery, shattered all illusions of sectional peace, and reordered the political landscape by destroying the Whig party, dividing the Democratic party, and creating the Republican party. Ironically, the author of this legislation was Senator Stephen A. Douglas, the very man who had pushed the earlier compromise through Congress.

As chairman of the Senate Committee on Territories, Douglas proposed that the area west of Iowa and Missouri—which had been set aside as a permanent Indian reservation—be organized as the Nebraska Territory and opened to white settlement. Douglas had sought to achieve this objective since 1844, but Southern congressmen had objected because Nebraska was located in the northern half of the Louisiana Purchase where the Missouri Compromise prohibited slavery. In order to forestall Southern opposition, Douglas's original bill ignored both the Missouri Compromise and the status of slavery in the Nebraska Territory. It simply provided that Nebraska, when admitted as a state, could enter the Union "with or without slavery," as its "constitution may prescribe."

Southern senators, however, demanded that Douglas add a clause specifically repealing the Missouri Compromise and stating that the question of slavery would be determined on the basis of popular sovereignty. For reasons still in dispute, Douglas relented to Southern pressure. In its final form Douglas's bill created two territories, Kansas and Nebraska, and declared that the Missouri Compromise was "inoperative and void." With solid support from Southern Whigs and Southern Democrats and the votes of half of the Northern Democratic congressmen, the measure passed. On May 30, 1854, President Pierce signed the measure into law.

Why did Douglas risk reviving the slavery question? His critics accused him of yielding to the Southern pressure because of his presidential ambitions and a desire to enhance the value of his holdings in Chicago real estate and western lands. They charged that the Illinois senator's chief interest in opening up Kansas and Nebraska was to secure a right of way for a transcontinental railroad that would make Chicago the transportation center of mid-America.

Douglas's supporters, on the other hand, pictured him as a statesman laboring for western development and a sincere believer in popular sovereignty as a solution to the problem of slavery in the western territories. Douglas had long insisted that the democratic solution to the slavery issue was to allow the people who actually settled a territory to decide whether slavery would be permitted or forbidden. Popular sovereignty, he believed, would allow the nation to "avoid the slavery agitation for all time

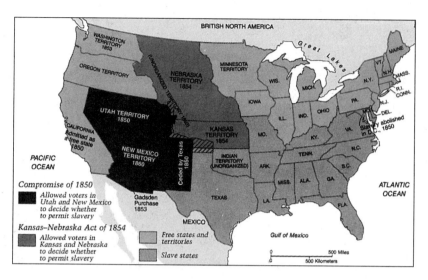

Compromise of 1850/Kansas-Nebraska Act

to come." Moreover, he believed that because of climate and geography slavery could never be extended into Kansas and Nebraska anyway.

In order to understand why Douglas introduced the Kansas-Nebraska Act, it is important to realize that by 1854 political and economic pressure to organize Kansas and Nebraska had become overwhelming. Midwestern farmers agitated for new land. A southern rail route had been completed through the Gadsden Purchase in December 1853, and promoters of a northern route for a transcontinental railroad viewed territorial organization as essential. Missouri slaveholders, already bordered on two sides by free states, believed that slavery in their state was doomed if they were surrounded by a free territory. All wanted to see the region opened to settlement.

Revival of the Slavery Issue

Neither Douglas nor his Southern supporters anticipated the extent and fury of Northern opposition to the Kansas-Nebraska Act. Douglas predicted that the "storm will soon spend its fury," but it did not subside. Northern Free-Soilers regarded the Missouri Compromise line as a "sacred compact" that had forever excluded slavery from the northern half of the Louisiana Purchase. Now they feared that under the guise of popular sovereignty, the Southern slave power threatened to spread slavery across the entire western frontier.

No single piece of legislation ever passed by Congress had more far-reaching political consequences. The Kansas-Nebraska Act brought about nothing less than a dramatic realignment of the two-party system. Conservative Whigs abandoned their party and joined the Democrats, while Northern Democrats with free-soil sentiments repudiated their own elected representatives.

The chief beneficiary of these defections was a new political organization, the Republican party. A combination of diverse elements, the Republican party stood for the belief that slavery must be barred from the western territories. It contained antislavery radicals, Free-Soilers, Whigs, Jacksonian Democrats, nativists, and antislavery immigrants.

In the fall of 1854 the new party contested congressional elections for the first time and won 46 seats in the House of Representatives. It included a number of men, like William H. Seward of New York, who believed that blacks should receive civil rights including the right to vote. But the new party also attracted many individuals, like Ohio senator Salmon P. Chase and Abraham Lincoln, who favored colonization as the only workable solution to slavery. Despite their differences, however, all of these groups shared a conviction that the western territories should be saved for free labor. "Free labor, free soil, free men," was the Republican slogan.

The Gathering Storm

Because the Kansas-Nebraska Act stated that the future status of slavery in the territories was to be decided by popular vote, both antislavery Northerners and proslavery Southerners competed to win the region for their section. Since Nebraska was too far north to attract slave owners, Kansas became the arena of sectional conflict. For six years, proslavery and antislavery factions fought in Kansas as popular sovereignty degenerated into violence.

"Bleeding Kansas" and "Bleeding Sumner"

Across the drought-stricken Ohio and Mississippi valleys, thousands of land-hungry farmers hoped to stake a claim to part of Kansas's 126,000 square miles of territory. Along with these pioneers came a small contingent of settlers whose express purpose was to keep Kansas free soil. Even before the 1854 act had been passed, the New England Emigrant Aid Company was promoting the emigration of antislavery New Englanders to Kansas to "vote to make it free." By the summer of 1855 more than 9,000 pioneers—mainly midwestern Free-Soilers—had settled in Kansas.

Slaveholders from Missouri expressed alarm at the activities of the Emigrant Aid Society. In response, they formed "Social Bands" and "Sons of the South" to "repel the wave of fanaticism which threatens to break upon our border." One Missouri lawyer told a cheering crowd that he would hang any "free soil" emigrant who came into Kansas.

Competition between proslavery and antislavery factions reached a climax on May 30, 1855, when Kansas held territorial elections. Although only 1,500 men were registered to vote, 6,000 ballots were cast, many of them by proslavery "border ruffians" from Missouri. As a result, a proslavery legislature was elected, which passed a series of laws protecting the "peculiar institution" in Kansas.

Free-Soilers called the election a fraud and held their own "Free State" convention which drew up a constitution that not only prohibited slavery in Kansas but also barred free blacks from the territory. Like the Free-Soilers who settled California and Oregon, most Northerners in Kansas wanted the territory to be free and white.

When Congress convened in January 1856, it was confronted by two rival governments in Kansas. President Pierce threw his support behind the proslavery legislature and asked Congress to admit Kansas to the Union as a slave state.

Violence broke out between Northern and Southern settlers over rival land claims, town sites, railroad routes—and, most dangerous of all, the question of slavery. In one episode, when a proslavery grand jury indicted several members of the Free-Soil Topeka government for high treason, 800 proslavery men marched into Lawrence, Kansas, to arrest the leaders of the antislavery government. The posse burned the local hotel, looted a number of houses, destroyed two antislavery printing presses, and killed one man.

On May 19, 1856—two days before the "sack of Lawrence"—Senator Charles Sumner of Massachusetts began a two-day speech in which he denounced "The Crime Against Kansas." In his speech Sumner charged that there was a Southern conspiracy to make Kansas a slave state. He proceeded to argue that a number of Southern senators, including Senator Andrew Butler of South Carolina, stood behind this conspiracy. Launching into a bitter personal diatribe, Sumner accused Senator Butler of taking "the harlot, Slavery," for his "mistress."

Two days later Butler's nephew, Congressman Preston Brooks of South Carolina, entered a nearly empty Senate chamber determined to "avenge the insult to my State." Sighting Sumner at his desk, Brooks charged at him and began striking the Massachusetts senator over the head with a cane. He swung so hard that the cane broke into pieces.

Although it would take Sumner three years to recover from his injuries and return to his Senate seat, he promptly became a martyr to the cause of freedom in the North, where a million copies of his "Crime

Clutching a pen in one hand and a copy of his "Crime Against Kansas" speech in the other, Senator Charles Sumner attempts to defend himself against an attack by South Carolina Congressman Preston Brooks.

Against Kansas" speech were distributed. In the South, Brooks was hailed as a hero. Merchants in Charleston bought the congressman a new cane, inscribed "Hit him again." A vote to expel Brooks from Congress failed because every Southern representative but one voted against the measure. Instead, Brooks was censured. He promptly resigned his seat and was immediately reelected.

The episode had repercussions in strife-torn Kansas. John Brown, a devout Bible-quoting Calvinist who believed that he had a personal responsibility to overthrow slavery, announced that the time had come "to fight fire with fire" and "strike terror in the hearts of proslavery men." The next day, in reprisal for the "sack of Lawrence" and the assault on Sumner, Brown and six companions dragged five proslavery men and boys from their beds at Pottawatomie Creek, split open their skulls with a sword, cut off their hands, and laid out their entrails.

A war of revenge erupted in Kansas. Columns of proslavery Southerners ransacked free farms while they searched for Brown and the other "Pottawatomie killers." Armed bands looted enemy stores and farms. At Osawatomie, proslavery forces attacked John Brown's headquarters, leaving a dozen men dead. John Brown's men killed four Missourians, and proslavery forces retaliated by blockading the free towns of Topeka and Lawrence. Before it was over, guerrilla warfare in Kansas would leave 200 dead.

The Election of 1856

The presidential election of 1856 took place in the midst of Kansas's civil war. President Pierce hoped for renomination to a second term in office, but Northern indignation over the Kansas-Nebraska Act led the Democrats to seek out a less controversial candidate. Northern and western Democrats succeeded in winning the nomination for James Buchanan, a 65-year-old Pennsylvania bachelor. The dying Whig party and the Southern wing of the Know-Nothing party nominated former President Millard Fillmore.

The Republican party held its first national convention in Philadelphia in June, nominating the dashing young explorer and soldier John C. Frémont for president. Frémont was a romantic figure who had led more than a dozen major explorations of the Rocky Mountains and Far West. After accepting the Republican nomination, he declared that Kansas should be admitted to the Union as a free state. This was his only public utterance during the entire 1856 campaign. A few weeks later the Northern wing of the Know-Nothing party threw its support behind Frémont.

The election was one of the most bitter in American history and the first in which voting divided along rigid sectional lines. The Democratic strategy was to picture the Republican party as a hotbed of radicalism. Democrats called the Republicans the party of disunion and described Frémont as a "black abolitionist" who would destroy the Union. Republicans responded by accusing the Democrats of being accomplices in a conspiracy to extend slavery.

Although Buchanan garnered only 45 percent of the popular vote, because of the presence of Fillmore he narrowly carried five Northern states, giving him a comfortable margin of victory in the electoral college. Buchanan won 174 electoral college votes to 114 for Frémont and 8 for Fillmore.

The election showed how polarized the nation had become. The South, except for Maryland, voted solidly Democratic. Frémont did not receive a single vote south of the Mason-Dixon line. At the same time, the northernmost states were solidly Republican.

In their first presidential campaign the Republicans had made an extraordinarily impressive showing. Eleven free states voted for Frémont. If only two more states had voted in his favor, the Republicans would have won the election.

The Supreme Court Speaks

In his inaugural address Buchanan declared that "the great object of my administration will be to arrest . . . the agitation of the slavery question in the North." He then predicted that a forthcoming Supreme Court decision would once and for all settle the controversy over slavery in the western territories. Two days after Buchanan's inauguration, the high court handed down its decision.

On March 6, 1857, the Supreme Court finally decided a question that Congress had evaded for decades: whether Congress had the power to prohibit slavery in the territories. Repeatedly, Congress had declared that this was a constitutional question that the Supreme Court should settle. Now, for the first time, the Supreme Court offered its answer.

The case originated in 1846, when a Missouri slave, Dred Scott, sued to gain his freedom. Scott argued that while he had been the slave of an army surgeon, he had lived for four years in Illinois, a free state, and Wisconsin, a free territory, and that his residence on free soil had erased his slave status. By a 7-2 margin the Court ruled that Dred Scott had no right to sue in federal court, that the Missouri Compromise was unconstitutional, and that Congress had no right to exclude slavery from the territories. All nine justices rendered separate opinions, but Chief Justice Taney delivered the opinion that expressed the position of the Court's majority. His opinion represented a judicial defense of the most extreme proslavery position.

The chief justice made two sweeping rulings. The first was that Dred Scott had no right to sue in federal court because neither slaves nor free blacks were citizens of the United States. At the time the Constitution was adopted, the chief justice wrote, blacks had been "regarded as beings of an inferior order" with "no rights which the white man was bound to respect."

Second, Taney declared that any law excluding slaves from the territories was a violation of the Fifth Amendment prohibition against the seizure of property without due process of law. The Missouri Compromise was unconstitutional, the Court declared, because it prohibited slavery north of 36° 30'.

In a single decision the Court sought to resolve all the major constitutional questions raised by slavery. It declared that the Declaration of Independence and the Bill of Rights were not intended to apply to black Americans. It stated that the Republican party platform—barring slavery from the western territories—was unconstitutional. And it ruled that Stephen Douglas's doctrine of "popular sovereignty"—which stated that territorial governments had the power to prohibit slavery—was also unconstitutional.

Republicans reacted with scorn. Radical abolitionists called for secession. Many Republicans—including an Illinois politician named Abraham Lincoln—regarded the decision as part of a slave power conspiracy to legalize slavery throughout the United States.

The Dred Scott decision was a major political miscalculation. In its ruling, the Supreme Court sought to solve the slavery controversy once and for all. Instead the Court intensified sectional strife, undercut possible compromise solutions to the divisive issue of the expansion of slavery, and weakened the moral authority of the judiciary.

The Lecompton Constitution: "A Swindle and a Fraud"

Late in 1857 President Buchanan faced a major test of his ability to suppress the slavery controversy. In September proslavery forces in Kansas met in Lecompton, the territorial capital, to draft a constitution that would bring Kansas into the Union as a slave state. Recognizing that a proslavery constitution would be defeated in a fair election, proslavery delegates offered voters a referendum on whether they preferred "the constitution with slavery" or "the constitution without slavery." In either case, however, the new constitution guaranteed slave ownership as a sacred right. Free-Soilers boycotted the election and, as a result, "the constitution with slavery" was approved by a 6,000 vote margin.

President Buchanan—afraid that the South would secede if Kansas were not admitted to the Union as a slave state—accepted the proslavery Lecompton constitution as a satisfactory application of the principle of popular sovereignty. He then demanded that Congress admit Kansas as the sixteenth slave state.

After a rancorous debate, the Senate passed a bill that admitted Kansas as a slave state under the Lecompton constitution. But the House of Representatives rejected this measure and instead substituted a compromise, which allowed Kansans to vote on the proslavery constitution. As a thinly veiled bribe to encourage Kansans to ratify the document, the bill offered Kansas a huge grant of public land if it approved the Lecompton constitution. While federal troops guarded the polls, Kansas voters overwhelmingly rejected the proslavery constitution.

The bloody battle for Kansas had come to an end. Free-Soilers took control of the territorial legislature and repealed Kansas's territorial slave code. Stripped of any legal safeguards for their slave property, most Kansas slave owners quickly left the territory. When the federal census was taken in 1860, just two slaves remained in Kansas.

But the nation would never be the same. To antislavery Northerners, the Lecompton controversy showed that the slave power was willing to subvert democratic processes in an attempt to force slavery on a free people. In Kansas, they charged, proslavery forces had used violence, fraud, and intimidation to expand the territory open to slavery. To the more extreme opponents of slavery in the North, the lesson was clear. The only way to preserve freedom and democratic procedures was to destroy slavery and the slave power through force of arms.

Crisis of the Union

By 1858, a growing number of Northerners were convinced that two fundamentally antagonistic societies had evolved in the nation, one dedicated to freedom, the other opposed. They had come to believe that their society was locked in a life and death struggle with a Southern society dominated by an aggressive slave power, which had seized control of the federal government and imperiled the liberties of free people. Declared the *New York Tribune:* "We are not one people. We are two peoples. We are a people for Freedom and a people for Slavery. Between the two, conflict is inevitable."

At the same time, an increasing number of Southerners expressed alarm at the growth of antislavery and anti-Southern sentiment in the North. They were convinced that Republicans would not only insist on halting slavery's expansion but would also seek to undermine the institution where it already existed. As the decade closed, the dominant question of American political life was whether the nation's leaders could find a peaceful way to resolve the differences separating the North and South.

The Lincoln-Douglas Debates

The critical issues dividing the nation—slavery versus free labor, popular sovereignty, and the legal and political status of African Americans—were brought into sharp focus in a series of debates during the 1858 election campaign for U.S. senator from Illinois. The campaign pitted a little-known lawyer from Springfield named Abraham Lincoln against Senator Stephen A. Douglas, the front-runner for the Democratic presidential nomination in 1860. (Senators, at the time, were elected by state legislators, and Douglas and Lincoln were actually campaigning for candidates from their party for the state legislature.)

The contest received intense national publicity. One reason for the public attention was that the political future of Stephen Douglas was at stake. Douglas had openly broken with the Buchanan administration over the proslavery Lecompton constitution and had joined with Republicans to defeat the admission of Kansas to the Union as a slave state. Many wondered if Douglas would now assume the leadership of the Free-Soil movement.

The public knew little about the man the Republicans selected to run against Douglas. Lincoln had been born in 1809 and had grown up on the wild Kentucky and Indiana frontier. At the age of 21 he moved to Illinois where he worked as a clerk in a country store, became a local postmaster and a lawyer, and served four terms in the lower house of the Illinois General Assembly. A Whig in politics, Lincoln was elected in 1846 to the U.S. House of Representatives, but his stand against the Mexican War had made him too unpopular to win reelection. After the passage of the Kansas-Nebraska Act in 1854 Lincoln reentered politics, and in 1858 the Republican party nominated him to run against Douglas for the Senate.

Lincoln accepted the nomination with the famous words: " 'A house divided against itself cannot stand.' I believe this Government cannot endure permanently half slave and half free." He did not believe the Union would fall, but he did predict that it would cease to be divided. Lincoln proceeded to argue that Stephen Douglas's Kansas-Nebraska Act and the Supreme Court's Dred Scott decision were part of a conspiracy to make slavery lawful "in all the States, old as well as new—North as well as South."

For four months Lincoln and Douglas crisscrossed Illinois, traveling nearly 10,000 miles and participating in seven face-to-face debates before crowds of up to 15,000. During the course of the debates Lincoln and Douglas presented two sharply contrasting views of the problem of slavery. Douglas argued that slavery was a dying institution that had reached its natural limits and could not thrive where climate and soil were inhospitable. He asserted that the problem of slavery could be resolved if it was treated as a local problem. Lincoln, on the other hand, regarded slavery as a dynamic, expansionistic institution, hungry for new territory. He argued that if Northerners allowed slavery to spread unchecked, slave owners would make slavery a national institution and would reduce all laborers, white as well as black, to a state of virtual slavery.

The sharpest difference between the two candidates involved the issue of African Americans' legal rights. Douglas was unable to conceive of blacks as anything but inferior to whites, and he was unalterably opposed to Negro citizenship. "I want citizenship for whites only," he declared. Lincoln said that he, too, was opposed to granting free blacks full legal rights. But he insisted that black Americans were equal to Douglas and "every living man" in their right to life, liberty, and the fruits of their own labor.

At Freeport, Illinois, Lincoln asked Douglas to reconcile the Supreme Court's Dred Scott decision, which denied Congress the power to exclude slavery from a territory, with popular sovereignty. Could the residents of a territory "in any lawful way" exclude slavery prior to statehood? Douglas replied by stating that the residents of a territory could exclude slavery by refusing to pass laws protecting slaveholders' property rights. "Slavery cannot exist a day or an hour anywhere," he declared, "unless it is supported by local police regulations."

Any way he answered, Douglas was certain to alienate Northern Free-Soilers or proslavery Southerners. The Dred Scott decision had given slave owners the right to take their slavery into any western territories. Now Douglas said that territorial settlers could exclude slavery, despite what the Court had ruled. Douglas won reelection, but his cautious statements antagonized Southerners and Northern Free-Soilers alike.

Although Lincoln failed to win a Senate seat, his battle with Stephen Douglas had catapulted him into the national spotlight and made him a serious presidential possibility in 1860. As Lincoln himself noted, his defeat was "a slip and not a fall."

Harpers Ferry

Up until the Kansas-Nebraska Act, abolitionists were averse to the use of violence. Opponents of slavery hoped to use moral suasion and other peaceful means to eliminate slavery. But by the mid-1850s the abolitionists' aversion to violence had begun to fade. In 1858 William Lloyd Garrison complained that his followers were "growing more and more warlike." On the night of October 16, 1859, violence came and John Brown was its instrument.

Brown's plan was to capture the federal arsenal at Harpers Ferry, Virginia (now West Virginia), and arm slaves from the surrounding countryside. His long-range goal was to drive southward into Tennessee and Alabama, raiding federal arsenals and inciting slave insurrections. Failing that, he hoped to ignite a sectional crisis that would destroy slavery.

At eight o'clock Sunday evening, October 16, John Brown led a raiding party of approximately 21 men into Harpers Ferry, where they captured the lone night watchman and cut the town's telegraph lines. Encountering no resistance, Brown's men seized the federal arsenal, an armory, and a rifle works. Brown then sent out several detachments to round up hostages and liberate slaves.

But Brown's plans soon went awry. As news of the raid spread, angry townspeople and local militia companies cut off Brown's escape routes and trapped his men in the armory. Twice Brown sent men carrying flags of truce to negotiate. On both occasions, drunken mobs, yelling "Kill them, Kill them," gunned the men down. Two days later U.S. Marines commanded by Colonel Robert E. Lee arrived in Harpers Ferry. Brown and his men took refuge in a fire engine house and battered holes through the building's brick wall to shoot through. Colonel Lee's marines stormed the engine house and rammed down its doors. Five of Brown's party escaped, ten were killed, and seven, including Brown himself, were taken prisoner.

A week later John Brown was put on trial in a Virginia court, even though his attack had occurred on federal property. He was found guilty of treason, conspiracy, and murder, and was sentenced to die on the gallows.

On December 2 Brown was hanged, a martyr to his cause. Across the North church bells tolled, flags flew at half-mast, and buildings were draped in black bunting. Ralph Waldo Emerson compared Brown to Jesus Christ and declared that his death had made "the gallows as glorious as the cross."

As Robert E. Lee's marines broke through the brick walls of John Brown's stronghold at Harper's Ferry, Brown "felt the pulse of his dying son with one hand and held his rifle with the other, and commanded his men with the utmost composure."

Prominent Northern Democrats and Republicans, including Stephen Douglas and Abraham Lincoln, spoke out forcefully against Brown's raid and his tactics. Lincoln expressed the views of the Republican leadership when he denounced Brown's raid as an act of "violence, bloodshed, and treason" that deserved to be punished by death. But Southern whites refused to believe that politicians like Lincoln and Douglas represented the true opinion of most Northerners. These men condemned Brown's "invasion," observed a Virginia senator, "only because it failed."

Conclusion

For 40 years the debate over the extension of slavery had divided North and South. National leaders had tried on several occasions to reach a permanent, workable solution to the problem, without success. With the collapse of the Whigs and the rise of the Republicans, the nation's first sectional party, the American political process could no longer contain the fierce antagonisms and mutual distrust which separated the two regions.

In 1859 John Brown's raid convinced many white Southerners that a majority of Northerners wished to free the slaves and incite a race war.

Chronology of Key Events

1850	Compromise of 1850
1852	Harriet Beecher Stowe publishes *Uncle Tom's Cabin*
1853	Gadsden Purchase from Mexico
1854	Ostend Manifesto; Commodore Matthew Perry negotiates a treaty opening Japan to American trade; Kansas-Nebraska Act reignites sectional controversy over slavery; "Bleeding Kansas" begins; Republican party formed
1856	"Sack of Lawrence;" "Bleeding Sumner"—Congressman Preston Brooks of South Carolina beats Senator Charles Sumner of Massachusetts; John Brown's raid on Pottawatomi Creek, Kansas
1857	Dred Scott decision
1858	Kansas voters reject the Lecompton constitution; Lincoln-Douglas debates
1859	John Brown's raid at Harpers Ferry

Southern extremists, known as "fire-eaters," told large crowds that John Brown's attack on Harpers Ferry was "the first act in the grand tragedy of emancipation, and the subjugation of the South in bloody treason." After Harpers Ferry, Southerners increasingly believed that secession and creation of a slaveholding confederacy were now the South's only options. A Virginia newspaper noted that there were "thousands of men in our midst who, a month ago, scoffed at the idea of a dissolution of the Union as a madman's dream, but who now hold the opinion that its days are numbered." The final bonds that had held the Union together had come unraveled.

Suggestions for Further Reading

Good overviews of the period include William W. Freehling, *The Road to Disunion: Secessionists at Bay* (1990); Michael Holt, *The Political Crisis of the 1850s* (1978); David M. Potter, *The Impending Crisis* (1976). See also Kenneth M. Stampp, *America in 1857* (1990).

For analyses of Southern attitudes on the eve of the Civil War see William J. Cooper, *Liberty and Slavery* (1983); David Brion Davis, *The Slave Power Conspiracy and the Paranoid Style* (1970). For information on Northern attitudes consult Eric Foner, *Free Soil, Free Labor, Free Men* (1970); William E. Gienapp, *Origins of the Republican Party* (1987).

For information on the Dred Scott Case see Don E. Fehrenbacher, *The Dred Scott Case* (1978). On foreign policy, see P. B. Wiley and Korogi Ichiro, *Yankees in the Lands of the Gods* (1990); Robert E. May, *The Southern Dream of a Caribbean Empire* (1974). Good biographical studies include Robert W. Johannsen, *Stephen A. Douglas* (1973); Stephen B. Oates, *To Purge This Land with Blood: A Biography of John Brown*, 2d ed., (1984).

Chapter **15**

A Nation Shattered by Civil War, 1860–1865

L ooking eastward from Sharpsburg into the mountains of western Maryland, General Robert E. Lee uttered the fateful words: "We will make our stand." Behind him was the Potomac River and to his front was Antietam Creek. Having invaded Union territory in early September 1862, Lee dispersed his Army of Northern Virginia, some 50,000 strong, across the countryside to capture strategic points and to rally the citizens of this border, slaveholding state behind the Confederate cause. Now he issued orders for his troops to reassemble with all haste at Sharpsburg. A major battle was in the making. General George B. Mc-Clellan's Army of the Potomac, numbering nearly 100,000 soldiers, was rapidly descending upon Lee's position.

Early on the morning of September 17 the great battle began. As the day progressed, Union forces attacked in five uncoordinated waves, which allowed Lee to maneuver his heavily outnumbered troops from point to point to meet each assault. As darkness fell, the Confederates still held their lines. Lee knew, however, that if McClellan attacked again the next morning, the Southern army might well be annihilated.

Among those rebel troops who marched into Maryland was 25-year-old Thomas Jefferson Rushin. He had grown up secure in his social station as the second son of Joel Rushin, a prospering west Georgia cotton planter who owned 21 slaves. Anxious to show that Southern gentlemen would never shrink from battle in defense of their way of life, he enlisted in Company K of the Twelfth Georgia Volunteers in June 1861. At 5:30 A.M. on September 17, 1862, Sergeant Rushin waited restlessly north of Sharpsburg—where the first Union assault occurred.

As dawn beckoned, Rushin and his comrades first heard skirmish fire, then the booming of cannons. Out in an open field they soon engaged Yankee troops appearing at the edge of a nearby woods. The Twelfth Georgia Volunteers stood their ground until they pulled back at 6:45 A.M. By the time that order came, 62 Georgians lay dead or wounded, among them the lifeless body of Thomas Jefferson Rushin.

At 9:00 A.M. General Ambrose E. Burnside's Union soldiers prepared to cross a stone bridge over Antietam Creek. On the other side was sharply rising ground, on top of which troops in gray waited, ready to shoot at any person bold enough to venture onto what became known as Burnside Bridge.

The Eleventh Connecticut Volunteers were among those poised for the advance. Included in their number was 18-year-old Private Alvin Flint, Jr., who had enlisted a few months before in Company D. He was from Hartford where his father, Alvin, Sr., worked in a papermaking factory. Flint's departure from home was sorrowful because his mother had

The human toll of the Civil War was overwhelming for contemporaries and remains so for later generations. Thomas Jefferson Rushin (left) and Alvin Flint, Jr. (right), were young casualties at the Battle of Antietam.

just died of consumption. A few weeks later he received word that his younger sister had succumbed to the same disease.

Flint's own sense of foreboding must have been overwhelming as he charged toward the bridge. In an instant, he became part of the human carnage, as minié balls poured down from across the bridge. Bleeding profusely from a mortal wound, he died before stretcher-bearers could reach him.

Flint never knew that his father and younger brother had recently joined another Connecticut regiment. By January, the two remaining Flints also would be dead, the victims of typhoid fever.

With 23,000 dead and wounded soldiers, Antietam turned out to be the bloodiest one-day action of the Civil War. And before the slaughter ended in 1865, total casualties reached 1.2 million people, including 620,000 dead—more than the total number of United States troops who lost their lives in World Wars I and II combined. Back in April 1861 when the Confederates fired on Fort Sumter, no one foresaw such carnage. No one imagined bodies as "thick as human leaves" decaying in fields around Sharpsburg, or how "horrible" looking would be "the faces of the dead."

The coming of the Civil War could be compared to a time bomb ready to explode. The fundamental issue was slavery and the question of whether the "peculiar institution" would be allowed to spread across the American landscape. Southerners feared that Northern leaders would use federal authority to declare slavery null and void throughout the land. Invoking the principle of states' rights, the South voted to secede. The North, in response, went to war to save the Union. Lurking in the background was the issue of permitting the continued existence of slavery. The carnage of the war settled the matter. A few days after Antietam, President Abraham Lincoln announced the Emancipation Proclamation, which transformed the Civil War into a struggle to end slavery—and the way of life it supported—as a means of destroying Confederate resistance and preserving the federal Union.

From Secession to Full-Scale War

On April 23, 1860, the Democratic party gathered in Charleston, South Carolina, to select a presidential candidate. No nominating convention faced a more difficult task. The delegates argued bitterly among themselves. In a rehearsal of what was to come, many Southern delegates left the convention. The breaking up of the Democratic party cleared the way for Lincoln's election, which in turn provoked the secession of seven Southern states by February 1861.

Electing a New President

Even before the Democratic convention met, there was evidence that the party was crumbling. Early in 1860 Jefferson Davis of Mississippi introduced a series of resolutions in the U.S. Senate calling for federal protection of slavery in all western territories. More extreme "fire-eaters," such as William L. Yancey of Alabama, not only embraced Davis's proposal but announced that he and others would leave the convention if the party did not defend their inalienable right to hold slaves and nominate a Southerner for president. Playing to cheering galleries in Charleston, the center of secessionist sentiment, delegates from eight Southern states walked out after the convention rejected an extreme proslavery platform.

Those who remained tried to nominate a candidate, but after dozens of ballots no one received a two-thirds majority. So the delegates gave up and agreed to reconvene in Baltimore in another six weeks. But that convention also failed to produce a consensus. Finally, in two separate meetings, Northern delegates named Stephen A. Douglas as their candidate while Southern delegates chose John C. Breckinridge of Kentucky.

To confuse matters further, a short-lived party, the Constitutional Union, emerged. This coalition of former Whigs, Know-Nothings, and pro-Union Democrats nominated John Bell of Tennessee. The party enjoyed support among moderates in the border states, enabling Bell to draw votes away from both Douglas and Breckinridge and making it easier for the sectional Republican party to carry the election.

When the Republicans gathered in Chicago in mid-May, they were very optimistic, especially with the Democrats hopelessly divided. Delegates constructed a platform that included high tariffs in an appeal to gain the support of Northern manufacturers and a homestead law in a bid to win the backing of citizens wanting free farmland. On the slave expansion issue there was no hint of compromise, although the platform did not call for an end to the institution of slavery in states where it already existed. To help ensure victory, Republican party regulars rejected front-runner William H. Seward, a strong antislavery advocate, in favor of Abraham Lincoln, a relative unknown.

According to custom, Lincoln stayed at home during the campaign and let others speak for him. His supporters inflamed sectional tensions by bragging that slavery would never survive their candidate's presidency. As a result, the 1860 presidential campaign took place in a lightning-charged atmosphere of threats and fears bordering on hysteria. Rumors of slave revolts, town burnings, and the murder of women and children swept the South. In one Alabama town a mob hanged a stranger, thinking him to be an abolitionist.

On election day, November 6, 1860, Lincoln won only 39.9 percent of the popular vote, but he received 180 electoral college votes, 57 more than the combined total of his opponents. The vote was purely sectional; Lincoln's name did not appear on the ballots of ten Southern states. Even when totaling all the popular votes against him, Lincoln still would have won in the electoral college by 17 votes because he carried the most populous states—all in the North. His election dramatically demonstrated to Southerners their minority status.

Secession Rends the Union

Lincoln told one friend during the campaign that Southerners "have too much good sense, and good temper, to attempt the ruin of the govern-

Table 15.1			
Election of 1860			
Candidate	*Party*	*Popular Vote*	*Electoral Vote*
Abraham Lincoln	Republican	1,865,593	180
John C. Breckinridge	Democratic Southern	848,356	72
Stephen A. Douglas	Democratic Northern	1,382,713	12
John Bell	Constitutional Union	592,906	39

ment." He explained to others that he would support a constitutional amendment protecting slavery where it already existed, but Southerners believed otherwise. Convinced that a Republican administration would seek to abolish slavery, South Carolina's legislature unanimously called for a secession convention. On December 20, 1860, the delegates voted unanimously to leave the Union. The rationale had long since been developed by John C. Calhoun. State authority was superior to that of the nation, and as sovereign entities, states could leave the Union as freely as they had joined.

By early February 1861 the Deep South states of Georgia, Florida, Alabama, Mississippi, Louisiana, and Texas had also voted in favor of secession. Representatives from the seven states first met in Montgomery, Alabama, on February 8 and proclaimed a new nation, the Confederate States of America. They elected Jefferson Davis provisional president and wrote a plan of government, which, except for emphasizing states' rights, they modeled on the federal Constitution. The Confederate constitution limited the president to a single six-year term, required a two-thirds vote of Congress to admit new states or enact appropriations bills, and forbade protective tariffs and government funding of internal improvements.

Some Northerners believed that the South should be allowed to "depart in peace." Senator John J. Crittenden of Kentucky proposed another alternative: to enshrine the old Missouri Compromise line of 36° 30' in a constitutional amendment that would also promise no future restrictions on slavery where it existed. Neither idea appealed to Lincoln. Secession was unconstitutional, he maintained, and appeasement, especially any plan endorsing the spread of slavery, was unacceptable.

President-elect Lincoln decided to do nothing until after his inauguration. He continued to hope that pro-Unionist sentiment in the South would win out over secessionist feelings. Also, eight slave states remained in the Union; controversial statements might have pushed some or all of them into the Confederate camp. Lincoln would make his moves prudently, indeed so carefully that some leading Republicans misread him as an inept fool. William Seward, his future secretary of state, even politely offered to run the presidency on Lincoln's behalf.

Lincoln Takes Command

On March 4 Lincoln took the oath of office as the nation's sixteenth president. His inaugural address contained a powerful but simple message: the Union was "perpetual," and secession was illegal. To resist federal authority was "insurrectionary." As president, he would support the Union by maintaining possession of federal properties in the South. Then Lincoln appealed to the Southern people: "We are not enemies, but friends." And he warned: "In your hands, my dissatisfied countrymen, and not in mine, is the momentous issue of civil war. . . . You can have no conflict without yourselves being the aggressors."

Even as he spoke, Lincoln knew that the seceding states had taken possession of all federal military installations within their borders—with the principal exceptions of Fort Sumter, guarding the entrance to Charleston harbor, and Fort Pickens at Pensacola. The next day Lincoln received an ominous report. Major Robert Anderson, in command of Fort Sumter, was running out of provisions and would have to abandon his position within six weeks unless resupplied.

Realizing that he had overestimated the extent of pro-Union feeling in the South, Lincoln ordered the navy to take provisions to Fort Sumter. Just before the expedition left, he sent a message to South Carolina's governor, notifying him that "if such attempt be not resisted, no effort to throw in men, arms, or ammunition, will be made." It was up to the rebels, from the president's point of view, to decide whether they wanted war.

Knowing that help for the Union garrison was on the way, Confederate General P. G. T. Beauregard ordered the cannonading of Fort Sumter. The firing commenced at 4:30 A.M. on April 12, 1861. Thirty-four hours later Major Anderson surrendered. On April 15 Lincoln announced that an "insurrection" existed and called for 75,000 volunteers to put down the Southern rebellion. The Civil War had begun.

An Accounting of Resources

The firing on Fort Sumter caused both jubilation and consternation. Most citizens thought that a battle or two would quickly end the conflict, so they rushed to enlist, not wanting to miss the action. The emotional outburst was particularly strong in the South where up to 200,000 enthusiasts tried to join the fledgling Confederate military machine. Several thousand had to be sent home because it was impossible to muster them into the service in so short a time with even the bare essentials of war—uniforms, weapons, camp equipment, and food rations.

Professional military men like Lieutenant Colonel Robert E. Lee, who had experienced combat in the Mexican War, were less enthusiastic. "I see only that a fearful calamity is upon us," he wrote. Lee was anxious "for the preservation of the Union," but he felt compelled to defend the "honor" of Virginia, should state leaders vote for secession.

Virginians seceded (April 17) in direct response to Lincoln's declaration of an insurrection. By late May, North Carolina, Tennessee, and Arkansas had also voted to leave the Union. In all, 11 states containing a population of nearly 9 million people, including 3.5 million slaves, proclaimed their independence. On the other hand, four slaveholding states bordering the North—Delaware, Maryland, Kentucky, and Missouri—equivocated about secession. Lincoln understood that sustaining the loyalty of the border states was critical. Besides making it more difficult for the Confederates to carry the war into the North, their presence gave the Union, with 23 million people, a major asset should there be a prolonged military struggle.

Secession

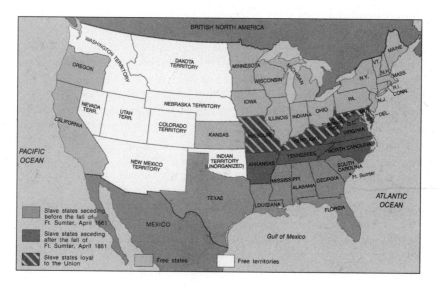

The North possessed overwhelming advantages going into the war. The value of Northern property was twice that of the South; the banking capital advantage was ten to one, and it was eight to one in investment capital. The North could easily underwrite the production of war goods, whereas the South would have to struggle, given its scarce capital resources and an industrial capacity far below that of the North. By other crucial resource measures, such as railroad mileage, representing the capacity to move armies and supplies easily, the Union was far ahead of the Confederacy. The North had 22,000 miles of track, as compared to 9,000 for the South. In 1860 U.S. manufacturers produced 470 locomotives, only 17 of which were built in the South. That same year the North produced 20 times as much pig iron, 17 times the clothing, and 32 times as many firearms.

With this imbalance, it is incredible that the South performed so well in the early stages, and that the North fared so poorly. Among the Southern assets, at least in 1861, was sheer geographic size. As long as the Confederacy maintained a defensive military posture, the North would have to demonstrate an ability to win more than an occasional battle. It would have to conquer a massive region, and this factor alone emboldened Southern leaders. In analogies alluding to the American Revolution, they discussed how the British, with superior resources, had failed to reconquer the colonies. If Southerners maintained their resolve, something more likely to happen when soldiers were defending homes and families, nothing, it appeared, could extinguish their desire for national independence.

In addition, the South held an initial advantage in generalship. Mature senior commanders like Albert Sidney Johnston, Joseph E. Johnston, and Robert E. Lee quickly gravitated to the top of the new Confederate command structure. The Union structure, however, was already in place, with the aging hero of the Mexican War, 74-year-old Winfield Scott, serving as general-in-chief in April 1861. Men like Ulysses S. Grant and William Tecumseh Sherman, who would later win renown as Union generals, were not even in the service at the outset of the war. It would take Grant and Sherman time to work through the pack of lackluster military professionals in line ahead of them.

Then there was the matter of civilian leadership. At the outset the South appeared to have the advantage. Jefferson Davis, the Confederacy's new president, possessed superb qualifications. Besides being a wealthy slaveholder, he had a West Point education, had fought in the Mexican War, had served in Congress, and had been Franklin Pierce's secretary of war. Davis proved to be a hardworking but ineffective administrator. He would not delegate authority and became tangled up in details; he surrounded himself with weak assistants; he held strong opinions on all subjects; and he was invariably rude to those who disagreed with him. Perhaps worst of all, he was not an inspirational leader, something the South desperately needed after war weariness set in.

Abraham Lincoln, by comparison, lacked the outward demeanor of a cultured gentleman. He had little formal schooling; he had spent an impoverished childhood in Kentucky and Indiana before moving to Illinois and succeeding as a country lawyer; he had served only one term in Congress; and he had virtually no military experience, except for brief duty as a militia captain during the Black Hawk War. But Northerners soon found that Lincoln viewed himself as a man of the people, eager to do anything necessary to save the Union. They saw him bear up under savage criticism. Even those who disagreed with him came to admire his ability to reflect and think through the implications of proposed actions—then move forward decisively. Lincoln emerged as an inspirational leader in the North's drive for victory.

"Forward to Richmond!" and "On to Washington!"

War hysteria was pervasive after Fort Sumter, and Southerners and Northerners alike exuded confidence. The populace clearly wanted a fight. Throughout the North the war cry was "Forward to Richmond!," referring to the Virginia city 100 miles south of Washington that had been selected as the permanent capital of the Confederacy. Throughout the South anyone shouting "On to Washington!" could expect to hear cheering voices in return. The land between the two capitals soon became a major combat zone, and the bloodshed began after President Lincoln, bowing in mid-July to pressure for a demonstration of Union superiority in arms, ordered General Irvin McDowell and 30,000 half-trained "Billy Yanks" to engage General P. G. T. Beauregard and his "Johnny Rebs," who were gathering at sleepy Manassas Junction, lying near a creek called Bull Run 25 miles southwest of the federal capital.

The Battle of Bull Run (First Manassas) occurred on Sunday, July 21. Citizens of Washington packed picnic lunches and went out to observe the engagement. Because the battlefield soon became shrouded in smoke, they saw little except Union soldiers finally breaking off and fleeing past them in absolute panic for their lives. Bull Run had its glorious moments, such as when Virginians under Thomas J. Jackson held onto a key hill, despite a crushing federal assault. This earned Jackson his nickname, "Stonewall," and he became the South's first authentic war hero. There were no heroes for the North. As Union troops straggled back into Washington, they "looked pretty well whipped." Bull Run, with 2,700 Union and 2,000 Confederate casualties, proved to Lincoln that the warring sections were in for a long-term struggle.

Planning the Union Offensive

Bull Run showed the deficiencies of both sides. Union troops had not been trained well enough to stand the heat of battle. The Confederates were so disorganized after sweeping their adversaries from the field that they could not take advantage of the rout and strike a mortal blow at Washington. Lincoln now realized, too, that he had to develop a comprehensive strategy—a detailed war plan—to break the Southern will of resistance. Also, he needed to find young, energetic generals who could organize Union forces and guide them to victory. Devising a war strategy proved to be much easier than locating military leaders with the capacity to execute those plans.

Civil War, 1861–1862

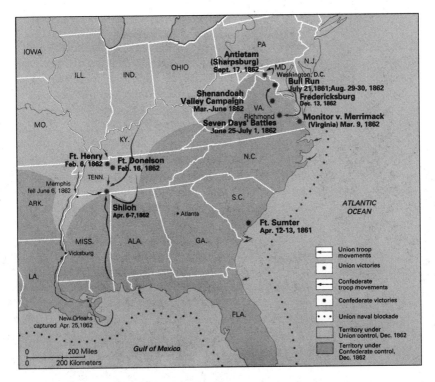

Well before Bull Run, Lincoln turned to Winfield Scott for an overall strategic design, and the general came up with the "Anaconda Plan"— which like the snake was intended to squeeze the resolve out of the Confederacy. The three essential coils included a full naval blockade of the South's coastline to cut off shipments of war goods and other supplies from Europe; a campaign to gain control of the Mississippi River, thereby splitting the Confederacy into two parts; and a placement of armies at key points to ensure that Southerners could not wiggle free.

Lincoln liked certain features of the strategic plan. He ordered the blockade, a seemingly impossible assignment, given a southern coastline stretching for 3,550 miles and containing 189 harbors and navigable rivers. In early 1861 the U.S. Navy had only 7,600 seamen and 90 warships, 21 of which were unusable. But with a burst of energy under Secretary Gideon Welles, the navy ultimately grew to 650 vessels and 100,000 sailors. Lincoln's "paper blockade," as detractors called it, became more effective with each passing month, and it also was a political success. Neutral powers generally respected the blockade, which seriously hampered Southern efforts to gain essential war matériel from abroad.

Lincoln also concluded that splitting the Confederacy was critical. He ordered Generals Henry W. Halleck, headquartered in St. Louis, and Don Carlos Buell, based in Louisville, to build great armies for the western theater. The president likewise worked with the Navy Department to devise the means to gain control of the Mississippi River. The latter effort resulted in the risky campaign of Captain David G. Farragut, whose fleet captured New Orleans on April 25, 1862. Farragut's triumph was a major first step in cutting the South apart and crippling dreams of independence.

The third aspect of the Anaconda Plan, Lincoln thought, was naive. Fort Sumter convinced him that the slaveholding elite had too strong a grip on the Southern populace to expect any significant rallying of pro-Unionists. Nor should armies sit on the sidelines or train endlessly and wait for a decisive battle. After Bull Run Lincoln got Congress to authorize the enlistment of 500,000 additional volunteer troops, far beyond the number recommended by Scott.

For a man with no formal training in military strategy, Lincoln was way ahead of the generals immediately surrounding him. As he explained to one of them, "we have the *greater* numbers," and if "superior forces" could strike "at *different* points at the *same* time," breakthroughs would occur. Lincoln's thinking pointed toward unrestrained total war, implying the complete destruction of the South, if need be, to save the Union. What the former militia captain needed were ranking officers of like mind. Lincoln hoped that he found such a person in George B. McClellan.

Yankee Reverses and Rebel Victories

George McClellan was a man of great bravado who had finished second in his West Point class and written a book on the art of war. Skilled at organizing and training troops, he was also an inspiring leader. With his usual brashness McClellan told Lincoln: "I can do it all." Unfortunately, the cocksure commander was incapable of using effectively what he had built.

Lincoln gave McClellan everything necessary to do the job. Not only did the president name him commander of the Army of the Potomac, which at peak strength numbered 150,000 troops, but he made him general-in-chief after Winfield Scott retired in the fall of 1861. The problem was McClellan's unwillingness to move his showcase force into combat. When Lincoln called for action, McClellan demanded more soldiers. The rebels, he claimed from spy reports, had 220,000 troops at Manassas Junction—the actual number was closer to 36,000. To counter this mythical force, McClellan wanted at least 273,000 men before entering the field. Lincoln, convinced that only crushing victories on several fronts could break the Confederate will, believed that McClellan had contracted a bad case of "the slows."

To give McClellan his due, his approach to the war was different from Lincoln's. He intended to maneuver his army but avoid large battles. He wanted to save soldiers' lives, not expend them, and he thought that he could threaten Southerners into submission by getting them to realize the futility of standing up to so superior a force—and so brilliant a general in command.

In March 1862, McClellan finally began the Peninsula campaign, transporting his army down through Chesapeake Bay to the peninsula formed by the York and James rivers, about 75 miles southeast of Richmond. In May his army moved forward at a snail's pace, which allowed the Confederates time to mass 70,000 troops before him. By the end of the month his advance units were approaching the outskirts of Richmond. Rebel forces under Joseph E. Johnston struck the main Union army near the Chickahominy River on May 31 and June 1. The Battle of Seven Pines cost a total of 10,000 casualties, among them a seriously wounded General Johnston.

Johnston's misfortune opened the way for Robert E. Lee to assume command of the Army of Northern Virginia. Lee called in "Stonewall" Jackson's corps from the Shenandoah Valley and went after the Union army aggressively. McClellan all but panicked. Insisting that his army now faced 200,000 rebels (the number was 90,000), he retreated after two inconclusive fights north of the Chickahominy. What ensued was the Battle of the Seven Days (June 25–July 1) in which combined casualties reached 30,000, two-thirds sustained by the Confederates. Still, Lee's offensive punches prevailed—and saved Richmond. McClellan soon boarded his troops on waiting transport ships and returned to Washington.

At first, Robert E. Lee was an adviser to Jefferson Davis. Then, on June 1, 1862, Davis appointed him to command the Confederate Army of Northern Virginia. After the war, Lee encouraged reconciliation between the North and South.

The aggressive Lee, meantime, sensed other opportunities. In defending Richmond the rebels had abandoned their advanced post at Manassas Junction. A Union force numbering 45,000 under General John Pope had moved into position there. Having just come in from the western theater, Pope was as blind to danger as McClellan was cautious. Lee, once sure of McClellan's decision to retreat, wheeled about and rushed northward toward Pope.

Dividing his force in half, Lee sent Jackson's corps in a wide, looping arc around Pope. On August 29 Jackson began a battle known as Second Bull Run (Second Manassas). When Pope turned to face Jackson, Lee hit him from the other side. The battle raged for another day and ended with Union troops again fleeing for Washington.

Lee led his victorious troops into Maryland in early September, toward another rendezvous with McClellan. The two armies met at Antietam on September 17, the bloodiest day of the war. Despite a numerical advantage, the Union army never got its punches coordinated, and could manage no better than a draw. Two days later Lee's army retreated back into Virginia.

Federal Breakthrough in the West

In the West the Union offensive fared much better. Brigadier General Ulysses S. Grant devised a plan to cut through the rebel defensive line, which was under the command of General Albert Sidney Johnston, thus opening states like Tennessee to full-scale invasion. In February 1862 Grant launched a successful land and river offensive against Forts Henry and Donelson, two rebel strongholds guarding the Tennessee and Cumberland rivers in northwestern Tennessee.

After breaking the Confederate line, Grant's army of 40,000 poured into Tennessee, following after Johnston, who retreated all the way to Corinth in northern Mississippi. Cautioned by General Halleck "to strike no blow until we are strong enough to admit no doubt of the result," Grant settled his army in at Pittsburg Landing, 25 miles north of Corinth along the Tennessee River—with advanced lines around a humble log church bearing the name Shiloh. There he waited for reinforcements. Flushed with confidence, Grant did not bother to order a careful posting of picket guards.

When Johnston received additional troops under General Beauregard, he decided to attack. At dawn on April 6, 40,000 rebels overran Grant's outer lines, and for two days the battle raged before the Federals drove off the Confederates. The Battle of Shiloh (Pittsburg Landing) resulted in 20,000 combined casualties. General Johnston died the first day from a severe leg wound, which cost the South a valued commander. Grant, so recently hailed as a war hero, now faced severe criticism for not having secured his lines. Some even claimed that he was drunk when the rebels first struck, undercutting—at least for the moment—thoughts of elevating him to higher command.

Ulysses S. Grant was criticized for his command tactics early in the war, but Lincoln remained supportive of him throughout. Grant later became the eighteenth president of the United States.

To and From Emancipation: The War on the Home Front

Keeping up morale—and the will to endure at all costs—was a major challenge for both sides, once citizens at home accepted the reality of a long and bloody conflict. Issues threatening to erode popular resolve were different in the North and the South. How civilian leaders handled these problems had a direct bearing on the outcome of the conflict; and Northern leaders, drawing on greater resources, proved more adept at finding solutions designed to keep up morale while breaking the Southern will to continue the war.

An Abundance of Confederate Shortages

With their society lacking an industrial base, Southern leaders understood the need for securing material aid from Europe, just as the American colonists had received foreign support to sustain their rebellion against Britain. Secessionists thought that Europe's dependence on cotton would assure them unofficial assistance, if not diplomatic recognition as an independent nation. "Cotton," predicted the *Charleston Mercury,* "would bring England to her knees." It did not. There was already a glut in the European marketplace, and textile manufacturers after 1861 turned to Egypt, India, and Brazil as sources for new supplies of cotton.

Despite concerted diplomatic efforts, Great Britain and other European nations officially ignored the Confederacy. What secessionists had not fully considered was that European countries were just as dependent on Northern grain crops to help feed their populace. In addition, nations like Britain, having long since abandoned slavery, had serious moral qualms about publicly recognizing a slave power.

The Confederacy, however, received small amounts of secret aid from Europe. By 1865 blockade runners brought an estimated 600,000 European-produced weapons into Southern ports, and in 1862 English shipyards built two commerce raiders, the *Florida* and *Alabama,* before protests from the Lincoln administration ended such activity. The Richmond government also received about $710 million in foreign loans, secured by promises to deliver cotton; but the tightening Union naval blockade made the exportation of cotton difficult, discouraging further European loans because of the mounting risk of never being paid back.

From the very outset Union naval superiority was a critical factor in isolating the South. The Confederacy simply lacked the funds to build a fleet of any consequence, which allowed the Union navy to dominate the sea lanes. The effects of cutting the South off from external support were profound. By the spring of 1862 citizens at home were experiencing many shortages—and getting mad about it. Such common items as salt, sugar, and coffee had all but disappeared, and shoes and clothing were at a premium. In 1863 bread riots broke out in several Southern cities, including Richmond. Shortages abetted rapid inflation, as did the overprinting of Confederate dollars. Between 1861 and 1865 prices spiraled upward on the average of 7,000 percent.

Most Southerners, in trying to comprehend so many difficulties, blamed their central government. When the Confederate Congress enacted a conscription act in 1862—the first draft law in U.S. history—because of rapidly declining enlistments, many Southerners accused their government of trampling on the principle of states' rights, the very issue that had caused them to secede. Moreover, the draft law allowed individuals to purchase substitutes, and, with rapid inflation, avoiding service became a wealthy man's prerogative. When the central government in October 1862 exempted from the draft all those managing 20 or more slaves, ordinary citizens started referring to the contest as "a rich man's war and a poor man's fight."

Directing the Northern War Effort

Although Abraham Lincoln focused most of his energies on military matters, he did not neglect other vital areas, including diplomatic relations and domestic legislation. His foreign policy was designed to keep European nations from supporting the Confederacy, and his domestic goal was to maintain high levels of popular support for the war effort. Lincoln was successful on both counts, but he took many risks, the most dramatic being his announcement of an emancipation proclamation.

Unlike Jefferson Davis, Lincoln delegated authority whenever he could. In foreign affairs he relied heavily on Secretary of State William Seward, whom European leaders came to regard as hotheaded but effective. There were some intense diplomatic moments, such as in November 1861 when the U.S. warship *San Jacinto* intercepted a British packet vessel, the *Trent*, and seized two Confederate envoys, James M. Mason and John Slidell, who were on their way to the courts of Europe. England vehemently protested such an overt violation of maritime law—stopping and searching neutral vessels on the high seas. Lincoln smoothed matters over by apologizing for the *Trent* affair and releasing the envoys from jail.

A few months later Seward received reports that English shipyards were completing two ironclad ram vessels for the Confederacy. This time the United States threatened serious repercussions, and British officials confiscated the ironclads, thus averting another crisis. With Europe maintaining a posture of neutrality the North could fully focus its energies on defeating the South.

Also helping the Yankee cause was wartime prosperity, which Lincoln and a Republican-dominated Congress tried to sustain. In 1862 Congress passed the Homestead Act, which granted 160 acres free to individuals who agreed to farm that land for at least five years; the Morrill Land Grant Act, which offered huge parcels of public land to states that established agricultural colleges; and the Pacific Railway Act, which laid the basis for constructing a transcontinental railroad after the war. Further, to protect the North's manufacturing interests from foreign competition, the Republican Congress approved tariff acts that raised import duties nearly 50 percent.

Under the watchful eye of Treasury Secretary Salmon P. Chase, the government likewise resorted to various expedients to finance the war effort. In 1861 Congress approved a modest income tax with rates that only fell on the wealthy. The government also taxed the states, borrowed heavily (around $2.2 billion), and issued "greenbacks," a currency that, like Confederate dollars, had no backing in gold or silver but held its value because of slowly growing confidence in the Union war effort.

Historians have debated whether the economic boom in the North generated by the Civil War sped up the process of industrialization in the United States. By some measures, such as the annual rate of economic growth during the 1860s, the war injured the economy, if destruction of property in the South is included. By the war's end in 1865 two-fifths of all Southern livestock had been killed; more than half of the Confederacy's farm machinery had been destroyed; and countless plantations and family farms had been ruined. In the North, by comparison, per capita commodity output rose by 56 percent during the decade of the 1860s, and the amount of working capital to underwrite business activity increased by 50 percent. Entrepreneurs, John D. Rockefeller and Andrew Carnegie among them, made monumental profits from war contracts. Their newfound capital base and methods of large-scale business organization certainly foreshadowed the rapid postwar transition to a full-scale industrial economy.

The intense level of governmental activity resulted in charges that Lincoln's true purpose was to become a dictator. These accusations started soon after Fort Sumter when the new president, acting by himself since Congress was not then in session, declared an insurrection and began a military buildup. Shortly thereafter, secessionist-minded Marylanders attacked Yankee troops moving through Baltimore. To quell such turbulence, Lincoln suspended the writ of habeas corpus in Maryland and ordered the arrest of leading advocates of secession.

In a federal circuit court case, *Ex Parte Merryman,* Supreme Court Chief Justice Roger B. Taney proclaimed Lincoln's action in Maryland illegal by arguing that only Congress had the authority to suspend writs of habeas corpus in times of rebellion. Lincoln ignored Taney's ruling, and John Merryman, one of those arrested, languished in a military prison with no set trial date on vague charges of having incited Marylanders to secede from the Union.

During the war Lincoln authorized the arrest of some 14,000 dissidents and had them jailed without any prospect for trials. He was careful, however, not to go after his political opponents, particularly leading members of the Democratic party. The president worked to have open and fair elections, operating on a distinction between legitimate dissent in support of the nation and willful attempts to subvert the Union. Most agree that Lincoln, given the tense wartime climate, showed sensitivity toward basic civil rights. At the same time he clearly tested the limits of presidential powers.

Issuing the Emancipation Proclamation

Abraham Lincoln believed fervently in the ideals of the Declaration of Independence, which gave Americans "the right to rise" out of poverty, as he described his own experience, and "get through the world respectably." Although he believed that chattel slavery was inconsistent with the ideals of the American Revolution, as president he had promised not to interfere with the institution in the Southern states. When the fighting commenced, he seemed to move with indecisive steps toward emancipation. His only war aim, he claimed well into the spring of 1862, was to save the Union. When in August 1861 General John C. Frémont, then heading federal military operations in Missouri, declared an end to slavery in that state, the president not only rescinded the proclamation but removed Frémont from command.

For a man who despised slavery, Lincoln held back in resolving the emancipation question for many reasons. First, he did not want to drive slaveholding border states like Missouri into the Confederacy. Second, he worried about pervasive racism; white Northerners had willingly taken up arms to save the Union, but he wondered whether they would keep fighting to liberate the black population. Third, if he moved too fast, he reasoned, he might lose everything, including the Union itself, should Northern peace advocates seize upon popular fears of emancipation and create an overwhelming demand to stop the fighting in favor of Southern independence. Fourth, he had personal doubts as to whether blacks and whites could ever live together harmoniously in freedom.

By the summer of 1862 Lincoln had finally made up his mind. The death toll, he now reasoned, had become too great; all the maiming and killing had to have some larger purpose, transcending the primary war aim of preserving the Union. For Lincoln the military contest had become a test to see whether the republic, at long last, had the capacity to live up to the ideals of the American Revolution, which could only be determined by announcing the Emancipation Proclamation.

Lincoln knew he was gambling with Northern morale at a time when Union victories were all but nonexistent, when enlistments were in decline, and when war weariness had set in. He was aware that racists would spread their poison far and wide. So the president waited for the right moment, such as after an important battlefield triumph, to quiet his critics who would surely say that emancipation was a desperate measure designed to cover up presidential mismanagement of the war.

As a shrewd politician, Lincoln began to prepare white Northerners for what was coming. He explained in late August: "If I could save the Union without freeing *any* slave, I would do it; and if I could save it by freeing *all* the slaves, I would do it; and if I could save it by freeing some and leaving others alone, I would also do that." Thus avoiding the pronouncement of high ideals in public, the president decided to treat his assault on slavery as a war measure designed to ensure total military victory.

On September 22, 1862, five days after the Battle of Antietam, Lincoln announced his preliminary Emancipation Proclamation, which called upon Southerners to lay down their arms and return to the Union by year's end or to accept the abolition of slavery. Getting no formal response, on January 1, 1863, he declared all slaves in the Confederacy "forever free," although slavery could continue to exist in the four Union border states—to assure a united front against the rebels.

Emancipation Tests Northern Resolve

In the Confederacy the planter elite played on traditional racist themes and used the proclamation to rally white citizens wavering in their resolve. Here was proof, shouted planter leaders, that every indignity the South had suffered was part of a never-ending abolitionist plot to stir up slave rebellions and "convert the quiet, ignorant black son of toil into a savage incendiary and brutal murderer."

Reaction to the proclamation in the North varied widely. With Democrats in Congress calling for Lincoln's impeachment, some cabinet members urged the president to reconsider. Republicans also feared repercussions in the upcoming November elections. They did lose seats, but they still controlled Congress, despite the efforts of many Democrats to smear "Black Republican" candidates. Certainly, too, frustration with so many battlefield reverses, as much as news of the proclamation, hurt Republican candidates at the polls.

On the other hand, many criticized Lincoln for not going far enough. Abolitionists chided him for failing to eradicate slavery in all the states. Foreign opinion generally applauded Lincoln, although a few commentators made caustic remarks about a curious new "principle" that no American would henceforth be allowed to own slaves "unless he is loyal to the United States."

Northern blacks, however, were jubilant. Frederick Douglass stated: "We shout for joy that we live to record this righteous decree." Up until this point blacks had found the war frustrating. Federal officials had blocked their attempts to enlist. Not wanting to stir up racial violence, Lincoln had danced around the issue. Most early black enlistments were in the navy. Finally in 1862 Secretary of War Edwin M. Stanton, with the president's backing, called for the enlistment of blacks—North and South. In a model program, Colonel Thomas W. Higginson, a radical abolitionist, worked with former slaves in the Sea Island region of South Carolina, an area under Union control, to mold them into a well-trained regiment. Higginson's troops fought effectively, demonstrating that blacks could master the art of war.

No regiment proved that more dramatically than the 54th Massachusetts Infantry. Like all other black regiments, the 54th trained separately from white units and received its commands from white officers. On July 18, 1863, the 54th, Massachusetts led by Robert Gould Shaw, the 25-year-old scion of a prominent antislavery family, launched an early evening assault against Fort Wagner, a major bastion protecting Charleston harbor for the Confederacy. Eventually repulsed after fierce fighting, the 54th experienced more than a 40 percent casualty rate. Shaw, who was shot dead in the charge, became a martyred war hero in the North.

Before the war ended, 179,000 blacks, most of them former slaves, served in the Union army, and another 29,000 were in the navy. Some 44,000 died fighting to save the Union and to defend the prize of freedom for African Americans. Twenty-four blacks received the Congressional Medal of Honor for extraordinary bravery in battle. Among them was Sergeant William H. Carney of the 54th Massachusetts, whose citation praised him for grabbing the regimental flag after its bearer was shot down and leading the troops forward into the outer works of Fort Wagner. Carney, a runaway slave from Virginia, then planted the flag and engaged in hand-to-hand combat. Severely wounded, he reluctantly retreated with flag in hand, not suspecting that he would become the first black Medal of Honor recipient in the Civil War—and American history.

Despite the Emancipation Proclamation, African Americans received lower military pay until protests ended such discrimination in 1864; and they quite often drew menial work assignments, such as digging latrines and burying the dead after battle. Emancipation, blacks soon realized, was just the beginning of an awesome struggle that lay ahead—beyond the Civil War—to overcome the prejudice and hatred that had locked them in slavery for over two centuries.

Breaking Confederate Resistance, 1863–1865

During the spring of 1863 Union war sentiment sagged to a new low point. Generals kept demanding more troops; yet with the exception of black enlistees, there were few new volunteers. Congress faced up to reality in March and passed a Conscription Act, which provided for the drafting of males between the ages of 20 and 45. Draftees could buy exemptions for $300—an average wage for half a year—or hire substitutes. All told, federal conscription produced 166,000 soldiers, roughly three-fourths of whom were substitutes.

Conscription infuriated many Northerners, particularly day laborers who lacked the income to buy their way out of the service. Riots took place in several cities, and the worst were in New York where Irish workers, sensing a plot to force them into the Union army so that newly freed slaves would get their jobs, vented their rage in mid-July 1863. The rampaging started when workers assaulted a building in which a draft lottery was taking place. For a week the streets were not safe, particularly for blacks, who in a few cases were beaten to death or hanged by roaming mobs. Only the intervention of federal troops ended the New York draft riots, but not before 100 or more persons had died.

The Tide Turns: Gettysburg and Vicksburg

After the Battle of Antietam, Lincoln had had enough of McClellan's cautious tactics. He named Ambrose E. Burnside to head the eastern army. Burnside did not have "the slows." He rushed his troops south and, on December 13, 1862, foolishly engaged Lee in a frontal assault at Fredericksburg, Virginia. His force outnumbered Lee's by a ratio of three to two; but Burnside's casualties that day were nearly 11,000, as compared to under 5,000 for the Army of Northern Virginia.

Shattered by the defeat, Burnside offered strong hints to Lincoln about finding a replacement. Lincoln accommodated him and elevated "Fighting Joe" Hooker, whose ambitions to command the Army of the Potomac were well known. Moving south in late April 1863, Hooker got 75,000 troops across the Rappahannock River and quickly squared off with Lee's Confederates in early May in what became a bloody brawl known as the Battle of Chancellorsville. The intense action resulted in a combined casualty count of 21,000 before Hooker pulled back across the

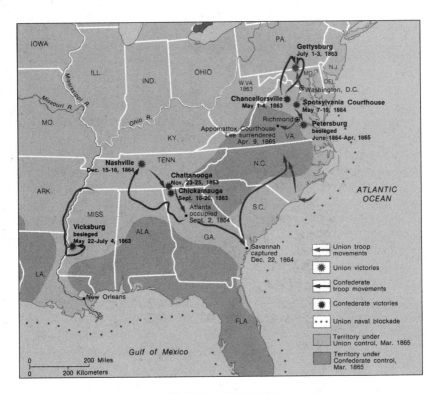

Civil War, 1863–1865

Rappahannock on the evening of May 5. "Stonewall" Jackson, shot accidentally by his own pickets during the engagement, died a few days later, costing General Lee and the South an authentic military genius. As for Hooker, the embarrassment of Chancellorsville soon brought to an end his command of the Army of the Potomac.

At this juncture, Lee asked Jefferson Davis for permission to lead his troops northward into Pennsylvania. There they could disrupt rail traffic, live off the land, and, most important, try to win a battle so overwhelming that Lincoln would be forced to consider peace terms favorable to the Confederacy. During June, Lee executed his plan. Late in the month Lincoln asked George G. Meade, a lackluster but competent general, to assume command of the Army of the Potomac, and on July 1, 1863, the two armies squared off against each other just west of a small Pennsylvania town called Gettysburg.

The Battle of Gettysburg, lasting three days, was the bloodiest engagement of the war, with combined casualties of more than 50,000. On the third day, hoping that he could split and rout his adversary, Lee massed soldiers under General George E. Pickett for an assault on the center of the Union line. Some 13,000 rebels charged across a mile of open, gradually rising fields, but were thrown back with 7,000 casualties. Late the next day Lee retreated, his army battered but not yet broken. Nonetheless, Gettysburg was a decisive battle. Never again would Lee have the troop strength to carry the war into enemy territory.

Meanwhile, in the western theater, the South suffered another major setback. After repeated attempts to seize Vicksburg, the Confederacy's last major stronghold on the Mississippi, from the north, General Grant had moved 75,000 troops south through eastern Arkansas into Louisiana, then swept east across the Mississippi River and slowly turned west in a wide arc, securing his lines against rebel marauders along the way. By late May, Grant had Vicksburg under siege, and his artillery bombarded that city and its defenders for six weeks. Reduced to living in caves and eating rats, Confederate troops and local citizens held on valiantly until they could take no more. On July 4, 1863, the day after Pickett's Charge, Grant accepted Vicksburg's surrender. Union forces had finally severed the Confederacy.

With these triumphs the war had turned against the South. Still, the combat was far from over, as Lincoln knew only too well as he rode a train to Gettysburg to dedicate a national memorial cemetery before a large crowd in November 1863. At Gettysburg he urged all citizens to "resolve that these dead shall not have died in vain;. . . and that government of the people, by the people, for the people, shall not perish from the earth."

Crushing Blows from Grant and Sherman

Vicksburg revived Grant's tarnished reputation, and after Union forces suffered an embarrassing defeat at the Battle of Chickamauga in northwestern Georgia on September 19–20, 1863, Lincoln named him overall commander of western forces. Grant quickly restored federal fortunes in the campaign to capture Chattanooga, Tennessee (November 1863). Now it was possible to plunge an army into Georgia to cut away at the heart of the Confederacy.

Early in 1864 Lincoln decided to name Grant general-in-chief. Vowing to end the war in a year, Grant planned to pursue the enemy deep inside the Confederacy, destroying all property that could be used to support the rebel armies. The general-in-chief called upon his old ally, General William Tecumseh Sherman, now commanding western forces, to march to Atlanta and destroy key Southern railheads there. As Sherman proceeded, he was to challenge the Confederate Army of Tennessee under General Joseph E. Johnston, now recovered from wounds suffered in defending Richmond back in the spring of 1862.

Grant and Sherman began operations in May 1864. Grant moved south across the Rappahannock River and engaged Lee in the Battle of the Wilderness (May 5–6). Union forces took a beating, but instead of retreating they rolled southeastward in what became the month-long campaign for Virginia. Again and again Johnny Rebs and Billy Yanks clashed at such places as Spotsylvania Court House (May 7–19) and Cold Harbor (June 1–3), within a few miles of Richmond. Finally, the two exhausted armies settled along siege lines at Petersburg, 20 miles southeast of the Confederate capital, with Grant waiting for Lee's army to disintegrate.

There had been nothing quite like the Virginia campaign before. Grant started with 120,000 soldiers, and half of them were casualties by early June. By the time Lee reached the Petersburg trenches in mid-June, his army had been reduced by more than a third to 40,000.

In the North, Peace Democrats called Grant a "butcher," but the general-in-chief, with Lincoln's backing, held tight to the war plan. Winning was now only a matter of time since the president, as the manager of the Union's superior resources, could supply more troops. The South, however, had no manpower left to give. Of an estimated 1.2 million white males between the ages of 16 and 50, some 90 percent had already seen Confederate military service; the comparable figure for the North was 40 percent.

In late 1864 Jefferson Davis admitted the South's need for new manpower when he called for the conscription of slaves. The Richmond government in March 1865 mandated the enlistment of 300,000 slaves; but by that time it was too late for Southerners "to gain our independence," as a Georgian noted with irony, "by the valor of our slaves." The war was over before black regiments could be organized.

If the Confederacy had any hope for survival in the fall of 1864, it centered on the upcoming presidential election. The Republicans, calling themselves the National Union party, renominated Lincoln in June with a new vice-presidential running mate, Andrew Johnson, a Democrat who had served as Tennessee's Union war governor after Grant's invasion of that state in early 1862. The Democrats nominated General George B. McClellan, running on a platform promising a negotiated end to the war, even if that meant independence for the Confederacy—a position McClellan himself thought too extreme to support. A despairing Lincoln, looking at the horrible casualty figures in Virginia, feared repudiation at the polls by a populace too sickened by the carnage to let him finish the fight.

Lincoln's pessimism proved groundless. He had not counted on General Sherman, moving slowly toward Atlanta in the face of stout rebel resistance. News of the capture of this major Confederate railroad and manufacturing center thrilled Northerners. The South was obviously in serious trouble. Voters gave Lincoln a resounding victory. On November 8, 1864, he received 55 percent of the popular vote and 212 electoral college votes, as compared to just 21 for McClellan.

Total War Forces Surrender

In the eighteenth century warfare rarely affected the whole populace. Armies were small, and combat could be conducted in war zones away from population centers. By comparison, the Civil War touched nearly every American life. Families gave fathers and sons to the armed services; and women assumed the management of farms or moved to the cities and took jobs to keep factories going in the production of war goods. Hundreds of women on both sides became nurses, and they fought to save thousands of lives. Dorothea Dix, superintendent of Union army nurses, and Clara Barton, who later founded the American Red Cross (1881), endured incredible personal privation to comfort those in pain. For the Confederacy, Sally L. Tompkins ran a clean, well-managed hospital in Richmond, Virginia.

In forcing an end to all the suffering and killing, General Sherman, after taking Atlanta, proposed to march his troops eastward to Savannah, Georgia, then north toward Grant's army in Virginia. Before year's end his soldiers cut a swath through Georgia 60 miles wide, and then in January 1865 they entered South Carolina, which they thought of as "the birth place of Dark Treason" against the Union. In systematic fashion Sherman's army broke the Southern capacity to keep fighting by burning and leveling everything in sight.

As word of Sherman's devastating march reached Lee's troops in the Petersburg trenches, they deserted in droves, wanting to get back home to protect their loved ones. By late March Lee's army had fewer than 35,000 troops, compared to Grant's total of 115,000. The situation was all but hopeless, so the Confederate commander ordered a retreat to the west. Grant's soldiers moved quickly to encircle the disintegrating rebel army, and on April 9, 1865, Lee met with Grant and surrendered at Appomattox. Grant graciously allowed the Confederates to keep their horses—they had to give up their arms—so that they could more easily plow their fields and plant crops after returning home. Lee's surrender served as a signal to other Confederate commanders to lay down their arms. The Civil War, at long last, had ended.

Conclusion

At noon on Good Friday, April 14, 1865, a crowd gathered to watch Major General Robert Anderson raise over Fort Sumter the very same U.S. flag that he had surrendered four years before. A genuinely moved Anderson said: "I thank God that I have lived to see this day." Then he hoisted up the "weather-beaten, frayed, and shell-torn old flag" as Union

Chronology of Key Events

1860   Abraham Lincoln elected sixteenth president; Crittenden Compromise fails; South Carolina secedes

1861   Six Deep-South States secede; Confederate States of America formed; Fort Sumter falls to Confederates; South wins First Battle of Bull Run (First Manassas)

1862   Union victory at Battle of Shiloh; Confederacy adopts a draft law; Homestead Act; Morrill Act; South wins Battle of the Seven Days and Second Battle of Bull Run (Second Manassas); Union victory at Battle of Antietam (Sharpsburg); Lincoln issues preliminary Emancipation Proclamation; Battle of Fredericksburg results in Southern victory

1863   Lincoln suspends habeas corpus for draft resisters; Battle of Gettysburg; siege of Vicksburg ends with Union victory; New York City draft riots occur

1864   Virginia campaign; siege of Petersburg begins; Sherman marches through Georgia

1865   Lee surrenders at Appomattox; John Wilkes Booth assassinates Lincoln; Andrew Johnson becomes seventeenth president

naval vessels out in Charleston harbor fired their cannons in salute. Citizens at the fort wept and cheered, realizing that the national tragedy was finally over, a tragedy that had forever sealed the fate of secession. The states, while far from reunited, would continue together as a nation.

Just a few hours later another shot rang out, this time in the nation's capital. John Wilkes Booth, a Confederate sympathizer and racist fanatic, gained access to the presidential box at Ford's Theater and assassinated the president at point-blank range. The next morning, four years to the day after he had declared an insurrection and called up federal troops, Lincoln died at the age of 56.

In his last days Lincoln felt the elation of knowing that a war begun to preserve the Union had achieved its objective. He took pride in the elimination of slavery from the American landscape, which he called the "act" that would put "my name . . . into history." Lincoln had also started to speak openly of citizenship for blacks as part of his reconstruction plans. Even as the American people mourned his passing, they too turned to the difficult task of how best to bring the South—defeated, destroyed, but still with a resolute streak of defiance—back into the nation.

Suggestions for Further Reading

Three valuable surveys of the Civil War are Shelby Foote, *The Civil War,* 3 vols. (1958–1974); James M. McPherson, *Battle Cry of Freedom* (1988); Allan Nevins, *The War for the Union,* 4 vols. (1959–1971).

Specialized military studies of the Civil War include Michael C. C. Adams, *Our Masters the Rebels* (1978); Joseph T. Glatthaar, *Partners in Command: Relationships Between Leaders in the Civil War* (1993); Paddy Griffith, *Battle Tactics of the Civil War* (1989); Gerald F. Linderman, *Embattled Courage: Combat in the American Civil War* (1987); Charles Royster, *The Destructive War: Sherman, Jackson, and the Americans* (1991); Steven E. Woodworth, *Jefferson Davis and His Generals: The Failure of Confederate Command in the West* (1990). The lives of common soldiers are the focus of Bell I. Wiley, *The Life of Johnny Reb* (1943), and *The Life of Billy Yank* (1952). On the role of African Americans during the war consult Joseph T. Glatthaar, *Forged in Battle: The Civil War Alliance of Black Soldiers and White Officers* (1990).

On the politics of the war effort, see LaWanda Cox, *Lincoln and Black Freedom* (1981); Paul D. Escott, *After Secession: Jefferson Davis* (1978); Eric Foner, *Politics and Ideology in the Age of the Civil War* (1980); Mark E. Neely, Jr., *The Fate of Liberty: Abraham Lincoln and Civil Liberties* (1991).

On the home front and American society during the conflict see Iver Bernstein, *The New York City Draft Riots* (1990); Randall C. Jimerson, *The Private Civil War: Popular Thought During the Sectional Conflict* (1988); Phillip Shaw Paludan, *"A People's Contest"* (1988); George C. Rable, *Civil Wars: Women and the Crisis of Southern Nationalism* (1989).

Valuable biographies of the period include Douglas S. Freeman, *R. E. Lee: A Biography,* 4 vols. (1934–1935); William S. McFeely, *Grant: A Biography* (1981); Stephen W. Sears, *George B. McClellan* (1988).

Chapter 16

The Nation Reconstructed: North, South, and the West, 1865–1877

A s Thomas Pinckney approached El Dorado, his plantation in South Carolina, he felt a quiver of apprehension. Pinckney, a captain in the defeated Confederate army, had stayed the night with neighbors before going to reclaim his land. "Your negroes sacked your house," they reported. "They got it in their heads that the property of whites belongs to them." Pinckney remembered the days when he had been met with cheerful greetings from his slaves; now he was welcomed with an eerie silence. In the house, a single servant seemed genuinely glad to see him, but she pleaded ignorance as to the whereabouts of the other freed persons. He lingered about the house until after the dinner hour. Still no one appeared, so he informed the servant that he would return in the morning.

The next day Pinckney returned and summoned his former slaves. Their sullen faces reflected their defiant spirits. Pinckney told them, "I do not wish to interfere with your freedom. But I want my old hands to work my lands for me. I will pay wages." The freed persons remained silent as he gave further reassurances. Finally one responded. They would never again work for a white man, he told his former master. Pinckney seemed confused and asked how they expected to support themselves and where they would go. They quickly informed him that they intended to stay and work the land themselves.

Pinckney had no intention of allowing his former slaves to lay claim to his property. He joined with his neighbors in an appeal to the Union commander at Charleston, who sent a company of troops. The freed persons still refused to work under his terms, so Pinckney denied them access to food and supplies. Soon his head plowman begged food for his hungry family, claiming he wanted to work. Slowly, other former slaves drifted back. "They had suffered," he later recalled, "and their ex-master had suffered with them."

All over the South this scenario was acted out with variations, as former masters and slaves sought to define their new relationships. Whites tried to keep the freed persons a dependent labor source; African Americans struggled to win as much independence as possible. At the same time the other sections of the nation faced similar problems of determining the status of heterogeneous populations whose interests were sometimes in conflict with the majority. The war had reaped a costly harvest in lives and property, but at the same time it accelerated the modernization of the economy and society. Western expansion forced Americans to deal with the often hostile presence of the Plains Indians; the resumption of large-scale immigration raised issues of how to adapt to a society made up of many different ethnic and religious groups. Complicating these issues were unresolved questions about federal authority, widespread racial prejudice in both North and South, and strongly held beliefs in the sanctity of property rights.

Reconstruction offered an opportunity to balance conflicting interests with justice and fairness. In the end, however, the government was unwilling to establish ongoing programs and permanent mechanisms to protect the rights of minorities. As on Pinckney's plantation, economic power usually became the determining factor in establishing relationships. Authorities sacrificed the interests of both African Americans and the Indians of the West to the goals of national unity and economic growth. Yet in the ashes of failure were left two cornerstones on which the future could be built—the Fourteenth and Fifteenth Amendments to the Constitution.

Postwar Conditions and Issues

The war had exacted a heavy price on Americans, but its costs were not borne equally. Many segments of the Northern economy were stimulated by wartime demands and had benefited from federal programs enacted to aid industrial growth. Virtually exempt from the devastation of the battlefield, the North built railroads and industries and increased agricultural production. At the same time torn-up Southern rails were twisted around trees, Southern factories were put to the torch, and Southern farmland lay choked with weeds.

In 1865 Southerners were still reeling from the bitter legacy of total war. General Philip Sheridan announced that after his troops had finished in the Shenandoah Valley even a crow would have to carry rations to fly over the area. One year after the war Carl Schurz noted that along the path of Sherman's march the countryside still "looked for many miles like a broad black streak of ruin and desolation." Southern cities suffered the most. Much of what was not destroyed was confiscated, and emancipation divested Southerners of another $2 billion to $4 billion in assets. The decline of Southern wealth has been estimated at more than 40 percent during the four years of war.

The War's Impact on Individuals

Returning soldiers and their wives had to reconstruct relationships disrupted by separation—and the assumption of control by the women on farms and plantations. Southerners worried about how to meet their obligations, since Confederate currency and bonds were now worthless. Many white Southerners also feared that the end of slavery would bring a night-mare of black revenge, rape, and pillage unless whites retained social control.

For four million former slaves, emancipation had come piecemeal, following the course of the Northern armies. It was not finalized until the ratification of the Thirteenth Amendment in December 1865. By then most border states had voluntarily adopted emancipation, but the amendment destroyed the remnants of slavery in Delaware and Kentucky. Most slaves waited patiently for the day of freedom, continuing to work the plantations but speaking up more boldly. Sometimes the Yankees came, proclaimed them free, and then left them to the mercy of their masters. Most, therefore, reacted cautiously in testing the limits of their new freedom.

Many African Americans had to leave their plantations, at least for a short time, to feel liberated. A few were not sure about the meaning of freedom and thought they would never have to work again. Soon, most learned they had gained everything—and nothing. As Frederick Douglass noted, the freed person "was free from the individual master but a slave of society. He had neither money, property, nor friends. He was free from the old plantation, but he had nothing but the dusty road under his feet. . . . He was turned loose, naked, hungry, and destitute to the open sky."

The wartime plight of homeless and hungry blacks as well as whites impelled Congress to take unprecedented action, establishing on March 3, 1865, the Freedmen's Bureau within the War Department. The bureau was to provide "such issues of provisions, clothing, and fuel" as were needed to relieve "destitute and suffering refugees and their wives and children." Never before had the national government assumed responsibility for relief. Feeding and clothing the population had not been deemed its proper function. Considered a drastic measure warranted only by civil war, the bureau was to operate for only a year.

The bureau was more than a relief agency. It had its own courts to deal with land and labor disputes. Agents in every state provided rations and medical supplies and helped to negotiate labor contracts between former slaves and landowners. The quality of the service rendered to the freed persons depended on the ability and motivation of the individual agents. Some courageously championed the freed persons' cause; others sided with the former masters. One of the most lasting benefits of the Freedmen's Bureau was the schools it established, frequently in cooperation with such Northern agencies as the American Missionary Association. During and after the war, African Americans of all ages flocked to these schools. The freed persons shrewdly recognized the keys to the planters' power—land, literacy, and the vote. The white South legally denied all three to African Amerians in slavery, and many former slaves were determined to have them all.

During the war General Sherman had been plagued with swarms of freed persons following his army, and in January 1865 he issued an order setting aside a strip of abandoned coastal lands from Charleston, South Carolina, to Jacksonville, Florida, for the exclusive use of freed blacks who were to be given title to 40-acre lots. Three months later the bill establishing the Freedmen's Bureau gave the agency control of thousands of acres of abandoned and confiscated lands to be rented to former slaves for three-year periods with an option to buy at a later date. By June 1865, 40,000 African Americans were cultivating land. In the Sea Islands and elsewhere they proved they could succeed as independent farmers. Yet land reform was not a popular cause among whites. Although a few congressmen continued to advocate land confiscation and redistribution, most freed persons never realized the dream of "forty acres and a mule."

Unresolved Issues

At war's end many questions remained unanswered. The first of these concerned the status of the former slaves. They were indeed free, but were

Former slaves realized that education was one key to real freedom and flocked to schools opened by the Freedmen's Bureau, the American Missionary Association, and various religious and human rights groups.

they citizens? The Dred Scott decision had denied citizenship to all African Americans. Even if it were decided that they were citizens, what rights were conferred by that citizenship? Would they be segregated as free blacks in the antebellum North had often been? Also, citizenship did not automatically convey suffrage rights; women were proof of that. Were the freed persons to be given the ballot? Racial prejudice as well as constitutional and partisan questions complicated these weighty matters.

The Constitution had been severely tested by civil war, and many felt it had been twisted by the desire to save the Union. Once the emergency was over, how were constitutional balance and limits to be restored? Except during the terms of a few strong presidents, Congress had been the most powerful branch of government during the nation's first 70 years. Lincoln had assumed unprecedented powers, and Congress was determined to regain its ascendency. The ensuing battle directly influenced Reconstruction policies and their implementation.

Secession was dead, but what about states' rights? Almost everyone agreed that a division of power between the national and state governments was crucial to the maintenance of freedom. The fear of centralized tyranny remained strong. There was reluctance to enlarge federal power into areas traditionally controlled by the states, even though action in some of those areas was essential to craft the kind of peace many desired. Hesitation to reduce states' rights produced timid and compromised solutions to such issues as suffrage. Also of concern was federal action in the realm of social welfare, a new and controversial role for the national government.

Another constitutional question concerned the status of the former Confederate states and how they were to be readmitted to the Union. There was no constitutional provision for failed secession, and many people debated whether the South had actually left the Union. Southerners and their Democratic party sympathizers now argued that the states had never legally separated from the rest of the nation, thus denying validity to the Confederacy in order to quickly regain their place in the Union. Extremists on the other side—Radical Republicans—insisted that the South had reverted to the status of conquered territory, forfeiting all rights as states. Lincoln and others believed that the Confederate states had remained in the Union but had forfeited their rights. This constitutional hairsplitting grew out of a struggle between the executive and legislative branches to determine which had the power to readmit the states and on what terms. It also reflected the hostility of some Northerners toward the "traitorous rebels" and the unwillingness of some Southerners to accept the consequences of defeat.

Affecting all these questions was partisan politics. The Republican party had very few adherents in the South. Its continued existence was dubious in the face of the probable reunion of the Northern and Southern wings of the Democratic party. Paradoxically, the political power of the

South, and in turn the Democratic party, was increased by the abolition of slavery. As freed persons, all African Americans would be counted for representation; as slaves only three-fifths of them had been counted. Thus the Republican party's perceived need to make itself a national party also influenced the course of Reconstruction.

Presidential Reconstruction

Early in the conflict questions regarding the reconstruction of the nation were secondary to winning the war—without victory there would be no nation to reconstruct. Nonetheless, Lincoln had to take some action as Union forces pushed into the South. Authority had to be imposed in the reclaimed territory, so the president named military governors for Tennessee, Arkansas, and Louisiana in 1862 after federal armies occupied most of those states. Lincoln also began formulating plans for civilian governments for those states and for other Confederate areas once they came under the control of Union forces.

Lincoln's Plan

Called the 10 percent plan, Lincoln's provisions were incredibly lenient. Rebels could receive presidential pardon by merely swearing their future allegiance to the Union and their acceptance of the end of slavery. Only a few people were excluded from pardons: Confederate military and civilian officers; United States judges, congressmen, and military officers who had resigned their posts to serve the Confederacy. Nevertheless, Lincoln did not require the new state governments to bar such people from future voting or officeholding. Moreover, after only 10 percent of the number who had voted in 1860 had taken the oath of allegiance, a state could form a civilian government. When such states produced a constitution outlawing slavery, Lincoln promised to recognize them as reconstructed. He did not demand any provisions for protecting black rights or allowing black suffrage.

The president's generosity outraged Radical Republicans, such as Representative Thaddeus Stevens of Pennsylvania and Senator Charles Sumner of Massachusetts. They thought the provisions did not adequately punish Confederate treason, restructure Southern society, protect the rights of African Americans, or aid the Republican party. The Radicals were in a minority, but Lincoln's leniency also dismayed many moderate Republicans. They shared the Radical view that Reconstruction was a congressional, not a presidential, function.

Congress then drew up a plan of its own: the Wade-Davis Bill. Its terms were much more stringent, yet not unreasonable. A majority, rather than 10 percent, of each state's voters had to declare their allegiance to form a government. Only those taking "ironclad" oaths of their past Union loyalty were allowed to participate in the making of new state constitutions. Barely a handful of high-ranking Confederates, however, were to be permanently barred from political participation. The only additional requirement imposed by Congress was the repudiation of the Confederate debt; Northerners did not want Confederate bondholders to benefit from their "investment in treason" at the cost to northern taxpayers. Congress would determine when a state had met these requirements.

A constitutional collision was postponed by Lincoln's pocket veto of the bill and his assassination on April 14, 1865. His successor, Andrew Johnson, was a Tennessee Democrat and Unionist. Of humble origins and illiterate until adulthood, he was the only Southerner to remain in the Senate after his state seceded. As with the Radical wing of the Republican party Johnson hated the planter class, but it was their aristocratic domination of the South, not their slaveholding, that he disliked. He was a firm believer in black inferiority and did not support the Radical aim of black legal equality. He also advocated strict adherence to the Constitution and strongly supported states' rights.

Johnson's Plan

In the end Johnson did not reverse Lincoln's lenient policy. Congress was not in session when Johnson became president so he had about eight months to pursue policies without congressional interference. He issued his own proclamation of amnesty in May 1865 and issued about 13,000 pardons. The most important aspect of the pardons was Johnson's claim that they restored all rights, including property rights. Thus many freed persons with crops in the ground suddenly found their masters back in charge—a disillusioning first taste of freedom that foreclosed further attempts at widespread land redistribution.

Johnson also announced plans for the reconstruction of North Carolina—a plan that was to set the pattern for all Southern states. A native Unionist was named provisional governor with the power to call a constitutional convention elected by loyal voters. Omitting Lincoln's 10 percent provision, Johnson did eventually require ratification of the Thirteenth Amendment, repudiation of Confederate debts, and state constitutional provisions abolishing slavery and renouncing secession. He also recommended limited suffrage for African Americans, primarily to stave off congressional attempts to give the vote to all black males.

The presidential plan fell short of the Radicals' hopes, but many moderates might have accepted it had the South complied with the letter

Andrew Johnson was the only president of the United States to be impeached. His successful defense centered on the legitimate uses of his executive powers.

and the spirit of Johnson's proposals. Instead, Southerners seemed determined to ignore their defeat. The state governments, for the most part, met the minimum requirements, but their apparent acceptance grew out of a belief that very little had actually changed. Thus Southerners proceeded to show almost total disregard for Northern sensibilities. Presenting themselves, like prodigal sons, for admission to Congress were four Confederate generals, six Confederate cabinet officials, and as the crowning indignity, Confederate Vice President Alexander H. Stephens. Most Northerners were not exceedingly vindictive. Still, the North wanted signs of change and indications of repentence by the former rebels.

Black Codes in the South

At the very least, Northerners expected adherence to the abolition of slavery, but the South was blatantly forging new forms of bondage. African Americans were to be technically free, but Southern whites expected them to work and live as they had before emancipation. To accomplish this purpose, the new state governments enacted a series of laws known as the Black Codes. This legislation granted certain rights denied to slaves. Freed persons had the right to marry, own property, sue and be sued, and testify in court. However, Black Codes in all states prohibited racial inter-marriage, and some forbade freed persons from owning certain types of property, such as alcoholic beverages and firearms. Most so tightly re-stricted black legal rights that they were practically nonexistent. Black Codes imposed curfews on African Americans, segregated them, and out-lawed their right to congregate in large groups.

The Black Codes also sought to fashion a labor system as close to slavery as possible. Some laws required that African Americans obtain spe-cial licenses for any job except agricultural labor or domestic service. Most mandated the signing of yearly labor contracts, which sometimes required African Americans to call the landowner "master" and allowed withhold-ing wages for minor infractions. Mississippi even prohibited black owner-ship or rental of land. Mandatory apprenticeship programs took children away from their parents, and vagrancy laws allowed authorities to arrest blacks and use them on chain gangs or rent them out to planters for as long as a year at a time.

Most Northerners would not have insisted on black equality or suf-frage, but the South had regressed too far. Some Black Codes were virtually identical to the old slave codes, with the word *negro* substituted for *slave.* At the same time, reports of white violence against blacks filtered back to Washington. As a result, Congress refused to seat the representatives and senators from the former Confederate states when it reconvened in De-cember 1865 and instead proceeded to investigate conditions in the South.

Congressional Reconstruction

To discover what was really happening in the South, Congress established the Joint Committee on Reconstruction, which conducted inquiries and interviews that provided graphic and chilling examples of white repres-sion and brutality toward African Americans. Prior to the committee's final report, even moderates came to believe that action was necessary. In early 1866 Congress passed a bill to extend the life of the Freedmen's Bu-reau, but Johnson vetoed it, claiming that the bureau was constitutional only as a wartime measure. Congress then passed the Civil Rights Act, granting citizenship to all persons born in the United States. Once again, Johnson used his veto power to kill a bill that he deemed both unconsti-tutional and unwise. This time, however, Congress overrode the veto. It then passed a slightly revised Freedmen's Bureau bill in July and enacted it over Johnson's veto. Even though the South had ignored much of Johnson's advice, such as granting limited suffrage to blacks, the president stubbornly held to his conviction that reconstruction was complete and labeled his congressional opponents as "traitors."

Johnson's language did not create a climate of cooperation. Congress did not care about the constitutional questions that he raised and his challenge to congressional authority. Determined to establish an alternate program of reconstruction, Congress drafted the Fourteenth Amendment. Undoubtedly the most significant legacy of Reconstruction, the first article of the amendment defined citizenship and its basic rights. Every person born in the United States and subject to its jurisdiction was declared a citizen. The amendment also forbade any state from abridging the rights of citizenship or from depriving any person of "due process of law." Although 100 years would pass before its provisions were enforced as intended, the amendment has been interpreted to mean that states as well as the federal government are bound by the Bill of Rights—an important constitutional change that paved the way for the civil rights decisions and laws of the twentieth century.

The amendment did not require black suffrage but reduced the "basis of representation" proportionately for those states not allowing it. Former Confederate leaders were also barred from holding office unless pardoned by Congress—not the president. Finally, neither Confederate war debts nor compensation to former slaveholders were ever to be paid. Congress adopted the amendment, in June 1866 and then sent it to the states for ratification.

President Johnson bristled at this assault on his perceived powers and urged the Southern states not to ratify the amendment. All but Tennessee decided to take his advice and wait for further congressional action. Johnson took to the campaign trail, urging voters to oust the Radicals in the 1866 congressional elections. He met with heckling and humiliation during his "swing around the circle." The campaign was vicious, characterized by appeals to racial prejudice by the Democrats and charges of Democratic treason by the Republicans. The Republicans won overwhelming victories, which they interpreted as a mandate for congressional reconstruction.

"Radical" Reconstruction

The election results along with Southern intransigence finally gave the Radicals the upper hand. In 1867 Congress passed the Military Reconstruction Act that raised the price of readmission. This act declared all existing "Johnson governments," except Tennessee's, void and divided the

South into five military districts headed by military governors who were to be granted broad powers. Following the ratification of a new state constitution that provided for black suffrage, elections were to be held and the state would be required to ratify the Fourteenth Amendment. When that amendment became part of the Constitution and Congress approved the new state constitutions, the states would be granted representation in Congress once again.

Obviously, Johnson disliked the congressional plan; he vetoed it, only to see his veto overridden. Nevertheless, as commander-in-chief he reluctantly appointed military governors, and by the end of 1867 elections had been held in every state except Texas. Because many white Southerners boycotted the elections, the South came under the control of Republicans supported by Union forces. In a way, however, Southerners had brought more radical measures upon themselves by their inflexibility.

Congress realized the plan it had enacted was unprecedented and subject to challenge by the other two branches of government. To check Johnson's power, Congress also passed the Tenure of Office Act, which required Senate consent for the removal of any official whose appointment had required the Senate's confirmation. It was meant in part to protect Secretary of War Edwin M. Stanton, who supported the Radicals.

When the president attempted to remove Stanton, the House of Representatives voted to impeach Johnson. In the Senate trial that followed radical prosecutors argued that Johnson had committed "high crimes and misdemeanors" and asserted that a president could be removed for political reasons, even without being found legally guilty of crimes—a position James Madison had supported during the drafting of the Constitution.

The vote for conviction fell one short of the required two-thirds majority, when seven Republicans broke ranks and voted against conviction. This action set the precedent that a president must be guilty of serious misdeeds to be removed from office. The outcome was a political blow to the Radicals, costing them some support. On the other hand, Johnson's brush with impeachment did make him more cooperative for the last months of his presidency.

Black Suffrage

In the 1868 presidential election the Republicans won with Ulysses S. Grant, whose Civil War victories made his name a household word. His slogan, "Let us have peace," was appealing, but his election was less than a ringing endorsement for Radical policies. The military hero who had seemed invincible barely won the popular vote in several key states.

While a few Radicals had long favored black suffrage, only after the Republicans' electoral close call in 1868 did the bulk of the party begin to consider a suffrage amendment. Many were swayed by the political certainty that the black vote would be theirs and might give them the margin of victory in future close elections. Others were embarrassed by the hypocrisy of forcing black suffrage on the South while only 7 percent of Northern African Americans could vote. Still others believed that granting African Americans the vote would relieve whites of any further responsibility to protect black rights.

Suffrage supporters faced many objections to such an amendment. One was based on the lack of popular support. At that time only seven Northern states granted blacks the right to vote, and, since 1865, referendum proposals for black suffrage in eight states had been voted down. The amendment was so unpopular that, ironically, it could never have won adoption without its ratification by the Southern states, where black suffrage already existed. A more serious challenge was the question of whether Congress could legislate suffrage at all. Before Reconstruction the national government had never taken any action regarding the right to vote; suffrage had been considered not a right but a privilege which only the states could confer.

The issue of an amendment guaranteeing black suffrage also raised the question of whether women should be granted the franchise. As leaders of the Women's Loyal League, Elizabeth Cady Stanton and Susan B. Anthony had both worked hard for the adoption of the Thirteenth Amendment, only to be rewarded by inclusion of the word *male* in the Fourteenth Amendment of the Constitution—the first time that word appears. Some women, such as Lucy Stone of the American Woman Suffrage Association, accepted the plea of longtime women's suffrage supporter Frederick Douglass that it was the "Negro's hour," and worked for ratification. Anthony, however, vowed to "cut off this right arm of mine before I will ever work for or demand the ballot for the Negro and not the woman." Such differences played a role in splitting the women's movement in 1869 between those working for a national suffrage amendment and those who concentrated their efforts on the state level. Anthony and Stanton founded the National Woman Suffrage Association to fight for a constitutional amendment and other feminist reforms. Others became disillusioned with that approach and established the American Woman Suffrage Association, which focused on obtaining suffrage on a state-by-state basis.

Actually, women did not lose much by not being included in the Fifteenth Amendment. To meet the various objections, compromise was necessary. The resulting amendment did not grant the vote to anyone. It merely stated that the vote could not be denied "on account of race, color, or previous condition of servitude." Suffrage was still essentially to be controlled by the states, and other bases of exclusion would not be deemed unconstitutional. These loopholes would eventually allow white Southerners to make a mockery of the amendment.

Although congressional reconstruction was labeled "radical," compromise and caution had prevailed. What Congress did *not* do is as important as what it did. It did not even guarantee the right to vote. There was only one execution for war crimes and only Jefferson Davis was imprisoned for more than a few months. For all but a handful, ex-Confederates were not permanently barred from voting or holding office. Most local Southern governments were undisturbed. Land as well as rights were restored to former rebels, eliminating the possibility of extensive land redistribution. The only attempt by the national government to meet the basic needs of African-American citizens was the temporary Freedmen's Bureau—justified only as an emergency measure. The cautious nature of Reconstruction doomed it as an opportunity to provide means for the protection of minority rights.

Such congressional moderation reflected the spirit of the age. Long-cherished beliefs in the need for strict construction of the Constitution and in states' rights presented formidable barriers to truly radical changes. Property rights were considered sacrosanct—even for "traitors." Cherished ideals of self-reliance and the conviction that a person determined his or her own destiny led many to believe that African Americans should take care of themselves.

Tainting every action was the widespread racist conviction that African Americans were not equal to whites. Many Northerners were more concerned with keeping blacks in the South than with abstract black rights. Even Radical Representative George Julian admitted to his Indiana constituents, "the real trouble is that *we hate the negro.* It is not his ignorance that offends us, but his color."

The plan for Reconstruction evolved fitfully, buffeted first one way and then another by the forces of the many unresolved issues at war's end. If permanent changes were very limited, nonetheless precedents had been set for later action, and for a brief time congressional reconstruction brought about the most democratic governments the South had ever seen—or would see for another hundred years.

Reconstruction in the South

Regardless of the specific details hammered out in Washington, any dictated peace would probably have been unpalatable to Southern whites. They were especially leery of any action that seemed to threaten white supremacy. Most Southerners condemned the Freedmen's Bureau, believing that its agents were partial to African Americans. Actually there was great diversity in the background and goals of bureau agents. Some were idealistic young New England men and women who came south to aid in the transition to freedom. Others were army officers whose first priority was to maintain order, often by siding with the landowners.

The results of bureau actions were mixed in regard to conditions for African Americans. The agents helped to negotiate labor contracts that African Americans had to sign to obtain rations. Frequently the wages were well below the rate at which slaves had been hired out by their owners before the war. Although money was scarce at the time, these contracts helped to keep African Americans on the farm—someone else's farm. On the other hand, between 1865 and 1869 the bureau issued over 21 million rations, of which about 5 million went to whites. The bureau also operated more than 40 hospitals, opened hundreds of schools, and accomplished the herculean task of resettling some 30,000 people displaced by the war. The agency showed that the federal government could establish and administer a massive relief program, as it would again do during the depression of the 1930s.

Carpetbaggers, Scalawags, and Black Republicans

After the passage of the Reconstruction Acts in 1867, Republican officeholders joined bureau agents in directing the course of Reconstruction. Northerners who came to the South during or after the war and became engaged in politics were called "carpetbaggers" by resentful Southerners. They supposedly arrived with a few meager belongings in their carpetbags, which they would fill with their ill-gotten gains from looting an already devastated South. Probably what most infuriated whites was the carpetbaggers' willingness to cooperate with African Americans. Native whites accused the carpetbaggers of cynically exploiting the freed persons for their own gain.

White Southerners who voted for Republicans were labeled "scalawags." The term had been used previously as a synonym for a loafer or rascal. Such men were said to have "sold themselves for office" and become a "subservient tool and accomplice" of the carpetbaggers. Some scalawags were members of the old commercial elite of bankers and merchants who, as former Whigs, favored the economic policies of the Republican party. The majority of Southern white Republican voters were yeoman farmers and poor whites from areas where slavery had been unimportant. They had long resented planter domination and had opposed secession.

Northerners who engaged in politics in the South before or after the war were called carpetbaggers. This cartoon shows Ulysses S. Grant and Union soldiers propping up carpetbag rule with bayonets, while the "Solid South" staggers under the weight.

Most detested by white Southerners were the black Republicans. They loathed the prospect of African Americans in authority. They feared that the former slaves would exact payment for their years of bondage. Democrats also knew that racism was their best rallying cry to regain power. Whites claimed that ignorant freed persons, incapable of managing their own affairs, were allowed to run the affairs of state with disastrous results.

Such myths persisted for a long time. Southern whites had determined even before Reconstruction began that it would be "the most galling tyranny and most stupendous system of organized robbery that is to be met with in history." The truth was, as black leader W. E. B. Du Bois later wrote, "There is one thing that the white South feared more than negro dishonesty, ignorance, and incompetency, and that was negro honesty, knowledge, and efficiency." To a surprising degree they got what they most feared.

Black voters were certainly as fit to vote as the millions of illiterate whites enfranchised by Jacksonian democracy. Black officials as a group were as qualified as their white counterparts. In South Carolina two-thirds of them were literate, and in all states most of the acknowledged leaders were well educated and articulate. They usually had been members of the Northern or Southern free black elite or part of the slave aristocracy of skilled artisans and household slaves. Hiram Revels, a U.S. senator from Mississippi, was the son of free blacks who had sent him to college in the North. James Walker Hood, the presiding officer of the North Carolina constitutional convention of 1867, was a Pennsylvania native and an African Methodist Episcopal missionary. Some, such as Francis Cardoza of South Carolina, were the privileged mulatto sons of white planters. Cardoza had been educated in Scottish and English universities. During Reconstruction 14 such men served in the U.S. House of Representatives and two in the Senate. By 1901, six others were elected to the House, before Southern black political power was effectively demolished.

In a historic first, seven African Americans were elected to the Forty-first and Forty-second Congresses. Between 1869 and 1901, two African Americans became senators and 20 served in the House.

Even if black Republicans had been incompetent, they could hardly be held responsible for the perceived abuses of so-called black reconstruction. Only in South Carolina did African Americans have a majority of the delegates to the constitutional convention provided for by the Reconstruction Acts. Neither did they dominate the new governments; only for a two-year period in South Carolina did blacks control both houses of the legislature. When the vote was restored to ex-Confederates, African Americans comprised only one-third of the voters of the South, and only in two states did they have a majority.

Actually, carpetbaggers dominated most Republican governments. They accounted for less than one percent of the party's voters but held a third of the offices. Their power was especially obvious in the higher offices. Over half of all Southern Republican governors and almost half of the Republican congressmen and senators were former Northerners. Although some carpetbaggers did resemble their stereotypes, most did not. Many had come south before black enfranchisement and could not have predicted political futures based on black votes. Most were Union veterans; some brought with them much-needed capital for local investments. A few came with a sense of mission to educate blacks and reform Southern society.

Since African Americans constituted only a third of the population and carpetbaggers less than one percent, those two groups had to depend on the votes of a sizable number of native white Southerners to obtain political offices in some regions of the South. To win the scalawags' vote (most of whom were poor whites) the Republicans appealed to class interests, playing on traditional lower-class resentment of the planter aristocracy. Many Southerners, won over by campaign promises of debtor relief, accepted such arguments and joined African Americans to put Republicans into office. The coalition, however, was always shaky, given the racism of poor whites. The scalawags actually represented a swing vote that finally moved toward the Democratic party of white supremacy later in the 1870s.

Character of Republican Rule

While the coalition lasted, the Republican governments became the most democratic that the South had ever had. More people could vote for more offices; all remaining property requirements for voting and officeholding were dropped; representation was made fairer through reapportionment; and more offices became elective rather than appointive. Salaries for public officials made it possible to serve without being wealthy. Most important, universal male suffrage was enacted with the support of black legislators. Ironically, by refusing to deny Southern whites what had been denied to them—the vote—African Americans sowed the seeds of their own destruction.

The Republican state constitutions, which brought the South firmly into the mainstream of national reform, often remained in effect years after the end of Reconstruction. Legislatures abolished automatic imprisonment for debt and reduced the use of the death penalty. More institutions for the care of the indigent, orphans, mentally ill, deaf, and blind were established. Tax structures were overhauled, reducing head taxes and increasing property taxes to relieve somewhat poorer taxpayers. At the same time, Southern railroads, harbors, and bridges were rebuilt.

Black legislators had the most success in laying the foundations for public education. Antebellum provisions for public schools below the Mason-Dixon line were meager to nonexistent. In every state African Americans were among the main proponents of state-supported schools, but most accepted segregated facilities as necessary compromises. Some black parents did not even desire integration; they believed their children could not flourish in environments tainted by white supremacy. By 1877 some 600,000 blacks were in schools, but only the University of South Carolina and the public schools of New Orleans were integrated.

As desirable as many of the new social services were, they required money and money was scarce. The war had destroyed not only railroads and bridges but also much of the Southern tax base. The necessary tax increases were unpopular, as were soaring state debts. Both were blamed on corruption, with some justification. Louisiana Governor Henry C. Warmouth netted some $100,000 during a year in which his salary was only $8,000. One black man was paid $9,000 to repair a bridge with an original cost of only $500. Contracts for rebuilding and expanding railroads, subsidies to industries, and bureaucracies for administering social services offered abundant opportunities for graft and bribery.

When these scandals came to light, Southern whites were quick to point an accusing finger at freed persons who, they claimed, were unfit for positions of authority. Actually, although African Americans received a large share of the blame, they received little of the profit. A smaller percentage of blacks than whites were involved in the scandals. Also the corruption that the Democrats denounced at every turn was rather meager in comparison to the shenanigans of some Democratic regimes in the North. In the aftermath of the war an orgy of national corruption seemed to infect both political parties.

Black and White Adaptation

The "tyranny" that so distressed Southern whites did not include wholesale disfranchisement or confiscation of their lands. Just as the ex-slaves on Thomas Pinckney's plantation had learned, freed persons everywhere soon realized that the economic power of whites had diminished little. If anything, land became more concentrated in the hands of a few. In one Alabama county the richest 10 percent of landowners increased their share of landed wealth from 55 to 63 percent between 1860 and 1870. Some African Americans, usually through hard work and incredible sacrifice, were able to obtain land. The percentage of blacks who owned property increased from less than 1 to 20 percent. Indeed, African Americans seemed to fare better than poor whites, for whom the percentage of land ownership dropped from 80 to 67 percent.

Most poor blacks and whites worked on someone else's land as sharecroppers. Under this system, landowners gave tenants a plot of land to work in return for a share of the crops. African Americans preferred the sharecropping system because working in gangs as contract and wage laborers under white supervision smacked too much of slavery. Anxious to obtain as much autonomy as possible, some freed persons hitched mule teams to their old slave cabins and carried them off to their assigned acres.

Sharecropping at first seemed to be a good bargain for African Americans. Receiving a half share of the crops they produced, they were making more for working less. Fewer family members worked and black men labored shorter hours; as a group African Americans worked one-third fewer hours than under slavery.

But sharecropping proved to be disastrous for most blacks and poor whites. They needed more than land to farm; they also required seeds, fertilizers, and provisions to live on until they harvested their crops. To obtain these necessities they often borrowed against their share of the crops. Falling crop prices, high credit rates, and, in later years, laws favoring creditors left many to harvest a growing burden of debt with each crop.

If most freedmen did not win economic freedom, they benefited from freedom in other ways. Since it was no longer illegal to learn to read and write, African Americans pursued education with much zeal. A growing number also sought higher education. Between 1860 and 1880 over 1,000 African Americans earned college degrees. Some went north to college, but most attended one of the 13 Southern colleges established by the American Missionary Association or by black and white churches with the assistance of the Freedmen's Bureau. Such schools as Howard University and Fisk University were a permanent legacy of Reconstruction.

African Americans were also able to enjoy and expand their rich cultural heritage. Religion was a central focus for most, just as it had been in slavery. Church membership in such antebellum denominations as the African Methodist Episcopal soared. In essence, black Christians declared their religious independence, and their churches became centers of political and social activities as well as religious ones.

The very changes that gave African Americans hope during Reconstruction distressed poor whites. Black political equality rankled them, but much more serious was their own declining economic status. As their land ownership decreased, more whites became dependent on sharecropping and low-wage jobs, primarily in the textile industry.

Ironically, although nearly everyone perceived poor whites as the group most hostile to blacks, the two shared many aspects of a rich Southern cultural heritage. In religion and recreation their experiences were similar. At camp meetings and revivals poor whites practiced a highly emotional religion, just as many black Southerners did. Both groups spun yarns and sang songs that reflected the perils of their existence and provided folk heroes. They also shared many superstitions as well as useful folk remedies. Race, however, was a potent wedge between them that upper-class whites frequently exploited for their own political and economic goals.

Planters no longer dominated the white elite; sharecropping turned them and others into absentee landlords. The sons of the old privileged families joined the growing ranks of lawyers, railroad entrepreneurs, bankers, industrialists, and merchants. In some ways, the upper and middle classes began to merge, but in many places the old elite and their children still enjoyed a degree of deference and political leadership. Their hostility toward African Americans was not as intense, largely because they possessed means of control. When their control slipped, however, they also became strident racists.

Violent White Resistance

Large numbers of whites of all classes engaged in massive resistance to Reconstruction. In 1866 some young men in Pulaski, Tennessee, organized the Ku Klux Klan, which began as a social club with all the trappings of fraternal orders—secret rituals, costumes, and practical jokes. They soon learned that their antics intimidated African Americans; thenceforth the Klan grew into a terrorist organization, copied all over the South under various names. A major goal of the Klan was to intimidate Republican voters and restore Democrats to office. In South Carolina, when blacks working for a scalawag began to vote, Klansmen visited the plantation and "whipped every nigger man they could lay their hands on." The group's increasing lawlessness alarmed many people and led to congressional action. The Klan was broken up by three Enforcement Acts that gave the president the right to suspend habeas corpus against "armed combinations" interfering with any citizen's right to vote. In 1871 Grant did so in nine South Carolina counties. Disbanding the Klan, however, did little to decrease Southern violence or the activities of similar terrorist groups.

Some black Southerners were probably never allowed to vote freely. At the peak of Reconstruction, fewer than 30,000 federal troops were stationed in the entire South, hardly enough to protect the rights of 4.5 million African Americans. As troops were being withdrawn, Democrats sought to regain control of their states. Without secret ballots landowners could threaten sharecroppers with eviction for "improper" voting. In addition to economic intimidation, violence against freed persons escalated in most states as the Democrats increased their political power. When victory seemed close, Democrats justified any means to "redeem" the South and rid it of Republican influence. In six heavily black counties in Mississippi such tactics proved highly successful, reducing Republican votes from more than 14,000 in 1873 to only 723 in 1876. Beginning with Virginia and Tennessee in 1869, by 1876 all but three states—Louisiana, Florida, and South Carolina—had Democratic "Redeemer" governments. The final collapse of Reconstruction became official the following year with the withdrawal of federal troops from the three unredeemed states.

Reconstruction in the North and West

In the end, the South could be said to have lost the war but won the peace. After 1877 Southern whites found little resistance to their efforts to forge new institutions to replace both the economic benefits and racial control of slavery. By 1910 they had devised a system of legalized repression that gave whites many of the benefits of slavery without all the responsibilities. Surely this pattern was not what the North had envisioned after Appomattox in 1865; nonetheless, as the years passed, civil rights for African Americans ceased to become a Northern priority. A shifting political climate, economic hard times, increasing preoccupation with other issues, and continued racism combined to make most Northerners retreat from any responsibility for the protection of black rights.

Northern Shifts in Attitudes

When Grant won the presidency in 1868, the voters had chosen a war hero who had no political record or experience. They voted not so much for a program, but for Grant's campaign slogan: "Let us have peace." The victorious general proved to be a poor choice. Politically inexperienced, haunted by a fear of failure, and socially insecure, Grant was too easily influenced by men of wealth and prestige. He made some dismal appointments and remained loyal to individuals who did not merit his trust. The result was a series of national political scandals. Grant was not personally involved, but his close association with the perpetrators blemished both his and his party's image. The first major scandal involved the Crédit Mobilier, a dummy construction company used to milk money from railroad investors in order to line the pockets of a few insiders, including Vice President Schuyler Colfax and a number of other prominent Republicans. Later, bribes and kickback schemes surfaced that involved Indian trading posts, post office contracts, and commissions for tax collection. Such revelations as well as the corruption in some Southern Republican governments did little to enhance the public image of the party, and Democrats were quick to make corruption a major issue in both the North and the South.

In the 1872 presidential election disenchantment with the Grant administration prompted a group calling themselves Liberal Republicans to form a separate party and nominate their own candidate, *New York Tribune* editor Horace Greeley. Among Greeley's campaign pledges was a more moderate Southern policy. Even with the Democrats also nominating Greeley, Grant easily won reelection, but Republican dominance was slipping. That year the Democrats captured the House and made gains in the Senate, following further revelations of Republican corruption.

At least as detrimental to Republican political fortunes was a depression that followed the panic of 1873, which resulted from overinvestment in railroads and risky financial deals. Lasting six years, the depression was the most serious economic downturn the nation had yet experienced. Whatever their cause, depressions usually result in "voting the rascals out." Yet economic distress had an even wider impact on Reconstruction. People's attention became focused on their pocketbooks rather than on abstract ideals of equality and justice. Economic scrutiny brought such issues as currency and tariffs to the forefront. As the depression deepened, many questioned Republican support for "sound money" backed by gold and the retirement of the legal-tender "greenback" paper money that had been issued during the war.

Those greenbacks had increased the money supply needed to finance postwar economic expansion. Yet many Republicans were suspicious of any money not backed by specie—that is, gold or silver. One of the last actions of the Republican-controlled Congress was to pass the Resumption Act of 1875. This bill provided for the gradual redemption of greenbacks in gold. The resulting deflation favored creditors over debtors because debtors were forced to repay loans with money that was worth more than when they borrowed it. Many Americans, especially farmers, were already in debt, and deflation coupled with a depression brought economic distress.

Actually, the panic of 1873 brought into clearer focus the vast changes occurring in the North during Reconstruction. The United States was experiencing the growing pains of economic modernization and westward expansion, the effects of which, such as the completion of the first transcontinental railroad in 1869, overshadowed Reconstruction-related issues. By the late 1870s the Republican party had foresaken its reformist past to become a protector of railroad and business interests rather than a guarantor of basic rights.

Racism and American Indians

The major reason for the decline of Reconstruction was the pervasive belief in white supremacy. There could be little determination to secure equal rights for those who were considered unequal in all other respects. Reconstruction represented a failed opportunity to resolve justly the status of one minority, and the climate of racism almost ensured failure for others as well. Westward expansion not only diverted attention from Reconstruction but also raised the question of what was to be done about the Plains Indians. They, too, were considered inferior to whites. Although Reconstruction at first offered hope to African Americans, for the American Indian hope was fading.

In the end, African Americans were oppressed; Native Americans were exterminated or pushed onto shrinking reservations. Because most Africans, like Europeans, depended on agriculture rather than hunting, they adapted more easily to agricultural slavery. Black labor was valuable, if controlled; Indians stood as barriers to expansion.

When settlers first began moving onto the Great Plains, they encountered about 250,000 Plains Indians and 13 million buffalo. Some tribes, including the Zuñi, Hopi, Navaho, and Pawnee, had fixed settlements and depended on gardening and farming. Such tribes as the Sioux, Apache, and Cheyenne, however, were nomadic hunters who followed the buffalo herds over vast tracts of land.

Cultural differences caused misunderstandings between settlers and Native Americans and ultimately led to conflict. Among Anglo-Americans capitalism fostered competition and frontier living promoted individualism. On the other hand, Plains Indians lived in tribes based on kinship ties. As members of an extended family that included distant cousins, Indians were taught to place the welfare of the group over the interests of the individual. The emphasis within a tribe was on cooperation rather than competition. Some tribes might be richer than others, but there was seldom a large gap between the rich and the poor within a tribe.

The two cultures' widely divergent forms of political organization also caused problems. Among the Indian tribes, power as well as wealth was usually shared. Chiefs seldom had much individual power, but were generally religious and ceremonial leaders. Whites incorrectly believed that an Indian chief could make decisions and sign treaties that would be considered legal and binding by fellow tribal members.

Another major cultural difference between the newly arriving settlers and the Plains tribes was their attitude toward the land. Most Indians had no concept of private property. They refused to draw property lines and borders because of how they viewed the place of people in the world. Whites tended to see land, plants, and animals as resources to be exploited. Indians, on the other hand, stressed the unity of all life. Most of the Plains Indians believed that land could be utilized, but never owned. The idea of owning land was as absurd as owning the air people breathed. As Chief Joseph of the Nez Percé tribe said, "The earth and myself are of one mind." Thus people were not meant to dominate the rest of nature; they were a part of it.

Although some tribes could coexist peacefully with settlers, nomadic Indians had a way of life that was incompatible with miners, railroad developers, cattle ranchers, and farmers. Most had no desire for assimilation; they merely wanted to be left alone. To Anglo-Americans the Indians were barriers to expansion. They agreed with Theodore Roosevelt that the West was not meant to be "a game reserve for squalid savages." Thus U.S. Indian policy focused on getting more territory for white settlement. Prior to Reconstruction the federal government signed treaties that divided land between Indians and settlers and restricted the movement of each on the lands of the other. Frequently Indian consent was fraudulently obtained, and white respect for Indian land depended on how desirable it was for settlement.

During the Civil War, Sioux, Cheyenne, and Arapaho warriors rejected the land cessions made by their chiefs. Violence against settlers erupted as frontier troop strength was reduced to fight the Confederacy. The war also provided an excuse to nullify previous treaties and pledges with the tribes resettled in Oklahoma by Andrew Jackson's Indian removal. Some Native Americans did support the Confederacy, but all suffered the consequences of Confederate defeat. Settlers moved into the most desirable land, pushing the Indians farther south and west. Some Indians began to resist.

In 1864 the territorial governor of Colorado persuaded most of the warring Cheyennes and Arapahoes to come to Fort Lyon on Sand Creek, promising them protection. Colonel J. M. Chivington's militia, however, attacked an Indian camp flying a white flag and the American flag and killed hundreds of Indian men, women, and children. The following year Congress established a committee to investigate the causes of conflict. Its final report in 1867 led to the creation of an Indian Peace Commission charged with negotiating settlements. At two conferences in 1867 and

1868 Indian chiefs were asked to restrict their tribes to reservations in the undesirable lands of Oklahoma and the Black Hills of the Dakotas in return for supplies and assistance from the government.

Most Indians did not consider the offer very generous, but those who refused to acquiesce soon found that resistance was futile. Railroads had penetrated the West, bringing in both settlers and federal troops more rapidly. The destruction of the buffalo herds by hunters was a particularly important factor in the subjugation of the Indian tribes. These herds played a crucial role in most Plains Indians' culture—providing almost all the basic necessities. Indians ate the buffalo meat, made clothing and tepees out of the hides, used the fats for cosmetics, fashioned the bones into tools, made thread from the sinews, and even burned dried buffalo droppings as fuel. Without the buffalo, most Indians became dependent on the federal government for food and clothing, and submitted peacefully to the new reservation policy.

In 1874 gold was discovered in the Black Hills Indian reservation in the present-day Dakotas. The area suddenly became tempting to whites, and miners began pouring into lands guaranteed to the Indians only five years before. In June 1876 federal troops were sent in to crush an uprising of Chief Sitting Bull's Sioux warriors and their Cheyenne allies. Instead, the warring tribes won their greatest victory against white encroachment when Indians overwhelmed and killed Lieutenant Colonel George A. Custer and 264 men at Little Bighorn. The battle had little long-term effect, however, except to strengthen white resolve in dealing with the "Indian problem."

The treatment of both Indians and African Americans would be justified by the increasingly virulent racism of whites, which was given "scientific" support by scholars of the late nineteenth century. One point was clear by 1876: Northerners who believed that the only good Indian was a dead Indian could hardly condemn Southern whites for their treatment of African Americans.

Final Retreat from Reconstruction

By 1876, fewer Americans championed black rights than had at the close of the Civil War. Some of the old abolitionist Radicals had grown tired of what had become a protracted and complex situation. Radical Republicans such as Thaddeus Stevens and Charles Sumner, who had labored to guarantee civil rights for African Americans, were dead. By 1876, all the elements were present for a national retreat on Reconstruction: the distraction of economic distress, a deep desire for unity among whites, the respectability of racism, a frustrated weariness with black problems by former allies, a growing conservatism on economic and social issues, a changing political climate featuring a resurgence of the Democratic party, and finally a general public disgust with the failure of Reconstruction.

The presidential election of that year sealed the fate of Reconstruction and brought this chapter in American history to a close.

Corruption was a major issue in the 1876 election. The Democrats chose Samuel J. Tilden, a New Yorker whose claim to fame was breaking up the notorious Boss Tweed Ring in New York City. The Republicans nominated Rutherford B. Hayes, a man who had offended few, largely by doing little. The election itself was so riddled with corruption and violence that no one can ever know what would have happened in a fair election. Tilden won the popular vote and led Hayes in undisputed electoral votes 184 to 165. However, 185 votes were needed for election, and 20 votes were disputed—19 of them from Louisiana, Florida, and South Carolina. These were the only Southern states still under Republican rule with the backing of federal troops. In each, rival election boards sent in different returns.

With no constitutional provision for such an occurrence, the Republican Senate and Democratic House established a special commission to decide which returns were valid. Composed of eight Republicans and seven Democrats, the Electoral Commission proceeded to vote along party lines, and gave all the disputed votes to Hayes. Democrats were outraged, and a constitutional crisis seemed in the making if a united Democratic front in the House voted to reject the commission's findings.

A series of agreements between Hayes's advisers and Southern Democratic congressmen averted the crisis. In what came to be called the "Compromise of 1877," Hayes agreed to support federal aid for Southern internal improvements, especially a transcontinental railroad. He also promised to appoint a Southern Democrat to his cabinet and to allow Southern Democrats a say in the allocation of federal offices in their region. Most important, however, was his pledge to remove the remaining federal troops from the South. In return, Southern Democrats promised to protect black rights and to support the findings of the Electoral Commission. On March 2 the House declared Hayes the presidential winner by an electoral vote of 185 to 184. After taking office, Hayes removed the

Table 16.1

Election of 1876

Candidate	Party	Uncontested Electoral Vote	Popular Vote	Electoral Vote
Ruthford B. Hayes	Republican	165	4,034,311	185
Samuel J. Tilden	Democratic	184	4,288,546	184
Peter Cooper	Greenback	—	75,973	—

troops, and the remaining Republican governments in the South soon collapsed.

Scholars once considered the Compromise of 1877 an important factor in the end of Reconstruction. Actually, its role was more symbolic than real; it merely buried the corpse. The battle for the Republican party's soul had been lost by its abolitionist faction well before the election of 1876. The Democratic party had never sought to extend or protect black rights. The Supreme Court began to interpret the Fourteenth and Fifteenth Amendments very narrowly, stripping them of their strength. Thus one by one many African-American rights were lost during the next four decades.

Conclusion

As the Civil War ended, many unresolved issues remained. The most crucial involved the status of former slaves and of the former Confederate states. The destinies of both were inextricably intertwined. Anything

*C*hronology of Key Events

1863	Lincoln proposes 10 percent plan for Reconstruction
1864	Lincoln vetoes Wade-Davis Bill; Sand Creek Massacre
1865	Freedmen's Bureau established; Lincoln assassinated; Andrew Johnson becomes seventeenth president; Thirteenth Amendment ratified, abolishing slavery
1866	Civil Rights Act
1867	Reconstruction Act divides South into five military districts
1868	President Johnson impeached; Fourteenth Amendment, guarenteeing citizenship to African Americans, ratified; Ulysses S. Grant elected eighteenth president
1870	Fifteenth Amendment ratified, outlaws exclusion from voting on basis of race
1870–71	Ku Klux Klan Acts passed
1876	Custer defeated at Little Bighorn
1877	Compromise of 1877; Rutherford B. Hayes becomes nineteenth president

affecting the status of one influenced the fate of the other. Quick read-mission of the states with little change would doom black rights. Enforced equality of African Americans under the law would create turbulence and drastic change in the South. This difficult problem was further complicated by constitutional, economic, and political considerations, ensuring that the course of Reconstruction would be chaotic and contradictory.

Presidential Reconstruction under both Lincoln and Johnson favored rapid reunification and white unity more than changes in the racial structure of the South. The South, however, refused to accept a meaningful end to slavery, as the Black Codes blatantly demonstrated. Congressional desire to reestablish legislative supremacy and the Republican need to build a national party combined with this Southern intransigence to unite Radical and moderate Republicans in the need to protect black rights and to restructure the South. What emerged from congressional reconstruction were Republican governments that expanded democracy and enacted needed reforms which many Southern whites deeply resented. At the core of that resentment was not disgust over incompetence or corruption but hostility to black political power in any form.

Given the pervasiveness of racial prejudice, what was remarkable was not that the Freedmen's Bureau, the constitutional amendments, and the civil rights legislation failed to produce permanent change but that these actions were taken at all. Cherished ideas of property rights, limited government, and self-reliance, as well as an almost universal belief in black inferiority, virtually guaranteed that the experiment would fail. The first national attempt to resolve fairly and justly the question of minority rights in a pluralistic society was abandoned in less than a decade. Indians, blacks, and women saw the truth of the Alabama planter's words of 1865: "Poor elk—poor buffaloe—poor Indian—poor Nigger—this is indeed a white man country." Nevertheless, less than a century later, seeds planted by the Reconstruction era amendments would finally germinate, flower, and be harvested.

Suggestions for Further Reading

Effective overviews of the Reconstruction period are Eric Foner, *Reconstruction: America's Unfinished Revolution* (1988); Leon Litwack, *Been in the Storm So Long* (1979); James McPherson, *Ordeal by Fire* (1982); Kenneth M. Stampp, *The Era of Reconstruction* (1965).

For information on the Johnson and Grant presidencies see Michael Les Benedict, *The Impeachment of Andrew Johnson* (1973); William S. McFeely, *Grant: A Biography* (1981); Eric McKitrick, *Andrew Johnson and Reconstruction* (1960).

Conditions in the South during Reconstruction are examined in Stephen J. DeCanio, *Agriculture in the Postbellum South* (1974); Herbert G. Gutman, *The Black Family in Slavery and Freedom* (1976); Thomas Holt, *Black over White* (1977); Jay R. Mandle, *The Roots of Black Poverty* (1978); Michael Perman, *The Road to Redemption: Southern Politics, 1869–1879* (1984); George C. Rable, *But There Was No Peace* (1984); James Roark, *Masters Without Slaves* (1977).

On the West during the Reconstruction period see Robert F. Berkhofer, *The White Man's Indian* (1978); Eugene H. Berwanger, *The West and Reconstruction* (1981); Francis Paul Prucha, *American Indian Policy in Crisis* (1975); Wilcomb E. Washburn, *The Indian in America* (1975).

Appendix

The Declaration of Independence

When in the Course of human events, it becomes necessary for one people to dissolve the political bands which have connected them with another, and to assume among the Powers of the earth, the separate and equal station to which the Laws of Nature and of Nature's God entitle them, a decent respect to the opinions of mankind requires that they should declare the causes which impel them to the separation.

We hold these truths to be self-evident, that all men are created equal, that they are endowed by their Creator with certain unalienable Rights, that among these are Life, Liberty and the pursuit of Happiness. That to secure these rights, Governments are instituted among Men, deriving their just powers from the consent of the governed. That whenever any Form of Government becomes destructive of these ends, it is the Right of the People to alter or to abolish it, and to institute new Government, laying its foundation on such principles and organizing its powers in such form, as to them shall seem most likely to effect their Safety and Happiness. Prudence, indeed, will dictate that Governments long established should not be changed for light and transient causes; and accordingly all experience hath shown, that mankind are more disposed to suffer, while evils are sufferable, than to right themselves by abolishing the forms to which they are accustomed. But when a long train of abuses and usurpations, pursuing invariably the same Object evinces a design to reduce them under absolute Despotism, it is their right, it is their duty, to throw off such Government, and to provide new Guards for their future security.—Such has been the patient sufferance of these Colonies; and such is now the necessity which constrains them to alter their former Systems of Government. The history of the present King of Great Britain is a history of repeated injuries and usurpations, all having in direct object the establishment of an absolute Tyranny over these States. To prove this, let Facts be submitted to a candid world.

He has refused his Assent to Laws, the most wholesome and necessary for the public good.

He has forbidden his Governors to pass Laws of immediate and pressing importance, unless suspended in their operation till his Assent should be obtained; and when so suspended, he has utterly neglected to attend to them.

He has refused to pass other Laws for the accommodation of large districts of people, unless those people would relinquish the right of Representation in the Legislature, a right inestimable to them and formidable to tyrants only.

He has called together legislative bodies at places unusual, uncomfortable, and distant from the depository of their Public Records, for the sole purpose of fatiguing them into compliance with his measures.

He has dissolved Representative Houses repeatedly, for opposing with manly firmness his invasions on the rights of the people.

He has refused for a long time, after such dissolutions, to cause others to be elected; whereby the Legislative Powers, incapable of Annihilation, have returned to the People at large for their exercise; the State remaining in the mean time exposed to all the dangers of invasion from without, and convulsions within.

He has endeavoured to prevent the population of these States; for that purpose obstructing the Laws of Naturalization of Foreigners; refusing to pass others to encourage their migration hither, and raising the conditions of new Appropriations of Lands.

He has obstructed the Administration of Justice, by refusing his Assent to Laws for establishing Judiciary Powers.

He has made Judges dependent on his Will alone, for the tenure of their offices, and the amount and payment of their salaries.

He has erected a multitude of New Offices, and sent hither swarms of Officers to harass our People, and eat out their substance.

He has kept among us, in times of peace, Standing Armies without the Consent of our legislature.

He has affected to render the Military independent of and superior to the Civil Power.

He has combined with others to subject us to a jurisdiction foreign to our constitution, and unacknowledged by our laws; giving his Assent to their acts of pretended legislation:

For quartering large bodies of armed troops among us;

For protecting them, by a mock Trial, from Punishment for any Murders which they should commit on the Inhabitants of these States;

For cutting off our Trade with all parts of the world;

For imposing taxes on us without our Consent;

For depriving us in many cases, of the benefits of Trial by Jury;

For transporting us beyond Seas to be tried for pretended offences;

For abolishing the free System of English Laws in a neighbouring Province, establishing therein an Arbitrary government, and enlarging its Boundaries so as to render it at once an example and fit instrument for introducing the same absolute rule into these Colonies;

For taking away our Charters, abolishing our most valuable Laws, and altering fundamentally the Forms of our Governments;

For suspending our own Legislature, and declaring themselves invested with Power to legislate for us in all cases whatsoever.

He has abdicated Government here, by declaring us out of his Protection and waging War against us.

He has plundered our seas, ravaged our Coasts, burnt our towns, and destroyed the lives of our people.

He is at this time transporting large armies of foreign mercenaries to compleat the works of death, desolation and tyranny, already begun with circumstances of Cruelty & perfidy scarcely paralleled in the most barbarous ages, and totally unworthy the Head of a civilized nation.

He has constrained our fellow Citizens taken Captive on the high Seas to bear Arms against their Country, to become the executioners of their friends and Brethren, or to fall themselves by their Hands.

He has excited domestic insurrections amongst us, and has endeavoured to bring on the inhabitants of our frontiers, the merciless Indian Savages, whose known rule of warfare, is an undistinguished destruction of all ages, sexes and conditions.

In every stage of these Oppressions We have Petitioned for Redress in the most humble terms: Our repeated Petitions have been answered only by repeated injury. A Prince, whose character is thus marked by every act which may define a Tyrant, is unfit to be the ruler of a free People.

Nor have We been wanting in attention to our British brethren. We have warned them from time to time of attempts by their legislature to extend an unwarrantable jurisdiction over us. We have reminded them of the circumstances of our emigration and settlement here. We have appealed to their native justice and magnanimity, and we have conjured them by the ties of our common kindred to disavow these usurpations, which, would inevitably interrupt our connections and correspondence. They too have been deaf to the voice of justice and of consanguinity. We must, therefore, acquiesce in the necessity, which denounces our Separation, and hold them, as we hold the rest of mankind, Enemies in War, in Peace Friends.

We, therefore, the Representatives of the united States of America, in General Congress, Assembled, appealing to the Supreme Judge of the world for the rectitude of our intentions, do, in the Name, and by Authority of the good People of these Colonies, solemnly publish and declare, That these United Colonies are, and of Right ought to be Free and Independent States; that they are Absolved from all Allegiance to the British Crown, and that all political connection between them and the State of Great Britain, is and ought to be totally dissolved; and that as Free and Independent States, they have full Power to levy War, conclude Peace, contract Alliances, establish Commerce, and to do all other Acts and Things which Independent States may of right do. And for the support of this Declaration, with a firm reliance on the Protection of Divine

Providence, we mutually pledge to each other our Lives, our Fortunes and our sacred Honor.

John Hancock,
Josiah Bartlett, Wm Whipple, Saml Adams, John Adams, Robt Treat Paine, Elbridge Gerry, Steph. Hopkins, William Ellery, Roger Sherman, Samel Huntington, Wm Williams, Oliver Wolcott, Matthew Thornton, Wm Floyd, Phil Livingston, Frans Lewis, Lewis Morris, Richd Stockton, Jno Witherspoon, Fras Hopkinson, John Hart, Abra Clark, Robt Morris, Benjamin Rush, Benja Franklin, John Morton, Geo Clymer, Jas Smith, Geo. Taylor, James Wilson, Geo. Ross, Caesar Rodney, Geo Read, Thos M:Kean, Samuel Chase, Wm Paca, Thos Stone, Charles Carroll of Carrollton, George Wythe, Richard Henry Lee, Th. Jefferson, Benja Harrison, Thos Nelson, Jr., Francis Lightfoot Lee, Carter Braxton, Wm Hooper, Joseph Hewes, John Penn, Edward Rutledge, Thos Heyward, Junr., Thomas Lynch, Junor., Arthur Middleton, Button Gwinnett, Lyman Hall, Geo Walton.

The Constitution of the United States of America

We the people of the United States, in Order to form a more perfect Union, establish Justice, insure domestic Tranquility, provide for the common defence, promote the general Welfare, and secure the Blessings of Liberty to ourselves and our Posterity, do ordain and establish this CONSTITUTION for the United States of America.

Article I

Section 1.

All legislative Powers herein granted shall be vested in a Congress of the United States, which shall consist of a Senate and House of Representatives.

Section 2.

The House of Representatives shall be composed of Members chosen every second Year by the People of the several States, and the Electors in each State shall have the Qualifications requisite for Electors of the most numerous Branch of the State Legislature.

No Person shall be a Representative who shall not have attained to the Age of twenty-five Years, and been seven Years a Citizen of the United States, and who shall not, when elected, be an Inhabitant of that State in which he shall be chosen.

Representatives and direct Taxes shall be apportioned among the several States which may be included within this Union, according to their respective Numbers, which shall be determined by adding to the whole Number of free

Persons, including those bound to Service for a Term of Years, and excluding Indians not taxed, three fifths of all other Persons. The actual Enumeration shall be made within three Years after the first Meeting of the Congress of the United States, and within every subsequent Term of ten Years, in such Manner as they shall by Law direct. The Number of Representatives shall not exceed one for every thirty Thousand, but each State shall have at Least one Representative; and until such enumeration shall be made, the State of New Hampshire shall be entitled to chuse three, Massachusetts eight, Rhode-Island and Providence Plantations one, Connecticut five, New-York six, New Jersey four, Pennsylvania eight, Delaware one, Maryland six, Virginia ten, North Carolina five, South Carolina five, and Georgia three.

When vacancies happen in the Representation from any State, the Executive Authority thereof shall issue Writs of Election to fill such Vacancies.

The House of Representatives shall chuse their Speaker and other Officers; and shall have the sole Power of Impeachment.

Section 3.

The Senate of the United States shall be composed of two Senators from each State, chosen by the Legislature thereof, for six Years; and each Senator shall have one Vote.

Immediately after they shall be assembled in Consequence of the first Election, they shall be divided as equally as may be into three Classes. The Seats of the Senators of the first Class shall be vacated at the Expiration of the second Year, of the second Class at the Expiration of the fourth Year, and of the third Class at the Expiration of the sixth Year, so that one-third may be chosen every second Year; and if Vacancies happen by Resignation, or otherwise, during the Recess of the Legislature of any State, the Executive thereof may make temporary Appointments until the next Meeting of the Legislature, which shall then fill such Vacancies.

No Person shall be a Senator who shall not have attained to the Age of thirty Years, and been nine Years a Citizen of the United States, and who shall not, when elected, be an Inhabitant of that State in which he shall be chosen.

The Vice President of the United States shall be President of the Senate, but shall have no vote, unless they be equally divided.

The Senate shall chuse their other Officers, and also a President pro tempore, in the absence of the Vice President, or when he shall exercise the Office of the President of the United States.

The Senate shall have the sole Power to try all Impeachments. When sitting for that purpose, they shall be on Oath or Affirmation. When the President of the United States is tried, the Chief Justice shall preside: And no person shall be convicted without the Concurrence of two thirds of the Members present.

Judgment in Cases of Impeachment shall not extend further than to removal from Office, and disqualification to hold and enjoy any Office of honor, Trust, or Profit under the United States: but the Party convicted shall nevertheless be liable and subject to Indictment, Trial, Judgment, and Punishment, according to Law.

Section 4.

The Times, Places and Manner of holding Elections for Senators and Representatives, shall be prescribed in each state by the Legislature thereof; but the Congress may at any time by Law make or alter such Regulations, except as to the Places of Chusing Senators.

The Congress shall assemble at least once in every Year, and such Meeting shall be on the first Monday in December, unless they shall by Law appoint a different Day.

Section 5.

Each House shall be the Judge of the Elections, Returns and Qualifications of its own Members, and a Majority of each shall constitute a Quorum to do Business; but a smaller number may adjourn from day to day, and may be authorized to compel the Attendance of absent Members, in such Manner, and under such Penalties, as each House may provide.

Each House may determine the Rules of its Proceedings, punish its Members for disorderly Behavior, and, with the Concurrence of two thirds, expel a Member.

Each House shall keep a Journal of its Proceedings, and from time to time publish the same, excepting such Parts as may in their Judgment require Secrecy; and the Yeas and Nays of the Members of either House on any question shall, at the Desire of one fifth of those Present, be entered on the Journal.

Neither House, during the Session of Congress, shall, without the Consent of the other, adjourn for more than three days, nor to any other Place than that in which the two Houses shall be sitting.

Section 6.

The Senators and Representatives shall receive a Compensation for their Services, to be ascertained by Law, and paid out of the Treasury of the United States. They shall in all Cases, except Treason, Felony, and Breach of the Peace, be privileged from arrest during their Attendance at the Session of their respective Houses, and in going to and returning from the same; and for any Speech or Debate in either House, they shall not be questioned in any other Place.

No Senator or Representative shall, during the Time for which he was elected, be appointed to any civil Office under the Authority of the United States, which shall have been created, or the Emoluments whereof shall have been increased, during such time; and no Person holding any Office under the United States shall be a Member of either House during his continuance in Office.

Section 7.

All Bills for raising Revenue shall originate in the House of Representatives; but the Senate may propose or concur with Amendments as on other bills.

Every Bill which shall have passed the House of Representatives and the Senate, shall, before it become a Law, be presented to the President of the United States; If he approve he shall sign it, but if not he shall return it, with his Objections, to that House in which it shall have originated, who shall enter the Objections at large on their Journal, and proceed to reconsider it. If after such Reconsideration two thirds of that House shall agree to pass the bill, it shall be sent, together with the objections, to the other House, by which it shall likewise be reconsidered, and if approved by two thirds of that House, it shall become a Law. But in all such Cases the Votes of both Houses shall be determined by Yeas and Nays, and the Names of the Persons voting for and against the Bill shall be entered on the Journal of each House respectively. If any Bill shall not be returned by the President within ten Days (Sundays excepted) after it shall have been presented to him, the Same shall be a Law, in like Manner as if he had signed it, unless the Congress by their Adjournment prevent its Return, in which Case it shall not be a Law.

Every Order, Resolution, or Vote to which the Concurrence of the Senate and House of Representatives may be necessary (except on a question of Adjournment) shall be presented to the President of the United States; and before the Same shall take Effect, shall be approved by him, or being disapproved by him, shall be repassed by two thirds of the Senate and House of Representatives, according to the Rules and Limitations prescribed in the Case of a Bill.

Section 8.

The Congress shall have Power To lay and collect Taxes, Duties, Imposts and Excises, to pay the Debts and provide for the common Defence and general Welfare of the United States; but all Duties, Imposts and Excises shall be uniform throughout the United States;

To borrow money on the credit of the United States;

To regulate Commerce with foreign Nations, and among the several States, and with the Indian Tribes;

To establish an uniform Rule of Naturalization, and uniform Laws on the subject of Bankruptcies throughout the United States;

To coin Money, regulate the Value thereof, and of foreign Coin, and fix the Standard of Weights and Measures;

To provide for the Punishment of counterfeiting the Securities and current Coin of the United States;

To establish Post Offices and post Roads;

To promote the Progress of Science and useful Arts, by securing for limited Times to Authors and Inventors the exclusive Right to their respective Writings and Discoveries;

To constitute Tribunals inferior to the Supreme Court;

To define and punish Piracies and Felonies committed on the high Seas, and Offences against the Law of Nations;

To declare War, grant Letters of Marque and Reprisal, and make Rules concerning Captures on Land and Water;

To raise and support Armies, but no Appropriation of Money to that Use shall be for a longer Term than two Years;

To provide and maintain a Navy:

To make Rules for the Government and Regulation of the land and naval forces;

To provide for calling forth the Militia to execute the Laws of the Union, suppress Insurrections and repel Invasions;

To provide for organizing, arming, and disciplining the Militia, and for governing such Part of them as may be employed in the Service of the United States, reserving to the States respectively, the Appointment of the Officers, and the Authority of training the Militia according to the discipline prescribed by Congress;

To exercise exclusive Legislation in all Cases whatsoever, over such District (not exceeding ten Miles square) as may, by Cession of particular States, and the acceptance of Congress, become the Seat of Government of the United States, and to exercise like Authority over all Places purchased by the Consent of the Legislature of the State in which the Same shall be, for the Erection of Forts, Magazines, Arsenals, dock-Yards, and other needful Buildings;—And

To make all Laws which shall be necessary and proper for carrying into Execution the foregoing Powers, and all other Powers vested by this Constitution in the government of the United States, or in any Department or Officer thereof.

Section 9.

The Migration or Importation of such Persons as any of the States now existing shall think proper to admit, shall not be prohibited by the Congress prior to the Year one thousand eight hundred and eight, but a tax or duty may be imposed on such Importation, not exceeding ten dollars for each Person.

The privilege of the Writ of Habeas Corpus shall not be suspended, unless when in Cases of Rebellion or Invasion the public Safety may require it.

No Bill of Attainder or ex post facto Law shall be passed.

No capitation, or other direct, Tax shall be laid unless in Proportion to the Census or Enumeration herein before directed to be taken.

No Tax or Duty shall be laid on Articles exported from any State.

No Preference shall be given by any Regulation of Revenue to the Ports of one State over those of another: nor shall Vessels bound to, or from, one State, be obliged to enter, clear, or pay Duties in another.

No Money shall be drawn from the Treasury, but in Consequence of Appropriations made by Law; and a regular Statement and Account of the Receipts and Expenditures of all public Money shall be published from time to time.

No Title of Nobility shall be granted by the United States: And no Person holding any Office of Profit or Trust under them, shall, without the Consent of the Congress, accept of any present, Emolument, Office, or Title, of any kind whatever, from any King, Prince, or foreign State.

Section 10.

No State shall enter into any Treaty, Alliance, or Confederation; grant Letters of Marque and Reprisal; coin Money; emit Bills of Credit; make any Thing but gold and silver Coin a Tender in Payment of Debts; pass any Bill of Attainder, ex post facto Law, or Law impairing the Obligation of Contracts, or grant any Title of Nobility.

No State shall, without the Consent of the Congress, lay any Imposts or Duties on Imports or Exports, except what may be absolutely necessary for executing its inspection Laws: and the net Produce of all Duties and Imposts, laid by any State on Imports or Exports, shall be for the Use of the Treasury of the United States; and all such Laws shall be subject to the Revision and Control of the Congress.

No State shall, without the Consent of Congress, lay any duty of Tonnage, keep Troops, or Ships of War in time of Peace, enter into any Agreement or Compact with another State, or with a foreign Power, or engage in War, unless actually invaded, or in such imminent Danger as will not admit of delay.

Article II

Section 1.

The executive Power shall be vested in a President of the United States of America. He shall hold his Office during the Term of four years, and, together with the Vice President, chosen for the same Term, be elected, as follows:

Each State shall appoint, in such Manner as the Legislature thereof may direct, a Number of Electors, equal to the whole Number of Senators and Representatives to which the State may be entitled in the Congress; but no Senator or Representative, or Person holding an Office of Trust or Profit under the United States, shall be appointed an Elector.

The Electors shall meet in their respective States, and vote by Ballot for two persons, of whom one at least shall not be an Inhabitant of the same State with themselves. And they shall make a List of all the Persons voted for, and of the Number of Votes for each; which List they shall sign and certify, and transmit sealed to the Seat of the Government of the United States, directed to the President of the Senate. The President of the Senate shall, in the Presence of the Senate and House of Representatives, open all the Certificates, and the Votes shall then be counted. The Person having the greatest Number of Votes shall be the President, if such Number be a Majority of the whole Number of Electors appointed; and if there be more than one who have such Majority, and have an equal Number of Votes, then the House of Representatives shall immediately chuse by Ballot one of them for President; and if no Person have a Majority, then from the five highest on the List the said House shall in like Manner chuse the President. But in chusing the President, the votes shall be taken by States, the Representation from each State having one Vote; a quorum for this Purpose shall consist of a Member or Members from two-thirds of the States, and a Majority of all the States shall be necessary to a Choice. In every Case, after the Choice of the President, the Person having the greatest Number of Votes of the Electors shall be the Vice President. But if there should remain two or more who have equal votes, the Senate shall chuse from them by Ballot the Vice President.

The Congress may determine the time of chusing the Electors, and the Day on which they shall give their Votes; which Day shall be the same throughout the United States.

No person except a natural-born Citizen, or a Citizen of the United States, at the time of the Adoption of this Constitution, shall be eligible to the Office of President; neither shall any Person be eligible to that Office who shall not have attained to the Age of thirty-five years, and been fourteen Years a Resident within the United States.

In Case of the Removal of the President from Office, or of his Death, Resignation, or Inability to discharge the Powers and Duties of the said Office, the same shall devolve on the Vice President, and the Congress may by Law provide for the Case of Removal, Death, Resignation, or Inability, both of the President and Vice President, declaring what Officer shall then act as President, and such Officer shall act accordingly, until the disability be removed, or a President shall be elected.

The President shall, at stated Times, receive for his Services a Compensation, which shall neither be increased nor diminished during the Period for which he shall have been elected, and he shall not receive within that Period any other Emolument from the United States, or any of them.

Before he enter on the execution of his Office, he shall take the following Oath or Affirmation:—"I do solemnly swear (or affirm) that I will faithfully execute the Office of President of the United States, and will, to the best of my Ability, preserve, protect, and defend the Constitution of the United States."

Section 2.

The President shall be Commander in Chief of the Army and Navy of the United States, and of the Militia of the several States, when called into the actual Service of the United States; he may require the Opinion, in writing, of the principal Officer in each of the executive Departments, upon any subject relating to the Duties of their respective Offices, and he shall have Power to Grant Reprieves and Pardons for Offences against the United States, except in Cases of Impeachment.

He shall have Power, by and with the Advice and Consent of the Senate, to make Treaties, provided two thirds of the Senators present concur; and he shall nominate, and by and with the Advice and Consent of the Senate, shall appoint Ambassadors, other public Ministers and Consuls, Judges of the supreme Court, and all other Officers of the United States, whose Appointments are not herein otherwise provided for, and which shall be established by Law: but the Congress may by Law vest the Appointment of such inferior Officers, as they think proper, in the President alone, in the Courts of Law, or in the Heads of Departments.

The President shall have Power to fill up all Vacancies that may happen during the Recess of the Senate, by granting Commissions which shall expire at the End of their next Session.

Section 3.

He shall from time to time give to the Congress Information of the State of the Union, and recommend to their Consideration such Measures as he shall judge necessary and expedient; he may, on extraordinary occasions, convene both Houses, or either of them, and in Case of Disagreement between them, with respect to the Time of Adjournment, he may adjourn them to such Time as he shall think proper; he shall receive Ambassadors and other public Ministers; he shall take Care that the Laws be faithfully executed, and shall Commission all the Officers of the United States.

Section 4.

The President, Vice President and all civil Officers of the United States, shall be removed from Office on Impeachment for, and Conviction of, Treason, Bribery, or other high Crimes and Misdemeanors.

Article III

Section 1.

The judicial Power of the United States, shall be vested in one supreme Court, and in such inferior Courts as the Congress may from time to time ordain and establish. The Judges, both of the supreme and inferior Courts, shall hold their Offices during good Behaviour, and shall, at stated Times, receive for their Services, a Compensation, which shall not be diminished during their Continuance in Office.

Section 2.

The judicial Power shall extend to all Cases, in Law and Equity, arising under this Constitution, the Laws of the United States, and treaties made, or which shall be made, under their Authority;—to all Cases affecting ambassadors, other public ministers and consuls;—to all cases of admiralty and maritime

Jurisdiction;—to Controversies to which the United States shall be a Party;—to Controversies between two or more States;—between a State and Citizens of another State;—between Citizens of different States,—between Citizens of the same State claiming Lands under Grants of different States, and between a State, or the Citizens thereof, and foreign States, Citizens or Subjects.

In all Cases affecting Ambassadors, other public Ministers and Consuls, and those in which a State shall be Party, the supreme Court shall have original Jurisdiction. In all the other Cases before mentioned, the supreme Court shall have appellate Jurisdiction, both as to Law and Fact, with such Exceptions, and under such Regulations as the Congress shall make.

The trial of all Crimes, except in Cases of Impeachment, shall be by Jury; and such Trial shall be held in the State where the said Crimes shall have been committed; but when not committed within any State, the Trial shall be at such Place or Places as the Congress may by Law have directed.

Section 3.

Treason against the United States, shall consist only in levying War against them, or in adhering to their Enemies, giving them Aid and Comfort. No Person shall be convicted of Treason unless on the testimony of two Witnesses to the same overt Act, or on Confession in open Court.

The Congress shall have power to declare the Punishment of Treason, but no Attainder of Treason shall work Corruption of Blood, or Forfeiture except during the Life of the Person attained.

Article IV

Section 1.

Full Faith and Credit shall be given in each State to the public Acts, Records, and judicial Proceedings of every other State. And the Congress may by general Laws prescribe the Manner in which such Acts, Records and Proceedings shall be proved, and the Effect thereof.

Section 2.

The Citizens of each State shall be entitled to all Privileges and Immunities of Citizens in the several States.

A Person charged in any State with Treason, Felony, or other Crime, who shall flee from Justice, and be found in another State, shall on demand of the executive Authority of the State from which he fled, be delivered up, to be removed to the State having Jurisdiction of the crime.

No Person held to Service or Labour in one State, under the Laws thereof, escaping into another, shall, in Consequence of any Law or Regulation therein, be discharged from such Service or Labour, but shall be delivered up on Claim of the Party to whom such Service or Labour may be due.

Section 3.

New States may be admitted by the Congress into this Union; but no new State shall be formed or erected within the Jurisdiction of any other State; nor any State be formed by the Junction of two or more States, or parts of States, without the Consent of the Legislatures of the States concerned as well as of the Congress.

The Congress shall have Power to dispose of and make all needful Rules and Regulations respecting the Territory or other Property belonging to the United States; and nothing in this Constitution shall be so construed as to Prejudice any Claims of the United States, or of any particular State.

Section 4.

The United States shall guarantee to every State in this Union a Republican Form of Government, and shall protect each of them against Invasion; and on Application of the Legislature, or the Executive (when the Legislature cannot be convened) against domestic Violence.

Article V

The Congress, whenever two-thirds of both Houses shall deem it necessary, shall propose Amendments to this Constitution, or, on the Application of the Legislatures of two-thirds of the several States, shall call a Convention for proposing Amendments, which, in either Case, shall be valid to all Intents and Purposes, as part of this Constitution, when ratified by the Legislatures of three-fourths of the several States, or by Conventions in three-fourths thereof, as the one or the other Mode of Ratification may be proposed by the Congress; Provided that no Amendment which may be made prior to the Year One thousand eight hundred and eight shall in any Manner affect the first and fourth Clauses in the Ninth Section of the first Article; and that no State, without its Consent, shall be deprived of its equal Suffrage in the Senate.

Article VI

All Debts contracted and Engagements entered into, before the Adoption of this Constitution, shall be as valid against the United States under this Constitution, as under the Confederation.

This Constitution, and the Laws of the United States which shall be made in Pursuance thereof; and all Treaties made, or which shall be made, under the

Authority of the United States, shall be the supreme Law of the Land; and the Judges in every State shall be bound thereby, any Thing in the Constitution or Laws of any State to the Contrary notwithstanding.

The Senators and Representatives before mentioned, and the Members of the several State Legislatures, and all executive and judicial Officers, both of the United States and of the several States, shall be bound by Oath or Affirmation to support this Constitution; but no religious Test shall ever be required as a qualification to any Office or public Trust under the United States.

Article VII

The ratification of the conventions of nine States shall be sufficient for the establishment of this Constitution between the States so ratifying the same.

Done in Convention by the unanimous consent of the States present, the seventeenth day of September in the year of our Lord one thousand seven hundred and eighty-seven and of the Independence of the United States of America the twelfth. In witness whereof we have hereunto subscribed our names.

George Washington,
President and Deputy from Virginia

New Hampshire
John Langdon
Nicholas Gilman

Massachusetts
Nathaniel Gorham
Rufus King

Connecticut
William S. Johnson
Roger Sherman

New York
Alexander Hamilton

New Jersey
William Livingston
David Brearley
William Paterson
Jonathan Dayton

Pennsylvania
Benjamin Franklin
Thomas Mifflin
Robert Morris
George Clymer
Thomas Fitzsimons
Jared Ingersoll
James Wilson
Gouverneur Morris

Delaware
George Read
Gunning Bedford, Jr.
John Dickinson
Richard Bassett
Jacob Broom

Maryland
James McHenry
Daniel of St. Thomas
 Jenifer
Daniel Carroll

Virginia
John Blair
James Madison, Jr.

North Carolina
William Blount
Richard Dobbs Spraight
Hu Williamson

South Carolina
J. Rutledge
Charles C. Pinckney
Pierce Butler

Georgia
William Few
Abraham Baldwin

Amendments to the Constitution

*A*rticles in Addition to, and Amendment of, the Constitution of the United States of America, Proposed by Congress, and Ratified by the Legislatures of the Several States, Pursuant to the Fifth Article of the Original Constitution.

Amendment I [1791]

Congress shall make no law respecting an establishment of religion, or prohibiting the free exercise thereof; or abridging the freedom of speech, or of the press; or the right of the people peaceably to assemble, and to petition the Government for a redress of grievances.

Amendment II [1791]

A well regulated Militia, being necessary to the security of a free State, the right of the people to keep and bear Arms shall not be infringed.

Amendment III [1791]

No Soldier shall, in time of peace, be quartered in any house, without the consent of the Owner, nor in time of war, but in a manner to be prescribed by law.

Amendment IV [1791]

The right of the people to be secure in their persons, houses, papers, and effects, against unreasonable searches and seizures, shall not be violated, and no Warrants shall issue, but upon probable cause, supported by Oath or affirmation, and particularly describing the place to be searched, and the persons or things to be seized.

Amendment V [1791]

No person shall be held to answer for a capital or otherwise infamous crime, unless on a presentment or indictment of a Grand Jury, except in cases arising in the land or naval forces, or in the Militia, when in actual service in time of War or public danger; nor shall any person be subject for the same offence to be twice put in jeopardy of life or limb; nor shall be compelled in any criminal case to be a witness against himself, nor be deprived of life, liberty, or property, without due process of law; nor shall private property be taken for public use, without just compensation.

Amendment VI [1791]

In all criminal prosecutions, the accused shall enjoy the right to a speedy and public trial, by an impartial jury of the State and district wherein the crime shall have been committed, which district shall have been previously ascertained by law, and to be informed of the nature and cause of the accusation; to be confronted with the witnesses against him; to have compulsory process for obtaining witnesses in his favor, and to have the Assistance of Counsel for his defence.

Amendment VII [1791]

In suits at common law, where the value in controversy shall exceed twenty dollars, the right of trial by jury shall be preserved, and no fact tried by a jury, shall be otherwise reexamined in any Court of the United States, than according to the rules of the common law.

Amendment VIII [1791]

Excessive bail shall not be required, nor excessive fines imposed, nor cruel and unusual punishments inflicted.

Amendment IX [1791]

The enumeration in the Constitution, of certain rights, shall not be construed to deny or disparage others retained by the people.

Amendment X [1791]

The powers not delegated to the United States by the Constitution, nor prohibited by it to the States, are reserved to the States respectively, or to the people.

Amendment XI [1798]

The Judicial power of the United States shall not be construed to extend to any suit in law or equity, commenced or prosecuted against one of the United States by Citizens of another State, or by Citizens or Subjects of any Foreign State.

Amendment XII [1804]

The Electors shall meet in their respective States and vote by ballot for President and Vice-President, one of whom, at least, shall not be an inhabitant of the same State with themselves; they shall name in their ballots the person voted for as President, and in distinct ballots the person voted for as Vice-President, and they shall make distinct lists of all persons voted for as President, and of all persons voted for as Vice-President, and of the number of votes for each, which lists they shall sign and certify, and transmit sealed to the seat of the government of the United States, directed to the President of the Senate;—The President of the Senate shall, in the presence of the Senate and House of Representatives, open all the certificates and the votes shall then be counted;—The person having the greatest number of votes for President, shall be the President, if such number be a majority of the whole number of Electors appointed; and if no person have such majority, then from the persons having the highest numbers not exceeding three on the list of those voted for as President, the House of Representatives shall choose immediately, by ballot, the President. But in choosing the President, the votes shall be taken by states, the representation from each state having one vote; a quorum for this purpose shall consist of a member or members from two-thirds of the states, and a majority of all the states shall be necessary to a choice. And if the House of Representatives shall not choose a President whenever the right of choice shall devolve upon them, before the fourth day of March next following, then the Vice-President shall act as President, as in the case of the death or other constitutional disability of the President.—The person having the greatest number of votes as Vice-President, shall be the Vice-President, if such number be a majority of the whole number of Electors appointed, and if no person have a majority, then from the two highest numbers on the list, the Senate shall choose the Vice-President; a quorum for the purpose shall consist of two-thirds of the whole number of Senators, and a majority of the whole number shall be necessary to a choice. But no person constitutionally ineligible to the office of President shall be eligible to that of Vice-President of the United States.

Amendment XIII [1865]

Section 1.

Neither slavery nor involuntary servitude, except as a punishment for crime whereof the party shall have been duly convicted, shall exist within the United States, or any place subject to their jurisdiction.

Section 2.

Congress shall have power to enforce this article by appropriate legislation.

Amendment XIV [1868]

Section 1.

All persons born or naturalized in the United States, and subject to the jurisdiction thereof, are citizens of the United States and of the State wherein they reside. No State shall make or enforce any law which shall abridge the privileges or immunities of citizens of the United States; nor shall any State deprive any person of life, liberty, or property, without due process of law; nor deny to any person within its jurisdiction the equal protection of the laws.

Section 2.

Representatives shall be apportioned among the several States according to their respective numbers, counting the whole number of persons in each State, excluding Indians not taxed. But when the right to vote at any election for the choice of electors for President and Vice-President of the United States, Representatives in Congress, the Executive and Judicial officers of a State, or the members of the Legislature thereof, is denied to any of the male inhabitants of such State, being twenty-one years of age, and citizens of the United States, or in any way abridged, except for participation in rebellion, or other crime, the basis of representation therein shall be reduced in the proportion which the number of such male citizens shall bear to the whole number of male citizens twenty-one years of age in such State.

Section 3.

No person shall be a Senator or Representative in Congress, or elector of President and Vice-President, or hold any office, civil or military, under the United States, or under any State, who, having previously taken an oath, as a member of Congress, or as an officer of the United States, or as a member of any State legislature, or as an executive or judicial officer of any State, to support the

Constitution of the United States, shall have engaged in insurrection or rebellion against the same, or given aid or comfort to the enemies thereof. But Congress may by a vote of two-thirds of each House, remove such disability.

Section 4.

The validity of the public debt of the United States, authorized by law, including debts incurred for payment of pensions and bounties for services in suppressing insurrection or rebellion, shall not be questioned. But neither the United States nor any State shall assume or pay any debt or obligation incurred in aid of insurrection or rebellion against the United States, or any claim for the loss or emancipation of any slave; but all such debts, obligations, and claims shall be held illegal and void.

Section 5.

The Congress shall have the power to enforce, by appropriate legislation, the provisions of this article.

Amendment XV [1870]

Section 1.

The right of citizens of the United States to vote shall not be denied or abridged by the United States or by any State on account of race, color, or previous condition of servitude—

Section 2.

The Congress shall have power to enforce this article by appropriate legislation.

Amendment XVI [1913]

The Congress shall have power to lay and collect taxes on incomes, from whatever source derived, without apportionment among the several States, and without regard to any census or enumeration.

Amendment XVII [1913]

The Senate of the United States shall be composed of two Senators from each State, elected by the people thereof, for six years; and each Senator shall have one vote. The electors in each State shall have the qualifications requisite for electors of the most numerous branch of the State legislatures.

When vacancies happen in the representation of any State in the Senate, the executive authority of such State shall issue writs of election to fill such vacancies: *Provided,* That the legislature of any State may empower the executive thereof to make temporary appointments until the people fill the vacancies by election as the legislature may direct.

This amendment shall not be so construed as to affect the election or term of any Senator chosen before it becomes valid as part of the Constitution.

Amendment XVIII [1919]

Section 1.

After one year from the ratification of this article the manufacture, sale, or transportation of intoxicating liquors within, the importation thereof into, or the exportation thereof from the United States and all territory subject to the jurisdiction thereof for beverage purposes is hereby prohibited.

Section 2.

The Congress and the several States shall have concurrent power to enforce this article by appropriate legislation.

Section 3.

This article shall be inoperative unless it shall have been ratified as an amendment to the Constitution by the legislatures of the several States, as provided in the Constitution, within seven years from the date of the submission hereof to the States by the Congress.

Amendment XIX [1920]

The right of citizens of the United States to vote shall not be denied or abridged by the United States or by any State on account of sex.

Congress shall have power to enforce this article by appropriate legislation.

Amendment XX [1933]

Section 1.

The terms of the President and Vice-President shall end at noon on the 20th day of January, and the terms of Senators and Representatives at noon on the 3d day of January, of the years in which such terms would have ended if this article had not been ratified; and the terms of their successors shall then begin.

Section 2.

The Congress shall assemble at least once in every year, and such meeting shall begin at noon on the 3d day of January, unless they shall by law appoint a different day.

Section 3.

If, at the time fixed for the beginning of the term of the President, the President elect shall have died, the Vice-President elect shall become President. If a President shall not have been chosen before the time fixed for the beginning of his term, or if the President elect shall have failed to qualify, then the Vice President elect shall act as President until a President shall have qualified; and the Congress may by law provide for the case wherein neither a President elect nor a Vice-President elect shall have qualified, declaring who shall then act as President, or the manner in which one who is to act shall be selected, and such person shall act accordingly until a President or Vice-President shall have qualified.

Section 4.

The Congress may by law provide for the case of the death of any of the persons from whom the House of Representatives may choose a President when ever the right of choice shall have devolved upon them and for the case of the death of any of the persons from whom the Senate may choose a Vice-President whenever the right of choice shall have devolved upon them.

Section 5.

Sections 1 and 2 shall take effect on 15th day of October following the ratification of article.

Section 6.

This article shall be inoperative unless it shall have been ratified as an amendment to the Constitution by the legislatures of three-fourths of the several States within seven years from the date of its submission.

Amendment XXI [1933]

Section 1.

The eighteenth article of amendment to the Constitution of the United States is hereby repealed.

Section 2.

The transportation or importation into any State, Territory, or possession of the United States for delivery or use therein of intoxicating liquors, in violation of the laws thereof, is hereby prohibited.

Section 3.

This article shall be inoperative unless it shall have been ratified as an amendment to the Constitution by conventions in the several States, as provided in the Constitution, within seven years from the date of the submission hereof to the States by the Congress.

Amendment XXII [1951]

No person shall be elected to the office of the President more than twice, and no person who has held the office of President, or acted as President, for more than two years of a term to which some other person was elected President shall be elected to the office of the President more than once.

But this Article shall not apply to any person holding the office of President when this Article was proposed by the Congress, and shall not prevent any person who may be holding the office of President, or acting as President, during the term within which this Article becomes operative from holding the office of President or acting as President during the remainder of such term.

Amendment XXIII [1961]

Section 1.

The District constituting the seat of Government of the United States shall appoint in such manner as the Congress may direct:

A number of electors of President and Vice President equal to the whole number of Senators and Representatives in Congress to which the District would be entitled if it were a State, but in no event more than the least populous State; they shall be in addition to those appointed by the States, but they shall be considered, for the purposes of the election of President and Vice President, to be electors appointed by a State; and they shall meet in the District and perform such duties as provided by the twelfth article of amendment.

Section 2.

The Congress shall have power to enforce this article by appropriate legislation.

Amendment XXIV [1964]

Section 1.

The right of citizens of the United States to vote in any primary or other election for President or Vice President, for electors for President or Vice President, or for Senator or Representative in Congress, shall not be denied or abridged by the United States or any State by reason of failure to pay any poll tax or other tax.

Section 2.

The Congress shall have the power to enforce this article by appropriate legislation.

Amendment XXV [1967]

Section 1.

In case of the removal of the President from office or his death or resignation, the Vice President shall become President.

Section 2.

Whenever there is a vacancy in the office of the Vice President, the President shall nominate a Vice President who shall take the office upon confirmation by a majority vote of both houses of Congress.

Section 3.

Whenever the President transmits to the President pro tempore of the Senate and the Speaker of the House of Representatives his written declaration that he is unable to discharge the powers and duties of his office, and until he transmits to them a written declaration to the contrary, such powers and duties shall be discharged by the Vice President as Acting President.

Section 4.

Whenever the Vice President and a majority of either the principal officers of the executive departments, or of such other body as Congress may by law provide, transmit to the President pro tempore of the Senate and the Speaker of the House of Representatives their written declaration that the President is unable to discharge the powers and duties of his office, the Vice President shall immediately assume the powers and duties of the office as Acting President.

Thereafter, when the President transmits to the President pro tempore of the Senate and the Speaker of the House of Representatives his written declaration that no inability exists, he shall resume the powers and duties of his office unless the Vice President and a majority of either the principal officers of the executive departments, or of such other body as Congress may by law provide, transmit within four days to the President pro tempore of the Senate and the Speaker of the House of Representatives their written declaration that the President is unable to discharge the powers and duties of his office. Thereupon Congress shall decide the issue, assembling within 48 hours for that purpose if not in session. If the Congress, within 21 days after receipt of the latter written declaration, or, if Congress is not in session, within 21 days after Congress is required to assemble, determines by two-thirds vote of both houses that the President is unable to discharge the powers and duties of his office, the Vice President shall continue to discharge the same as Acting President; otherwise, the President shall resume the powers and duties of his office.

Amendment XXVI [1971]

Section 1.

The right of citizens of the United States, who are 18 years of age or older, to vote shall not be denied or abridged by the United States or any state on account of age.

Section 2.

The Congress shall have the power to enforce this article by appropriate legislation.

[Amendment XXVII] [1992]

No law varying the compensation for the services of the Senators and Representatives shall take effect, until an election of Representatives shall have intervened.

Presidential Elections, 1789–1992

Year	Candidates	Party	Popular Vote*	Electoral Vote**
1789	**George Washington**			69
	John Adams			34
	Others			35
1792	**George Washington**			132
	John Adams			77
	George Clinton			50
	Others			5
1796	**John Adams**	Federalist		71
	Thomas Jefferson	Democratic Republican		68
	Thomas Pinckney	Federalist		59
	Aaron Burr	Democratic Republican		30
	Others			48
1800	**Thomas Jefferson**	Democratic Republican		73
	Aaron Burr	Democratic Republican		73
	John Adams	Federalist		65
	Charles C. Pinckney	Federalist		64
1804	**Thomas Jefferson**	Democratic Republican		162
	Charles C. Pinckney	Federalist		14

Year	Candidates	Party	Popular Vote*	Electoral Vote**
1808	**James Madison**	Democratic Republican		122
	Charles C. Pinckney	Federalist		47
	George Clinton	Independent Republican		6
1812	**James Madison**	Democratic Republican		128
	DeWitt Clinton	Federalist		89
1816	**James Monroe**	Democratic Republican		183
	Rufus King	Federalist		34
1820	**James Monroe**	Democratic Republican		231
	John Quincy Adams	Independent Republican		1
1824	**John Quincy Adams**	Democratic Republican	108,704 (30.5%)	84
	Andrew Jackson	Democratic Republican	153,544 (43.1%)	99
	Henry Clay	Democratic Republican	47,136 (13.2%)	37
	William H. Crawford	Democratic Republican	46,618 (13.1%)	41
1828	**Andrew Jackson**	Democratic	647,231 (56.0%)	178
	John Quincy Adams	National Republican	509,097 (44.0%)	83
1832	**Andrew Jackson**	Democratic	687,502 (55.0%)	219
	Henry Clay	National Republican	530,189 (42.4%)	49
	William Wirt	Anti-Masonic		7
	John Floyd	National Republican		11
1836	**Martin Van Buren**	Democratic	761,549 (50.9%)	170
	William H. Harrison	Whig	549,567 (36.7%)	73
	Hugh L. White	Whig	145,396 (9.7%)	26
	Daniel Webster	Whig	41,287 (2.7%)	14

(continues)

* Because only the leading candidates are listed, popular vote percentages do not always total 100.

** The elections of 1800 and 1824, in which no candidate received an electoral vote majority, were decided in the House of Representatives.

Year	Candidates	Party	Popular Vote*	Electoral Vote**
1840	**William H. Harrison (John Tyler,** 1841)	Whig	1,275,017 (53.1%)	234
	Martin Van Buren	Democratic	1,128,702 (46.9%)	60
1844	**James K. Polk**	Democratic	1,337,243 (49.6%)	170
	Henry Clay	Whig	1,299,068 (48.1%)	105
	James G. Birney	Liberty	62,300 (2.3%)	
1848	**Zachary Taylor (Millard Fillmore,** 1850)	Whig	1,360,101 (47.4%)	163
	Lewis Cass	Democratic	1,220,544 (42.5%)	127
	Martin Van Buren	Free Soil	291,263 (10.1%)	
1852	**Franklin Pierce**	Democratic	1,601,474 (50.9%)	254
	Winfield Scott	Whig	1,386,578 (44.1%)	42
1856	**James Buchanan**	Democratic	1,838,169 (45.4%)	174
	John C. Frémont	Republican	1,335,264 (33.0%)	114
	Millard Fillmore	American	874,534 (21.6%)	8
1860	**Abraham Lincoln**	Republican	1,865,593 (39.8%)	180
	Stephen A. Douglas	Democratic	1,382,713 (29.5%)	12
	John C. Breckinridge	Democratic	848,356 (18.1%)	72
	John Bell	Constitutional Union	592,906 (12.6%)	39
1864	**Abraham Lincoln (Andrew Johnson,** 1865)	Republican	2,206,938 (55.0%)	212
	George B. McClellan	Democratic	1,803,787 (45.0%)	21
1868	**Ulysses S. Grant**	Republican	3,013,421 (52.7%)	214
	Horatio Seymour	Democratic	2,706,829 (47.3%)	80

Year	Candidates	Party	Popular Vote*	Electoral Vote**
1872	**Ulysses S. Grant**	Republican	3,596,745 (55.6%)	286
	Horace Greeley	Democratic	2,843,446 (43.9%)	66
1876	**Rutherford B. Hayes**	Republican	4,036,572 (48.0%)	185
	Samuel J. Tilden	Democratic	4,284,020 (51.0%)	184
1880	**James A. Garfield**	Republican	4,449,053 (48.3%)	214
	(Chester A. Arthur, 1881)			
	Winfield S. Hancock	Democratic	4,442,035 (48.2%)	155
	James B. Weaver	Greenback Labor	308,578 (3.4%)	
1884	**Grover Cleveland**	Democratic	4,874,986 (48.5%)	219
	James G. Blaine	Republican	4,851,981 (48.2%)	182
	Benjamin F. Butler	Greenback Labor	175,370 (1.8%)	
1888	**Benjamin Harrison**	Republican	5,444,337 (47.8%)	233
	Grover Cleveland	Democratic	5,540,050 (48.6%)	168
1892	**Grover Cleveland**	Democratic	5,554,414 (46.0%)	277
	Benjamin Harrison	Republican	5,190,802 (43.0%)	145
	James B. Weaver	People's	1,027,329 (8.5%)	22
1896	**William McKinley**	Republican	7,035,638 (50.8%)	271
	William Jennings Bryan	Democratic; Populist	6,467,946 (46.7%)	176
1900	**William McKinley**	Republican	7,219,530 (51.7%)	292
	(Theodore Roosevelt, 1901)			
	William Jennings Bryan	Democratic; Populist	6,356,734 (45.5%)	155

* Because only the leading candidates are listed, popular vote percentages do not always total 100.

** The elections of 1800 and 1824, in which no candidate received an electoral vote majority, were decided in the House of Representatives.

(continues)

Year	Candidates	Party	Popular Vote*	Electoral Vote**
1904	**Theodore Roosevelt**	Republican	7,628,834 (56.4%)	336
	Alton B. Parker	Democratic	5,084,401 (37.6%)	140
	Eugene V. Debs	Socialist	402,460 (3.0%)	
1908	**William H. Taft**	Republican	7,679,006 (51.6%)	321
	William Jennings Bryan	Democratic	6,409,106 (43.1%)	162
	Eugene V. Debs	Socialist	420,820 (2.8%)	
1912	**Woodrow Wilson**	Democratic	6,286,820 (41.8%)	435
	Theodore Roosevelt	Progressive	4,126,020 (27.4%)	88
	William H. Taft	Republican	3,483,922 (23.2%)	8
	Eugene V. Debs	Socialist	897,011 (6.0%)	
1916	**Woodrow Wilson**	Democratic	9,129,606 (49.3%)	277
	Charles E. Hughes	Republican	8,538,221 (46.1%)	254
1920	**Warren G. Harding** (Calvin Coolidge, 1923)	Republican	16,152,200 (61.0%)	404
	James M. Cox	Democratic	9,147,353 (34.6%)	127
	Eugene V. Debs	Socialist	919,799 (3.5%)	
1924	**Calvin Coolidge**	Republican	15,725,016 (54.1%)	382
	John W. Davis	Democratic	8,385,586 (28.8%)	136
	Robert M. La Follette	Progressive	4,822,856 (16.6%)	13
1928	**Herbert C. Hoover**	Republican	21,392,190 (58.2%)	444
	Alfred E. Smith	Democratic	15,016,443 (40.8%)	87
1932	**Franklin D. Roosevelt**	Democratic	22,809,638 (57.3%)	472
	Herbert C. Hoover	Republican	15,758,901 (39.6%)	59
	Norman Thomas	Socialist	881,951 (2.2%)	

Year	Candidates	Party	Popular Vote*	Electoral Vote**
1936	**Franklin D. Roosevelt**	Democratic	27,751,612 (60.7%)	523
	Alfred M. Landon	Republican	16,681,913 (36.4%)	8
	William Lemke	Union	891,858 (1.9%)	
1940	**Franklin D. Roosevelt**	Democratic	27,243,466 (54.7%)	449
	Wendell L. Willkie	Republican	22,304,755 (44.8%)	82
1944	**Franklin D. Roosevelt**	Democratic	25,602,505 (52.8%)	432
	(Harry S Truman, 1945)			
	Thomas E. Dewey	Republican	22,006,278 (44.5%)	99
1948	**Harry S Truman**	Democratic	24,105,812 (49.5%)	303
	Thomas E. Dewey	Republican	21,970,065 (45.1%)	189
	J. Strom Thurmond	States' Rights	1,169,063 (2.4%)	39
	Henry A. Wallace	Progressive	1,157,172 (2.4%)	
1952	**Dwight D. Eisenhower**	Republican	33,936,234 (55.2%)	442
	Adlai E. Stevenson	Democratic	27,314,992 (44.5%)	89
1956	**Dwight D. Eisenhower**	Republican	35,590,472 (57.4%)	457
	Adlai E. Stevenson	Democratic	26,022,752 (42.0%)	73
1960	**John F. Kennedy**	Democratic	34,227,096 (49.9%)	303
	(Lyndon B. Johnson, 1963)			
	Richard M. Nixon	Republican	34,108,546 (49.6%)	219
1964	**Lyndon B. Johnson**	Democratic	43,126,233 (61.1%)	486
	Barry M. Goldwater	Republican	27,174,989 (38.5%)	52

* Because only the leading candidates are listed, popular vote percentages do not always total 100.
** The elections of 1800 and 1824, in which no candidate received an electoral vote majority, were decided in the House of Representatives.

(continues)

Year	Candidates	Party	Popular Vote*	Electoral Vote**
1968	**Richard M. Nixon**	Republican	31,783,783 (43.4%)	301
	Hubert H. Humphrey	Democratic	31,271,839 (42.7%)	191
	George C. Wallace	Amer. Independent	9,899,557 (13.5%)	46
1972	**Richard M. Nixon**	Republican	45,767,218 (60.6%)	520
	(**Gerald R. Ford**, 1974)			
	George S. McGovern	Democratic	28,357,668 (37.5%)	17
1976	**Jimmy Carter**	Democratic	40,828,657 (50.6%)	297
	Gerald R. Ford	Republican	39,145,520 (48.4%)	241
1980	**Ronald Reagan**	Republican	43,899,248 (51%)	489
	Jimmy Carter	Democratic	36,481,435 (41%)	49
	John B. Anderson	Independent	5,719,437 (6%)	
1984	**Ronald Reagan**	Republican	54,455,075 (59%)	525
	Walter F. Mondale	Democratic	37,577,185 (41%)	13
1988	**George Bush**	Republican	48,881,221 (54%)	426
	Michael Dukakis	Democratic	41,805,422 (46%)	111
1992	**Bill Clinton**	Democratic	43,728,375 (43%)	370
	George Bush	Republican	38,167,416 (38%)	168
	H. Ross Perot	Independent	19,237,247 (19%)	

* Because only the leading candidates are listed, popular vote percentages do not always total 100.

** The elections of 1800 and 1824, in which no candidate received an electoral vote majority, were decided in the House of Representatives.

Presidential Administrations

Washington, 1789–1797

Vice-President	John Adams	1789–1797
Secretary of State	Thomas Jefferson	1789–1793
	Edmund Randolph	1794–1795
	Timothy Pickering	1795–1797
Secretary of War	Henry Knox	1789–1794
	Timothy Pickering	1795–1796
	James McHenry	1796–1797
Secretary of Treasury	Alexander Hamilton	1789–1795
	Oliver Wolcott, Jr.	1795–1797
Postmaster General	Samuel Osgood	1789–1791
	Timothy Pickering	1791–1794
	Joseph Habersham	1795–1797
Attorney General	Edmund Randolph	1789–1793
	William Bradford	1794–1795
	Charles Lee	1795–1797

John Adams, 1797–1801

Vice-President	Thomas Jefferson	1797–1801
Secretary of State	Timothy Pickering	1797–1800
	John Marshall	1800–1801
Secretary of War	James McHenry	1797–1800
	Samuel Dexter	1800–1801
Secretary of Treasury	Oliver Wolcott, Jr.	1797–1800
	Samuel Dexter	1800–1801
Postmaster General	Joseph Habersham	1797–1801
Attorney General	Charles Lee	1797–1801
Secretary of Navy	Benjamin Stoddert	1798–1801

Jefferson, 1801–1809

Vice-President	Aaron Burr	1801–1805
	George Clinton	1805–1809

(continues)

Secretary of State	James Madison	1801–1809
Secretary of War	Henry Dearborn	1801–1809
Secretary of Treasury	Samuel Dexter	1801
	Albert Gallatin	1801–1809
Postmaster General	Joseph Habersham	1801
	Gideon Granger	1801–1809
Attorney General	Levi Lincoln	1801–1805
	Robert Smith	1805
	John C. Breckinridge	1805–1806
	Caesar A. Rodney	1807–1809
Secretary of Navy	Robert Smith	1801–1809

Madison, 1809–1817

Vice-President	George Clinton	1809–1813
	Elbridge Gerry	1813–1817
Secretary of State	Robert Smith	1809–1811
	James Monroe	1811–1817
Secretary of War	William Eustis	1809–1812
	John Armstrong	1813–1814
	James Monroe	1814–1815
	William H. Crawford	1815–1817
Secretary of Treasury	Albert Gallatin	1809–1813
	George W. Campbell	1814
	Alexander J. Dallas	1814–1816
	William H. Crawford	1816–1817
Postmaster General	Gideon Granger	1809–1814
	Return J. Meigs, Jr.	1814–1817
Attorney General	Caesar A. Rodney	1809–1811
	William Pinkney	1811–1814
	Richard Rush	1814–1817
Secretary of Navy	Paul Hamilton	1809–1813
	William Jones	1813–1814
	Benjamin W. Crowninshield	1814–1817

Monroe, 1817–1825

Vice-President	Daniel D. Tompkins	1817–1825
Secretary of State	John Quincy Adams	1817–1825
Secretary of War	George Graham	1817
	John C. Calhoun	1817–1825
Secretary of Treasury	William H. Crawford	1817–1825
Postmaster General	Return J. Meigs, Jr.	1817–1823
	John McLean	1823–1825
Attorney General	Richard Rush	1817
	William Wirt	1817–1825
Secretary of Navy	Benjamin W. Crowninshield	1817–1818
	Smith Thompson	1818–1823
	Samuel L. Southard	1823–1825

John Quincy Adams, 1825–1829

Vice-President	John C. Calhoun	1825–1829
Secretary of State	Henry Clay	1825–1829
Secretary of War	James Barbour	1825–1828
	Peter B. Porter	1828–1829
Secretary of Treasury	Richard Rush	1825–1829
Postmaster General	John McLean	1825–1829
Attorney General	William Wirt	1825–1829
Secretary of Navy	Samuel L. Southard	1825–1829

Jackson, 1829–1837

Vice-President	John C. Calhoun	1829–1832
	Martin Van Buren	1833–1837
Secretary of State	Martin Van Buren	1829–1831
	Edward Livingston	1831–1833
	Louis McLane	1833–1834
	John Forsyth	1834–1837
Secretary of War	John H. Eaton	1829–1831
	Lewis Cass	1831–1837
	Benjamin Butler	1837
Secretary of Treasury	Samuel D. Ingham	1829–1831
	Louis McLane	1831–1833
	William J. Duane	1833
	Roger B. Taney	1833–1834
	Levi Woodbury	1834–1837
Postmaster General	William T. Barry	1829–1835
	Amos Kendall	1835–1837
Attorney General	John M. Berrien	1829–1831
	Roger B. Taney	1831–1833
	Benjamin F. Butler	1833–1837
Secretary of Navy	John Branch	1829–1831
	Levi Woodbury	1831–1834
	Mahlon Dickerson	1834–1837

Van Buren, 1837–1841

Vice-President	Richard M. Johnson	1837–1841
Secretary of State	John Forsyth	1837–1841
Secretary of War	Joel R. Poinsett	1837–1841
Secretary of Treasury	Levi Woodbury	1837–1841
Postmaster General	Amos Kendall	1837–1840
	John M. Niles	1840–1841
Attorney General	Benjamin F. Butler	1837–1838
	Felix Grundy	1838–1840
	Henry D. Gilpin	1840–1841
Secretary of Navy	Mahlon Dickerson	1837–1838
	James K. Paulding	1838–1841

(continues)

William Harrison, 1841

Vice-President	John Tyler	1841
Secretary of State	Daniel Webster	1841
Secretary of War	John Bell	1841
Secretary of Treasury	Thomas Ewing	1841
Postmaster General	Francis Granger	1841
Attorney General	John J. Crittenden	1841
Secretary of Navy	George E. Badger	1841

Tyler, 1841–1845

Vice-President	None	
Secretary of State	Daniel Webster	1841–1843
	Hugh S. Legare	1843
	Abel P. Upshur	1843–1844
	John C. Calhoun	1844–1845
Secretary of War	John Bell	1841
	John C. Spencer	1841–1843
	John M. Porter	1843–1844
	William Wilkins	1844–1845
Secretary of Treasury	Thomas Ewing	1841
	Walter Forward	1841–1843
	John C. Spencer	1843–1844
	George M. Bibb	1844–1845
Postmaster General	Francis Granger	1841
	Charles A. Wickliffe	1841
Attorney General	John J. Crittenden	1841
	Hugh S. Legaré	1841–1843
	John Nelson	1843–1845
Secretary of Navy	George Badger	1841
	Abel P. Upshur	1841
	David Henshaw	1843–1844
	Thomas W. Gilmer	1844
	John Y. Mason	1844–1845

Polk, 1845–1849

Vice-President	George M. Dallas	1845–1849
Secretary of State	James Buchanan	1845–1849
Secretary of War	William L. Marcy	1845–1849
Secretary of Treasury	Robert J. Walker	1845–1849
Postmaster General	Cave Johnson	1845–1849
Attorney General	John Y. Mason	1845–1846
	Nathan Clifford	1846–1848
	Isaac Toucey	1848–1849
Secretary of Navy	George Bancroft	1845–1846
	John Y. Mason	1846–1849

Taylor, 1849–1850

Vice-President	Millard Fillmore	1849–1850
Secretary of State	John M. Clayton	1849–1850
Secretary of War	George W. Crawford	1849–1850
Secretary of Treasury	William M. Meredith	1849–1850
Postmaster General	Jacob Collamer	1849–1850
Attorney General	Reverdy Johnson	1849–1850
Secretary of Navy	William Preston	1849–1850
Secretary of Interior	Thomas Ewing	1849–1850

Fillmore, 1850–1853

Vice-President	None	
Secretary of State	Daniel Webster	1850–1852
	Edward Everett	1852–1853
Secretary of War	Charles M. Conrad	1850–1853
Secretary of Treasury	Thomas Corwin	1850–1853
Postmaster General	Nathan K. Hall	1850–1852
	Sam D. Hubbard	1852–1853
Attorney General	John J. Crittenden	1850–1853
Secretary of Navy	William A. Graham	1850–1852
	John P. Kennedy	1852–1853

Secretary of Interior	Thomas M. T. McKennan	1850
	Alexander H. H. Stuart	1850–1853

Pierce, 1853–1857

Vice-President	William R. King	1853
Secretary of State	William L. Marcy	1853–1857
Secretary of War	Jefferson Davis	1853–1857
Secretary of Treasury	James Guthrie	1853–1857
Postmaster General	James Campbell	1853–1857
Attorney General	Caleb Cushing	1853–1857
Secretary of Navy	James C. Dobbins	1853–1857
Secretary of Interior	Robert McClelland	1853–1857

Buchanan, 1857–1861

Vice-President	John C. Breckinridge	1857–1861
Secretary of State	Lewis Cass	1857–1860
	Jeremiah S. Black	1860–1861
Secretary of War	John B. Floyd	1857–1861
	Joseph Holt	1861
Secretary of Treasury	Howell Cobb	1857–1860
	Philip F. Thomas	1860–1861

(continues)

Postmaster General	John A. Dix	1861
	Aaron V. Brown	1857–1859
	Joseph Holt	1859–1861
	Horatio King	1861
Attorney General	Jeremiah S. Black	1857–1860
	Edwin M. Stanton	1860–1861
Secretary of Navy	Isaac Toucey	1857–1861
Secretary of Interior	Jacob Thompson	1857–1861

Lincoln, 1861–1865

Vice-President	Hannibal Hamlin	1861–1865
	Andrew Johnson	1865
Secretary of State	William H. Seward	1861–1865
Secretary of War	Simon Cameron	1861–1862
	Edwin M. Stanton	1862–1865
Secretary of Treasury	Samuel P. Chase	1861–1864
	William P. Fessenden	1864–1865
	Hugh McCulloch	1865
Postmaster General	Horatio King	1861
	Montgomery Blair	1861–1864
	William Dennison	1864–1865
Attorney General	Edward Bates	1861–1864
	James Speed	1864–1865
Secretary of Navy	Gideon Welles	1861–1865
Secretary of Interior	Caleb B. Smith	1861–1863
	John P. Usher	1863–1865

Andrew Johnson, 1865–1869

Vice-President	None	
Secretary of State	William H. Seward	1865–1869
Secretary of War	Edwin M. Stanton	1865–1867
	Ulysses S. Grant	1867–1868
	John M. Schofield	1868–1869
Secretary of Treasury	Hugh McCulloch	1865–1869
Postmaster General	William Dennison	1865–1866
	Alexander W. Randall	1866–1869
Attorney General	James Speed	1865–1866
	Henry Stanbery	1866–1868
	William M. Evarts	1868–1869
Secretary of Navy	Gideon Welles	1865–1869
Secretary of Interior	John P. Usher	1865
	James Harlan	1865–1866
	Orville H. Browning	1866–1869

Grant, 1869–1877

Vice-President	Schuyler Colfax	1869–1873
	Henry Wilson	1873–1875
Secretary of State	Elihu B. Washburne	1869
	Hamilton Fish	1869–1877

Secretary of War	John A. Rawlins	1869
	William T. Sherman	1869
	William W. Belknap	1869–1876
	Alphonso Taft	1876
	James D. Cameron	1876–1877
Secretary of Treasury	George S. Boutwell	1869–1873
	William A. Richardson	1873–1874
	Benjamin H. Bristow	1874–1876
	Lot M. Morrill	1876–1877
Postmaster General	John A. J. Creswell	1869–1874
	James W. Marshall	1874
	Marshall Jewell	1874–1876
	James N. Tyner	1876–1877
Attorney General	Ebenezer R. Hoar	1869–1870
	Amos T. Ackerman	1870–1871
	G. H. Williams	1871–1875
	Edwards Pierrepont	1875–1876
	Alphonso Taft	1876–1877
Secretary of Navy	Adolph E. Borie	1869
	George Robeson	1869–1877
Secretary of Interior	Jacob D. Cox	1869–1870
	Columbus Delano	1870–1875
	Zachariah Chandler	1875–1877

Hayes, 1877–1881

Vice-President	William A. Wheeler	1877–1881
Secretary of State	William B. Evarts	1877–1881
Secretary of War	George W. McCrary	1877–1879
	Alexander Ramsey	1879–1881
Secretary of Treasury	John Sherman	1877–1881
Postmaster General	David M. Key	1877–1880
	Horace Maynard	1880–1881
Attorney General	Charles Devens	1877–1881
Secretary of Navy	Richard W. Thompson	1877–1880
	Nathan Goff, Jr.	1881
Secretary of Interior	Carl Schurz	1877–1881

Garfield, 1881

Vice-President	Chester A. Arthur	1881
Secretary of State	James G. Blaine	1881
Secretary of War	Robert T. Lincoln	1881
Secretary of Treasury	William Windom	1881
Postmaster General	Thomas L. James	1881
Attorney General	Wayne MacVeagh	1881

(continues)

| Secretary of Navy | William H. Hunt | 1881 |
| Secretary of Interior | Samuel J. Kirkwood | 1881 |

Arthur, 1881–1885

Vice-President	None	
Secretary of State	Frederick T. Frelinghuysen	1881–1885
Secretary of War	Robert T. Lincoln	1881–1885
Secretary of Treasury	Charles J. Folger	1881–1884
	Walter Q. Gresham	1884
	Hugh McCulloch	1884–1885
Postmaster General	Timothy O. Howe	1881–1883
	Walter Q. Gresham	1883–1884
	Frank Hatton	1884–1885
Attorney General	Benjamin H. Brewster	1881–1885
Secretary of Navy	William H. Hunt	1881–1882
	William E. Chandler	1882–1885
Secretary of Interior	Samuel J. Kirkwood	1881–1882
	Henry M. Teller	1882–1885

Cleveland, 1885–1889

Vice-President	Thomas A. Hendricks	1885
Secretary of State	Thomas F. Bayard	1885–1889
Secretary of War	William C. Endicott	1885–1889
Secretary of Treasury	Daniel Manning	1885–1887
	Charles S. Fairchild	1887–1889
Postmaster General	William F. Vilas	1885–1888
	Don M. Dickinson	1888–1889
Attorney General	Augustus H. Garland	1885–1889
Secretary of Navy	William C. Whitney	1885–1889
Secretary of Interior	Lucius Q. C. Lamar	1885–1888
	William F. Vilas	1888–1889
Secretary of Agriculture	Norman J. Colman	1889

Benjamin Harrison, 1889–1893

Vice-President	Levi P. Morton	1889–1893
Secretary of State	James G. Blaine	1889–1892
	John W. Foster	1892–1893
Secretary of War	Redfield Proctor	1889–1891
	Stephen B. Elkins	1891–1893
Secretary of Treasury	William Windom	1889–1891
	Charles Foster	1891–1893
Postmaster General	John Wanamaker	1889–1893
Attorney General	William H. H. Miller	1889–1891
Secretary of Navy	Benjamin F. Tracy	1889–1893
Secretary of Interior	John W. Noble	1889–1893
Secretary of Agriculture	Jeremiah M. Rusk	1889–1893

Cleveland, 1893–1897

Vice-President	Adlai E. Stevenson	1893–1897
Secretary of State	Walter Q. Gresham	1893–1895
	Richard Olney	1895–1897
Secretary of War	Daniel S. Lamont	1893–1897
Secretary of Treasury	John G. Carlisle	1893–1897
Postmaster General	Wilson S. Bissell	1893–1895
	William L. Wilson	1895–1897
Attorney General	Richard Olney	1893–1895
	Judson Harmon	1895–1897
Secretary of Navy	Hilary A. Herbert	1893–1897
Secretary of Interior	Hoke Smith	1893–1896
	David R. Francis	1896–1897
Secretary of Agriculture	Julius Sterling Morton	1893–1897

McKinley, 1897–1901

Vice-President	Garret Hobart	1897–1899
	Theodore Roosevelt	1901
Secretary of State	John Sherman	1897–1898
	William R. Day	1898
	John M. Hay	1898–1901
Secretary of War	Russell A. Alger	1897–1899
	Elihu Root	1899–1901
Secretary of Treasury	Lyman J. Gage	1897–1901
Postmaster General	James A. Gary	1897–1898
	Charles E. Smith	1898–1901
Attorney General	Joseph McKenna	1897–1898
	John W. Griggs	1898–1901
	Philander C. Knox	1901
Secretary of Navy	John D. Long	1897–1901
Secretary of Interior	Cornelius N. Bliss	1897–1899
	Ethan A. Hitchcock	1899–1901
Secretary of Agriculture	James Wilson	1897–1901

Theodore Roosevelt, 1901–1909

Vice-President	Charles Warren Fairbanks	1905–1909
Secretary of State	John M. Hay	1901–1905
	Elihu Root	1905–1909
	Robert Bacon	1909
Secretary of War	Elihu Root	1901–1904
	William Howard Taft	1904–1908
	Luke E. Wright	1908–1909

(continues)

Secretary of Treasury	Lyman J. Gage	1901–1902
	Leslie M. Shaw	1902–1907
	George B. Cortelyou	1907–1909
Postmaster General	Charles Emory Smith	1901–1902
	Henry C. Payne	1902–1904
	Robert J. Wynne	1904–1905
	George B. Cortelyou	1905–1907
	George von L. Meyer	1907–1909
Attorney General	Philander C. Knox	1901–1904
	William H. Moody	1904–1906
	Charles J. Bonaparte	1906–1909
Secretary of Navy	John D. Long	1901–1902
	William H. Moody	1902–1904
	Paul Morton	1904–1905
	Charles J. Bonaparte	1905–1906
	Victor H. Metcalf	1906–1908
	Truman H. Newberry	1908–1909
Secretary of Interior	Ethan A. Hitchcock	1901–1907
	James R. Garfield	1907–1909
Secretary of Agriculture	James Wilson	1901–1909
Secretary of Labor and Commerce	George B. Cortelyou	1903–1904
	Victor H. Metcalf	1904–1906
	Oscar S. Straus	1906–1909

Taft, 1909–1913

Vice-President	James S. Sherman	1909–1912
Secretary of State	Philander C. Knox	1909–1913
Secretary of War	Jacob M. Dickinson	1909–1911
	Henry L. Stimson	1911–1913
Secretary of Treasury	Franklin MacVeagh	1909–1913
Postmaster General	Frank H. Hitchcock	1909–1913
Attorney General	George W. Wickersham	1909–1913
Secretary of Navy	George von L. Meyer	1909–1913
Secretary of Interior	Richard A. Ballinger	1909–1911
	Walter Lowrie Fisher	1911–1913
Secretary of Agriculture	James Wilson	1909–1913
Secretary of Labor and Commerce	Oscar S. Straus	1909
	Charles Nagel	1909–1913

Wilson, 1913–1921

Vice-President	Thomas R. Marshall	1913–1921
Secretary of State	William Jennings Bryan	1913–1915
	Robert Lansing	1915–1920
	Bainbridge Colby	1920–1921
Secretary of War	Lindley M. Garrison	1913–1916

Secretary of Treasury	Newton D. Baker	1916–1921
	William Gilbert McAdoo	1913–1918
	Carter Glass	1918–1920
	David F. Houston	1920–1921
Postmaster General	Albert Sidney Burleson	1913–1921
Attorney General	James Clark McReynolds	1913–1914
	Thomas Watt Gregory	1914–1919
	A. Mitchell Palmer	1919–1921
Secretary of Navy	Josephus Daniels	1913–1921
Secretary of Interior	Franklin Knight Lane	1913–1920
	John Barton Payne	1920–1921
Secretary of Agriculture	David F. Houston	1913–1920
	Edwin T. Meredith	1920–1921
Secretary of Commerce	William C. Redfield	1913–1919
Secretary of Labor	William Bauchop Wilson	1913–1921

Harding, 1921–1923

Vice-President	Calvin Coolidge	1921–1923
Secretary of State	Charles Evans Hughes	1921–1923
Secretary of War	John W. Weeks	1921–1923
Secretary of Treasury	Andrew W. Mellon	1921–1923
Postmaster General	Will H. Hays	1921–1922
	Hubert Work	1922–1923
	Harry S. New	1923
Attorney General	Harry M. Daugherty	1921–1923
Secretary of Navy	Edwin Denby	1921–1923
Secretary of Interior	Albert B. Fall	1921–1923
	Hubert Work	1923
Secretary of Agriculture	Henry C. Wallace	1921–1923
Secretary of Commerce	Herbert C. Hoover	1921–1923
Secretary of Labor	James J. Davis	1921–1923

Coolidge, 1923–1929

Vice-President	Charles G. Dawes	1925–1929
Secretary of State	Charles Evans Hughes	1923–1925
	Frank B. Kellogg	1925–1929
Secretary of War	John W. Weeks	1923–1925
	Dwight F. Davis	1925–1929
Secretary of Treasury	Andrew W. Mellon	1923–1929

(continues)

Postmaster General	Harry S. New	1923–1929
Attorney General	Harry M. Daugherty	1923–1924
	Harlan Fiske Stone	1924–1925
	John G. Sargent	1925–1929
Secretary of Navy	Edwin Derby	1923–1924
	Curtis D. Wilbur	1924–1929
Secretary of Interior	Hubert Work	1923–1928
	Roy O. West	1928–1929
Secretary of Agriculture	Henry C. Wallace	1923–1924
	Howard M. Gore	1924–1925
	William M. Jardine	1925–1929
Secretary of Commerce	Herbert C. Hoover	1923–1928
	William F. Whiting	1928–1929
Secretary of Labor	James J. Davis	1923–1929

Hoover, 1929–1933

Vice-President	Charles Curtis	1929–1933
Secretary of State	Henry L. Stimson	1929–1933
Secretary of War	James W. Good	1929
	Patrick J. Hurley	1929–1933
Secretary of Treasury	Andrew W. Mellon	1929–1932
	Ogden L. Mills	1932–1933
Postmaster General	Walter F. Brown	1929–1933

Attorney General	William D. Mitchell	1929–1933
Secretary of Navy	Charles F. Adams	1929–1933
Secretary of Interior	Ray L. Wilbur	1929–1933
Secretary of Agriculture	Arthur M. Hyde	1929–1933
Secretary of Commerce	Robert P. Lamont	1929–1932
	Roy D. Chapin	1932–1933
Secretary of Labor	James J. Davis	1929–1930
	William N. Doak	1930–1933

Franklin D. Roosevelt, 1933–1945

Vice-President	John Nance Garner	1933–1941
	Henry A. Wallace	1941–1945
	Harry S Truman	1945
Secretary of State	Cordell Hull	1933–1944
	Edward R. Stettinius, Jr.	1944–1945
Secretary of War	George H. Dern	1933–1936
	Henry A. Woodring	1936–1940
	Henry L. Stimson	1940–1945
Secretary of Treasury	William H. Woodin	1933–1934
	Henry Morgenthau, Jr.	1934–1945
Postmaster General	James A. Farley	1933–1940
	Frank C. Walker	1940–1945

Attorney General	Homer S. Cummings	1933–1939
	Frank Murphy	1939–1940
	Robert H. Jackson	1940–1941
	Francis Biddle	1941–1945
Secretary of Navy	Claude A. Swanson	1933–1940
	Charles Edison	1940
	Frank Knox	1940–1944
	James V. Forrestal	1944–1945
Secretary of Interior	Harold L. Ickes	1933–1945
Secretary of Agriculture	Henry A. Wallace	1933–1940
	Claude R. Wickard	1940–1945
Secretary of Commerce	Daniel C. Roper	1933–1939
	Harry L. Hopkins	1939–1940
	Jesse H. Jones	1940–1945
	Henry A. Wallace	1945
Secretary of Labor	Frances Perkins	1933–1945

Truman, 1945–1953

Vice-President	Alben W. Barkley	1949–1953
Secretary of State	Edward R. Stettinius, Jr.	1945
	James F. Byrnes	1945–1947
	George C. Marshall	1947–1949
	Dean G. Acheson	1949–1953
Secretary of War	Robert P. Patterson	1945–1947
	Kenneth C. Royall	1947
Secretary of Treasury	Fred M. Vinson	1945–1946
	John W. Snyder	1946–1953
Postmaster General	Frank C. Walker	1945
	Robert E. Hannegan	1945–1947
	Jesse M. Donaldson	1947–1953
Attorney General	Tom C. Clark	1945–1949
	J. Howard McGrath	1949–1952
	James P. McGranery	1952–1953
Secretary of Navy	James V. Forrestal	1945–1947
Secretary of Interior	Harold L. Ickes	1945–1946
	Julius A. Krug	1946–1949
	Oscar L. Chapman	1949–1953
Secretary of Agriculture	Clinton P. Anderson	1945–1948
	Charles F. Brannan	1948–1953
Secretary of Commerce	Henry A. Wallace	1945–1946
	W. Averell Harriman	1946–1948
	Charles W. Sawyer	1948–1953
Secretary of Labor	Lewis B. Schwellenbach	1945–1948
	Maurice J. Tobin	1948–1953
Secretary of Defense	James V. Forrestal	1947–1949
	Louis A. Johnson	1949–1950
	George C. Marshall	1950–1951
	Robert A. Lovett	1951–1953

(continues)

Eisenhower, 1953–1961

Vice-President	Richard M. Nixon	1953–1961
Secretary of State	John Foster Dulles	1953–1959
	Christian A. Herter	1959–1961
Secretary of Treasury	George M. Humphrey	1953–1957
	Robert B. Anderson	1957–1961
Postmaster General	Arthur E. Summerfield	1953–1961
Attorney General	Herbert Brownell, Jr.	1953–1958
	William P. Rogers	1958–1961
Secretary of Interior	Douglas McKay	1953–1956
	Fred A. Seaton	1956–1961
Secretary of Agriculture	Ezra Taft Benson	1953–1961
Secretary of Commerce	Sinclair Weeks	1953–1958
	Lewis L. Strauss	1958–1959
	Frederick H. Mueller	1959–1961
Secretary of Labor	Martin P. Durkin	1953
	James P. Mitchell	1953–1961
Secretary of Defense	Charles E. Wilson	1953–1957
	Neil H. McElroy	1957–1959
	Thomas S. Gates, Jr.	1959–1961
Secretary of Health, Education, and Welfare	Oveta Culp Hobby	1953–1955
	Marion B. Folsom	1955–1958
	Arthur S. Flemming	1958–1961

Kennedy, 1961–1963

Vice-President	Lyndon B. Johnson	1961–1963
Secretary of State	Dean Rusk	1961–1963
Secretary of Treasury	C. Douglas Dillon	1961–1963
Postmaster General	J. Edward Day	1961–1963
	John A. Gronouski	1963
Attorney General	Robert F. Kennedy	1961–1963
Secretary of Interior	Stewart L. Udall	1961–1963
Secretary of Agriculture	Orville L. Freeman	1961–1963
Secretary of Commerce	Luther H. Hodges	1961–1963
Secretary of Labor	Arthur J. Goldberg	1961–1962
	W. Willard Wirtz	1962–1963
Secretary of Defense	Robert S. McNamara	1961–1963
Secretary of Health, Education, and Welfare	Abraham A. Ribicoff	1961–1962
	Anthony J. Celebrezze	1962–1963

Lyndon Johnson, 1963–1969

Vice-President	Hubert H. Humphrey	1965–1969
Secretary of State	Dean Rusk	1963–1969
Secretary of Treasury	C. Douglas Dillon	1963–1965
	Henry H. Fowler	1965–1969

Postmaster General	John A. Gronouski	1963–1965
	Lawrence F. O'Brien	1965–1968
	Marvin Watson	1968–1969
Attorney General	Robert F. Kennedy	1963–1964
	Nicholas Katzenbach	1965–1966
	Ramsey Clark	1967–1969
Secretary of Interior	Stewart L. Udall	1963–1969
Secretary of Agriculture	Orville L. Freeman	1963–1969
Secretary of Commerce	Luther H. Hodges	1963–1964
	John T. Connor	1964–1967
	Alexander B. Trowbridge	1967–1968
	Cyrus R. Smith	1968–1969
Secretary of Labor	W. Willard Wirtz	1963–1969
Secretary of Defense	Robert F. McNamara	1963–1968
	Clark Clifford	1968–1969
Secretary of Health, Education, and Welfare	Anthony J. Celebrezze	1963–1965
	John W. Gardner	1965–1968
	Wilbur J. Cohen	1968–1969
Secretary of Housing and Urban Development	Robert C. Weaver	1966–1969
	Robert C. Wood	1969
Secretary of Transportation	Alan S. Boyd	1967–1969

Nixon, 1969–1974

Vice-President	Spiro T. Agnew	1969–1973
	Gerald R. Ford	1973–1974
Secretary of State	William P. Rogers	1969–1973
	Henry A. Kissinger	1973–1974
Secretary of Treasury	David M. Kennedy	1969–1970
	John B. Connally	1971–1972
	George P. Shultz	1972–1974
	William E. Simon	1974
Postmaster General	Winton M. Blount	1969–1971
Attorney General	John N. Mitchell	1969–1972
	Richard G. Kleindienst	1972–1973
	Elliot L. Richardson	1973
	William B. Saxbe	1973–1974
Secretary of Interior	Walter J. Hickel	1969–1970
	Rogers Morton	1971–1974
Secretary of Agriculture	Clifford M. Hardin	1969–1971
	Earl L. Butz	1971–1974
Secretary of Commerce	Maurice H. Stans	1969–1972
	Peter G. Peterson	1972–1973
	Frederick B. Dent	1973–1974
Secretary of Labor	George P. Shultz	1969–1970
	James D. Hodgson	1970–1973
	Peter J. Brennan	1973–1974

(continues)

Secretary of Defense	Melvin R. Laird	1969–1973
	Elliot L. Richardson	1973
	James R. Schlesinger	1973–1974
Secretary of Health, Education, and Welfare	Robert H. Finch	1969–1970
	Elliot L. Richardson	1970–1973
	Caspar W. Weinberger	1973–1974
Secretary of Housing and Urban Development	George W. Romney	1969–1973
	James T. Lynn	1973–1974
Secretary of Transportation	John A. Volpe	1969–1973
	Claude S. Brinegar	1973–1974

Ford, 1974–1977

Vice-President	Nelson A. Rockefeller	1974–1977
Secretary of State	Henry A. Kissinger	1974–1977
Secretary of Treasury	William E. Simon	1974–1977
Attorney General	William B. Saxbe	1974–1975
	Edward H. Levi	1975–1977
Secretary of Interior	Rogers C. B. Morton	1974–1975
	Stanley K. Hathaway	1975
	Thomas S. Kleppe	1975–1977
Secretary of Agriculture	Earl L. Butz	1974–1976
	John A. Knebel	1976–1977

Secretary of Commerce	Frederick B. Dent	1974–1975
	Rogers C. B. Morton	1975–1976
	Elliot L. Richardson	1976–1977
Secretary of Labor	Peter J. Brennan	1974–1975
	John T. Dunlop	1975–1976
	W. J. Usery, Jr.	1976–1977
Secretary of Defense	James R. Schlesinger	1974–1975
	Donald H. Rumsfeld	1975–1977
Secretary of Health, Education, and Welfare	Caspar W. Weinberger	1974–1975
	F. David Mathews	1975–1977
Secretary of Housing and Urban Development	James T. Lynn	1974–1975
	Carla Anderson Hills	1975–1977
Secretary of Transportation	Claude S. Brinegar	1974–1975
	William T. Coleman, Jr.	1974–1977

Carter, 1977–1981

Vice-President	Walter F. Mondale	1977–1981
Secretary of State	Cyrus R. Vance	1977–1980
	Edmund S. Muskie	1980–1981
Secretary of Treasury	W. Michael Blumenthal	1977–1979
	G. William Miller	1979–1981

Attorney General	Griffin B. Bell	1977–1979
	Benjamin R. Civiletti	1979–1981
Secretary of Interior	Cecil D. Andrus	1977–1981
Secretary of Agriculture	Robert Bergland	1977–1981
Secretary of Commerce	Juanita M. Kreps	1977–1979
	Philip M. Klutznick	1979–1981
Secretary of Labor	F. Ray Marshall	1977–1981
Secretary of Defense	Harold Brown	1977–1981
Secretary of Health, Education, and Welfare	Joseph A. Califano, Jr.	1977–1979
	Patricia Roberts Harris	1979
Secretary of Health and Human Services	Patricia Roberts Harris	1979–1981
Secretary of Housing and Urban Development	Patricia Roberts Harris	1977–1979
	Moon Landrieu	1979–1981
Secretary of Transportation	Brock Adams	1977–1979
	Neil E. Goldschmidt	1979–1981
Secretary of Energy	James R. Schlesinger, Jr.	1977–1979
	Charles W. Duncan, Jr.	1979–1981
Secretary of Education	Shirley M. Hufstedler	1979–1981

Reagan, 1981–1989

Vice-President	George Bush	1981–1989
Secretary of State	Alexander M. Haig, Jr.	1981–1982
	George P. Shultz	1982–1989
Secretary of Treasury	Donald T. Regan	1981–1985
	James A. Baker, III	1985–1988
	Nicholas F. Brady	1988–1989
Attorney General	William French Smith	1981–1985
	Edwin A. Meese, III	1985–1988
	Richard Thornburgh	1988–1989
Secretary of Interior	James C. Watt	1981–1983
	William P. Clarke, Jr.	1983–1985
	Donald P. Hodel	1985–1989
Secretary of Agriculture	John R. Block	1981–1986
	Richard Lyng	1986–1989
Secretary of Commerce	Malcolm Baldrige	1981–1987
	C. William Verity, Jr.	1987–1989
Secretary of Labor	Raymond J. Donovan	1981–1985
	William E. Brock	1985–1987
	Ann D. McLaughlin	1987–1989
Secretary of Defense	Caspar W. Weinberger	1981–1987
	Frank C. Carlucci	1987–1989

(continues)

Secretary of Health and Human Services	Richard S. Schweiker	1981–1983
	Margaret M. Heckler	1983–1985
	Otis R. Bowen	1985–1989
Secretary of Housing and Urban Development	Samuel R. Pierce, Jr.	1981–1989
Secretary of Transportation	Andrew L. Lewis, Jr.	1981–1983
	Elizabeth Hanford Dole	1983–1987
	James H. Burnley	1987–1989
Secretary of Energy	James B. Edwards	1981–1982
	Donald P. Hodel	1982–1985
	John S. Herrington	1985–1989
Secretary of Education	Terrel H. Bell	1981–1985
	William J. Bennett	1985–1988
	Lauro F. Cavazos	1988–1989

Bush, 1989–1993

Vice President	J. Danforth Quayle	1989–1993
Secretary of State	James A. Baker III	1989–1992
Secretary of Treasury	Nicholas Brady	1989–1993
Attorney General	Richard Thornburgh	1989–1991
	William P. Barr	1991–1993
Secretary of Interior	Manuel Lujan	1989–1993
Secretary of Agriculture	Clayton K. Yeutter	1989–1991
	Edward Madigan	1991–1993
Secretary of Commerce	Robert Mosbacher	1989–1992
	Barbara Franklin	1992–1993
Secretary of Labor	Elizabeth Hanford Dole	1989–1991
	Lynn Martin	1991–1993
Secretary of Defense	Richard Cheney	1989–1993
Secretary of Health and Human Services	Louis W. Sullivan	1989–1993
Secretary of Education	Lauro F. Cavazos	1989–1991
	Lamar Alexander	1991–1993
Secretary of Housing and Urban Development	Jack F. Kemp	1989–1993
Secretary of Transportation	Samuel K. Skinner	1989–1992
	Andrew H. Card Jr.	1992–1993
Secretary of Energy	James D. Watkins	1989–1993
Secretary of Veterans Affairs	Edward J. Derwinski	1989–1993

Clinton, 1993–

Vice President	Albert Gore	1993–
Secretary of State	Warren Christopher	1993–
Secretary of Treasury	Lloyd Bentsen	1993–
Attorney General	Janet Reno	1993–

Secretary of Interior	Bruce Babbitt	1993–
Secretary of Agriculture	Michael Espy	1993–
Secretary of Commerce	Ronald Brown	1993–
Secretary of Labor	Robert B. Reich	1993–
Secretary of Defense	Les Aspin	1993–1994
	William Perry	1994–
Secretary of Health and Human Services	Donna Shalala	1993–
Secretary of Housing and Urban Development	Henry G. Cisneros	1993–
Secretary of Education	Richard W. Riley	1993–
Secretary of Transportation	Federico Peña	1993–
Secretary of Energy	Hazel R. O'Leary	1993–
Secretary of Veterans Affairs	Edward J. Derwinski	1993–

Supreme Court Justices

Chief Justices in italics.

	Term of Service	Years of Service
John Jay	1789–1795	5
John Rutledge	1789–1791	1
William Cushing	1789–1810	20
James Wilson	1789–1798	8
John Blair	1789–1796	6
Robert H. Harrison	1789–1790	—
James Iredell	1790–1799	9
Thomas Johnson	1791–1793	1
William Paterson	1793–1806	13
*John Rutledge**	1795	—
Samuel Chase	1796–1811	15
Oliver Ellsworth	1796–1800	4
Bushrod Washington	1798–1829	31
Alfred Moore	1799–1804	4
John Marshall	1801–1835	34
William Johnson	1804–1834	30
H. Brockholst Livingston	1806–1823	16
Thomas Todd	1807–1826	18
Joseph Story	1811–1845	33
Gabriel Duval	1811–1835	24
Smith Thompson	1823–1843	20
Robert Trimble	1826–1828	2

Justice	Term of Service	Years of Service	Justice	Term of Service	Years of Service
John McLean	1829–1861	32	William Strong	1870–1880	10
Henry Baldwin	1830–1844	14	Joseph P. Bradley	1870–1892	22
James M. Wayne	1835–1867	32	Ward Hunt	1873–1882	9
Roger B. Taney	1836–1864	28	Morrison R. Waite	1874–1888	14
Philip P. Barbour	1836–1841	4	John M. Harlan	1877–1911	34
John Catron	1837–1865	28	William B. Woods	1880–1887	7
John McKinley	1837–1852	15	Stanley Matthews	1881–1889	7
Peter V. Daniel	1841–1860	19	Horace Gray	1882–1902	20
Samuel Nelson	1845–1872	27	Samuel Blatchford	1882–1893	11
Levi Woodbury	1845–1851	5	Lucius Q. C. Lamar	1888–1893	5
Robert C. Grier	1846–1870	23	Melville W. Fuller	1888–1910	21
Benjamin R. Curtis	1851–1857	6	David J. Brewer	1890–1910	20
John A. Campbell	1853–1861	8	Henry B. Brown	1890–1906	16
Nathan Clifford	1858–1881	23	George Shiras, Jr.	1892–1903	10
Noah H. Swayne	1862–1881	18	Howell E. Jackson	1893–1895	2
Samuel F. Miller	1862–1890	28	Edward D. White	1894–1910	16
David Davis	1862–1877	14	Rufus W. Peckham	1895–1909	14
Stephen J. Field	1863–1897	34	Joseph McKenna	1898–1925	26
Salmon P. Chase	1864–1873	8	Oliver W. Holmes, Jr.	1902–1932	30
			William R. Day	1903–1922	19

*Never confirmed as Chief Justice

(continues)

Name	Term of Service	Years of Service	Name	Term of Service	Years of Service
William H. Moody	1906–1910	3	Felix Frankfurter	1939–1962	23
Horace H. Lurton	1910–1914	4	William O. Douglas	1939–1975	36
Charles E. Hughes	1910–1916	5	Frank Murphy	1940–1949	9
Willis Van Devanter	1911–1937	26	*Harlan F. Stone*	1941–1946	5
Joseph R. Lamar	1911–1916	5	James F. Byrnes	1941–1942	1
Edward D. White	1910–1921	11	Robert H. Jackson	1941–1954	13
Mahlon Pitney	1912–1922	10	Wiley B. Rutledge	1943–1949	6
James C. McReynolds	1914–1941	26	Harold H. Burton	1945–1958	13
Louis D. Brandeis	1916–1939	22	*Fred M. Vinson*	1946–1953	7
John H. Clarke	1916–1922	6	Tom C. Clark	1949–1967	18
William H. Taft	1921–1930	8	Sherman Minton	1949–1956	7
George Sutherland	1922–1938	15	*Earl Warren*	1953–1969	16
Pierce Butler	1922–1939	16	John Marshall Harlan	1955–1971	16
Edward T. Sanford	1923–1930	7	William J. Brennan, Jr.	1956–1990	34
Harlan F. Stone	1925–1941	16	Charles E. Whittaker	1957–1962	5
Charles E. Hughes	1930–1941	11	Potter Stewart	1958–1981	23
Owen J. Roberts	1930–1945	15	Byron R. White	1962–	—
Benjamin N. Cardozo	1932–1938	6	Arthur J. Goldberg	1962–1965	3
Hugo L. Black	1937–1971	34	Abe Fortas	1965–1969	4
Stanley F. Reed	1938–1957	19	Thurgood Marshall	1967–1991	24

	Term of Service	Years of Service
Warren E. Burger	1969–1986	18
Harry A. Blackmun	1970–1994	24
Lewis F. Powell, Jr.	1971–1987	15
*William H. Rehnquist**￼*	1971–	—
John P. Stevens III	1975–	—
Sandra Day O'Connor	1981–	—
Antonin Scalia	1986–	—
Anthony M. Kennedy	1988–	—
David H. Souter	1990–	—
Clarence Thomas	1991–	—
Ruth Bader Ginsburg	1993–	—
Stephen Breyer	1994–	—

*Never confirmed as Chief Justice.
**Chief Justice from 1986 on.

Admission of States to the Union

State	Date of Admission
1 Delaware	December 7, 1787
2. Pennsylvania	December 12, 1787
3. New Jersey	December 18, 1787
4. Georgia	January 2, 1788
5. Connecticut	January 9, 1788
6. Massachusetts	February 6, 1788
7. Maryland	April 28, 1788
8. South Carolina	May 23, 1788
9. New Hampshire	June 21, 1788
10. Virginia	June 25, 1788
11. New York	July 26, 1788
12. North Carolina	November 21, 1789
13. Rhode Island	May 29, 1790
14. Vermont	March 4, 1791
15. Kentucky	June 1, 1792
16. Tennessee	June 1, 1796
17. Ohio	March 1, 1803
18. Louisiana	April 30, 1812
19. Indiana	December 11, 1816
20. Mississippi	December 10, 1817
21. Illinois	December 3, 1818
22. Alabama	December 14, 1819
23. Maine	March 15, 1820

State	Date of Admission
24. Missouri	August 10, 1821
25. Arkansas	June 15, 1836
26. Michigan	January 26, 1837
27. Florida	March 3, 1845
28. Texas	December 29, 1845
29. Iowa	December 28, 1846
30. Wisconsin	May 29, 1848
31. California	September 9, 1850
32. Minnesota	May 11, 1858
33. Oregon	February 14, 1859
34. Kansas	January 29, 1861
35. West Virginia	June 20, 1863
36. Nevada	October 31, 1864
37. Nebraska	March 1, 1867
38. Colorado	August 1, 1876
39. North Dakota	November 2, 1889
40. South Dakota	November 2, 1889
41. Montana	November 8, 1889
42. Washington	November 11, 1889
43. Idaho	July 3, 1890
44. Wyoming	July 10, 1890
45. Utah	January 4, 1896
46. Oklahoma	November 16, 1907
47. New Mexico	January 6, 1912
48. Arizona	February 14, 1912
49. Alaska	January 3, 1959
50. Hawaii	August 21, 1959

Credits

Unless otherwise acknowledged, all photographs are the property of Scott, Foresman and Company. Page abbreviations are as follows: (T)top, (C)center, (B)bottom, (L)left, (R)right.

Page 3, Courtesy of the Plymouth Society, Plymouth, Mass. **Page 13,** Rare Books and Manuscripts Division/New York Public Library, Astor, Lenox and Tilden Foundations **Page 20,** Copyright the British Museum **Page 35,** Courtesy American Antiquarian Society **Page 41,** Peabody Essex Museum, Salem **Page 46,** Collection of Tazwell Ellett III **Page 59,** Library of Congress **Page 81,** Spencer Collection/New York Public Library, Astor, Lenox and Tilden Foundations, **Page 89,** Library of Congress **Page 95,** Library of Congress **Page 108,** Courtesy of the Valley Forge Historical Society **Page 115,** Copyright Yale University Art Gallery **Page 134,** Historical Society of Pennsylvania **Page 135,** Library of Congress **Page 152,** Bowdoin Museum of Fine Arts, Bowdoin College **Page 164,** Library of Congress **Page 166,** Library of Congress **Page 171,** The Metropolitan Museum of Art, Gift of Colonel and Mrs. Edgar William Garbisch, 1963 **Page 182,** Copyright Yale University Art Gallery, Bequest of Oliver Burr Jennings, B.A. 1917 in memory of Miss Annie Burr Jennings, **Page 186,** Washington and Lee University **Page 195,** Library of Congress **Page 205L,** In the Collection of the Corcoran Gallery of Art **Page 213,** I.N. Phelps Stokes Collection/New York Public Library, Astor, Lenox and Tilden Foundations, **Page 234,** Library of Congress **Page 235,** Memphis Brooks Museum of Art **Page 255,** The Museum of the City of New York **Page 260,** Sophia Smith Collection, Smith College **Page 261,** The Metropolitan Museum of Art **Page 264T,** Library of Congress **Page 278,** Copyright Yale University Art Gallery, Gift of George Hoadley **Page 283,** Prints Division/New York Public Library, Astor, Lenox and Tilden Foundations **Page 293,** Prints Division/New York Public Library, Astor, Lenox and Tilden Foundations **Page 294,** Library of Congress **Page 305,** California Department of Parks and Recreation **Page 311,** The Bancroft Library, University of California **Page 322,** National Academy of Design **Page 348,** Prints Division/New York Public Library, Astor, Lenox and Tilden Foundations **Page 360L,** Courtesy Georgia Department of Archives & History **Page 360R,** John L. McGuire Collection **Page 371,** Library of Congress **Page 372,** Library of Congress **Page 390,** Valentine Museum **Page 401,** Library of Congress **Page 402,** Library of Congress **Page 421,** Edison National Historic Site/U.S. Dept. of the Interior **Page 430,** Culver Pictures **Page 431,** Culver Pictures **Page 432,** Brown Brothers **Page 435,** Mrs. Vincent Astor **Page 438,** Nebraska State Historical Society **Page 448,** Culver Pictures **Page 452,** Culver Pictures **Page 456,** From the Hultz Collection **Page 465,** The Granger Collection **Page 473,** Culver Pictures **Page 476,** The Museum of the City of New York **Page 480,** George Eastman House **Page 481,** Brown Brothers **Page 487,** Hogan Jazz Archives, **Page**

489, Library of Congress   **Page 500,** Culver Pictures   **Page 500B,** Courtesy American Antiquarian Society   **Page 510,** Harper's Weekly   **Page 514,** Culver Pictures   **Page 529,** Bettmann Archive   **Page 531,** Library of Congress   **Page 541,** Library of Congress   **Page 553,** National Park Service/U.S. Dept. of the Interior   **Page 559,** AP/Wide World   **Page 569,** Brown Brothers   **Page 576,** Library of Congress   **Page 590,** The Archives of Labor and Urban Affairs, Wayne State Univ.   **Page 592,** Music Division/ New York Public Library, Astor, Lenox and Tilden Foundations   **Page 602,** Brown Brothers   **Page 605,** Chicago Tribune-NY News Syndicate   **Page 611,** Culver Pictures   **Page 615,** Culver Pictures   **Page 620,** Ben Shahn, BARTHOLOMEO VANZETTI AND NICOLA SACCO (1931–32). Tempera on paper over composition board, 10 x 14; dp. Gift of Mrs. John D. Rockefeller, Jr. Collection, The Museum of Modern Art, New York   **Page 621,** Brown Brothers   **Page 631,** New York Times, October 25, 1929   **Page 638,** Culver Pictures   **Page 644,** Brown Brothers   **Page 649,** AP/Wide World   **Page 663,** Culver Pictures   **Page 668,** United Press International Photo   **Page 672,** Official U.S. Navy Photograph   **Page 681,** The National Archives   **Page 686,** The Franklin D. Roosevelt Library   **Page 690,** United States Air Force photo   **Page 697L,** James Whitmore/Life Magazine/Time Warner Inc.   **Page 697R,** Thomas D. McAvoy   **Page 712,** Bettmann Archive   **Page 715,** Film Stills Archive Collection/ The Museum of Modern Art   **Page 721,** AP/Wide World   **Page 729,** Bettmann Archive   **Page 735,** AP/Wide World   **Page 737,** Life Magazine/Time Warner Inc.   **Page 740,** Don Wright/Life Magazine/Time Warner Inc.   **Page 745,** Bettmann Archive   **Page 748,** Bettmann Archive   **Page 764,** Kent State University News Service   **Page 772,** AP/Wide World   **Page 778,** Charles Moore/Black Star   **Page 782,** John Launois/Black Star   **Page 784,** Constantine Manos/Magnum Photos   **Page 797,** Arthur Grace/Sygma   **Page 807,** Alex Webb/Magnum Photos   **Page 816,** Bill Fitzpatrick/The White House   **Page 818,** Special Features/SIPA-Press   **Page 829R,** Bossu/Sygma

Index

Presley, Elvis, 739–740
Press, freedom of. *See* Freedom of the press
Preston, Thomas, 95–96
Primogeniture, abolition of, 145
Princeton, NJ, and American Revolution, 118
Private city, in 19th century, 481–482
Proclamation of 1763, 83–84
Progress and Poverty (Henry George), 555
Progressive party, 566–567, 627–628
Progressivism
 accomplishments and failures of, 573–577
 international, 569–573
 moral, under Wilson, 568–569
 national, 564–569
 origins and appeal of, 553–557
 quiet, under Taft, 566–567
 state, 562–564
 and urban reform, 561–562, 573–574
 and voices for changes, 555–557
 winners and losers under, 575–577
Progressivists
 activism of, 557–564
 heterogeneity of, 557
Prohibition, 575, 617–618
 early seeds of, 512
 in Maine (1851), 254
 repeal of, 617
 during World War I, 593–594
Prohibitionism, 558
 and progressivism, 563
Property rights, 144, 399
Prosser, Gabriel, 298
Protestant ethic, 252
Protestant Reformation, 16–17, 34
Protestant Wind, 18
Providence, RI, 37
Pseudoscience, 273
 and slavery, 290
Public schools, 257
Public virtue, 136
Public Works Administration (PWA), 647
 effects on Native Americans, 657
Pueblo Indians, 312
 challenge to Spanish rule, 15
Pueblos, 6
Puerto Rico, American acquisition of, 544
Pulitzer, Joseph, 540
Pullman strike of 1894, 518–519, 532, 538
Punch, John, 28
Pure Food and Drugs Act, 565, 575

Puritans, 17, 24, 32, 56, 58
 in England, 33–34
 family life of, 40
 in New England, 32–39
 patriarchal values of, 42
PWA. *See* Public Works Administration

Quakers, 58–59
Quartering Act of 1765, 100
Quebec, 23
Quebec Act of 1774, 100–101
Quebec City, 1775 patriot attack on, 112
Queen Anne's War, 72
"Queen for a Day," 792
Quota systems, 788

Race relations
 in New South, 441–442
 and progressivism, 576–577
 in 1890s, 519–520
Racial discrimination
 in late 19th century, 512
 during 1920s, 612–614
Racial justice
 current state of, 788
 struggle for, 774–792
Racial prejudice, and Social Darwinism, 530
Racial separatism, 783
Racial violence, of 1890s, 519–520
Racism, 273, 731–734, 774, 785. *See
 also* Segregation
 and Emancipation Proclamation, 377
 in military, in Spanish-American War, 542
 and Native Americans, 409–411
 and Reconstruction, 399, 401–402
 in Revolutionary period, 148–149
 and slavery, 289–290
 during World War II, 676, 678–679
Radical Republicans, 391–392
Radical revolutionaries, 136–138
 beliefs of, 136
Radio, during 1920s, 623–624
Railroad Administration, during World
 War I, 589
Railroads
 early, 213
 in early 19th century, growth, 213–214
 in late 19th century, regulation, 509
 pools, in 19th century, 430–431
 regulation of, 565, 574

Sherman, William Tecumseh, 322, 366, 390
  march across Georgia, 383
  march to Atlanta, 381–382
Sherman Antitrust Act, 511, 552, 565
Sherman Silver Purchase Act, 511, 518
Shiloh, battle of, 372
Shinn, Everett, 486
Shippen, Nancy, 133–134, 134*f*
Shipping, during trade wars between France
  and Great Britain, 192
Shipping Board, during World War I, 589
Sicilian immigrants, 453
Sierra Leone, 259
Sigourney, Lydia, 272
Simmons, William Joseph, 619
Sinclair, Upton, 557, 565
Sioux Indians, 311, 409
  conflict with settlers, 410
  and Wounded Knee, 457
Sirhan, Sirhan B., 761
Sister Carrie (Theodore Drieser), 485
Sit-ins, 679, 775
Sitting Bull, 411, 457
Sixteenth Amendment, 568
Skyscrapers, 477
Slater, Samuel, 281
Slave insurrections, 241
Slave labor, 294–295
Slave ownership, prevalence of, 287, 289
Slave rebellions, in Stono River area of South
  Carolina, 49
Slavery, 259, 288, 292–300
  beginnings of, 45–46
  and Civil War, 361
  codes for, 291
  conspiracy theories of, 334–335
  and Constitution, 153–154
  controversy over, in Kansas, 346–348
  decline of, 336–337
  in 1790s, 277
  effects of cotton gin on, 277
  effects of Mexican War on, 329–330
  effects on Southern economy, 288–289
  in English North America, 28, 47–49
  expansion in West, controversy over,
   225–241
  and Great Britain, 373
  Jefferson and, 183
  Lincoln-Douglas debates over, 352–354
  and Missouri Compromise, 219–221

  in New Spain, 14–15
  political debate over, 329–330
   renewal of, 345–346
  and presidential election of 1860, 361–362
  prohibition in Mexico, 315
  resistance to, 298–299
  in Revolutionary period, 147–150
  Southern defense of, 289–290
Slaves. *See also* Freed slaves
  African, 14–15
  concentration of, in 1860, 337*f*
  in Continental Army, 120
  cultural expression of, 297–298
  diet of, 295
  emancipation of, by Lord Dunmore, 112–113
  family life of, 48–49, 296–297
  infant mortality among, 295
  legal status of, 292–294
  lodging of, 296
  material conditions of, 295–296
  motivation of, 294–295
  Native Americans as, 14
  regulation of, 291, 293–294
  religion of, 297–298
  southern, 48
Slavic immigrants, in 19th century, 451
Slidell, John, 323, 374
Sloan, John D., 485–486
Sloat, John D., 324
Slums, 255*f*
Smallpox, in 19th century, 479
Smith, Adam, 426
Smith, Alfred, 628
Smith, Francis, 109
Smith, Jedediah, 307
Smith, John, 22
Smith, Joseph, 320–321
Smith-Connally Act, 675
Snake Indians, 312
SNCC. *See* Student Nonviolent Coordinating
  Committee
Snyder Act of 1924, 458
Social Bands, 347
Social change, in Revolutionary period, 144–150
Social Darwinism, 530
  challenges to, in early 20th century, 555–556
  and industrialization, 424–426
Social Gospel movement, 556–557
Socialism, in early 20th century, 562
Social issues, in late 19th century, 512–513